Rogue Reels:
Oppositional Film
in Britain, 1945–90

Edited by Margaret Dickinson

 Publishing

First published in 1999 by the
British Film Institute
21 Stephen Street, London W1P 2LN

The British Film Institute is the UK national agency with
responsibility for encouraging the arts of film and television
and conserving them in the national interest.

Cover design: **ketchup**
Cover images: *Berlin Horse* (Malcolm Le Grice, 1970); *The Miners' Campaign
Video Tapes* (Miners' Campaign Tape Project, 1984)

Set by Wyvern 21 Ltd
Printed in Great Britain by St Edmundsbury Press, Bury St Edmunds, Suffolk

British Library Cataloguing-in-Publication Data
A catalogue record for this book is available from the British Library

ISBN 0–85170–727–0 (paperback)
    0–85170–728–9 (hardback)

Contents

PART III: ORAL HISTORIES

Acknowledgments

I would like to thank the many people who helped in the preparation of this book, of whom it is only possible to mention a small handful here. My greatest debt is to those who contributed the material for the group histories, which often involved searching through personal and company records as well as recording extensive interviews. Apart from those named in Part III, I also had particularly useful discussions with Esther Ronay on the London Women's Film Group, Peter Bell on the North Eastern Film Workshop, Stuart McKinnon on Trade, Maureen Blackwood on Sankofa, Chris Reeves and Lin Soloman on Platform Films and Sarah McCarthy on Swingbridge. I would like to acknowledge a major debt to the late Simon Hartog, who as colleague and friend was a key influence and source of ideas, information and inspiration. Special thanks are due to Sylvia Harvey whose writings are among the most important published sources for the subject and who gave extensive advice and much-needed encouragement during my research. For my account of the 50s and 60s I am grateful to several film-makers, among whom Dai Vaughan and the late Maurice Hatton were particularly helpful, and I am indebted to Bert Hogenkamp for discussing his own material and inviting me to 'gatecrash' some of his viewings of archive films. I am grateful to Jim Pines and Paul Willemen for discussing their involvement in the British film culture of the 70s; to William Raban for thoughts and documentation on the London Film-Makers' Co-op; to Simon Blanchard for his perspective on the IFA; to Paul Marris for comments on the IFA, the GLC and the cultural industries policy; to Alan Fountain and Rod Stoneman for help with the material on Channel Four; to Rob MacPherson for access to his research on independent film in Scotland; and to Michael Chanan, the late Marc Karlin, Julian Petley and Sam Rhodie for further background information and comment.

For access to documentation, I would like to thank the library staff in charge of the IFA archive at Sheffield Hallam University, the Feminist Archive in Bradford, the London Film-Makers' Co-op, Steve MacIntyre at the London Film and Video Agency, Irene Whitehead at the BFI and the staff of the special collections at the BFI Library. My thanks to Kate and Joe Parry for guidance on the younger reader's perception of recent history and to Jonathan Parry for advice on technical points of writing and for consoling me that even for authors more proficient than I, writing can be slow and laborious.

Introduction

You weren't trying to record history. You were trying to make history. ... The whole point of revolutionary film was to make the struggle. (Dave Douglass, Cinema Action)

We declared proudly that we wanted to make our own subjective account. We wanted to make films that were off the beaten track. We wanted to make 'ourstories'. (Lina Gopaul, Black Audio)

This is a study about how two passions, for film and politics, intersected over a period of recent British history to fuel a biting critique of the media industries and inspire models for a radically different kind of cinema and television.

At times, those models had considerable public impact. Their products reached the cinema screen and were broadcast nationally. Even specialist exhibition could mean projection to thousands of workers at mass meetings. Nevertheless, the results achieved by operating outside or on the edge of commercial structures were, inevitably, on a smaller scale than those of the industry they sought to challenge. On these grounds detractors often dismiss the work as insignificant, or defend it in a back-handed way that it is indirectly effective, through a process of trickle-down, because 'important' people are influenced or because the commercial media borrow its themes and take up some of its practitioners. While there is little doubt that elements of yesterday's avant-garde surface in today's mainstream, the argument misses the point in proposing, as a measure of success, incorporation into the system under attack. Certainly, when the enterprise is at its most vital, the aim is to contest the whole territory of the media, and any marginal operation is intended as a base, not a permanent ghetto. Certainly, there is a hazy boundary between incorporation and infiltration, and the relative merit of changing the industry from within or opposing it from outside was a recurring subject for debate. But the change envisaged is fundamental and structural. So, if the project is to be valued at all, it must be for the qualities the mainstream does not digest: for an anarchic variety; for running to extremes; for risking absurdity; for offering glimpses of unknown social worlds; for opening doors to new ways of perceiving what there is and of imagining what there might be.

However marginal the work, it relates to questions which preoccupy a very large public. The high profile given by the press to any shred of evidence about the effects of television testifies to the level of popular interest and suggests there is a widespread consensus that the media have significance beyond making money for their owners. The obsession with supposed bad effects – links with crime, poor school performance – indicates a prevalent distrust of the business as it is. But tabloid press coverage of these issues usually gives little encouragement for public concern to develop into anything but a vague anxiety or the negative reflex of calling for more censorship. The impulse to experiment, to make films and television differently, is a positive response which stems from that same shared distrust.

This movement for change encompasses a tangle of political, economic and aesthetic motivations which are not easily subsumed under a single term. The words used so far – 'film' and 'politics' – need some qualification. 'Film' has already appeared with two different functions: to refer to film-like audiovisual products created by any technology; and to single out the products of a photographic process. For the first meaning, 'moving pictures' would be accurate but cumbersome, and its short form, 'movies' is too strongly associated with classic cinema. So, I continue to use 'film' and rely on context to distinguish between them. 'Politics' is too broad. The relevant politics in this context are those of the left, premised on the objective of redistributing power, wealth and cultural capital, and informed by the principle: 'From each according to his abilities, to each according to his needs.'[1] Marx is a key intellectual influence, even when gender or race rather than class are stressed. Many, but not all, of the protagonists would consider themselves socialists.

The period covered runs roughly from the end of the Second World War to 1990, although there is a concentration on the years of intense activity between the late 60s and the early 80s. A previous wave of creativity in the 30s has been documented and discussed in Don Macpherson's collection, *Traditions of Independence*,[2] while Bert Hogenkamp's *Deadly Parallels*[3] provides a more comprehensive, if less theorised, history. As I embarked on this study I heard that Hogenkamp was researching a follow-up volume on the 40s and 50s, a discovery which has served as an excuse to cull my own material on these years. The year 1990 signals a convenient break, not only because it defines a tidy decade but also because associations which had formed a support structure for political film – IFVPA, SEFT, WFTVN – were wound up or scaled down in the last years of the 80s, bringing to a close a particular phase of organisation.

The aspect of the work which is most difficult to define is the quality of being outside and different. The term which has probably been most widely used is 'independent', as in the Independent Film-Makers' Association (IFA), which was formed in the 70s by film-makers working outside the mainstream. At a time when most television was made in-house and much corporate work was carried out by in-house industrial film units, the word had a stronger resonance than it does now. Even so, it was seen as problematic by commentators within the IFA. Some thought the problem could be solved by redefinition. Paul Willemen, for instance, writes in *Traditions of Independence*:

> Existing uses of the term independent, meaning either independent of state
> funding (as in 'Independent' TV) or independence of the duopoly controlling film
> exhibition (as in the Association of 'Independent Producers') were criticised as
> inadequate because solely founded on narrow economic considerations, or worse
> as misleading. The IFA proposed to define independence as an oppositional
> practice ...[4]

Sylvia Harvey and Simon Blanchard expressed stronger reservations in their essay, 'The Post-War Independent Cinema', which opens with a history of the word that points to 'a pedigree whose dominant values are "non-partisan", if not frankly "anti-political"'.[5] They argue that the term gained currency partly because it was vague, 'a convenient expression of the sector's vacillation'.[6] Despite these criticisms, the phrase 'independent sector' (usually shortened, as above, to 'sector') became standard usage by the 80s when it acquired a more precise meaning through institutional associations: namely, an area of film activity supported by the IFA, assisted by grant aid and covered by a special union agreement.

Apart from the non-committal 'independent', most terms either define the area by its economic base or focus on objectives and content. In the economic category 'grant-aided', which became popular in the 80s, is the least helpful. Grant aid was only a major factor for a comparatively brief period from the late 70s to the late 80s, and became so then mainly because there was a vigorous movement which fought for it. During the late 60s and early 70s, when that movement was gaining momentum, scarcely any of the work associated with it received public funding. Even when the grants began flowing they only provided partial support for some of the work. One motive for adopting such a misleading term was the practical need for an objective distinction between work done primarily to generate income and work done primarily for social or aesthetic purposes. The receipt of a grant supposedly provided some guarantee as to the purpose, and was conditional on the delivery of accounts which would reveal any profit element.

The phrase 'non-commercial' had the disadvantage that it was not based on a clear criterion. Sometimes it was used to distinguish low-earning areas like educational film from high-earning areas like features, sometimes to designate the work of non-profit distributing organisations, or sometimes to indicate that wages were being waived for a charitable or political cause. Like the phrase 'grant-aided' it was often used with reference to practical questions to do with rates of pay and rights, with implications similar to 'non-theatric', the formal term for a release outside the commercial cinema. In relation to film politics, 'non-commercial' is flawed, because it posits a somewhat dubious distinction between profitable and subsidised activity, which responds more to the ideology than the actuality of 'commercial' production. For the film business is notorious, on the one hand, for a market completely distorted by monopoly and, on the other, for unsound speculation. Thus much 'commercial' production is cross-subsidised by people paying to see other films (since big producers balance losses from failures against profits from successes); some is supported indirectly from the public purse through tax losses; and some, following bankruptcies, is paid for by involuntary contributions from workers and investors. As for television, the status of the BBC is highly ambiguous because of the licence fee, while 'commercial' TV could also be described as subsidised by advertising.

Equally, work called 'non-commercial', purely because it is conducted outside the standard commercial arrangements, is not necessarily unprofitable. A more accurate definition would have to reflect the actual methods of support, which have been extremely varied, including commissions and sales as well as voluntary contributions from individuals, charitable grants, grants from public funds and payments for services (to trade unions, schools, local authorities, etc.).

Terms focused on the product also have to encompass variety. Most of those that refer to political objectives – 'socialist', 'feminist', 'anarchist' – are too narrow. 'Revolutionary' might serve but, if used in a literal political sense, promises too much: in Britain there was no revolution. Another approach is to stress the quality of being different and/or ground-breaking: 'experimental', 'innovative', 'alternative', 'oppositional', 'avant-garde' – expressions which, to some extent, are all coloured by the contexts in which they have been used. 'Experimental' was popular in the 50s and 60s, when the BFI subsidised the Experimental Film Fund, the precursor of the Production Division. This fund was often justified in terms of providing research and development for the mainstream, but the grants were so small that the work initiated by it was effectively amateur film. This history has left slight overtones of the nursery, of an exercise which is not quite serious itself but may lead to higher things. 'Innovative' has been worn down by its frequent use in Channel Four publicity that claims to fulfil the much-quoted brief to be 'innovative in form and content'. By emphasising the value of being new rather than of trying out, it fits more comfortably than 'experimental' into the language of fashion and commerce, but both words share the disadvantage that they are politically and culturally neutral.

'Oppositional' and 'alternative' foreground a relationship with the mainstream which became increasingly relevant from the late 60s with the development of a systematic and complex critique of dominant cinema. The weaker form, 'alternative', linked to phrases like 'alternative society' and 'alternative lifestyle', suggests an extension of personal choice in a plural culture in which different values are not necessarily in conflict with one another. 'Oppositional' implies taking a position within a struggle, and comes closer to the meaning I intend, although in the 70s 'oppositional cinema' was often assumed to centre round deconstruction, only one of a number of strategies.

'Avant-garde' is favoured by writers like Paul Willemen and Peter Wollen who place British oppositional cinema within a continuing European or international tradition of revolutionary art. However, to describe a present and evolving movement as avant-garde has required a conscious struggle to free the phrase from its association with a particular kind of 20s cinema and, more generally, with modernism. Willemen argues that modernist and avant-garde are not only different tendencies but also opposing ones, that modernism 'reduces artistic practice to a set of formal characteristics, a set of procedures frozen into specific generic practice and suggesting that modernism is a period style', while the avant-garde 'is not prescriptive about the precise characteristics of any given art practice'.[7] Thus, modernism, being both conservative and conformist, becomes the antithesis of the avant-garde. The distinction made here is an important one and accurately reflects tensions within the independent film movement, highlighting a tendency for temporary and exploratory strategies to be hijacked and codified as prescriptive rules. But I am doubtful whether 'avant-garde' can be made to carry that particular distinction. Apart from the associations with the 20s and modernism, there is the difficulty that its role in criticism has more often been to make a different distinction: between film as political art – the avant-garde – and film which is just political. The distinction is often more implicit than explicit, apparent from the set of films included in discussions of the avant-garde.[8] The criteria for inclusion was contested in the IFA, and when it was necessary to refer to the whole range of films made by members, it became common to talk about the 'aesthetic avant-garde' and the 'political avant-garde', which inevitably undermined the political force of plain 'avant-garde'.

Whatever it is called, the subject is fluid and the boundaries always controversial. Both mainstream and avant-garde contain contradictory tendencies. Even if the former is shaped by the drive for profit it does not mean that, as individuals, the players are always or only maximising wealth, or a combination of wealth, power and prestige. Personal values, inclinations and interests are also important. Individual motivation may be very mixed, particularly as it is not self-evident how to maximise profit in a business characterised by rapid change and affected by ill-defined factors like taste and fashion. The need to steal a competitive lead over a rival can involve adopting an oppositional cause like feminism or race. But change usually has to be fought for even when it is good for business and individual careers are bound up in those struggles. Entry to, and advancement in, the industry is highly competitive, and one way that newcomers justify their inclusion or promotion is that they offer something different. So, taking an oppositional stand may be a good career move. If this is all it is, the stand may be modified once the promotion is secured; alternatively, a promotion may be used to advance oppositional objectives. Similarly, a decision to work outside the industry may be less to do with a struggle against capitalism than with career opportunities within other areas, such as education or the art world. It is often only as events and careers unfold that it becomes possible to identify how the minor conflicts fit into the larger pattern.

In this study I have tried to give a sense of the variety and range of practices and to trace the cross-currents of influence and co-operation rather than provide comprehensive documentation of a narrower field. The content was to some extent influenced by the pragmatic consideration that some areas are already well covered. Much of the most influential theory is available in collections and anthologies. Derek Jarman, undoubtedly one of the most important individual film-makers, has inspired three books[9] on different aspects of his life and work. There have been three recent contributions to the critical study of film and video art: Julia Knight's *Diverse Practices*,[10] Michael O'Pray's *The British Avant-Garde Film*[11] and the *Directory of Film and Video Artists*.[12] As already mentioned, Bert Hogenkamp has a book in progress on film and the labour movement from the 40s to the 60s. I complement these studies by concentrating on the period after 1968 and on collective action rather than the work of individual artists.

The book is divided into three sections. The first is a short, general history in which I look at the evolution of left politics, film politics and left film practices from the end of the war to the late 80s. Part II is a collection of articles and documents produced by the film culture of the 70s and 80s. Part III contains detailed oral histories of selected companies and workshops: the two distributors whose work forms a link between the traditions of the 30s and those of the 70s; three of the pioneering film groups formed at the end of the 60s; one of the first feminist groups formed in the early 70s and one of the first black workshops established in the early 80s. My analysis dissents from the orthodoxy of the 70s by attributing more importance to the struggles of the preceding decades, but accepts the view that the political ferment of the late 60s marked a watershed and germinated film practices which were both different from anything which had gone before and more profoundly critical of capitalist culture.

The interviews in Part III include some personal histories, an approach rarely employed in contemporary discussion, and one that was played down for practical and theoretical reasons. The requirements of collective work called for an assertion of unity and common objectives over potentially divisive differences, while there was a reluctance to give out personal details which might feed the mainstream media's obsession with personalities. Aspects of Marxist theory (some versions of economic determinism, in particular) could be interpreted as minimising the significance of individual biography, while the influence of the Women's Movement was contradictory: on the one hand, feminists promoted a concept of collective action extremely hostile to named leaders or representatives, and, on the other, launched the slogan, 'The personal is political', encouraging women to interrogate their own home life.

As I progressed with my research I became more and more interested in questions of personal motivation, a preoccupation which does not imply a denial of the social process but rather a recognition that individual experiences can contribute to an understanding of it. A question underlying many reformulations of Marxist theory, and of obvious importance to the activist, is how revolutionary change is possible, given an interdependence between society and thought. I am not suggesting that information about the background and politicisation of a few individuals provides answers to such a major question, but that it offers clues. I would also argue that everyone trails a weight of ideological baggage from their own past and that, while it may or may not be relevant to particular conflicts or alliances, it should form part of the analysis.

This position puts me under some obligation to come clean about my own background and connections with the subject, for I have been and am, in a minor way, a participant. The phrase 'red diaper baby' used by one of the founders of Angry Arts struck a chord with me, as my parents were also socialists and had been communists up to the Second World War. They were from the professional middle class, but not a moneyed subsection of it. I absorbed their values, only slowly noticing that they were not the usual ones of my class, at least not in the 50s in suburban Bristol, where we lived.

My relationship with the cinema was a far less placid affair. Childhood encounters with this supposed treat were an acute disappointment. Before the show, the screen would look suitably promising, draped with an illuminated curtain, slowly changing through the colours of the rainbow. When the lights dimmed there was a moment of magical suspense, but the film, with a very few exceptions, seemed to me to be silly, frightening or both, and certainly a let-down after the glowing curtains. With hindsight, this might be understood as an early experience of cultural colonisation, because what I remember disliking in cartoons were squawky American voices and the coy sweetness of female characters, quite unlike the hefty Pansy Potter or warped Keyhole Kate of my comics.[13] Nevertheless, the *idea* of the cinema remained attractive and I persevered, but not enough to internalise the Hollywood codes. A breakthrough came later on when I discovered a small cinema on the other side of town which showed 'Continental' films, alternating soft porn and classics. Probably, the reason for the first visit was the attraction of the 'X' certificate and being able to pass for sixteen. The picture was *Gervaise*, not one that figures in many people's lists of most memorable films, but at the time it was a shock and permanently changed my notion of what cinema might be.

Despite a growing fascination with the medium, the possibility of getting a job in film never crossed my mind at school, where I progressed obediently along an educational conveyer belt which led to Cambridge University. As soon as I arrived there in 1961 I joined the Socialist Society and the Film Society, and when I left, tried and failed for a BBC traineeship. I had assumed the film industry was inaccessible until a chance opening in a factory film unit in Bristol gave me an entry. I became an assistant editor, moved to London and began to get freelance jobs in the feature studios. This was the mid-60s, when an influx of American investment was creating a boom in freelance employment. Like a lot of other young technicians, I did a bit of work on my own, using borrowed equipment and short ends of film donated by the camera department. I went to meetings of the film trade union, ACTT, and was elected to the Editorial Section Committee, but film and politics remained rather separate until a commonplace incident jolted me into seeing a connection.

I was working as an assistant editor for an American company and the front office suddenly, and pointlessly, made a demand which would require the cutting room to work more or less round the clock. According to union rules we would be on double time until we got a twelve-hour break, and the editor cheerfully assumed the producer would back down when reminded how much his whim would cost. But compared with Hollywood technicians, we were cheap and the message came back, 'We'll pay. Just do it.' The experience gave meaning to the notion of economic and cultural colonialism and set me thinking in a new way about the industry I worked in.

At that time the union was in a position to extract a good price from unreasonable employers, and the proceeds from such jobs were indirectly responsible for an encounter with traditional, direct colonialism. The money enabled me to take a long break. In 1967 I set off with a friend to travel in Africa and through sheer serendipity we came to work as volunteers in Tanzania for the Mozambique Liberation Front (FRELIMO), which was conducting a guerrilla war across the border against the Portuguese colonial government. After that, film and politics came together in a different way, when I undertook to make a documentary about the struggle[14] and raising the money for it brought me into closer contact with London's left cultural networks. This was 1968–9 when the first film groups were forming, and I attended Angry Arts screenings, edited *All You Need Is an Excuse* for Liberation Films and worked on some collective productions, but, partly because I moved to Scotland, did not become a member of any group. Having returned to London, I became a founder member of the IFA.

When I began compiling this book I thought that having been a participant would be a considerable advantage. However, I soon realised that my own involvement was slight and that the movement was so scattered and varied that large parts of it had completely escaped my notice. Even events I had been involved in were usually recalled differently by other people, confirming the notoriously unreliable quality of memory. Thus my involvement was not a great practical help, and it certainly prevents me claiming the role of impartial observer. Fortunately, that is not my intention. The initial impetus for putting together this material was to make the experience of the past more easily available to those carrying on the oppositional tradition in the present.

This is not to suggest that the account provides lessons. The media business changes very fast and politics evolve. Trying to bring film and politics together in the run-up to the twenty-first century is a very different proposition from doing it in the 60s. Core objectives remain, but each expression is a new incarnation. However, digesting earlier incarnations can speed up an understanding of the present one. The past can be a stimulus, a provocation. On the negative side, misunderstandings can drag back the present. For example, the late 80s and 90s witnessed the demise of creative enterprises in the face of the withdrawal of public funds. It is easy to assume that the enterprises were established by those funds, whereas a longer perspective suggests a very different pattern.

Reflecting on the material, what is striking is, first, how much of what was achieved was set in motion merely by large inputs of voluntary labour; and second, what a high proportion of the individuals involved made quite distinctive contributions, whether they were part of collectives or working alone. That makes the subject constantly interesting but difficult to cover in a representative way. It has meant talking to a great many people just to get a sense of the range of activities which should be included. I am extremely grateful for the help and advice of all those I managed to approach, but am uncomfortably aware of many other people who played a significant role whom I should have consulted but did not. My defence is that I do not offer this as a comprehensive history but as a resource and basis for further discussion.

Even a provisional history, however, suggests some general observations. While compiling this one I have been asked with some frequency whether the movement 'achieved anything'. The question is difficult to answer when couched in terms of such generality. For we are not dealing with a single organisation pursuing a well-defined goal, but with loosely connected groups and individuals following partially compatible objectives in a complex and changing environment. Participants were drawn into the movement for a variety of reasons, and an important stimulus was provided by their own dissatisfaction with mainstream media. The interviews in Part III explore feelings of exclusion or being misled as consumers and frustrated as employees. A first step towards an oppositional practice was often the attempt to understand and articulate such experiences. In that context the general question about achievements can be treated as a series of more specific questions about the efficacy of action at specific times, in relation to the needs and aims of specific individuals and groups. Questions of that kind are raised and addressed throughout the text and most directly in Part III. For instance, there is evidence that the groups documented there at least temporarily provided for their members more satisfying working conditions than those that existed in the industry, and that they answered the needs of certain sections of the public. The film-makers were able to engage with diverse minorities – from teachers to employees of declining heavy industry, from women trade unionists to black students – and worked with them to construct images and meanings which were evidently of relevance to those people at the time.

Giving examples of such temporary practical successes is only a partial answer. It is possible to make a case that the practices described here were often resourceful, produced some highly creative work and catered effectively to a genuine demand, while dismissing the rationale for these practices. But the premise which gives coherence to the oppositional agenda is that there is a continuing struggle between dominant and dominated sections of society which takes place in the mind through language and communication as well as in the external world. (I choose this open formulation rather than adopting the classic Marxist terms of labour and capital, because there was always disagreement – explicit and implicit – about identifying the fundamental organising principles of society, while there was broad consensus that there are principles, including class, gender and race, producing inequality.) If the movement is perceived as trying to influence such a continuing process, then a key consideration will be whether its activities provided for continuity and development.

To take first the question of continuity, the period I cover falls into two distinct phases, with a change occurring round about the mid-60s. Before that the Communist Party is a central influence and film-related work revolves round developing the institutions of art cinema; afterwards a new generation with more varied leftist allegiances embarks on the project of creating a more assertively political cinema. While the practices of the 70s were not a direct development from those of the 50s, I argue in Chapter 1 that the latter prepared the ground and that, in particular, the diversity of films made available through film societies and art cinemas nurtured the cinematic imagination of subsequent generations. A striking testimony to such indirect influences occurs in the dossier on Black Audio in Part III, when John Akomfrah describes how his ideas about cinema developed after seeing programmes at the Paris Pullman, the showcase cinema run by Contemporary Films, a distribution company founded in the 50s by a communist who, as a member of Kino in the 30s, had been involved in an even earlier phase of the movement.[15]

During the 70s and the first half of the 80s the tradition becomes more continuous. There were waves of new activity associated with the entry into the arena of younger film-makers, but these new arrivals for the most part knew about work already going on and when they disagreed with more established film-makers, this disagreement was a result of assimilating and reacting to their ideas. By the end of the 80s, however, the movement was less cohesive, as the structures through which debate was carried on – associations, magazines, festivals – were disappearing. Looking beyond this point, threads of continuity did continue into the late 90s. The London Film-Makers' Co-op and London Electronic Arts (formerly London Video Arts) remained active and in 1997 jointly opened new premises at the Lux Centre.[16] Although two important magazines, *Undercut* and *Independent Media*, folded in 1990 and 1991 respectively, discussions about the fate of *Independent Media* led to the launch of a new magazine, *Vertigo*, with an agenda which reasserted the connection between politics, media politics and the avant-garde. Of the five workshops covered in Part III two are still active at the time of writing, and in the 90s new groups like Undercurrents carried forward the tradition of gathering and disseminating material on social action.[17]

Some correlation between continuity and development is to be expected, and history leaves little doubt that the movement developed, in the sense that there was a learning process – ideas and strategies were tried out, criticised and changed. Whether there was also development in terms of sustained progress is more diffi-cult to assess, since circumstances were always changing. There is certainly a more extensive and elaborated body of media theory available now than there was in the 40s. There is also a much larger and more varied body of practical political experi-ence to draw on: experience of different kinds of co-operative and collective decision-making; of different ways of allocating production tasks and distributing finished product; of a variety of relationships with mainstream television. Yet the picture presented at the end of Chapter 4 is one of diminishing effectiveness. This is accentuated by the decision to draw the story to a close at the point when several significant institutions were wound up. That this was not the end of oppositional activity has already been mentioned. Nevertheless, the loss of those institutions and the lack of obvious successors naturally cast some doubt over the future: is this a time of temporary retreat or have events undermined the movement's rationale?

The question has wide-ranging references – to the collapse of Soviet commu-nism, to the rise of religious fundamentalism, to controversies around free-market economics, to post-modernist theory. The oppositional rationale can be attacked on the grounds that there is no continuing struggle, that capitalism has no general tendencies or only liberating ones, that hierarchies of wealth and power are nat-ural, inevitable and/or beneficial, and at this level the objections need to be addressed from a far broader perspective than the one this study pretends to offer. However, arguments relating specifically to the media demand some comment, and here the factors most frequently invoked are the effects of the digital revolution and of globalisation.

One line of thought is that strategy centred round state intervention – regula-tion, nationalisation, grant aid – has no future because the process of globalisation is robbing the nation state of its political and cultural significance. Whether or not the latter part of this analysis is correct – and it is speculative, based on projecting forward selected trends – the relevance to oppositional film culture is highly ques-tionable. Film activists in the past were by no means unanimous in their attitude to the state and state funding. Many were anarchists or syndicalists who had little faith in any kind of centralised power structures. It is true that the left in the ACTT suggested nationalising the cinema in the 40s and again in the 70s, but even those proposals did not envisage handing the industry's assets over to monolithic state institutions.[18] Nor was support for nationalisation backed by a rhetoric of cultural nationalism. The aim was to secure a stable base for film-making in Britain, and to that extent the nation state was treated as a significant political/geographical unit. But that does not imply either that there is a homogeneous British culture or that films made in Britain would or should reflect it. As far as those notions played a part in the film debates, they were the currency of parliamentary speeches rather than oppositional tracts. Far from being fixated on the national, the oppositional tradition has always had a strong internationalist streak, while individual groups tended to have strong local allegiances. More importantly, the address to institutions, whether national, supra-national or local, was pragmatic and instrumental. The core of the oppositional strategy, described in the IFA foundation paper as the 'preservation and development of critical thought',[19] has to do precisely with obtaining through collective action a degree of autonomy from established centres of power.

Arguments about the digital revolution also involve projections into the future and prognoses tend to be based either on the growth of global monopoly, as personified by Rupert Murdoch, or on the open, interactive potential of the internet.[20] The latter holds out the promise of a new kind of image culture, no longer characterised by transmission from a privileged elite to the masses but by a free exchange naturally reflecting the diverse preoccupations and interests of the wired public. There would be no dominant agenda requiring concerted resistance, and the oppositional tradition could dissolve into a multiplicity of unconnected creative and critical strands. But the scenario remains hypothetical and coexists with that of global monopoly. So, are they compatible? Is one of the pictures based on a misreading of the present? Could there be monopoly transmission in one sphere and exchange in another? The very fact that present trends can appear so contradictory highlights the pressing need for continuing analysis. And if the purpose is to influence the situation, this would mean more than academics writing papers. It requires the combination of critical thought, practical politics and creative production which characterises the oppositional tradition.

The disintegration of the infrastructure associated with that tradition in the 80s is not necessarily the setback it seemed to be at the time. Each phase of the movement gave rise to structures which responded to the specific conditions and opportunities of the moment. As those conditions changed, the structures also changed and were adapted and abandoned for all kinds of reasons. Given the cumulative pressure from the right in Britain and the dramatic changes that took place throughout the world in the late 80s and early 90s, it is hardly surprising that an institutional framework which originated nearly twenty years earlier came under severe stress. A new situation requires a period of reflection, and this may be better served by scattered informal networks than by high-profile structures which take time and effort to maintain. It is too soon to make any confident assessment of the meaning of this last part of the story.

Notes

1. Karl Marx, 'Critique of the Gotha Programme', in *Karl Marx and Frederich Engels Selected Works Volume II* (Moscow: Foreign Languages Publishing House, 1962), p. 24.
2. Don Macpherson (ed.), *Traditions of Independence* (London: BFI Publishing, 1980).
3. Bert Hogenkamp, *Deadly Parallels* (London: Lawrence and Wishart, 1986).
4. Paul Willemen, 'Presentation', in Macpherson (ed.), *Traditions*, p. 1.

5. Simon Blanchard and Sylvia Harvey, 'The Post-War Independent Cinema – Structures and Organisation', in James Curran and Vincent Porter (eds), *British Cinema History* (London: Weidenfeld and Nicolson, 1983), p. 227.

6. Ibid., p. 241.

7. Paul Willemen, *Looks and Frictions* (London: BFI Publishing, 1994), p. 143.

8. See, for instance, David Curtis (ed.), *The Directory of British Film and Video Artists* (Luton: John Libbey Media, 1996).

9. Michael O'Pray, *Derek Jarman, Dream of England* (London: BFI Publishing, 1996); Roger Wollen (ed.), *Derek Jarman, a Portrait* (London: Thames and Hudson, 1996); Chris Lippard (ed.), *By Angels Driven: The Films of Derek Jarman* (Trowbridge, Wilts: Flicks Books, 1996).

10. Julia Knight (ed.), *Diverse Practices: A Critical Reader on British Video Art* (Luton: Arts Council/John Libbey Media, 1996).

11. Michael O'Pray, *The British Avant-Garde Film* (Luton: John Libbey Media, 1996).

12. David Curtis (ed.), *The Directory of British Film and Video Artists* (Luton: John Libbey Media, 1996).

13. See *Dandy Monster Comic* (Dundee: D. C. Thompson and Co., nd).

14. *Behind the Lines* (1970) was shot by John Fletcher, who had been a member of the Free Cinema group, edited by Ellen Adams, co-founder of the Angry Arts Film Society, and distributed by Contemporary Films. It therefore serves as an example of how interrelated the old and the new independent networks were.

15. For the background to the Paris Pullman, see p. 214; for John Akomfrah's account, see p. 302.

16. See Sarah Turner, 'The Lux Centre: Eastward Ho!', *Vertigo* issue 7, Autumn 1997, p. 9.

17. See James Hartzell, Robert Morris and Peter Sibley, 'Video Power', *Vertigo* issue 4, Winter 1994/5, p. 12.

18. See pp. 20–1 & 109.

19. See p. 135.

20. For a discussion about the implications of the internet, see John Wyver, 'Gardening the Net', Paul Walton and Brian Winston, 'Virtually Free' and Granville Williams, 'Media Meltdown' in *Vertigo* issue 6, Autumn 1996, pp. 26, 30, 32.

Part I

A Short History

Chapter One
Hope Deferred (1945–65)

The sudden flowering of oppositional film culture at the end of the 60s made the preceding era appear, by contrast, something of a desert. The theorists of the 70s were more interested in the left film activity of the 30s than in anything that happened after the war. As Paul Willemen put it in *Traditions of Independence*:

> The IFA embarked on a search for its precursors and found them in the 30s, the only time when film makers had presented an organised challenge to the dominant prejudices of the industry in directly political and ideological terms as well as in economic ones.[1]

Similarly, Bert Hogenkamp concluded his pre-war history by suggesting that the story effectively ends when all but one of the film groups were wound up during the war.[2] This is a judgment the author may revise in his own forthcoming book on the 40s and 50s, for the picture of a thirty-year break is, at the very least, an exaggeration. Lines of continuity can be traced through a number of distributors, as some of the 70s practitioners were well aware. Liberation Films, for instance, acknowledged significant support from distributors set up in the 50s, which themselves had links with the 30s.[3]

One reason for ignoring or discounting the work of the left in the post-war decades was that much of it was perceived as being purely cultural (like the promotion of European or Asian films) or purely economic (like the enforcement of minimum rates of pay) while the most overtly political aspect – the campaign for state control of the film industry – bore little fruit. Nevertheless, these activities were a continuation, in different circumstances, of what the pre-war left had been doing. The 30s tradition had not so much been extinguished as fragmented. The film groups then had been part of a broader network of political and cultural initiatives which embraced the film societies, the amateur film movement, the Documentary Movement (all well covered in *Traditions of Independence*) and the growth of trade unionism within the mainstream film industry.[4] While only one of the production groups lasted beyond the war, these other organisations and areas of activity survived, developed and helped shape the environment from which the radicalism of the late 60s emerged.

In some respects the work of the 40s and 50s was too directly a continuation of the pre-war tradition. Networks and structures evolved but the thinking behind them changed rather little except to adjust, often with difficulty, to a series of technological and institutional revolutions sweeping through the industry. The most far-reaching of these were, of course, connected with television. During these years BBC transmissions began (not counting the limited pre-war experiment): the BBC monopoly gave way to the BBC/ITV duopoly; the BBC acquired its second channel; and watching TV evolved from a rare novelty to an almost universal, daily pastime. Although less momentous, the switch from optical to magnetic recording for films and the introduction of lightweight, 16mm blimped cameras did much to change working practices and the expectations of audiences and critics.

From a chronological perspective, the period can roughly be divided into a very short but creative phase of radical optimism up to about 1948, a long phase of defensive adjustment lasting well into the 60s and, overlapping with this, another more creative period starting around the end of the 50s in which new forms of political expression and new political and cultural theories are beginning to make their mark. In the first period the left hoped to overturn the corporate control of the film industry and thereby change the mainstream; during the second and third phases it was a matter of keeping a few checks on the corporate owners and opening a few spaces outside their control.

Political Background

In the 30s the film activists had been closely linked to political parties, and this pattern continued into the 40s and 50s. Film practices were therefore defined to a great extent by national and international politics. The most directly influential political events were those affecting alignments within the left and particularly the position of the small but dynamic Communist Party. Many of the individuals prominent in the radical film politics of the 30s were communists and remained so after the war. Two such key figures, both active in the leadership of the Association of Cine-Technicians (ACT), were Ivor Montagu, who had founded the London Film Society in 1925 and later the Progressive Film Institute and Ralph Bond who, with Montagu and others, had set up the Federation of Workers' Film Societies and worked on some of the earliest workers' newsreels. Again, after the war, it was communists who took the initiative to re-establish a left film service – Stanley Forman with Plato Films and Charles Cooper with Contemporary Films. The interviews conducted with them in Part III illustrate some of the ways in which the position of the party impinged on their work.

The war left a mixed legacy for communists. Many sympathisers were shaken by the way the British Communist Party followed the Moscow line, first condemning the war as imperialist and then hailing it as progressive when Russia was invaded. Later on, the performance of the Red Army and the activities of communist partisans for the first time gave communism a moderately favourable press, but this began to change again towards the end of hostilities when the divisions of the cold war were taking shape. The transformation of Russia back from ally to enemy was, however, gradual and in 1945 other outcomes seemed possible.

The decisive Labour majority in the post-war election was unforeseen[5] and the wider implications were hard to predict, as this was the first ever Labour Government with a clear mandate and it was taking power in the first year of a re-ordered world. Socialists and communists made electoral gains all across Europe, holding out a utopian promise of a new democratic force aligned neither with Stalinism nor with free-market capitalism. However, the present reality was one of increasing tension between the western alliance and the Soviet Union, an uneasy relationship that in Britain separated Labour and Communist supporters. For Labour the priority was to implement the electoral programme; for the communists it was to support the Soviet Union and promote good British–Soviet relationships.[6]

Differences widened as the slide towards cold war continued. By 1946 it was becoming clear that the key division in Europe would be between communist and non-communist and that the Labour government was seeking alliance with the United States against the Soviet Union. But, again, it took time for the alignments to harden. Landmarks on the road to confrontation included the Berlin blockade of 1948, the signing of the Nato alliance in 1949 and the outbreak of the Korean War in 1950, all accompanied by an anti-communist rhetoric from politicians and press. The British Communist Party became increasingly defensive and closed. At the same time, the cold war accentuated differences within the Labour Party as the left wing continued to favour co-operation with the Soviet Union. Thus, by the time the next election was due, the Labour Party was divided internally and the Labour left was distanced from the communists.

Labour just scraped through in 1950, but a second election returned the Conservatives to power in 1951 and assured a further drift to the right. Labour's reforms were put into reverse, but it was done gently and the impact, unlike in the 80s, was softened by continued high levels of employment. Nor was the welfare state abolished. Changes in the terms of trade gave the economy an artificial boost and hastened the end of rationing. The Conservatives were returned again in 1955. Actual prosperity was exaggerated by a consumer boom which filled streets with cars and roofs with television aerials, so that those who remained poor could assume, even without the media, that everyone else was doing well. And the media certainly confirmed the impression with constant references to affluence. The irrelevance of socialism became a popular theme and was more and more taken for granted. When 1959 brought yet another Conservative victory, Hugh Gaitskell, then leader of the Labour Party, proposed abolishing Clause Four on social ownership. Unlike his successor of the 90s, he failed and the clause was retained after a long and bitter struggle.

Just when socialism seemed to be beaten at the polls and beaten even within the Labour Party, there were faint signs of revival. Two events in 1956 were significant, although possibly more as symptoms than cause. One was the invasion of Hungary by the Soviet Union. The British Communist Party refused to condemn the Soviet action and thousands of its members left in protest. The other was the abortive Anglo-French invasion of Egypt. Faced with Labour leaders who joined in the vilification of Nasser, many supporters were shocked into moving leftwards. Increasingly, people interested in socialism did not turn to either the Labour or the Communist Parties but looked for some other way of expressing their politics.[7] Some joined Trotskyist parties, while others threw their energies into single-issue campaigns, particularly CND and then Anti-Apartheid. The evident need to rethink socialist goals and strategies found expression in the growth of the New Left.

In many respects left film activity paralleled national politics. Work done in production and distribution reflects the divisions of the cold war and the increasing marginalisation of socialism. A partial exception, however, was a long-running campaign around official film policy.

The Campaign to Change the Mainstream

In 1945 virtually everyone on the left concerned with film united to put pressure on the new Labour government to bring the film industry under state control. The lobby included the Tribune Group in the Labour Party, the Workers' Film Association and the Documentary Movement, and a leading role was played by the ACT. Founded in 1933, the ACT was the youngest of the trade unions organising in the industry before the war and, unlike the Electrical Trades Union (ETU) and the National Association of Theatrical and Kinematograph Employees (NATKE), Actors' Equity and the Musicians' Union, it had been formed specifically to organise film workers. The membership included lighting cameramen, editors and directors, employees for whom creative frustration as much as economic insecurity was a motive for joining. Among them was an influential group of left-wingers who helped to keep policy issues on the agenda. Before and during the war the ACT was already promoting arguments for radical state intervention. In 1939 it published *Film Business Is Big Business*,[8] a political and economic analysis which emphasised the means by which American corporate interests controlled the British market. In 1941 a report recommending nationalisation was put to the membership and published in the union's journal as 'A State Film Industry?'.[9] This contains the basis of the arguments put forward in the first years of peace and, in certain respects, is more interesting than post-war contributions. It makes a stronger case for nationalisation as opposed to regulation, and yet acknowledges that state ownership by itself would be no guarantee of an industry more responsive to its workforce and its public:

> nationalisation, an economic method of organisation, is not in itself the solution
> to social difficulties. The democratic enlargement of the influence of the public on
> the operation of each national service and on the affairs of the State is
> indispensable.[10]

The authors already foresee the aggressive post-war strategy which Hollywood and the American State Department would adopt, and warn that protection could be 'effected completely only at a cost of a conflict with the incompatible US interests'.[11] They recommend imposing an import duty on American films but emphasise the need to introduce it slowly.[12] While putting the argument for complete nationalisation – or municipalisation – of exhibition, the report sets out, as a short-term strategy, the establishment of a state sector comprising a production enterprise, a distributor, studios and a credit organisation. Variants of this idea formed the basis of the left campaign immediately after the war.

In 1945 there seemed some realistic chance that such proposals could become policy, for the war years had provided new precedents for state control of the economy and for public patronage of culture and entertainment which fed into the post-war nationalisations and the creation of the Arts Council. In relation to cinema, the war had forced a rethink about notions of luxury and necessity, about the value of entertainment in general and film in particular, in which considerations of morale had been at least as important as those of propaganda. The government was quickly persuaded that cinemas should remain open despite air-raid risks and, with more difficulty, that film production should have the resources to ensure a continuing supply of home-produced entertainment.[13] In the early 40s, severe problems of foreign exchange put a new complexion on the issue and rekindled debate about the long-standing and well-publicised problem of American competition. Before the war, under pressure from an alliance of trade interests and protectionists, the government had passed Acts in 1927 and 1938 which obliged cinemas to show a quota of British films. Then during the war anxiety about the dollar cost of American films made the government consider more radical ways of cutting imports.[14] Although these were rejected, the discussions helped establish the view that the film trade was a matter for government concern. This notion received further support in 1944 from the influential Palache Report[15] on the growth of monopoly. This made public a situation well understood in the trade: namely, that the three large cinema circuits that dominated the market were linked with American distributors and gave preference to American product. A concept of independence was frequently invoked at this time, denoting commercial independence from the combines rather than anything more radical. Whether this kind of independence had any aesthetic or political implications was as arguable then as it is now, but it was often associated with a strategy of making modest pictures for the British market.

So, when the post-war discussions began, the case for state control was not only a left-wing cause but was also backed by an official report, by well-known feature producers like Michael Balcon, by the Documentary Movement and a body of moderate opinion outside the industry. In 1945 Stafford Cripps, as President of the Board of Trade, gave serious consideration to a memorandum from Paul Rotha that suggested the establishment of a Film Corporation with wide powers along the lines of the National Film Board of Canada.[16] The left meanwhile kept up the pressure in Parliament and the press. Two rather similar pamphlets of 1946 reiterated the arguments about monopoly: the ACT's *Monopoly: The Future of British Films*, by Ralph Bond, and *Films: An Alternative to Rank*, by Frederick Mullally, a member of the Tribune Group.

In the event, the government ignored most of the advice from the left.[17] The first major disappointment was the reorganisation of the official film service, which was placed under the new common services department, the Central Office of Information, instead of being set up as a separate organisation with a creative brief, as Rotha and others had advised. The first government action affecting the feature business was motivated almost entirely by fiscal considerations and proved to be a blunder which alienated almost everyone concerned with film. This was the hasty imposition, during the financial crisis of 1947, of a massive *ad valorem* import duty of 75 per cent on all imported films, the object of which was to save dollars rather than to protect British producers. The measure provoked an immediate boycott by the Motion Picture Export Association of America (MPEA), Hollywood's powerful trade association. Any hopes that the duty and the withdrawal of American films might stimulate British production were dashed when the duty was removed, equally hastily, in 1948 after a compromise, agreed with the MPEA, limiting the repatriation of earnings. Following the agreement, a flood of high-quality American films hit the market and the slump in British production, which followed in 1949, was so severe that technicians still talked about it twenty years later. The mismanagement of the whole affair by the Board of Trade and their protestations that they had been taken by surprise contrast sharply with the clarity with which the ACT had argued the need to prepare for a boycott in 1941. The ACT was also right in thinking that the MPEA would have the full backing of the State Department, for the banning of film quotas was one of the American objectives in the international trade negotiations of 1946 and 1947, as it was in the most recent round of GATT half a century later.

The slump of 1949 increased pressure on the government to provide assistance for producers, and a mass meeting of the ACT reiterated demands for a state distribution organisation and a state-owned cinema circuit.[18] By this time the government had decided against any major restructuring. The Films Act of 1948 had simply modified and renewed the regulations and screen quota which had been introduced before the war. A second Act of 1949 went some way to satisfying the independent lobby and the ACT by setting up a films' bank – the National Films' Finance Corporation (NFFC) – although with more limited powers than the union had called for.

Before the disappointments of the 40s had been fully absorbed, Labour was voted out of office and the long period of Conservative rule began. The direct effects on the film industry were comparatively minor. The Crown Film Unit was abolished and the powers of the NFFC restricted still further. Otherwise the framework of aid was kept in place and another plank was added: namely, a levy paid from cinema receipts to producers of British films. Known as the Eady levy, it began as a voluntary arrangement but became statutory in 1957. The screen quota, the levy and the NFFC formed the basis of the aid regime which lasted until the mid-80s.

The long period of Conservative rule in the 50s coincided with the spectacular decline of the cinema. It was also a feature of the decline that monopoly became even more deeply entrenched. Faced with this situation, the ACT's political interventions became more defensive. The old arguments against monopoly were repeated at intervals but with less and less chance of influencing action, and the ACT aligned itself with the other film unions and the employers in calling for the continuation of the existing regime of aid. During the more defensive phase of the campaign after 1949, demands centred round the organisation of an extra circuit – first of all a fourth circuit – then, when the existing three were reduced to two, a third circuit.[19] This notion of an independent circuit fed into the debates about parallel cinema in the late 60s which preceded the establishment of The Other Cinema.

Union Power

As the possibility of changing the industry receded, the union concentrated on the task of protecting its members' immediate interests in the business as it was. On this front it was reasonably successful. It moved in to organise independent television in 1955, adding the other 'T' to its name a year later; it was instrumental in setting up the Federation of Film Unions in 1956 to strengthen co-operation with the other British unions; it pursued foreign links and led the way to the formation of the International Federation of Audiovisual Workers' Unions (FISTAV) in 1974; and it maintained a post-entry closed shop, which helped to ensure that agreements were usually enforced. These agreements were often attacked in the 60s on the grounds that they inhibited artistic experiment by imposing unnecessarily large and expensive crews. They were criticised in the 70s by the left for maintaining a rigid division of labour and a hierarchy of status and pay. Both lines of criticism were based on a somewhat distorted picture of the situation. In the first case because, in practice, the crews on feature films nearly always exceeded the minimum, so that if experiment was inhibited, this was due more to decisions on the part of the producer than demands by the union. In the second case because, in practice, employment patterns were more hierarchical and rigid than the agreements. The fees employers were actually prepared to pay, the 'going rate', were usually well above the minimum for a director or lighting cameraman and only slightly, if at all, above the level for a clapper-loader or runner. Individuals experienced difficulties crossing grades and getting promotion because employers looked for a proven track record in one grade, not because union rules prevented mobility. The only restrictions imposed by the union were those sometimes placed temporarily on new entrants; otherwise, members were entitled to work in any job or at any grade. Both sets of critics failed to acknowledge that the union procedures were

designed to protect rather than police the members and that action was usually precipitated by a complaint. So, if all members on a production were content with
conditions, even if these flouted a few rules, the production was unlikely to be
stopped. Similarly, rules could be officially waived if employers made a good case
and their employees did not object. The whole rule book could be changed by the
members, and there was no fundamental objection to equal and flexible working
arrangements, as the evolution of the Workshop Agreement in the late 70s and early
80s was to show.[20] The older agreements for mainstream working, with their built-
in assumptions, were not invented by union officials in a vacuum but were the
outcome of protracted negotiations with employers who had modelled the industry to suit themselves and resisted any attempts to change it. The result was a
compromise which was certainly not egalitarian but at least gave employees some
control over how they worked and enforced some minimal redistribution from
profits and fees at the top to wages at the bottom. One by-product was that professionals could earn enough from commercial jobs to be free to work unpaid on
special projects from time to time and so contribute to the culture of sharing which
facilitated independent work.

Alternative Production

In the context of the the 40s and 50s 'alternative' seems a better term than 'independent' for work which was oppositional or marginal, because of the use of the
latter term in the monopoly debate for commercial feature companies. But 'alternative' makes a distinction not normally emphasised at the time. Even the left,
despite being concerned about issues of ownership and control, did not on the
whole question prevailing industry aesthetics or notions of professionalism. People
made films on minimal budgets using unorthodox methods for pragmatic reasons,
because that was the only way they could make them. Newcomers complained of
the industry's closed shop mentality, intellectuals attacked prevailing aesthetics and
activists pointed to political bias, but the relationship with the mainstream was not
deeply theorised. This goes some way to explaining why the IFA's paper, *Independent Film-Making in the 70s*, ignores almost all the alternative production of this
period, mentioning only Free Cinema. But there was a continuous, albeit erratic,
trickle of marginal productions: some, like Free Cinema, very much the product of
individual enterprise, but some responding to collective, political objectives.

There were attempts in the 40s and 50s to revive the practice of making films for
the labour movement and left causes, but production never became very organised.
Initially, practical and social factors were probably a disincentive: the continued
shortages and the sheer exhaustion and disruption caused by six years of war. The
main reasons, however, were almost certainly related to politics and to an assumption on the part of the moderate left after the election of 1945 that socialism was
no longer marginalised and that the government could be persuaded to sponsor a
more effective socialist film service than any shoestring operation by independents.

With hindsight and the benefit of a more sophisticated cultural theory, the expectation seems extraordinarily naive or self-serving, but we must remember that there
had been limited experience either of Labour governments or state-funded culture.

One pre-war left film organisation that survived into the 40s was the Workers'
Film Association, which had links with the co-operative movement. Its formation
in 1938 was the outcome of years of work by Joseph Reeves, Education Secretary
of the Royal Arsenal Co-operative Society, a member of the Independent Labour
Party (ILP) and an energetic and eloquent champion for co-operative education
and for film. He promoted a plan to develop the WFA into a labour movement film
service,[21] and in 1946 the WFA joined forces with the Co-operative Wholesale Society and Co-operative Union and was renamed the National Film Association
(NFA). Despite the combined experience available to the NFA and the presence of
a supposedly favourable government, the projected service did not take off. The
Co-operative Society produced and sponsored a steady flow of films, but they were
merely functional advertisements for products and services. The trade unions
hardly used film at all, and the Labour Party only commissioned official films for
election broadcasts. The NFA functioned as a film society and film education service but was disbanded in 1953. Alan Burton, on whose work this account is based,
puts the failure down to the labour movement becoming 'more placid' and having
a 'more limited vision'.[22] However, an examination of the few films which were
made suggests another explanation might be the extent to which the methods and
ethos of official sponsored film had been internalised, particularly by the professionals in the Co-operative Film Unit. For sponsored film had evolved according
to the requirements of the public relations industry, to convey messages from sponsor to public and promote favourable associations with products or service. It was
a model for top-down communication and avoidance of controversy which was ill-
designed for the needs of democratic organisations supposedly run by and for the
members.

Professional and creative conservatism arguably had a dampening effect on an
interesting initiative taken by the ACT. In 1950 the union set up its own production company in response to the crisis of 1949. The objective was pragmatic rather
than political, to make feature films that would provide jobs for unemployed
members. The other stated aims – 'to make 100 per cent British films' and 'to prove
that films of quality could be made on reasonable budgets while observing all the
appropriate union agreements'[23] – did not include any requirement about the kind
of products to be made. The accusation of creative conservatism may be slightly
unfair, since the company was constrained, like any other independent, by the difficulty of raising commercial finance and of obtaining a release, but the union's own
account of the work does not suggest a perspective which was original or challenging.[24] It mentions attempts to raise money for left subjects like the Tolpuddle
Martyrs or *The Ragged-Trousered Philanthropist* and efforts to persuade the trade
unions to use film, but the one union film which was made, *We Are the Engineers*

(1969), is a thoroughly conventional documentary in the sponsored film tradition. Nevertheless, the establishment and survival of a feature company owned by the film trade union had a certain political significance, and it is notable that most general histories of British cinema either do not mention the venture or refer to it misleadingly. George Perry, for instance, writes of the first production, *Green Grow the Rushes* (1950), 'its box-office failure brought a brave experiment in constructive trade unionism to an end',[25] even though he knew that the company was still in production ten years later, as he correctly names ACT Films as the producer of *The Kitchen* (1961).[26] In fact, despite the failure of *Green Grow the Rushes*, the company went on to make twelve second features, a children's film and four main features between 1951 and 1962, including *The Kitchen*, which was based on the play by Arnold Wesker and is one of the group of films sometimes referred to as the British New Wave.[27]

Outside the structures provided by the WFA and ACT Films various informal production ventures were started by individual left-wingers. During the first years of the 50s a group of communist film-makers got together under the banner New Era to make films about party activities. They were young men already working, or aiming to work, in the film industry and included Anthony Simmons, who went on to direct a number of independent shorts, numerous sponsored films and a few features. The group took silent footage of demonstrations and strikes and made at least two documentaries on youth festivals organised by the World Federation of Democratic Youth: *We Who Are Young* (1952) and *One Great Vision* (1953). In these two films the emphasis, reflecting the cold war and the Communist Party priorities, is on showing the party and its allies in a positive light. Recurring themes are international peace and friendship and the threat posed by American aggression. Stylistically, they are far from innovative and resemble other low-budget public relations films of the time, shot mute with naturalistic sound and music added afterwards and overlaid with a dominant narration. To give a more democratic feel than that of the standard sponsored film, the narration is written in the first person as if it were the personal story of a participant, but the effect is still that of someone reading words written after the event and has none of the immediacy of speech recorded on location. Such films, circulated through the party, and shown at branch meetings and youth groups, contributed to the distinctive culture of the party but did little to alleviate its isolation.

This was not the only model adopted by left film-makers. Beverly Robinson's *We Speak for Our Children* (1952),[28] about a campaign to prevent the closure of day nurseries in Kent, employs a style of montage that looks back to the techniques of earlier silent documentary and forward to the cine tracts of Cinema Action. Although a striking and potentially useful campaign film, it is doubtful whether it could have been used effectively at the time in the absence of a developed national nurseries campaign or a proactive exhibition strategy for seeking out relevant audiences and generating debate.

The only alternative films of the 50s to have a high profile in film history are those of the Free Cinema Movement, usually discussed without reference to the wider range of marginal production. Their special status can be justified by the subsequent fame of three of the directors, Lindsay Anderson, Karel Reisz and Tony Richardson, and by the fact that the films were comparatively polished products, conceptualised as art cinema. However, their reputation rests in part on the high critical profile they enjoyed at the time, which did not follow automatically from the qualities of the films but was achieved by a deliberate strategy of packaging the work as programmes for the National Film Theatre and issuing provocative press hand-outs.[29] In this respect the movement may be regarded as an exemplary exercise in cultural promotion. A key element was co-operation. The film-makers were a disparate group of individuals with distinct critical and aesthetic trajectories, but were able to identify a few shared ideas – principally an emphasis on personal expression and the need to portray contemporary society – which were built into a collective platform which journalists, reviewers and the public could relate to. Another factor was that the film-makers were also active in related disciplines, pursuing ideas and establishing a presence in critical writing and the live theatre.

The Free Cinema campaign was successful in ensuring that the programmes were reviewed in most of the daily papers and in periodicals like *Tribune* and the *New Statesman*, as well as generating longer articles in film magazines. The press also covered the subsequent careers of some of the films, noting that *Thursday's Children* (1953) won an Oscar but failed to obtain a circuit release, that *Every Day Except Christmas* (1957) won the documentary prize at Venice but was rejected by the BBC. Most reviewers were supportive, but the nature of their comment, whether favourable or hostile, speaks eloquently of the political attitudes of the time. A vitriolic reviewer in *Films and Filming* wrote:

> The deserving poor are no longer with us; and the antics of their undeserving and comfortably-well-off-thank-you descendants are of interest only to a duffle-coated minority.
>
> One cannot but feel sad for the conscience-stricken, affluent, middle-class socialist, lost in a changing world, with no miserable wretches to fight for with all the strength that tongue and pen can muster. But that, alas, is life.[30]

A sign of the gulf which, by this time, separated the far left from dominant culture was that these films, promoted by their makers as personal statements, were widely perceived as self-evidently socialist, because they reflected a renewed interest in representations of working-class life. The debate around these films reflects a repressive and conservative culture which, as some of the interviews in Part III testify,[31] lasted well into the 60s. Sexual hypocrisy was an element, but it was also a matter of not mentioning or showing whole areas of life to do with women, the working class, foreigners, blacks. Free Cinema marked the beginning of a reaction in the cinema against these exclusions, but the films which got exposure and the film-makers who got through to the industry represented a somewhat qualified reaction. Working-class characters and environments appear, but the focus is on consumption: the pub, the fairground, the dancehall, the bingo club. Working-class institutions like trade unions, co-operatives, the WEA, or actions like the nurseries campaign, recorded by Beverly Robinson, remain virtually invisible.

The Free Cinema films are alternative only by default. They are apprenticeship pieces, professional calling-cards for film-makers who were seeking entry to the industry and, although critical of individual people and films, were not proposing fundamental change. Of the directors who made it into features, Lindsay Anderson is the only one who was at all actively involved with the left and with left film-making and who remained persistently non-conformist. Up to a point, however, the group argued the advantages of working outside the industry, free from technical and social conventions. Their critique of industry methods was attached to quite traditional ideas about individual artistic expression, but encouraged a questioning of professional conservatism which had a radical potential at a time when rigid attitudes – from an unwillingness to consider a hand-held track to the inability to conceive of a woman gaffer – were affecting both left alternatives and the mainstream.

One consequence of the tradition-bound and closed character of the profession was that film enthusiasts who wanted to turn film-maker often took it up as amateurs. There was still a large amateur movement in the 50s and 60s which included people with an extensive knowledge of film history, a high level of technical competence and a clear vision of how to make a finished product with a purpose. Amateur film was also one of the routes into the business. Derek Hill, for instance, who founded the Short Film Service, started off as an amateur.[32] Amateur films could reach an audience in the amateur film world and occasionally got more public showings. The most exceptional case of an amateur project developing into a cinema feature was Kevin Brownlow's and Andrew Mollo's *It Happened Here*, a story of an imaginary German occupation of Britain. Shooting began in 1956 when Brownlow was eighteen and was only completed in 1963. The film finally opened in London in 1965, when it looked less subversive than it might have done if finished in the 50s. One of the most provocative touches, for example, is to place the death camp in an environment full of trappings which, in 50s films, represent a quintessential Englishness: a rural setting, a country house, motherly women serving cups of tea ...

The history of the British Free Cinema shorts and of *It Happened Here* demonstrates how extremely difficult it was for new film-makers to get a footing in the feature industry or for enterprising independents to find an audience, let alone make a living. Even though the films were shown and praised at festivals, received some public screenings and extensive press coverage, they did not open doors. None of them received a wide release in Britain. Despite remarkably low costs, considerable critical success and a well-attended, though brief, West End run, *It Happened Here* made no money for its makers.[33] Kevin Brownlow was unable to direct another film until the BFI-funded *Winstanley* in 1975. The Free Cinema directors who eventually managed to make features found that experience in the theatre carried more weight with producers than the abilities demonstrated by their short films.

These films were exceptional in winning prizes and critical acclaim but they were not exceptional for being made outside the industry framework. Rather, they were part of a practice which was quite widespread, whereby freelancers, amateurs, junior employees in the film industry or would-be entrants to it would embark on making films for fun or personal satisfaction, to advance their career or to support a cause, often paying for materials themselves and with no certainty that the results would ever be shown. The establishment of the BFI Experimental Film Fund in 1952 for the first time provided a regular source of public funding for such projects and some of the shorts shown in the Free Cinema programmes benefited from its grants. Apart from that, a support structure of a kind was provided by small companies specialising in making or servicing sponsored films. Because the feature industry was notoriously difficult to enter, people seeking a career in films usually looked to these companies for training. Some graduated to technical jobs in features; others stayed within sponsored film and moved on by setting up their own small companies. Grierson's views on sponsorship were a lingering influence and occasional successes perpetuated the dream that sponsors might pay for films that film-makers wanted to make. Some of the Free Cinema films were examples: Anderson's *Wakefield Express* (1952) was sponsored by the paper of the title and the Ford motor company paid for *Every Day Except Christmas* and *We Are the Lambeth Boys* (1959), documentaries which had little direct relevance to company objectives. Charities like Oxfam were beginning to experiment with film, offering the prospect of sponsors with aims which might coincide with those of socially committed film-makers. Even when experience showed that open-ended or socially committed commissions were a rarity, film-makers hoped that their companies would generate enough revenue to subsidise independent projects. So, there was a proliferation of companies with premises and equipment run by people who earned a living from run-of-the mill sponsored film but who harboured other ambitions themselves and were sympathetic towards freelancers or amateurs with similar ideas.

At the time Lindsay Anderson and Karel Reisz were making their first shorts, Leon Clore's company, Graphic, played an important role as producer of the Ford films and of several films directed by John Fletcher, a member of the Free Cinema group who established his own company, Dateline, in 1964. During the late 50s and early 60s several new companies were set up by film-makers with liberal to left sympathies, interested in the artistic, social and political potential of film. Those particularly known for helping newcomers and supporting innovative, experimental or socially committed production were Derrick Knight Associates; Mithras; Alan King Associates; Document, a spin-off from Alan King; Dateline; David Naden Associates; Tattooist. They were businesses operating, or trying to operate, in the marketplace, but at the same time they all supported some non-commercial, unfunded work. Some, like Alan King Associates, were in practice, if not in name, co-operatives, groups of freelancers sharing premises and facilities. Originally set up by Canadians, the company was important for pioneering the use of hand-held 16mm equipment in Britian and for developing an observational documentary style used to good effect in *Warrendale* (1966). Mithras was most associated with explicitly left subjects, as it obtained the contract to make films for the Labour Party in the run-up to the 1964 election, and one of its founders, Maurice Hatton, an active socialist, was director of photography on *Gala Day* (1963), about the Durham miners' gala, and director of *Praise Marx and Pass the Ammunition* (1968), a full-length feature about revolutionary activists.

The improvements in 16mm technology and the increasing acceptance of this gauge by television were important factors in the economy of these new enterprises. On the commercial side, the switch to 16mm resulted in a sudden demand from television for outside facilities. Thus, while most programmes continued to be produced in-house, it became quite normal to employ freelance crew and use outside cutting rooms. Although most of the television work was in the servicing category there were some opportunities for freelance directors. Sales of finished films to British television remained rare but were possible, and foreign stations represented a growing market. On the non-commercial side, the new equipment had a liberating effect rather like the coming of small digital video cameras in the 90s. With an Eclair and Nagra it was relatively easy, given the appropriate skills, for as few as two people working on their own in their spare time to make a professional-looking documentary.

There is no straightforward way to estimate the extent of professionally made but non-funded or semi-funded production, since films often remained unfinished or were never registered; some were presented as 'professional' and some as 'amateur'; and the distinction between these categories, supposedly defined by regulations and policed by the union, was often blurred. However, some evidence is provided by the records of the BFI Experimental Film Fund: most of the productions it supported, of which Free Cinema films constituted a small proportion, would count as semi-funded and every application for finishing costs indicates that someone had begun a film in unorthodox circumstances. My own experience from the 60s would suggest that projects sent to the BFI, let alone those funded by it, represent only the tip of an iceberg. Certainly, people making campaign films were unlikely even to apply for grants. Two scraps of anecdotal evidence support this: when I worked at MGM studios in 1966, three out of about twelve assistant editors known to me were making their own unfunded experimental films; and in 1968, while working at Dateline, all the people permanently associated with the company had worked for free on their own or other people's productions, and the cutting rooms were regularly borrowed at evenings or weekends by people making unfunded films, practices no one regarded as unusual.

Although this unofficial cottage industry was not linked directly with politics, it had a subversive influence, generating a culture of lending and giving which constituted a form of untheorised cultural politics – an implied critique of industry values and a denial of the market – which became more explicitly political when the borrowers were activists. Thus the help which the first film workshops received from within the industry, most dramatically the virtual donation of Lusia Film's equipment to Cinema Action,[34] came out of a pre-existing tradition.

A liberal/left strand in the alternative film culture became more pronounced from the late 50s with the growth of CND and the New Left. CND itself stimulated a wave of film activity and a series of films were made of the Aldermaston marches and the invasion of military bases organised by the Committee of a Hundred. The most successful was *March to Aldermaston* (1959), which was released in the Academy Cinema with Renoir's *La Grande illusion*. Like the old New Era films, this is a chronological account of one event but, stylistically, it marks a significant departure. The soundtrack is based on direct comments from the marchers and speakers, and the editing sustains interest through its rhythms and the use of expressive images, rather than by artificially imposing a personal story on the material. In part, the development can be put down to changes in the mainstream: improved sound technology; the influence of a stream of interviews and reportage on television; the reassertion against television of a more crafted cinematic practice. But the qualities also reflect the scale of the production, shot by several professional crews and edited by Lindsay Anderson. That in turn reflects the success of CND in becoming a mass movement able to call in favours from far beyond the confines of the narrow left.

CND did not go on to make other films on an equivalent scale but *March to Aldermaston* was a breakthrough which showed that a straight political documentary could interest the general public. It set a precedent for making films on single-issue campaigns which was followed intermittently through the 60s:[35] a distributor guarantees to promote the film; money for stock is raised from a few individuals, facilities companies lend equipment and technicians donate labour.

Independent Distribution

The most lasting achievement of the 50s was the development and expansion of the alternative distribution networks. New specialist distributors emerged to support the film societies and a growing number of arts cinemas. An oral history of the first of these, Plato and Contemporary (established in 1950 and 1951 respectively) appears in Part III. Both were run by members of the CPBG and both gave priority to importing films from communist countries, but Plato handled shorts and documentary while Contemporary concentrated on features, branched out into managing cinemas and developed an international rather than an Eastern European catalogue. Contemporary was swiftly followed by Connoisseur and Gala, which also dealt largely with foreign-language features. Then at the time the CND films were being made, one of Plato's employees set up the Concord Films Council to promote the CND films more effectively; Concord later grew into a very large distributor of educational films, an important supplier for schools and colleges and the main source for western films on political and social issues.

These distributors helped prepare the ground for the radical film movement of the late 60s. Some of the new film activists tapped into this pre-existing network and even those who made no direct use of it inherited a public familiar with the concept of showing films outside the cinema, and receptive to a wide range of film language. A less direct, but arguably more important, influence was that of the films these distributors made available. Several of the workshop members interviewed talk about the impact of films like *The Seventh Seal* or *Zéro de conduite*. For some, the passion for cinema was sparked off by such films; for others, first smitten in childhood by Hollywood serials, the love affair was confirmed and developed by a later experience of art cinema.

Few of the 70s radicals regarded art cinema as anything but a variant of the main-stream,[36] and, given key cultural debates of the time, this was to be expected. The critique of narrative was as applicable to most art cinema films as to Hollywood, and the audience of the Academy, the archetypal Arts Cinema in Oxford Street, was as guilty of passive consumption as that of an Odeon. The fact that the proprietor of Contemporary Films was a member of the CPBG, if anything, reinforced its establishment image, since the party still operated with a discredited realist aesthetic and a notion of influence untouched by Althusser. It was logical to class Contemporary as conservative in contrast to a notional revolutionary cinema and to some of the embryonic practices of the new workshops, but it made less sense in relation to practical strategy. The very fact that Contemporary was commercially successful, placed films in comfortable West End cinemas, won reviews in the quality press and reached large audiences while remaining independent and under left management represented a modest challenge to the hegemony of the corporate interests running the mainstream. It was of practical significance that Contemporary could provide a high-profile platform to films the circuits would never touch and would hire or lend cinemas to organisations and for purposes that, again, the circuits would not. At the very least, the presence of a politically sympathetic company on the edge of commercial cinema opened spaces and possibilities for the left that otherwise would not have existed.

Notes

1. Paul Willemen, 'Presentation', in Don Macpherson (ed.), *Traditions of Independence* (London: BFI Publishing, 1980), p. 2.
2. Bert Hogenkamp, *Deadly Parallels* (London: Lawrence and Wishart, 1986), p. 209.

3. Contemporary Films, founded by a former member of Kino; ETV, which had inherited films from Kino and the Progressive Film Institute; Concorde, started by a former employee of ETV.

4. See Michael Chanan, *Labour Power in the British Film Industry* (London: BFI Publishing, 1976).

5. See Chris Cook and Alan Sked, *Post-War Britain* (Harmondsworth: Penguin, 1979), p. 15.

6. Stalin had dissolved the Comintern in 1943 and dropped the strategy of world revolution in favour of consolidating communism in Eastern Europe.

7. Geoff Richman describes his experience of the Communist Party and small left groups (see p. 227).

8. ACT, *Film Business Is Big Business* (London: 1939).

9. ACT, 'A State Film Industry?', *The Cine-Technician* May/June 1941, p. 62.

10. Ibid., p. 69.

11. Ibid., p. 70.

12. Ibid., p. 71.

13. For an account of wartime industry–government relations, see Margaret Dickinson and Sarah Street, *Cinema and State* (London: BFI Publishing, 1985), Chapters 6 and 7.

14. Measures considered included changing the release pattern to reduce the total demand for product and setting up a films bank to boost the British supply.

15. Board of Trade, *Tendencies to Monopoly in the Cinematograph Film Industry*, report of a committee appointed by the Cinematograph Films Council (London: HMSO, 1944).

16. Paul Rotha, 'The Government and the Film Industry', in *Rotha on the Film* (London: Faber and Faber, 1958), pp. 261–75.

17. See Dickinson and Street, *Cinema and State*, Chapters 8 and 9.

18. ACT, *The Film Crisis* (London: ACT, 1949).

19. Important contributions include a joint union statement of 1956: ACT's *Film: Trade Union Policy* (London: ACT, 1956) and the ACTT's *Survival or Extinction: A Policy for British Films* (London: ACTT, 1964).

20. See pp. 58–9.

21. See Alan Burton, *The People's Cinema: Film and the Co-operative Movement* (London: National Film Theatre, 1994), pp. 47–9.

22. Ibid., p. 49.

23. ACTT, *Action. 50 Years in the Life of a Union* (London: ACTT, 1983), p. 79.

24. Ibid., pp. 82–3.

25. George Perry, *The Great British Picture Show* (London: Hart-Davis, MacGibbon Ltd, 1974), p. 159.

26. Ibid., p. 197.

27. John Hill's discussion of the representation of work in *The Kitchen* reads even more interestingly in the light of the production company's history. See John Hill, *Sex, Class and Realism: British Cinema 1956–1963* (London: BFI Publishing, 1986), pp. 139–40.

28. I am indebted to Bert Hogenkamp for drawing my attention to this film.

29. See Alan Lovell, 'Free Cinema' in Jim Hillier and Alan Lovell, *Studies in Documentary* (London: Secker and Warburg, 1972).

30. Matt McCarthy, 'Free Cinema – In Chains', *Films and Filming* vol. 5 no. 5, February
    1959, p. 10.

31. See, for instance, Murray Martin, pp. 247–8.

32. See Alan Cleave, 'Middleman with a Mission', *Movie Maker* September 1967, p. 508.

33. Kevin Brownlow, *New Statesman*, 3 August 1979.

34. See Part III p. 268.

35. My own film, *Behind the Lines* (1970), was an example.

36. Steve Neale, 'Art Cinema as Institution', *Screen* vol. 22 no. 1, 1981, p. 71.

Chapter Two
Confrontation and Community (1966–74)

In the late 60s, within two or three years, the concept and context of independent film was transformed by the rapid growth of film practices which were deliberately sited outside the mainstream. The very word 'independent' became a site of struggle between those who used it in this oppositional sense and those who applied it to small enterprises operating, or trying to operate, within the mainstream.

This upsurge of oppositional independent film-making, like that of the 30s, was inspired by and dependent on politics, but on a different kind of politics. The tradition of the 30s was centred around the labour movement and its main components, the Labour Party, the Communist Party, the trade unions and the co-operatives – all structured organisations, democratic but hierarchical with a mass membership, elected leadership and clearly defined procedures of meetings, debates, motions and votes. The film groups had been set up by committed members of one or more of these organisations, and were conceived of as part of a cultural wing playing a supporting role in a political and economic struggle.[1] The activism of the late 60s occurred to a large extent outside these traditional structures and was embraced enthusiastically by academic, professional and creative workers who tended to assign to cultural struggle a central rather than instrumental role in the revolutionary process.

New Politics

1968 was the year when political action erupted onto the streets and into the headlines, but the ideas which gained sudden prominence through that action had been evolving over the previous decade. An aspect of the culture seemingly detached from politics and particularly important in the late 50s and early 60s was the rejection, at an individual level, of the values of 'respectable' society. With it went an enthusiasm for art forms associated with marginal groups (black music, beat poetry); for a literature of alienation and exclusion (Sartre, Camus, Beckett, Genet); an assertion of sexual freedom at a time when there were strong social sanctions against sex outside marriage; and the use of cannabis when legal sanctions against mere possession were vigorously enforced. It was within this ambience that underground film began to find a following. Describing the context of the London Film-Makers' Co-operative, Steve Dwoskin writes that it 'began as one of the many liberating influences that hit Britain in the 'mid 'sixties, along with the Beatles, the miniskirt and "swinging London"', and goes on to list the beats, the hippies, the

Provos, marijuana, the underground press and the 'anti-university'.[2] It was a culture influenced by showbiz and high-society fashion, and although politically ambivalent, it was often associated with left politics. Those immersed in it were susceptible to politicisation through personal contact and common experiences of conflict with authority. There was a shared distrust of the police, encountered both at demonstrations and in the search for drugs. The issue of sexual freedom became political when it met with repression, as in 1970 with the prosecutions under the Obscene Publications Act of the editors of the *International Times* and *Oz*.

The more directly political influences came first, from developments mentioned in the last section: the formation of the New Left in the wake of Hungary and Suez, and the single-issue campaigns of CND and Anti-Apartheid. Intellectual leadership was provided by the *New Left Review*, founded by E. P. Thompson, Stuart Hall and Raymond Williams. A first collection of essays, *Out of Apathy*, published in 1960, was written as a call to action, using clear language to expose the inequalities of the supposedly affluent society and to dissect the prevailing ideology of pessimism. The New Left, however, split into separate tendencies after Perry Anderson took over as editor of the *Review* in 1962 and introduced a more analytical Marxism drawn primarily from Italy, France and Germany. An acrimonious debate ensued, fought over a battleground of English history.[3]

The controversy helped to attract young academics to Marxist theory, offered not as a closed system but as a choice between contrasting methods, each in itself stimulating. Anderson's position had the added appeal of being an outspoken attack on the citadels of British academia:

> The two great chemical elements of this blanketing English fog are traditionalism and empiricism; in it, visibility – of any social or historical reality – is always zero. ... A comprehensive, coagulated conservatism is the result, covering the whole of society with a thick pall of simultaneous philistinism (towards ideas) and mystagogy (towards institutions) for which England has justly won an international reputation.[4]

With the return to power of a Labour government under Harold Wilson in 1964 the centre of gravity shifted leftwards. Support for the far left increased as it became clear that the Labour leadership was planning only minor changes in foreign and economic policy. Conflict was muted at first, because the new government did not have an absolute majority. After 1966, however, when a second election produced a clear victory, the attacks and campaigns became more aggressive. E. P. Thompson and Raymond Williams, now ousted from *New Left Review*, launched their onslaught in the *May Day Manifesto 1968*, where they expressed the widespread disappointment:

> the official Labour Party, though by no means its whole membership, has redefined itself to fit in with new capitalism and managed politics. The party

created, as it was thought, to transform society, and still the party of the great
majority – some 60 to 70 percent – of the working people of Britain, faces us now
in this alien form: a voting machine; an effective bureaucracy; an administration
claiming no more than to run the existing system more efficiently.[5]

The new *New Left Review*, meanwhile, continued an all-out attack on British
intellectual life which was to exercise a major influence on film theory in the 70s.
To counter what Anderson regarded as an insular empiricism, the *Review* adopted
a platform that was self-consciously internationalist and theoretical, with three
main areas of concern: the critical reassessment of British culture; the third world;
and European critical theory. The coverage of the third world focused very heavily
on those parts of it, like Vietnam and South and Central America, where revolutionary struggles were taking place. The theory was predominantly concerned with
readings of Marx, with Marxist analysis of culture and with psychoanalysis. The
names which appear as authors or subjects read like a roll call of the radical heroes
of the time: Herbert Marcuse, R. D. Laing, Régis Debray, Gunnar Myrdal, André
Gorz, Marx, Sartre, Oscar Lewis, Baron and Sweezy, Althusser, Che Guevara,
Gramsci, Lacan, Walter Benjamin.

Much of this European theory reached Britain via the United States, where it had
been assimilated earlier. During the Third Reich the entire Frankfurt Institute of
Social Research established an identity in exile in the United States, from where its
members continued to elaborate the social and cultural theory known as the Frankfurt School. Two of its most important exponents, Theodor Adorno and Max
Horkheimer, returned to Germany in the 50s, where Adorno was to exercise a profound influence on Schlacke Lamche, one of the future key members of Cinema
Action. Herbert Marcuse remained behind to become one of the major gurus of
American radical politics. The book which popularised his ideas beyond an academic circle was *One Dimensional Man*, described by the blurb on the back of the
paperback edition as 'the most subversive book published in the United States this
century'. It is a surprising text to acquire such a reputation, a dense critique of late
capitalism which is more Hegelian than Marxist and tends towards the pessimistic
view that neither intellectual nor physical resistance is possible. But the argument
is driven by an emotional rejection of modern technological society which struck
a chord with young educated people, authorising their disaffection from a system
which appeared to be providing what most people wanted:

Here the social controls exact the overwhelming need for the production and
consumption of waste; the need for stupefying work where it is no longer a real
necessity; the need for modes of relaxation which soothe and prolong this
stupefaction; the need for maintaining such deceptive liberties as free competition
at administered prices, a free press which censors itself, free choice between brands
and gadgets.[6]

Marcuse confirmed a common perception of a convergence between the working class and the bourgeoisie and yet could be read as proposing a new revolutionary force: 'the substratum of the outcasts and outsiders, the exploited and persecuted of other races and other colours, the unemployed and the unemployable.'[7]

The writer who was widely regarded as speaking for the 'exploited of other races and other colours' was Franz Fanon, a Martinican who trained as a doctor in Paris, became head of the psychiatric department of a hospital in Algeria under French rule and spent the last years of his life working for the Algerian National Liberation Front (FLN). *The Wretched of the Earth* (1961), based on the years in Algeria, was extremely influential in Britain in the mid-60s and helped to place third world struggles on the socialist agenda together with a set of issues to do with the gulf between rich and poor nations, the need for nationalist revolutions to be socialist, the revolutionary potential of the peasantry and the efficacy of armed struggle.

Fanon was taken up by black activists in the United States and this in turn enhanced his reputation in Britain. Stokely Carmichael attended the Dialectics of Liberation Congress in London in 1967, where he referred to Fanon in his speech as his patron saint and offered simplified readings – or misreadings[8] – of his work. This conference, which took place just as the Vietnam Solidarity Campaign (VSC) was gathering momentum, represented a landmark in the development of a counter-culture. Carmichael was one among a disparate platform of political and academic stars who drew a predominantly youthful audience, including several of the film-makers interviewed in Part III.

Before the Vietnam War became a major cause, other events had confirmed the reality of imperialist aggression – the destabilisation of the Congo and murder of Lumumba in 1961; the fall of Nkrumah in 1965; the American invasion of the Dominican Republic in 1965 – and demonstrated the apparent efficacy of armed struggle – Castro's victory in Cuba in 1959; the Algerian war of independence, 1954–62. These events excited the left but had little effect on domestic politics, whereas the repercussions of the Vietnam conflict were on a different scale. The role of the VSC is explored in more detail in the interviews with members of Liberation Films in Part III, which testify to the influence of American expatriates and draft resisters.[9] They brought not only experiences from the American anti-war movement of violent confrontations with riot police but also experiences from the civil rights movement of low-key work in deprived communities, and both were recorded in the films of the Newsreel group. There were also Marxist intellectuals well versed in the Frankfurt School and women who had been involved in the early phase of Women's Liberation.

The VSC itself was not very different from earlier single-issue movements, based on a mass following with an executive committed to organising rallies and marches. Many of the individual supporters, however, became more interested in community action and the Women's Movement, in consciousness-raising, in revolutionising personal relationships, in the idea of taking politics into the home, the

neighbourhood and the workplace. These concerns found expression in the establishment of small magazines, organising street theatre and festivals, mural painting,
discussion groups and film shows. There was a shift away from the structured politics of parties and campaigns in favour of informal groups defined by participation
rather than membership, taking decision by consensus instead of majority vote.
Since activists tended either to have no party allegiance or belong to one of a variety of rival Marxist parties, there was no unifying structure, and informal
networking, assisted by the underground press, to some extent served as a substitute. In London, *Time Out*, started as a collective venture in 1969, began to
provide a vital service, giving unprecedented exposure to alternative politics and
culture.

The revolt in the universities took the traditional left by surprise. In the early 60s
the conservatism and political apathy of the student body was a constant theme of
complaint. By 1968 student revolution was a media cliché. The London School of
Economics (LSE) and Hornsey College of Art were in the forefront: at the LSE
problems surfaced in 1966 and led to an occupation in the spring of 1967, while at
Hornsey action peaked in the academic year 1967–8. The causes and political
potential of the upheaval were the subject of intense debate at the time,[10] but there
is no doubt that, whatever its wider meaning, the student movement was an important stimulus to the development of oppositional film culture. Throughout the 50s
and 60s university film societies provided a significant proportion of the audience
for the films distributed by independent distributors. So, the campus revolt had
quite direct implications in terms of – to use the business phrase – demand for
product. It was accompanied by a growing interest in fiction from third world
countries and in political documentary. Film shows were a part of the debates, sit-
ins and teach-ins. *The Organiser* (1964), for example, was screened during the first
LSE sit-in. There was also a more precise connection between student politics and
independent film in that several individuals active in the latter, were, or had been,
involved in the former. Early recruits to Cinema Action were David Adelstein, president of the LSE Students' Union, who was suspended during the 1967 conflict, and
two women, Dana Purvis and Jane Grant, who had edited a film about the LSE
action (*Student Power* (1968), produced and directed by Daniel Schechter, who was
also a member of the Stop It Committee formed by Americans in Britain against
the Vietnam War).

Local grievances were an important factor in the first student protests, but
activists were also inspired by a sense of being part of an international movement
of young intellectuals. The spring of 1968 brought unexpected, though short-lived,
triumphs in Czechoslovakia and France. The Prague Spring and its suppression had
long-term repercussions on British politics, but, understandably, the drama played
out just across the Channel, in a supposedly democratic state and within easy reach
of the media, had more immediate impact. In Paris, agitation by students at the
University of Nanterre escalated very rapidly, as other young activists became

involved. Then after the French riot police used truncheons and tear gas on peace-
ful marchers, the demonstrations turned into a nationwide campaign of direct
action against the de Gaulle government. By late May about ten million people had
come out on strike and the scale of the stoppages, demonstrations and occupations
of factories and colleges began to look like a revolution. De Gaulle then dissolved
the Assembly and called a general election. This proved an astute decision, for mass
support for the May movement did not translate into an electoral majority and de
Gaulle was able to win a decisive victory at the end of June. The movement sub-
sided without changing the basic social structure, but it did have a lasting effect on
ideas, attitudes and individual careers, which was to some extent passed on to the
British left.

As the 60s drew to a close in Britain the area of confrontation broadened as the
focus shifted away from the universities and Vietnam towards industrial politics
and Ireland, conflicts in which the government was more directly implicated.
Although these were issues on which Labour and Conservative were not fundamentally divided, the return of a Conservative government in 1970 nonetheless
heralded an escalation of conflict. The events of this period form the background
to the early work of Cinema Action.[11]

The movement for civil rights in Ulster was gathering momentum throughout
1968, and events moved towards civil war after the RUC broke up the People's
Democracy civil rights march in January 1969. In the summer of 1969 the Catholic
population of Derry put up barricades and called the area behind them 'Free Derry'.
In August British troops were sent in. Internment was introduced in 1971.

The Labour government entered into a conflict with the unions over the 1969
white paper *In Place of Strife*, but pressure from the TUC prevented the intended
legislation going through. The following year the Heath government provoked a
massive campaign against its more explicitly anti-union Industrial Relations Bill.
The passage of the bill into law was followed by the introduction of a statutory
prices and pay standstill in 1972. Inflation, rising unemployment and cuts in welfare provision contributed to trade union militancy, and there followed a series of
strikes, both official and unofficial, in defiance of the legislation. The miners were
also alienated by the policy of pit closures started under the previous government.
In 1972 they embarked on a long strike over pay and eventually won a settlement
substantially higher than the original offer. Among the provisions of the Industrial
Relations Act which incensed trade unionists were the restrictions on the right to
picket and the use of industrial courts. Just after the miners returned to work the
dockers struck over the imprisonment for contempt of court of three pickets who
had refused to appear before the Industrial Relations Court. In 1973 the
Arab–Israeli War led to an oil shortage and a rise in oil prices, which strengthened
arguments against pit closures. In November 1973 the miners embarked on an
overtime ban in defence of a pay claim. The government refused to meet it, dealing with the resulting shortage of power by restricting industry to a three-day week.

Hoping to receive a stronger mandate for the incomes policy, Heath called an election and lost.

New Cinema

Some of the relevant aspects of the film politics of the period are discussed in *Independent Film-Making in the 70s* reproduced in Part II as one of the key documents of the IFA. Since the committee responsible for the paper included writers who later contributed to *Traditions of Independence*, it is not surprising to find that the historical analysis similarly concentrates on the 30s, and makes no mention of the 50s other than a dismissive reference to Free Cinema. The commentary on the late 60s, a period when the authors themselves were beginning to get involved, is comprehensive, and there is no need to duplicate the account of the Short Film campaign, the New Cinema Club, the influence of underground film and of the Knocke Film Festival. However, the paper passes rather hastily over other developments which, in the present context, deserve more attention: the beginnings of what later became known as 'the workshop sector'; the influence of post-1968 French film culture; and the rethinking of film theory.

Much of the momentum behind the politicisation of film culture was provided by proto-workshops – small enterprises concerned simultaneously with production distribution and exhibition of films. Typically, they began with a few like-minded people getting together round shared objectives, and between 1966 and 1970 at least half a dozen such groups began functioning. The vocabulary associated with them – 'workshops' and 'integrated practice' – only gradually acquired currency with the need to describe and define what they were doing. The groups fell broadly into two types, which later became known as access workshops and collectives. The London Film-Makers' Co-op (LFMC), formed in 1966, was the first and most famous example of the former, a cultural centre and facility serving an open membership – in that case, a growing pool of individual film-makers. The collectives, like Cinema Action or Amber, consisted of fewer members who worked together as a team and also provided facilities and equipment to other people but on an ad hoc basis, and at the discretion of the team. Radical politics and a collective or co-operative ethos were influences on them all but otherwise the stimuli were varied. The LFMC, which was not only the first access workshop but also the first of any kind, was a direct spin-off from the New York Film-Makers' Co-operative;[12] most of its members were influenced by the American underground and American New Cinema; many were art-school trained and tended to see themselves as artists working with film. Angry Arts/Liberation Films grew out of the VSC and was modelled partly on American Newsreel, partly on the Canadian Film Board's Challenge for Change programme. Cinema Action was formed as a direct response to May 1968 in France. The Women's Film Group and Sheffield Film Co-op, formed in 1972 and 1973 respectively, were inspired by the Women's Movement.

Although these film groups played a central role in the development of independent film culture, little was written about them in their early years and, except in the case of the LFMC, not many retrospective accounts have been published. Part III contains oral histories of five of the groups: Liberation Films, Amber, Cinema Action, Sheffield Film Co-op and Black Audio. Other groups are mentioned subsequently in relation to the later development of the movement, but there is no attempt to list or classify them all.

From about 1970–1 new groups were to some extent influenced by the existing ones. In London TVX, a group which had particularly strong links with popular music and was important for pioneering work both in video art and in community video, was started in 1970 by John Hopkins, who had worked at the LFMC.[13] Berwick Street Collective, formed in 1970 by Marc Karlin, Richard Mordaunt and Humphrey Trevelyan, was a spin-off from Cinema Action, and took with it Mordaunt's company, Lusia Films, which is still in business at the end of the 90s, managed by Marc Karlin until his death in early 1999. Four Corners, formed in 1973, developed an interestingly varied practice informed by avant-garde traditions, by the political work of Cinema Action and by feminism. One of its members, Mary Pat Leece, was on the staff of the LFMC, while another, Ron Peck, directed a full-length cinema feature in 1975, *Nighthawks*, remarkable for its pioneering treatment of a gay theme and for being made by a dedicated cast and crew on a tiny budget raised from private sources. Newsreel, formed in 1974, took American Newsreel as a model but, unlike Liberation Films, concentrated very much on campaign films. Out of London, early and long-lasting groups included Leeds Animation and Trade Films in Newcastle; Birmingham was distinctive for strong trade union links; Nottingham as an access workshop which was, in many ways, more typical than the LFMC, smaller, and relating more to a film than a fine arts tradition.

Initially the group productions were made entirely outside the industry framework. The work was unpaid or only minimally paid, and only a few of those engaged in it were film professionals or members of the ACTT. However, an interesting but temporary phenomenon associated with the years of militancy was that a series of films were made on a similar basis by ACTT members as a contribution to the campaign against the Industrial Relations Bill. The union's General Council agreed to a proposal from the left that members should be officially allowed to work unpaid on these projects, known as Free Prop films.[14] Although there was a precedent from the work done for CND at the end of the 50s, it was a significant step for the union to take, cutting across the traditional reluctance to put political, social or cultural objectives before wages. However, in the event, the only film to receive much exposure was a conventional documentary of the TUC march against the bill, and the experiment did not outlive that particular campaign.

Apart from the film groups, the key institution of the 70s was the distributor, The Other Cinema. Its genesis was complicated, as it emerged from meetings attended by a disparate mix of industry film-makers involved in the Third Circuit

and Short Film campaigns who were looking for outlets for their films, by representatives of film societies looking for product as well as by activists who envisaged
a more overtly political mission.[15] When it was formed in 1970 it was one of three
new political distributors, the others being Politkino and Liberation Films,[16] which
all had aspirations to develop political cinema. Politkino, however, proved a short-
lived venture in that form,[17] and Liberation Films concentrated more on education
and production. So, The Other Cinema remained as by far the most important
new distributor, although its pre-eminence was achieved by adopting a relatively
conventional mode of operation not fundamentally different from that of Contemporary.[18] Renting foreign cinema features to arts cinemas and film societies
represented a major part of the business, although the catalogue also offered a wide
range of political documentary and British independent films of value to a more
explicitly political clientele. Structurally, The Other Cinema was set up as a trust,
with a council of management which, in the mid-70s, included people active in
independent film culture, such as Steve Dwoskin, Marc Karlin and Laura Mulvey.
The staff – Peter Sainsbury, Paul Marris, Tony Kirkhope – were also part of that
culture, and these personal connections help to explain why The Other Cinema
played a more central role in the 70s than any of the older companies. The films
acquired, particularly the Godard features and a large Latin American collection,
were in tune with the preoccupations of a politicised youthful audience and with
the critics they respected. Despite this advantage, the company was unable to
achieve financial stability, let alone generate capital for expansion. One of its early
problems was that it lacked a cinema that might serve as an outlet and showcase
for its films. Unable to finance such a venture independently, it applied for and
received a grant from the BFI and opened a cinema on a site just off Charlotte
Street. (Interestingly enough, the building had once housed the Scala Cinema used
by the British Soviet Friendship Society in the 40s[19] and was to become the first
headquarters of Channel Four Television.) The operation was under-financed, and
after only eighteen months the cinema was forced to close, leaving a burden of debt
and recrimination.

The 1968 events in France had an immense impact on British film culture, partly
because film-makers and critics were among the French professions most conspicuously politicised by 1968, and partly because the prestige attached to the French
film culture, and particularly to *Cahiers du cinéma*, ensured that the process of
politicisation was closely followed in Britain. The role of the French film world in
the events is covered in detail in Sylvia Harvey's *May '68 and Film Culture*,[20] but a
brief summary may be helpful here. The film studios, the national film school and
the state-controlled television station, ORTF, went on strike. The action at the
ORTF was provoked partly by the government's attempts to interfere with coverage
of the demonstrations. A number of professional and student film-makers set about
making their own record of the events, which led, in some cases, to the formation
of political production groups, the most famous being SLON, associated with Chris

Marker, and the Vertov Group, associated with Godard. A series of mass meetings were called, known as the États Généraux du Cinéma, to debate the future of the film and television industries. In film theory, the increasing influence of Marxism was signalled by a shift in the editorial policy of *Cahiers du cinéma* and the founding of a new film magazine, *Cinéthique*. The new theory was taken up by the British theoretical journal *Screen*, and the example of the film groups reinforced the idea that co-operative production was the way forwards. The ideas put forward at the États Généraux du Cinéma exercised an important influence on deliberations within the ACTT about whether to press for nationalisation.

Making the French debates available to its readers was part of a wider project by *Screen* to revolutionise British film theory. *Screen* had evolved from an educational project. It was published by the Society for Education in Film and Television (SEFT), an association for film teachers which had a quasi-official status as a grant-in-aid body of the BFI, and was funded, initially, to serve the needs of teachers and academics. There were constant tensions about the interpretation of this brief, and in 1971 a major change of direction was signalled by the appointment of an editorial board with a strong left contingent including the editor, Sam Rhodie, Peter Wollen and Ben Brewster, who were all contributors to *New Left Review*, and Paul Willemen, Simon Hartog and Sylvia Harvey, who were associated with the emergent independent film movement. The new board determined that the development of critical theory was to take precedence over the discussion of educational practice, a policy outlined in the editorial of their first issue in 1971.[21] Under its new board, *Screen* became deeply involved in independent film culture, commenting on the events, discussing some of the films, providing a platform for debates and elaborating a body of theory which the *Screen* writers hoped would inform the film-makers. Directly and indirectly the journal was to play a major role in the movement, although, as I argue in the next chapter, many of the film-makers did not share the views and judgments associated with it.

Notes

1. See Trevor Ryan, 'Film and Political Organisation in Britain 1929–1939', in Don Macpherson (ed.), *Traditions of Independence* (London: BFI Publishing, 1980), pp. 58–9.
2. Steve Dwoskin, *Film Is* (London: Peter Owen, 1975), p. 62.
3. See Perry Anderson, 'Origins of the Present Crisis', and Tom Nairn, 'The British Political Elite', *New Left Review* no. 23, January/February 1964, pp. 19–25; Tom Nairn, 'The English Working Class', *NLR* no. 24, March/April 1964, pp. 43–57; 'The Anatomy of the Labour Party', *NLR* no. 27, September/October 1964, pp. 38–65 and *NLR* no. 28, November/December 1964, pp. 33–62; E. P. Thompson, 'Peculiarities of the English', *Socialist Register* no. 2, 1965; Perry Anderson, 'Socialism and Pseudo-empiricism', *NLR* no. 35, January/February 1966, pp. 2–24.
4. Anderson, 'The Present Crisis', p. 40.
5. Raymond Williams (ed.), *The May Day Manifesto 1968* (Harmondsworth: Penguin, 1968), p. 155.

6. Herbert Marcuse, *One Dimensional Man* (London: Sphere Books, 1968), p. 23.

7. Ibid., p. 200.

8. Misreadings according to David Caute, *Fanon* (London: Fontana, 1970), pp. 36, 95.

9. See Part III, pp. 227–8.

10. See Robin Blackburn and Alexander Cockburn (eds), *Student Power – Problems, Diagnosis, Action* (Harmondsworth: Penguin 1969).

11. See Part III, pp. 268, 270–3.

12. See Bob Cobbing, 'Report', *Cinim* 1, 1966, p. 8 and Malcolm Le Grice, 'A Reflection on the History of the London Film-Makers' Co-op', in *Light Years: 20 Years of the LFMC,* 1986, p. 26.

13. See interviews with early video-makers, John Hopkins, Steve Herman and Chris Evans, 'The Last Nine Years of Video UK', in *Film and Video Extra* no. 9, Spring 1978.

14. See 'The Strike . . . The March . . . and the Movies', *Film and Television Technician* vol. 36 no. 307, December 1970, p. 8.

15. See comments by Ron Orders on his disappointment with the outcome, Part III, pp. 238, 240.

16. The three are described and compared in a contemporary article by Jim Pines, 'Left Film Distributors', *Screen* vol. 13 no. 4, Winter 1972/3, p. 116.

17. Politkino was absorbed by The Other Cinema, but the owners, Pam and Andi Engel, later established a more conventional distribution company, Artificial Eye.

18. For a detailed retrospective history, see a series of interviews with employees: Sylvia Harvey, 'The Other Cinema – A History: Part I 1970–1977', *Screen* vol. 26 no. 6, November/December 1985, p. 40, and 'Part II', *Screen* vol. 27 no. 2, March/April, 1986.

19. See interview with Stanley Forman pp. 216–7.

20. Sylvia Harvey, *May '68 and Film Culture* (London: BFI Publishing, 1978).

21. *Screen* vol. 12 no. 1, 1971.

Chapter Three
Assault on the Mainstream (1974–80)

In the mid-70s, several of the separate elements of counter-cinema coalesced under the banner of the IFA. Its formation was part of a more general process of networking and proselytising in which the IFA occupied a central place, providing a base for a series of campaigns aimed at the cultural establishment, the mainstream industry and, ultimately, the government.

The National Context

Looking back, it is difficult to view the second half of the 70s without anticipating Thatcherism. But the perspective at the time was one of conflict rather than incipient reaction. Industrial and social unrest suggested that the post-war settlement was under stress, but the pressure was coming from the left as well as the right. Margaret Thatcher, already adopting a high profile as a right-winger, became Conservative leader from 1975, and within the Labour Party, left-wingers, like Michael Foot, were prominent.

The election of February 1974 was a setback for Heath's policy of industrial confrontation, but it did not represent a clear victory for the unions or Labour either. No party gained an overall majority and Harold Wilson took office heading a minority government. A second election in October delivered a small working majority, subsequently eroded by a series of by-election losses. These, and losses in local elections, signalled the government's declining popularity and fuelled arguments within the party between those who called for a more decisively socialist programme and those who advocated a move towards the centre ground.

Although there was no immediate prospect of a socialist revolution being delivered through the ballot box, there were signs that the basis of consensus, as far as one remained, was shifting leftwards. Between 1964 and 1979 the Conservatives were in power for four years and Labour for eleven. The welfare state was taken for granted. The three main parties paid lip-service to equal opportunities, and Labour had taken steps to outlaw direct discrimination with the Equal Pay Act of 1970, the Sex Discrimination Act of 1975 and three Race Relations Acts between 1965 and 1976. The combined effects of comprehensive education, the expansion of the universities, the recent politicisation of the student body and the proliferation of women's networks were bringing into the professions and positions of influence a growing minority of feminists and people with left sympathies. While their presence helped promote an ideology of equality, sociologists were finding that there had been very little reduction in actual class inequalities and only a slight increase in mobility between classes.[1] The discovery undermined the view that economic growth and appropriate administrative measures would deliver a more equal society and strengthened the arguments of the far left that class struggle was essential.

The far left could also point to signs that the struggle was intensifying: voting behaviour in the elections of 1974 had revealed deep divisions between town and country and North and South; industrial confrontation continued throughout the 70s; fighting in Northern Ireland escalated; violence and discrimination against ethnic minorities were provoking an increasingly organised and militant response; the oil crisis of 1973 and high inflation were generating a sense of insecurity; unemployment was becoming an issue.

The problem of inflation became a focus of conflict within the labour movement, as the moderate wing tended to agree with the Conservatives that wage demands were the main culprit. During the election campaign of spring 1974 Wilson promoted the social contract as a solution. The idea was that, in return for the repeal of Heath's Industrial Relations Act and some measures to hold down prices, the TUC would persuade its member unions to co-operate with wage restraint. Within a matter of months the agreement was failing, but the term, 'social contract', continued to be used for ensuing attempts to impose an incomes policy. This is partly what the title of Cinema Action's unfinished film refers to,[2] although the name was almost certainly chosen, as presumably it was by Wilson, for its historical resonances of seventeenth-century England and the political theory of Locke and Hobbes.

The struggle within the Labour Party took a very public form round the leadership election which followed Wilson's resignation in 1976. By the final ballot, in a contest between Michael Foot and Jim Callaghan, Callaghan won, but only by 176 votes to 137. The left showed itself to be a significant force, while the immediate outcome was a middle-of-the-road government still committed to a managed economy with a large public sector. From the point of view of cultural activists this meant that arguments about regulating the media industries or spending on the arts could at least expect a hearing.

Lobbying around the media naturally intensified whenever the government was considering changes and the 70s witnessed three important developments. The first was the decision, taken during the Heath government, to allow experiments in local cable television. The focus fell on film in the mid-70s when Wilson initiated a series of inquiries into the industry which ran on into the review of the films legislation due for renewal in 1980. The decade ended with the debate on the fourth television channel, which became a major concern after the publication of the Annan Report on broadcasting in 1977.

For many activists the practical business of trying to foster a socialist culture was more important than pressure politics, and in this context the state of local government was particularly important. Before the rate-capping of the 80s, local authorities had enjoyed a fair degree of autonomy and would sometimes run the services under their control in a way which deviated quite significantly from central government policies. Thus, when one party was in power nationally, councils under the control of the other party could partially sabotage domestic legislation (Conservative councils, for instance, long resisted the abolition of the eleven-plus exam). The political spectrum was also wider in local politics, and the variation in services offered in different areas could provide a taste of what certain policies might mean at a national level. Local government was reorganised in 1972 by an Act which devolved wider powers to some regions by creating six very large authorities: the metropolitan counties of Tyne and Wear, South Yorkshire and West Yorkshire, Greater Manchester, Merseyside and West Midlands.

At the supra-national level Britain's entry into the EEC in 1973 had long-term implications for culture and particularly the film industry. The other large film producers in Europe aided their industries, and eventually all the regimes of aid would have to be harmonised. Unlike Britain, France and Italy treated film as culture rather than commerce and had devised aid regimes which were more complex and interventionist than the British system. Although much criticised in their own countries, the French and Italian approach answered some of the traditional demands of the British left, in that they set up more effective barriers against Hollywood competition. Thus, although sections of the British left opposed membership of Europe, there was growing interest in European cultural policies, particularly after Britain's membership was confirmed by a referendum in 1975.

Independent Film Culture – Consolidation

The independent film culture of the early 70s had a spontaneous and heterogeneous quality which has been somewhat obscured by a subsequent tendency to describe activities in terms of binary oppositions: alternative *or* mainstream; collective versus individual; theory versus practice; the political avant-garde *or* the aesthetic avant-garde; the Co-op kind of avant-garde *or* the European kind.[3] The use of such labels, even as a convenient shorthand, implies that films and film-makers could be tidily packaged as belonging to one kind of practice or another. In fact many people were active either simultaneously or serially across those distinctions. For example, Simon Hartog worked for a short spell at the BBC, was one of the first members of the LFMC, worked for the ACTT as a researcher and was subsequently a founding member of Spectre, a co-operative of film-makers whose work was closer to the European kind of avant-garde than to the Co-op kind; John Hopkins, founder of TVX, was a central figure in both underground culture and community video and yet had material broadcast on national television as early as 1970;[4] the LMFC was mainly known for film art, but some of its members covered the Grosvenor Square VSC demonstration, and Liberation Film's *End of a Tactic?* was included in the 1976 tenth anniversary screenings. The workshop histories in Part III offer other examples and the list could be extended over several pages.

So, at the individual level there was understanding, interest and mutual support across the divisions. The notion that political and aesthetic struggle were connected was not only held by participants; the security services, for instance, apparently viewed all independent film-makers as potentially subversive. They raided Cinema Action in 1971,[5] which might not seem surprising, given the overtly political nature of its work, but after the prevention of Terrorism Act was passed in 1974 the police turned their attention to the LFMC. Searching, not for drugs but explosives, they broke into the Co-op premises and mounted a classic dawn raid on the home of the then director of the workshop, William Raban, battering down his front door while the household slept.[6]

A sense of common purpose was reflected in a series of early attempts to bring together different strands around common aims and needs. The LFMC itself began in this spirit. John Hopkins set up the Centre for Advanced Television Studies (CATS)[7] to serve community video workers, and its first report, *Video in Community Development*, published in 1972, helped to define shared objectives. For those involved in community media, an important stimulus was provided by the government's deliberations about cable television, a technology with an interactive potential which added a new dimension to the long-running debate over public service versus private profit.[8] Excitement mounted with the decision, announced by the Minister for Posts and Telecommunications in 1972, to set up five local programming experiments at Bristol, Greenwich, Sheffield,[9] Swindon and Wellingborough.

The networking process evolved with the formation of representative organisations. Early in 1974 the Association of Community Artists was set up, while, more directly relevant to the film and video world, was the establishment of the IFA at the end of 1974 and the Independent Video Association (IVA) in 1975, both committed to developing radical alternatives to the mainstream. Of the two, the IFA proved the more active and eventually absorbed the video-makers in 1983 to become the IFVA. In 1976 the Association of Independent Producers (AIP), was formed by film-makers working in or on the edge of the mainstream. Unlike the IFA, which challenged the whole context in which films were made and shown, the AIP demands were focused on seeking adjustment to the films' legislation to encourage a more specifically British form of mainstream cinema: namely, locally produced, medium-budget feature films. The two associations subsequently provided a convenient way of defining the different kinds of independence they represented.

The IFA, which was to become the best-known institution of the oppositional kind of independent film culture, was born out of a quarrel with the BBC over a programme purporting to show independent films. A number of aggrieved film-makers called a meeting, which attracted a large and diverse audience, and the outcome was a decision to form the association. The letter calling the meeting is reprinted in Part II, followed by the paper, *Independent Film-Making in the 70s*, which was presented at the Association's first conference in May 1976 by the conference organising committee. The paper, written by a group including Simon Hartog, Paul Willemen and Claire Johnston, discusses the IFA's origins and activities since formation and attempts to define its purpose. Although never fully accepted by all the membership, it states a position around which future debate revolved, and in that sense can be regarded as the Association's foundation document.

While the formation of the IFA was a significant landmark, the movement had already been defining and promoting itself through one-off events like screenings, conferences and festivals, and these continued to play an important role, often, but not always, in association with the IFA. Major landmarks in the promotion of underground and avant-garde film were the screenings arranged by the LFMC at the Edinburgh Film Festival in 1969 and 1970; and the 1970 First International Underground Festival at the NFT and its sequel in 1973. The years 1975 and 1976 were extremely busy, with events which helped raise the profile of the independent film culture. Video Art made a breakthrough with the Video Show in May 1975 at the Serpentine Gallery in London, and the same year there was an exhibition of landscape film at the Haywood Gallery. The political wing was acknowledged in a series of screenings and discussions called 'Film and Community Action' at the ICA in 1976.[10] But the event which is most representative of the movement as a whole was the 1975 Bristol Festival of Independent Film, which chaotically embraced a range of work from the art installations of Ron Haselden to community productions like *Tunde's Film*. It was organised by Independent Cinema West at the Arnolfini Gallery, Bristol, and received encouragement and support from the IFA executive. The 'Polemic', reprinted in Part II, states the aims.

The Edinburgh Film Festival played a role which in some ways contrasts with that of Bristol. Edinburgh was a long-established international festival, devoted primarily to mainstream cinema, but with the appointment of Lynda Miles as festival director, the programme's focus was sharpened to include screenings and seminars informed by current film theory. There was a more decisive shift in policy in 1975, and the rationale for these changes is outlined in the introduction to the *Edinburgh '76 Magazine*, in Part II. The trajectory was influenced by a number of *Screen* contributors who were also active in the IFA, so that, as with Bristol, there was a close relationship between the festival and the IFA. However, while Bristol had celebrated diversity, the annual Edinburgh gatherings were more about advancing a unifying ideology.

Theory and Practice

One of the the central tenets of the IFA was the need to connect film theory with the practice of film-making, and to this end the association successfully encouraged an exchange between theorists and practitioners, albeit one which was often uneasy and unbalanced.

The theory promoted in *Screen* and through Edinburgh initially made little reference to British independent film but was focused on an analysis of mainstream work and foreign avant-garde films. This was a source of friction between the theorists and film-makers, aggravated by the difficulty the latter experienced in understanding the theory, much of which seemed counter-intuitive, perverse and, on top of that, was often presented in unfamiliar technical language borrowed from French Marxism and structuralism.[11] However, both sides made efforts to communicate, especially around the practical question of how to make political films. In this context a certain critique of the realist tradition was absorbed by many of the practitioners, to the extent that it acquired the status of an IFA orthodoxy.

Colin MacCabe's article on *Days of Hope* in Part II sets out some of the arguments about the inadequacy of mainstream drama techniques. The BBC series attracted special attention as the work of an established leftist writer/director team, Jim Allen and Ken Loach, and because of the special place that its subject, the General Strike, occupies in the memory of the left. Prior to the Edinburgh event which the article relates to,[12] the series had already been the subject of an exchange in *Screen* between MacCabe and Colin McArthur.[13] The MacCabe piece reproduced here exemplifies some of the qualities complained of by practitioners, in that a relatively straightforward analysis of *Days of Hope* is inserted within a puzzling and controversial exposition of empiricist Marxist and Freudian theories of memory.

The next two articles in Part II approach the question from the other side, by looking at two of the few British independent films which the theorists wrote about enthusiastically. Released within months of each other, Berwick Street Collective's *Nightcleaners* and Laura Mulvey and Peter Wollen's *Penthesilea* were written about extensively in the theoretical journals,[14] but the *Spare Rib* articles below (pp. 146–52) were intended to introduce the films to a potential audience beyond the *Screen* readership.

The two films use techniques which are almost polar opposites: *Penthesilea* was planned as a series of continuous takes which were joined together virtually unedited; *Nightcleaners* was shot as observational documentary and the material then elaborately restructured. More importantly, their relationship to theory was quite different. The makers of *Penthesilea* came to film-making from a background as teachers and theorists, primarily of Hollywood cinema. Peter Wollen had already made a reputation with *Signs and Meaning*,[15] but had yet to publish 'The Two Avant-Gardes'.[16] Laura Mulvey was known as a feminist intellectual but not, as yet, for 'Visual Pleasure and Narrative Cinema'.[17] *Nightcleaners*, on the other hand, was made by people engaged primarily in film-making and politics, two of whom, Marc Karlin and Humphrey Trevelyan, had been members of Cinema Action, while the third, James Scott, had worked at the LFMC.

Different production histories affected the way the two films were received and discussed. *Penthesilea* was seen as an authored film which reflected currents in feminist thinking but was not made for or with the Women's Movement. The authors were explicit that addressing the movement had not been a priority, that they knew they would restrict the audience 'by concentrating on radical aesthetic problems',[18] a decision justified on the grounds that

> The problem is that counter-institutions which lack a theory tend spontaneously to reflect the ideology in reaction to which they were formed. If you bounce a ball, the rebound is symmetrical in the same way. This means that a counter-cinema has to have a theoretical stand-point. This means making theoretical films for a theoretically aware audience in order to break out of that symmetry. You can't imagine theoretical films which don't make their own formal structure an object of investigation.[19]

The film provoked intense debate within the milieu of independent film culture but did little to carry the arguments beyond this predominantly university-educated circle.

Nightcleaners, however, began as a record of a strike, for which the makers had required co-operation and access from the strikers and had been in regular contact with a large support movement. They were seen to be working within the tradition of making films around labour struggles and circulating them through the labour movement. So, many people besides the film-makers had a vested interest in the film's career and there was a clear expectation that audiences would not be restricted to the 'theoretically aware'. When the film was released reactions were, sometimes literally, violent. The film was attacked and praised with a passion not normally evoked in Britain by a cultural event, and the debate unleashed then still rumbles on today. Brian Winston in his recent book on documentary ignores the independent movement except to single out *Nightcleaners* for attack:

> the collective's concerns with the nature of image production, while neither unimportant nor trivial, looked impossibly sterile and irrelevant when yoked with the raw material of a group of exploited women trying to organise a strike against the advice of their union. The result was to reduce the deconstructionist agenda to a bathetic formalism. The film was received with much hostility by most viewers. … At best the film bored; at worst it got in the way of the nightcleaners' struggle.[20]

The passage echoes, uncritically, assumptions of the time that, because the film was championed by *Screen*, it was an exercise in deconstruction and that because it looked odd and did not 'tell the story' of the strike it could not work for the political film circuit. Both were hasty and muddled judgments. For the film-makers were scarcely aware of deconstructionist theory when working on the project and, as Humphrey Trevelyan describes, were ambivalent about the *Screen* reaction:

> The film happened to express some of the things that some of the *Screen* people

were talking about and so it was taken over, assimilated by them and became a *cause célèbre*. We felt that one of the things we'd been wanting to do, speaking as film-makers, was to try to be exploratory. . . . It's an organic process and we felt that the *Screen* incorporation of *Nightcleaners* into their argument ignored that rather intuitive and organic process that we had had to go through.[21]

Humphrey acknowledges that there was intense hostility to the film from some of the people who had taken part in the campaign but not, significantly, from the nightcleaners themselves:

We showed it to several small groups of cleaners who came into Earlham Street. They didn't feel that it was weird or mad. I think they were just intensely interested in how they were represented and what was being said. I don't think they ever really thought that the film would have much influence on their lives and they took it very calmly, while everybody else was getting hot under the collar about it.[22]

The film's subsequent career indicates that, at the very least, it fared no worse on the political circuit than many conventional films:

It was shown in extraordinary places – extraordinary, given that initially difficult form that presents itself. The International Socialists used it a lot; a number of the trade unions used it; there was a couple of Workers' Education Colleges that showed it at shop-stewards' training sessions; some of those *Screen* people showed it in schools – imagine that, you wouldn't be able to do that now. It went the round of all the university socialist societies and was booked several times by some.[23]

As for the qualitative response, my evidence is anecdotal but includes the testimony of one observer that it was received with interest by a working-class audience in Doncaster. As he said, 'They did not expect a cartoon.'[24]

Gender and Race

The Women's Movement, as already noted, was an important influence in independent film before the formation of the IFA, and women, from the start, played a central role in the association, arguing successfully for a requirement in the constitution for 50 per cent representation for women on all committees. There were, however, different and sometimes conflicting, feminist positions within the movement, exemplified by the contrast between the Sheffield Co-op, featured in Part III, which saw itself as servicing the Women's Movement, and the London Women's Film Group, whose aim was to pursue a feminist agenda within film culture. The latter was formed in 1972 by women who already had a professional commitment to film, some of whom were working in the industry. Esther Ronay, Linda Dove and Sue Shapiro had made independent films before starting to work together in the group. Claire Johnston was already making a name as a film critic and theorist. The group quickly achieved a high profile in the independent film movement but was short-lived, disbanded as a result of internal tensions in 1977 after the production of *Rapunzel*, an ambitious short drama film funded by the BFI Production Board.

In 1976 the group produced a short account of their work, part of which is reproduced in Part II. It mentions that among their activities they joined with other women in the ACTT to persuade the union to take up the issue of discrimination in the industry. The action is indicative of the extent to which the group straddled the division between mainstream and alternative. The approach was in keeping with the programme of the Women's Movement, which was prosecuting a vigorous campaign for equal opportunities within existing institutions, while at the same time encouraging experimental women-only or non-patriarchal alternatives. But there were also pragmatic reasons for emphasising action around the industry. Esther Ronay was working as an assistant editor; Fran McLean had tried to get a job as an assistant camera operator. The women intended to work full time in film and, at a time when there was no possibility of doing this on grant aid, this meant earning their living through paid work in the industry.

The ACTT women's caucus proved extremely effective in putting equal opportunities on the union's agenda and one of the early results was the report, *Patterns of Discrimination* presented to the 1975 annual conference. This was the first document to provide comprehensive documentation about the severity of discrimination in the industry and it became an important reference point and stimulus for feminist action in all branches of the industry. The extract included in Part II draws attention to indirect discrimination, which is widely understood in the 90s but was only just being identified and discussed in 1975.

One of the aims of the London Women's Film Group had been to provide a distribution service for films by women and films on feminist issues, and after the group's dissolution the task was taken up by a new specialist distributor, Cinema of Women (COW). In 1979 a second women's distributor, Circles, was established, partly as a result of a conflict over the Film as Film exhibition of film art at the Haywood when women contributors, incuding Liz Rhodes and Felicity Sparrow, withdrew on the grounds that the event was inherently anti-feminist.[25] Circles initially set out to complement the work of COW by concentrating on experimental film by women and on the work of women directors from the past like Alice Guy and Germaine Deluc.

Race did not have a comparable impact on independent film culture until the 80s and the presence of a small number of black film-makers in the early 70s went relatively unnoticed. Jim Pines relates that the chief librarian at the BFI was extremely surprised by his article, reproduced in Part II, 'Black Film in White

Britain', and questioned whether those black film-makers could really exist, seeing that she had not heard of them![26] Despite a politics which foregrounded anti-racism and the importance of third world anti-imperialist struggles, despite support for the Campaign Against Racism in the Media (CARM), launched by members of the NUJ in 1976, independent film-makers only slowly began to connect with British black and Asian communities. Blacks were present as subjects in some films and participated in a number of community video projects, but did not get deeply involved with groups or in the IFA. The Ghanaian film-maker, Nii Kwate Owoo,[27] used Cinema Action facilities for his film, *You Hide Me,* and attended the 1976 IFA conference, where he distributed information from his group, Ifriquiyah, but that was as far as the contact went. The IFA remained almost entirely white until the early 80s, when newly formed black groups, initially Ceddo, Sankofa, Black Audio, Retake and Liverpool Black Media Group, began to participate forcefully in the Association and in related events and activities.

The IFA Campaigns

> While it appears that the Independent Film-makers' Association is already – or rapidly becoming – an established fixture in the minds of most people within or related to the independent film-makers' fraternity, the precise objectives of the organisation remain largely a mystery. (*IFA Newsletter*, August 1976)

The mystery, never completely solved, did not prevent the IFA becoming an effective pressure group which succeeded, between 1976 and 1982, in opening up professional opportunities for independent film-makers. But there was always an ambivalence about the process. Was the aim to hijack resources from the mainstream for a different enterprise, to change the mainstream from the inside or just to get into it? In practice it was never easy to predict where a particular initiative would lead.

The position articulated in 1976–7 was clear that the objective was to set up separate structures but that this required intervening in existing ones.[28] Discussion at the 1977 AGM focused heavily on relations with the funding agencies that independent film-makers were already dealing with, the BFI and the RAAs, and, to a lesser extent, the Arts Council. Nevertheless, state finance was not regarded as a panacea and the suspicion was frequently voiced that funding would be organised to recuperate independent activity to the mainstream.[29]

Lobbying was initially aimed at the BFI and, in particular, at the Production Division and the Regional Department. The Regional Department's main responsibility was for the regional film theatres, and the IFA's objective was to change the policy to one of supporting independent film in the regions.[30] The Production Division had a budget of £125,000 in 1976, £400,000 in 1979, just enough to invest in one or two very low-budget features but not enough to exert the financial clout in the industry that the NFFC had in its early days. The department's policy, or lack of policy, the individual funding decisions and the composition of the Production Board, the voluntary body which made those decisions, were subject to intense critical scrutiny.[31] An early success for the IFA was in securing representation on the Production Board; this was achieved through a characteristic British compromise, whereby the BFI agreed in principle that the governors, who appointed the board members, would select, as individuals, two people recommended by the IFA. If the IFA chose to elect those people, that was their business. The IFA nominees on the board concentrated on influencing the decision-making process in favour of IFA practices. A separate argument arose concerning control over the finished products: namely, whether the BFI or the film-maker would hold the rights and manage distribution. A sub-committee set to work to negotiate changes to the production contract.

While negotiating to improve practical conditions for its members the IFA was also trying to gain acceptance within the BFI for the IFA/*Screen* position on cinema. A sign of success is the catalogue for the 1979 and 1980 BFI productions. Produced under the title *The New Social Function of Cinema*, it is a substantial collection of articles and interviews designed as 'an attempt to offer an understanding of the role of independent film in social, political and historical contexts'.[32] Whereas the text is almost an IFA manifesto, the BFI productions described in it reflect more of an art cinema/experimental film agenda. IFA film-makers are well represented as individuals but there are no true workshop productions, and the co-op tradition is represented only by a celebrated American exponent, Yvonne Rainer. The selection to some extent reflects the interests on the board, but it is also indicative of the range of practices within the IFA, that many of its members were trying to extend and build on the traditions of mainstream cinema rather than oppose it absolutely.

The output of the board in the first years of the 80s continued to represent a compromise but with a tendency to polarisation, so that the money was divided between several major investments in arts features, like *The Draughtsman's Contract*, and a number of minor investments in films from the co-op tradition or from workshops. After *The Draughtsman's Contract* the department increasingly began to invest in feature-film co-productions with television, a policy made possible by an increase in funds and influenced by the decline of the NFFC, in principle a more appropriate funding agency for full-scale feature projects. It was clear that the IFA needed to extend its influence into the wider world of film and television.

It was an opportune moment for intervention in film policy, because the industry was enduring one of the bad phases of its permanent crisis, following the gradual impoverishment of the NFFC, a recent reduction in American investment and a continuing decline in cinema admissions. In the late 50s and early 60s the NFFC's revolving fund had supported over thirty productions a year. Between 1973 and 1981 it invested in thirty features in total and could no longer be regarded as a seri-

ous player in the industry. The brief to operate commercially prevented it from officially targeting its investment according to cultural criteria, although, unofficially,
critical preferences probably influenced support for films like Ken Loach's *Family
Life* (1971) and James Ivory's *The Europeans* (1979). The commercial implications
of the NFFC's decline were at first softened by increasing American investment, but
during the 70s there was a sharp drop, from nearly £21 million in 1969 to £4.8
million in 1973.

In 1975, in response to these problems, Harold Wilson appointed a committee
under the chairmanship of John Terry to 'consider the requirements of a viable and
prosperous British film industry over the next decade'.[33] Their recommendations,
contained in *The Future of the British Film Industry*, or the Terry Report, included
an injection of public money into the NFFC, or equivalent fund, and the establishment of a British Film Authority to take charge of all the functions then divided
between the Department of Trade and the Department of Education and Science.
The immediate result was the appointment of another committee, the Interim
Action Committee on the Film Industry, under the chairmanship of Harold Wilson, to make more detailed proposals for changes in the films' legislation due for
renewal in 1980. The AIP began to lobby intensely for minor modifications to the
proposals that would favour the production of British films rather than the servicing of American ones.[34] At this stage, in early 1978, the IFA became involved[35] and
prepared a document, *The Future of the British Film Industry*, which argued the case
for a network of state-funded workshops. Simon Hartog took a leading role in these
proceedings, and his own more detailed account of the proposal and its reception
is contained in *The Perils of Film Policy* in Part II.

While this attempt to influence films' policy was regarded as rather a long shot,
a serious and sustained effort was made to influence the constitution of the fourth
television channel recommended by the Annan Report of 1977. The story of the
background to Channel Four is long and complicated,[36] as discussions began prior
to the appointment of the Annan Committee and before the formation of the IFA,
and, following the publication of the committee's report, their recommendations
went through a series of transformations from the Open Broadcasting Authority
proposed by Annan to the Channel Four company finally established. Although a
minor player in the process, for its size, the IFA proved an effective one. There were
intense internal discussions about the Association's policy, several papers were
written and members were delegated to represent the IFA within the Channel Four
Group, an alliance of interests lobbying for the public service model rather than a
second ITV channel. The IFA's intervention helped secure the general requirement
to be innovative, although their specific proposal for a foundation designed to
promote innovative work was not taken up. Part II contains an account of the negotiations and the IFA's role: written for *Screen* by John Ellis, it was composed shortly
before the final decision on the foundation was taken. It is followed by an IFA
pamphlet, *Channel Four: Innovation or ITV2?*, describing briefly the idea for the

foundation. John Ellis's piece originally formed an introduction to two detailed IFA papers: *Channel Four and Innovation: The Foundation* (February 1980), and *British TV Today* (November 1980). The former represents an elaborated version of the pamphlet reproduced here, and among the additional details it contains is the recommendation that 10 per cent of the channel's budget should be used for the foundation. In the event, the Chief Executive, Jeremy Isaacs, rejected the idea of the foundation but, as a compromise, proposed the appointment of a commissioning editor with a brief for independent film. Alan Fountain, then an active member of the IFA in Nottingham, was appointed to the post in August 1981.

The IFA and the ACTT

The aspect of policy which caused most controversy within the IFA in the late 70s was whether the Association should seek closer relations with the ACTT. The question was raised at the 1977 conference, where it proved highly contentious. At this stage the issues presented were whether the IFA should declare support for the proposal for nationalising the film industry, which the union had by this time shelved; and whether to seek ACTT membership for film-makers working with grant aid. The second produced the main source of conflict, although the two were seen as related.[37] The argument was that joining the ACTT was difficult because prospective members had to find a job within the industry, but most jobs required applicants to be members already. Independent film-makers working unpaid or supported by small grants were ineligible. The argument for seeking a change in the rules was linked with the idea of enlisting the ACTT's support in the campaign for larger grants. Other advantages of union membership were that it would open doors to paid work in the industry and end an anomaly whereby some IFA members working with the labour movement did not belong to their own appropriate trade union. Some IFA members, however, regarded the union as largely irrelevant or even hostile to the independent film agenda.

The discussion proved inconclusive in 1977, but it was followed by an even more heated exchange at the next AGM in 1980, when the issue was settled in favour of unionisation. One of the concerns then was that the ACTT was worried on its own account about the status of grant-aided work and had already entered into discussions with the BFI about drawing up a Code of Practice to regularise conditions for such work. Some IFA members continued to have strong reservations and Simon Hartog, one of the main opponents of unionisation, made a last attempt to present the case against at the AGM the following year. His contribution is included in Part II.

Rapprochement with the ACTT certainly changed the IFA and the context of independent film. An important consequence was the elaboration of an entirely new union agreement, the Workshop Agreement, an extraordinary innovation which gave formal recognition to the principles of workshop practice and opened up the possibility of extending them as a basis for fully professional participation in the industry. Extracts containing the relevant clauses are reproduced in Part II. However, because of its specific origins, the document was designed more as an agreement for grant-aided groups than as an agreement for workshops in general. It evolved from the Code of Practice, at a time when public funding for film work had been rising. The ACTT was interested in unionising this expanding area of production without undermining its existing agreements or the post-entry closed shop, while the long-term objective of the IFA was the idea set out in the recommendations on films' policy to establish a public sector based on a network of workshops. The solution to the ACTT's anxieties was to restrict the agreement to workshops which not only fulfilled the conditions of being non-profit-making and managed by the workers but also employed at least four members of staff paid at a specified rate. Those that qualified were given a franchise by the union which meant they could produce work for the cinema or television under the Workshop Agreement. Although the wording of the agreement did not insist that income came from public funds, in practice the detailed provisions were such that it was difficult for groups to qualify unless they had long-term revenue grants. This was reasonable in relation to the IFA's plan for a publicly funded workshop sector, but had disadvantages in the context of cutbacks and privatisations in which the agreement was to be used. The rules excluded groups based on voluntary labour but also discouraged those generating much of their income from commissions and/or servicing the industry. The number of groups which were able to operate officially according to workshop principles therefore remained very small. The psychological effect was to elide the objectives of oppositional practice with a contingent dependency on state funding, an association of ideas which was reinforced by the general use of the term 'grant-aided', as in the ACTT London Grant-Aided Section.

Notes

1. See John H. Goldthorpe, *Social Mobility and Class Structure in Britain* (Oxford: Clarendon Press, 1980), pp. 251–2.
2. See pp. 278–9 and 283.
3. This last distinction is taken from Peter Wollen's 'The Two Avant-Gardes', *Studio International*, November/December 1975, pp. 171–175.
4. See Julia Knight (ed.), *Diverse Practices: A Critical Reader on British Video Art* (Luton: Arts Council/John Libbey Media, 1996), pp 28–30.
5. Reported in the *Morning Star*, 21 January 1971.
6. William Raban, interviewed in 1996.
7. See Knight (ed.), *Diverse Practices*, pp. 27, 34–7.
8. See Raymond Williams, *Technology and Cultural Form* (London: Fontana, 1974), p. 139.
9. The Sheffield station played a key role in the development of the Sheffield Film Co-op. See Part II p. 290.
10. See *Film and Video Extra*, no. 6, Spring 1976.
11. See, for example, the views of Sheffield Co-op member, Jenny Woodley, pp. 296–7,

and also Jonathan Curling and Fran McLean, 'The Independent Film-Makers'
Association – Annual General Meeting and Conference', *Screen* vol. 18 no. 1, Spring
1977, p. 116.

12. See also a further article about *Days of Hope* and the Edinburgh History event by Mark
    Nash and Steve Neale: 'Film History Production Memory', in 'Reports from the
    Edinburgh Festival', *Screen* vol. 18 no. 4, Winter 1977, p. 77.

13. Colin McArthur, 'Days of Hope', *Screen* vol. 16 no. 4, Winter 1975/6, p. 139 and Colin
    MacCabe, 'Days of Hope', *Screen* vol. 17 no. 1, Spring 1976, p. 98.

14. For *Penthesilea*, see Claire Johnston and Paul Willemen, 'Penthesilea, Queen of the
    Amazons', *Screen* vol. 15 no. 3, Autumn 1974, p. 120; Laura Mulvey and Peter Wollen,
    'A Written Discussion', *Afterimage* no. 6, 1976 p. 31. For *Nightcleaners* see Johnston
    and Willeman, *Screen* vol. 16 no. 4, 1975/6, p. 104.

15. Peter Wollen, *Signs and Meaning in the Cinema* (London: Secker and Warburg, 1969).

16. Wollen, 'Two Avant-Gardes', p. 171.

17. Laura Mulvay, 'Visual Pleasure and Narrative Cinema', *Screen* vol. 16 no. 3, Autumn
    1975, p. 6.

18. Mulvey and Wollen, 'Written Discussion', p. 32.

19. Ibid., p. 33.

20. Brian Winston, *Claiming the Real* (London: BFI Publishing, 1995), p. 199.

21. Interview with Humphrey Trevelyan recorded in 1996.

22. Ibid.

23. Ibid.

24. Interview with Dave Douglass, p. 274.

25. See Caroline Merz and Pratibha Parmar, 'Distribution Matters: Circles', *Screen* vol. 28
    no. 4, Autumn 1987, pp. 66–9.

26. Jim Pines, in interview, 1996.

27. See Nii Kwate Owoo, 'You Hide Me', *Vertigo* issue 2, Summer/Autumn 1993, p. 26, for
    a retrospective account by Nii Kwate Owoo of the making of his first film and other
    activities of the Ifriquiyah group.

28. See Curling and McLean, 'Independent Film-Makers' Association', pp. 107–17.

29. Ibid., pp. 109–11. Also see Jane Clarke for the IFA London Region, letter in *Screen*
    vol. 18 no. 1, Spring 1977, pp. 120–2.

30. See Alan Fountain, 'Questions of Democracy and Control in Film Culture', in Rod
    Stoneman and Hilary Thompson (eds), *The New Social Function of Cinema* (London:
    BFI, 1981), pp. 164–9.

31. See ibid., John Ellis, 'Selection by Committee' in *The New Social Function of Cinema*
    (London: BFI, 1981), pp. 12–18.

32. Rod Stoneman and Hilary Thompson (eds), *The New Social Function of Cinema:
    Catalogue of British Film Institute Productions 1979–1980* (London, BFI, 1981), p. 6.

33. *Future of the British Film Industry*, report of the Prime Minister's Working Party,
    January 1976, Cmnd 6372.

34. See AIP, *Recommendations to the Government following the Prime Minister's Working
    Party Report on the Future of the British Film Industry and the Interim Action
    Committee's Report on the Setting up of the British Film Authority* (London: AIP,
    1978).

35. See John Ellis, 'Art, Culture and Quality: Terms for a Cinema in the Forties and Seventies', *Screen* vol. 19 no. 3, Autumn 1978, pp. 9–49.

36. A brief, clear account of the history can be found in Simon Blanchard, 'Where Do New Channels Come From?', in Simon Blanchard and David Morley (eds), *What's This Channel Fo/ur?* (London: Comedia, 1982).

37. See Curling and McLean, 'Independent Film-Makers' Association', p. 113.

Chapter Four
Paradoxical Success (1980–90)

By 1984 many IFA activists were working for, or funded by, the new Channel Four. Film-makers who, previously, had circulated their work to audiences of tens or hundreds were now addressing hundreds of thousands, occasionally millions. It was a victory, a vindication of all that energy invested in discussion, writing and lobbying over the preceding decade. But it proved a limited and temporary victory. Scarcely a year after broadcasting began on Channel Four many of those commissioned were complaining bitterly of the discrepancy between the channel's rhetoric and its practice.[1] Even more disappointing in the long run was that the partial victory did not advance or strengthen the movement which had fought for it. Within ten years the IFA and nearly all the other structures which promoted oppositional film-making were gone.

Commentaries on this period, particularly those of participants, tend to be accusatory, seeking to allocate responsibility for the decline. Candidates for blame included individual commissioning editors at Channel Four,[2] the IFA film-makers and critics themselves,[3] outside pressures, Thatcherism or 'marketisation'. At its crudest and most judgmental, the question lurking in the background is, was there a sell-out? At a more interesting level the discussion explores a confusing and contradictory situation in which many different factors played a part.

After 1982 a major preoccupation for the IFA became monitoring developments within Channel Four, and, more specifically, trying to influence the policies of the Independent Film and Video Department. The emphasis was understandable, since the channel became a major source of finance for the IFA sector and the department was the one enclave in the mainstream media directly amenable to IFA influence. However, the concentration on this special relationship represented a shift in the IFA agenda from the time when the campaign for a sympathetic TV channel or at least one sympathetic department within the channel, had been merely a tactic in the wider strategy of transforming society and its media.

The Advance of the New Right
The politics of Thatcherism, like those of most governments, were marked by wide gaps between rhetoric and practice, promise and achievement. This fact hinders tidy generalisations, but it is widely accepted that the main thrust was towards deregulating and extending the market, that the methods were authoritarian by

British standards and the outcome was a society more divided than before in terms of wealth, opportunity and power.[4]

By the 1979 election the Conservatives had proclaimed their intention to roll back the state and break the unions. Their victory was a serious setback for Labour, but the most destructive aspect was that it exacerbated an internal struggle between left and right which led to the four most militant right-wingers leaving in 1981 to form the Social Democratic Party (SDP). In the following two elections, in 1983 and 1987, the SDP-Liberal Alliance successfully attracted support from Labour, enabling Thatcher to win with a declining share of the vote and smaller majorities than the one which had lost the Conservatives an election in 1964.[5]

The fact that extremely radical policies were implemented on the basis of such minimal electoral majorities is a feature of the Thatcher period after 1983, which was largely obscured by successful public relations. One of the keys to Thatcher's ability to silence opposition was that her government broke with the tradition of non-partisan public services and administration by appointing an unprecedented number of supporters to senior public posts and by relying for advice less on civil servants and more on independent experts and private think-tanks. The role of the right-wing popular press was another factor, particularly important at the time of the Falklands War, when the jingoistic coverage[6] helped to boost the government's popularity in time for the 1983 election campaign, diverting attention from a catastrophic rise in unemployment to over 13 per cent.

It was during the second Thatcher government that the power base of the labour movement was seriously undermined. Legislation curbing the rights of trade unionists to impose closed shops, take industrial action and join picket lines was tested by the miners' strike of 1984–5. The handling of this dispute set a pattern for confrontational tactics and aggressive policing. The failure of the NUM after a determined and protracted struggle was extremely damaging to the whole union movement, particularly as the miners had been divided and the press, with a few exceptions, had tended to portray the dispute as a struggle between two groups of workers rather than between the government and workers. In the following year a strike by print workers resisting the employers' terms for using new technology was defeated, again after violent struggles between police and pickets. The outcome reinforced the lesson of the miners that industrial action was no longer effective and that, consequently, unions had lost much of their power to protect their members and influence policy. Other main centres of resistance to Thatcherism, high-spending Labour local authorities, were partially removed when the largest, the metropolitan counties and the GLC, were abolished in 1986, while rate-capping reduced the smaller ones to relative impotence.

It was also during this government that assistance afforded to the film industry by the Films Acts was phased out and finally abolished in 1985. The short-term effects were comparatively minor, because the legislation, which had been changed only in detail since its introduction, was becoming increasingly irrelevant and no

longer provided significant incentives to producers of British films.[7] However, with
the aid regime went the structures for supervising the industry. The regulations for
quota and levy and for securing NFFC loans had required producers and exhibitors
to provide quite detailed information: the Cinematograph Films Council and the
NFFC both processed information and published statistics. When these structures
were dismantled it became more difficult to monitor what was happening in the
business, let alone intervene.

From the point of view of the IFA constituency, the films' legislation, designed
to benefit large commercial producers and administered by the Department of
Trade and Industry, was less relevant than changes in cultural and educational policy. Cuts in cultural funding presented a direct threat to one source of income, but
cuts to schools, colleges and adult education were at least as serious, because they
affected those institutions which had provided a growing market for independent
film, and the use of film in education not only provided a source of income but also
a rationale for grant aid. When schools and colleges had their funding cut, budgets
for extras like film hire were naturally among the first things to go, especially when
an obligatory curriculum was being designed which narrowed the choice of subjects and materials that teachers could use. When adult education was cut the
lowest priority tended to be the so-called 'recreational' courses, including the kind
of open-ended classes on current affairs, women's issues or media which frequently
used independent film. The effect cannot be judged only by the loss of existing business. Many ideas current at the beginning of the 80s about how to expand the use
of independent film revolved round educational networks and resources. For
example, the advent of tape created a potential for distribution through public
libraries and for using all kinds of public spaces – in hospitals, doctors' waiting
rooms, job centres as well as museums and libraries[8] – for showing material. But
just as such developments were becoming practically possible, libraries everywhere
were being closed and other institutions with public spaces but facing a cut in funding came under pressure to adopt more commercial modes of operation.

Technological Change

Political factors exercised a restraint on what could be done with new technology
just when changes associated with it were sweeping through the industry. Developments in video and computer systems, which had been extensively debated[9] but
used rather patchily in the 70s, were a major practical influence in the 80s. They
impinged even on the most basic administrative tasks, as the office revolution
brought about by the personal computer, fax and answer-phone began to transform the routines of the small film entrepreneur.

Of the technology more specifically affecting film and TV, cable and satellite television were the subject of much speculation,[10] but advances in video posed a more
immediate challenge. Artists and community workers had been experimenting
with the medium throughout the 70s, but they were not the customers the tech-

nology was designed for. Manufacturers were interested, on the one hand, in the domestic consumer market and on the other, in the television industry and corporate users. In Britain the domestic and professional markets both took off rapidly at the beginning of the 80s, creating a combination of anxiety and excitement in the mainstream industry and the independent sector. Betacam swiftly gained acceptance in broadcast television as an alternative to 16mm film, and the public began to buy VHS domestic VCRs on a massive scale. The latter development provoked a stream of articles in the trade press that tried to predict the likely effects on cinema-going and television viewing habits. By 1982 19 per cent of television homes had a VCR, by 1983 it was 30 per cent[11] and by 1986 42 per cent.[12] As it turned out, fears that video might drastically reduce the audience for the cinema or television and, equally, hopes that it might stimulate new kinds of production, proved largely unfounded. The main use VCRs were put to was to time-shift broadcast programmes and to view feature films recycled on tape. Video-rental outlets mushroomed, but the product they carried reflected, possibly reinforced, existing audience tastes.

The arrival of camcorders designed for amateur use began to change the nature of home-movie-making. The market for 8mm and super 8mm film declined as existing users, other than a small minority of enthusiasts, switched to tape. The relative cheapness of tape, the user-friendly quality of the camcorder and the ease with which the end product could be shown made video a far more popular medium. While shooting films (even casual, unedited records of the family) had been more of a specialist hobby than a regular part of domestic ritual, shooting tape soon came to be regarded as something anyone could have a go at, almost on a par with taking snaps with an instamatic.

For similar reasons video was quickly accepted in the field of sponsored and semi-professional film, replacing 16mm film in some areas but also serving new purposes for which the use of film would have been too costly or too difficult. A feature of this new video world was the variety of tape formats, from the video 8 and ½ inch VHS used by amateurs, through ¾ inch u matic low band and high band, to the betacam and 1 inch used in broadcasting. As with the different gauges of film, the range was associated with a hierarchy of price, quality and status, but the boundaries became more fluid as new arrivals, like hi 8, kept upsetting the pattern. The variety and the speed of change made for difficult planning decisions, since the difference in price between the systems was considerable, but outlets were severely restricted by opting for low-cost formats. A production shot on anything less than betacam would not be considered for broadcast; tape distribution would be jeopardised by the poor quality of copies if material was originated on anything less than high band.

The hierarchy of formats influenced developments within the independent sector. The qualities which made video more accessible than film applied most decisively to the use of formats at the bottom end of the scale, and to shooting rather than to the whole process of film-making. Cameras in the amateur and semi-professional categories were easier to use than a 16mm system, in that it was easier for the novice to obtain a readable image with an audible, synchronised soundtrack. But the advantages gained during production were to some extent offset by problems at the post-production stage, since editing with the linear systems of the 80s was fiddly and time-consuming. The usual procedure was to construct the programme using a basic edit deck, which produced a rough result like a film cutting copy. To get a version with balanced colour, a mixed soundtrack and optical effects it was necessary afterwards to do a final on-line edit at a facilities company, an expensive procedure comparable to negative cutting and grading a film. This became a major drawback only if the end product had to resemble a television programme. However, artists' objectives were rarely as straightforward as that, and many community users emphasised process over product, aiming to get people involved in continuing interactive projects rather than producing a final programme. Their attitude, in some ways echoing that of the artists, was to explore the possibilities of the medium – in this case social ones – rather than copying commercial uses. In the event, however, low-budget video systems encouraged an enormous expansion in all areas of independent production, and when the aim was to make a tape for agitational or educational use video could prove frustrating and confusing, as producers were constantly having to weigh up the benefits of low production costs against the likely outcome in terms of public reception and potential revenue.

When it came to the choice between film and video, aesthetic and political considerations were often emphasised over practical ones. Artists regarded video as an art form in its own right and were hostile to the notion that the two media were in any sense interchangeable.[13] Most were initially preoccupied with the specific properties of the medium, in the way that film artists were preoccupied with the properties of film. London Video Arts (renamed London Electronic Arts in 1994), an organisation founded at David Hall's initiative by a group of video artists, set out to raise the profile of video art and assert a medium-specific identity for it. However, by the 80s LVA had expanded to become an access facility serving a wider video constituency, while other initiatives like Film and Video Umbrella, started by Mike O'Pray in 1983, promoted video art alongside film art. These cross-connections with other video work on the one hand and with film art on the other, made it difficult to sustain a clear, separate identity, especially as video became increasingly used for distribution, irrespective of the medium of origin. Having said this, video art became a very important component of a wider independent video culture, which was celebrated at an annual Festival of Independent Video, held at South Hill Park Arts centre, Bracknell, from 1981. Bracknell was also the base for a magazine, *Independent Video* (renamed *Independent Media* in 1986), which was launched in 1982 by editors David Stewart and Barrie Gibson and continued to cover both art and community video for the next decade.

Community users tended to adopt a fairly pragmatic attitude to the choice of medium, and those who took a stand on the question were usually more interested in asserting the specific value of film than of video.[14] The choice was likely to be influenced by considerations relating to distribution. If the production was for video release, then video would be favoured; if it was for television, the decision would depend on relative costs and the skills and experience of the makers; only if there was likelihood of major screenings in cinemas or large halls would there be a clear preference for film. But the question of what kind of release to aim for was itself a political one, and the sudden proliferation of VCRs in homes and institutions meant rethinking the strategies which had characterised the 70s. Video had the advantage over film that it could be shown in many venues without bringing anything to the screening except the tape. Even if it was necessary to import a VCR and monitor, once they were set up, no skill was needed to run the tape. Gone were the nerve-racking reel changes, and if everything had worked satisfactorily during a rehearsal, there was little danger of a breakdown during the show. The disadvantage, in the 80s, was that video projectors were extremely rare, so that exhibition was effectively confined to the small screen, and unless there were several monitors it was difficult for a large audience to see and hear properly. For the purpose of generating discussion, using video with small groups could be more effective than screening a film before a large audience lined up in rows. But if an important aspect of group strategy was to send members of the group out with productions, there was the problem that it cost more in time and energy to organise a lot of small shows than one big one. In any case, by the 80s, the decline in organised political activity made it harder to sustain the kind of mobile cinema culture that Cinema Action had been associated with in the 70s. The increasing use of video was therefore one factor, among others, which encouraged a more conventional and impersonal style of distribution based on hiring and selling tapes to people with whom the group might have no other contact.

It is difficult to assess the political impact of this kind of distribution, as tapes may be viewed by an individual or very small group and there is unlikely to be any report back on the response. To expect a comparable impact to film would require a much larger number of sales or bookings. In theory, video has the merit that it can be viewed in the home by people who do not have the opportunity or motivation to attend a show. In practice, however, three related obstacles made it difficult for independents to reach either a large or a relatively uncommitted audience through direct sales or rentals. One was outlets. High-street video stores were not interested in carrying material made by little-known independents and assumed to have only a minority appeal. Business had to be conducted mainly by mail order, and that aggravated the next problem: price. The market was rarely large enough to bring down costs of copying and packaging sufficiently for tapes to be offered at prices comparable to those in the high-street store, even before the cost of postage was added on. Then there was publicity. For people to order a tape they needed to know about it, but large-scale advertising campaigns were far beyond the means of any small independent. As a result, tape distribution, like film distribution, depended very much on circulating information to known user groups and through political and professional networks.

Growth and Dispersal

The independent sector was growing fast at the end of the 70s, and continued to do so for much of the 80s. There were several reasons for this: first, it takes time for policy decisions to feed through into budgets; second, up to 1986 the large Labour authorities protected funding levels; and third, new income from Channel Four was many times higher than the income lost through cuts. As the movement grew and its component parts became larger, they also became more distinct and more autonomous, a process which reflected the wider influence of the politics of gender, ethnicity, sexuality and national or local identities. This diversity was a source of vitality but also, not surprisingly, of division. The range of ideas and practices represented within the independent sector meant that attempts to maintain a common representative body proved costly in time and energy. The IFA made the strongest bid to represent the sector as a whole, and successfully eroded technological barriers by bringing in video in 1983 and photographers in 1986, changing its initials first to IFVA and then to IFVPA. But technology was only one of several potentially divisive factors, and the mergers failed to secure a united front.

Throughout the IFA/IFVPA's existence its membership and the constituency it theoretically represented were changing. The most obvious factors were overall growth, growth out of London and a proliferation of workshops. The early membership, which prepared the 1976 conference, had been London-based, and the most active were theorists or film-makers associated with underground/avantgarde film. Even before 1976, however, many of the original members had drifted away, as the authors of *Independent Film-Making in the '70s* had noted, while many of the new members who joined after 1976 were from outside London. This change in regional balance reflected a growth of independent film outside London which is too early to be attributed to the IFA. As in London, social and political movements were a major stimulus and most of the work was voluntary. In some cases there was a modest financial input from a local council or RAA, a relatively new departure in the early 70s, but one which predated the IFA and can be attributed partly to the policy of decentralisation introduced by the 1964 Labour government[15] and partly to local pressure. The IFA became a factor at the end of the 70s, and a second wave of expansion in the early 80s was certainly encouraged by increased funds which the association had campaigned for, particularly those provided by the Independent Film and Video Department at Channel Four.

It is difficult to quantify these trends precisely because of the difficulty of defining independent practice and because those engaged in it did not necessarily join any organisation. One indicator is the increase in the number of practising workshops. In 1979 over thirty were listed at the Film Workshop conference in Bristol.

From 1983 the BFI handbook provides annual lists, but these almost certainly exaggerate the situation by including groups which were hardly active or active in only one area rather than the combination associated with workshops. Nevertheless, evidence from IFA reports, surveys and applications for funding suggests that during the 80s the lengthening list reflects a real increase in workshop practice, whereas in the 90s these figures become less helpful, because several groups had effectively closed down in all but name and an increasing proportion functioned only as resource centres. Figures for ACTT-franchised groups provide another measure, but one which underestimates by excluding those with an established practice but without the level of funding required for franchised status. We can assume that the number of functioning workshops lies somewhere between the total listed and the total franchised. In 1983 the BFI listed 44 , making no distinction; in 1984 the total was 67, of which 11 were franchised. In 1987 the total was 106, with 18 franchised.

Growth was unevenly distributed geographically, with London continuing to be over-represented. The North East was particularly well developed, and there was more activity in the North and the Midlands than in the South, excluding London. While the situation varied from one English region to another, the patterns were more distinct in Wales, Scotland and Northern Ireland. Independents in Wales were divided between those for whom Welsh films meant Welsh-speaking films and those who worked only, or primarily, in English. The former initially looked for support to the Welsh Film Board, set up in 1970, and in the 80s to S4C, and by 1987 there were two Welsh-language workshops. Most workshop production, however, was in English and the early development of community film and video around Chapter Arts Centre in Cardiff shared many of the characteristics found in the English regions.

Scotland was very much a separate case, because a fledgling film industry had been brought into being by the Scottish Film Council, an organisation set up under the influence of John Grierson to promote sponsored documentary.[16] The Council provided some patronage itself but mainly channelled private sponsorship to local film companies, distributed the products and, most importantly, negotiated with local cinemas for some of the films to be released as shorts. The 50s and 60s witnessed a proliferation of small companies subsisting on sponsored documentary but with ambitions to make independent films for the cinema. Bill Forsyth was one of the few who emerged from the system to make the breakthrough into features. In the 70s film politics were focused on attempts to consolidate and expand this embryo industry and to escape from the stranglehold of sponsorship. The objective was a film culture which was local and Scottish rather than one which was structurally different from the mainstream. The IFA concept of independence took root more slowly. The first workshop, the Edinburgh Film Workshop Trust, began as a photographic-based project in 1977 and gradually moved into super 8 and then video production. Four more workshops were founded during the 80s: a second one in Edinburgh, Video in Pilton (1981); the Glasgow Film and Video Workshop

(1983); Alva in Sterling in Sterling (1982); and Fradharc Ur in Lewis (1984), although the last two were small, rather insecure operations.

Northern Ireland presents a contrasting picture with its history of overt political conflict and lack of a local film tradition. Looking back at its past in 1988, the Northern Ireland branch of the IFVA noted that 'There have been subterranean currents of community media groups making their own videos on social and political issues and creating local screening and distribution outlets since 1972.'[17] But more formal organisation came relatively late, when three groups emerged: Belfast Independent Video, which evolved from the Northern Ireland Film and Video Association, formed in 1980; Double Band Film and Video, set up in Belfast in 1985; and the Derry Film and Video Collective, formed in 1984.

The expansion of the sector with all its separate local histories increased the difficulties of organising united action. The situation of independents outside London was naturally different from that of London-based practitioners, simply because the industry was concentrated in the capital. In their criticism of the mainstream the former tended to emphasise the failure to cater for regional or local voices and were generally more concerned with questions of access than issues of language. As well as geographical tensions there were generational ones, as older IFA members, or former members, sometimes assumed that the newcomers were merely opportunists[18] attracted by the prospect of paid work and an entry to the industry. Such suspicions were evidently unfair in relation to the newer collectives: Platform Films, Sankofa, Black Audio, Derry Film and Video, to mention only a few, all had distinct political aims. Whether the newer individual film-makers in the IFA were, on average, less politically committed than older members is also debatable, but they were, on the whole, younger, more of them had formal film training and fewer had either a foothold in the industry or an established independent practice.

There was, therefore, a growing constituency of film-makers, including many of the regional groups and a large contingent of recent film school graduates, who wanted to experiment or make films on political and social issues but had not been involved in, and were not necessarily interested in, the 70s debates. By this time some of the film artists and theorists who had promoted those debates had benefited from the new professional opportunities that had opened up outside the milieu of independent film. Film art was proving easier to promote through art structures than through film structures. Since 1972, when the 'Survey of the Avant-Garde' at Gallery House in London broke new ground by including film and video, there had been a series of exhibitions wholly or partly devoted to those forms: in Liverpool's Walker Art Gallery and Edinburgh's Scottish Arts Council Gallery in 1973; two major London events in 1975, 'British Landscape Films' at the Tate and the 'Video Show' at the Serpentine; 'Perspectives on British Avant-Garde Film' at the Haywood in 1976 and 'Film as Film', again at the Haywood in 1979. Gallery exhibition complemented rather than replaced screenings, but the implied recognition as high art had economic consequences. The Arts Council began to fund film and video artists, and to fund them in a way which segregated them from other film-makers. The Arts Council already had a budget for films *about* art, directed by independent film-makers, some influenced by the Continental avant-garde but all working in a film tradition. These were funded as low-budget professional productions with an ACTT crew. The film artists, on the other hand, were assumed to be working alone and were funded from a separate budget which gave much smaller grants to cover materials and services but not the artist's time. Both kinds of film might be screened in a gallery cinema, but the first would be presented as a variation on art criticism, while the second would be contextualised as works of art in their own right. Thus, just when the debate around 'The Two Avant-Gardes' (Wollen, 1975) was calling into question such a separation, institutional arrangements were reinforcing it. The connection between art and political action proposed in the mixture of work shown at Bristol and in IFA and workshop screenings was played down in favour of defining a distinct art tradition.

Parallel with the tendency for film art to move into galleries was the retreat of film theory into the academy. As more colleges and universities began to teach film and media studies the market for academic articles grew, as did the career opportunities opened up by them. Writers were also constrained by the publications available and funding, again, affected the options. Magazines combining a political agenda and a relatively popular address, like *Cinim* and *Cinema Rising* were short-lived; clearly not commercial propositions, neither could they attract support as educational publications. *Screen*, primarily a platform for academic writing, was comfortably subsidised. *Framework*, run from a university film department (first Warwick and then East Anglia), aimed to be more accessible and less doctrinaire than *Screen*, but the content was still pitched more towards the academic than the film-making community. *Afterimage*, more oriented towards film-makers, received only a tiny grant and came out very intermittently. *Undercut*, based at the London Film-makers' Co-op and concerned primarily with film art, was also fairly irregular. *Independent Video* covered both the art and the political traditions but was more of a newsletter for practitioners than a vehicle for general cultural debate. *Sight and Sound* was subsidised, came out regularly and addressed the general public, but concentrated on the mainstream and on topical reviews and news. There was no equivalent to the French critical magazines, written primarily by and for intellectuals in the film business, read by a public of cinephiles and concerned with cultural politics.

Some film artists and theorists resisted the trend towards isolated specialisms and tried to politicise the universities and galleries, using them to reach out to the public. The feminist exodus from the 'Film as Film' Haywood exhibition in 1979 is an example. But in the competitive environment of the 80s career considerations increasingly put pressure on academics to write for each other and artists to exhibit for each other and for professional critics, thus encouraging the development of discrete professional cultures, a world in which the aims of the early IFA appeared distinctly quixotic.

While practical circumstances began to undermine the IFA's inclusive character, the broadly Marxist, libertarian and internationalist assumptions of the early
70s were challenged by the growing emphasis on difference – differences of gender,
race, sexuality, language, ethnicity. The 80s saw an intensification of campaigning
by feminists and blacks, with a tendency for those working in the mainstream and
in the independent sector to form separate organisations. Thus the Women's
Broadcasting and Film Lobby (WBFL), launched in 1979, drew most of its members from television and included several prominent producers. The Women's Film
and Television Network (WFTVN), formed two years later, served a constituency
closer to that of the IFA, including students, women in the grant-aided sector and
those seeking entry to the industry. The membership of the two associations overlapped, but some of those in WFTVN regarding the WBFL as exclusive and too
concerned with the careers of women already established in the industry. There
was, similarly, a mainstream/independent divide between the Black Media Workers' Association, formed in 1981, and the Association of Black Workshops formed
in 1984.

The impact of the politics of difference was affected, possibly distorted, by the
broader context of a government profoundly hostile to state-funded culture and to
all manifestations of the labour movement. It was a time when funds were under
threat and funding agencies were forced to consider how to target their remaining
funds without courting direct conflict with the government. They proved receptive
to applications from women-only and black-only groups on the grounds that they
came from, or represented – the difference was often not made clear – marginalised
or oppressed sections of the population. When other projects were being cut these
successful applications set an example, encouraging ever-more specific minorities
to organise around their own experience of discrimination. It was a process which
underlined the complexity of the social fabric and of disadvantage, but it was also
divisive, emphasising competitive demands for special consideration rather than a
basis for solidarity. Rival claims were sometimes justified in terms which accorded
an absolute authority to personal subjective experience. Translated into a film-
making agenda, this became an argument for a degree of identity between film-
maker and subject which denied the value of research, analysis and imagination,
and, if taken to a logical conclusion, suggested that the only legitimate form of
expression was that of individuals talking about themselves. The argument was
often deployed tactically to exploit liberal guilt, but could backfire by endorsing
funding or commissioning policies which resulted in film-makers, whose aim was
to make films *from* their perspective but *about* any subject of their choice, finding
themselves restricted to a 'home territory' defined by the funder.

In the late 70s and early 80s the IFA failed to keep pace with the expansion of
the sector. Membership even declined for a while: in 1977 there were 280 members;
in 1981 there were only 190. By then about half the members were from outside
London, which made the association more nationally representative but aggravated

the practical difficulties. Pressure began to mount to shift decision-making away from London, and in 1980 the constitution was changed so that the executive committee was no longer elected by the AGM but was made up of representatives elected in the regions. From 1980 the AGMs and executive committee meetings were mostly held outside London. The following year administrative difficulties were eased by a BFI grant. The IFA had initially been run on a voluntary basis, with small grants to assist with the 1976 conference and 1977 AGM. In 1981 it obtained a grant of £10,000 from the BFI, which subsequently rose quite steeply. Membership picked up and climbed to above the 1977 figure but still did not reflect the growth of the sector, nor did it bring increased income to match the larger grants. In 1977 income (from January to August) was £1,123, of which about half (£559) comprised subscriptions; in 1982 income was £10,659 of which only £725 was represented by subscriptions; by 1987 income was £52,500, of which £1,615 or about 3 per cent, came from subscriptions.[19] One result was that the IFA became progressively more dependent on the BFI, while the apparent willingness to fund a small association quite generously no doubt set a precedent which encouraged more specialised pressure groups to form associations and apply for grants, so contributing to the fragmentation of the sector.

The conflict about relations with the ACTT described in the previous chapter opened up divisions within the IFA which were never satisfactorily resolved. The 1980 AGM settled the dispute but not the underlying tensions, which soon re-emerged in the debate about the purpose and future of the organisation discussed in Frank Abbott's article, 'The IFA – Film Club/Trade Association' (reproduced in Part II). *Rapprochement* with the ACTT strengthened the IFA's influence *vis à vis* the funding bodies and Channel Four but, in the long run, contributed to the centrifugal tendencies, as opponents had predicted. Those outside the union tended to drift away, because the IFA seemed too identified with the ACTT; those inside the union, faced with two sets of meetings, often transferred their allegiance.

To make matters worse the link with the union came too late to satisfy all those who had argued for it. Murray Martin, from Amber, concluded from the nature of the debate that the IFA would never be wholly committed to the workshop strategy. He began arguing for a new organisation and in 1983 eventually succeeded in bringing the workshops together to discuss the possibility. At the meeting there was considerable resistance to the idea of a workshop association, on the grounds that it would weaken the IFA. Despite the objections, in 1984 the National Organisation of Workshops (NOW) was finally launched, becoming, in some respects, a competitor to the IFA. During these deliberations the black groups identified a need for an organisation more wholeheartedly committed to advancing black film culture and formed the Association of Black Film and Video Workshops (ABW), also in 1984.

The Encounter with Channel Four

Most histories of Channel Four point out the contrast between the political climate in which the new channel was conceived and the reality into which it was born.[20] The outcome was that an institution reflecting a mix of liberal and radical politics temporarily enabled the IFA sector to prosper at a time when the abolition of the metropolitan counties, the onslaught on the trade unions and cuts in cultural funding and education were destroying the networks that had previously sustained their work. However, when Channel Four first came on the air the process had only just begun. The Thatcher government was only three years old, as yet a mere blip in the familiar pattern of consensus politics. The subsequent rightwards journey, leading to the extremes of the mid-90s, if forecast then, would have sounded like paranoid leftist scare-mongering.

At the time of Channel Four's birth, therefore, the more utopian expectations of 'difference' were not as unrealistic as they now seem with hindsight. The start was promising. The output of the first two to three years, compared to that of the other three channels before they adjusted to the competition, represented a significant shift in broadcasting culture. Undoubtedly, a high point in the history of the independent sector was the opening of the Independent Film and Video Department's *11th Hour* strand with Cinema Action's feature-length documentary *So That You Can Live* (one of the contemporary reviews is reprinted in Part II). Here was a film, given airtime and widely discussed and praised, which before, because of its unorthodox appearance, its politics and the political reputation of its producer, would have had virtually no chance of being broadcast. Furthermore, the strand went on to show material which might be regarded as more overtly radical. The first year included a season on that most sensitive of political topics – Ireland – and screened examples of the work of both kinds of avant-garde: Laura Mulvey and Peter Wollen's *Amy* and films by Malcolm Le Grice, Geoff Keen and Margaret Tait. In 1983 the department launched another strand, *People to People*, for 'programmes resulting from the unique collaboration between groups within geographical communities or "communities of interest" and programme producers committed to this form of television'.[21]

Discussion in the independent sector tended to focus on Independent Film and Video, but this was by no means the only department which commissioned IFA independents and other innovative or left-wing producers. For example, all the commissions obtained by Cinecontact, the company Ron Orders set up after leaving Liberation Films, were from other departments. There were, for a time, three commissioning editors with a brief for documentary, and two of them, Paul Madden and Carol Haslam, commissioned individual programmes which appeared in the *People to People* slot. Paul Madden commissioned some of the early programmes made by the Television History Workshop, a production group closely linked with the oral history movement. Despite its name this is an ordinary production company set up by producers whose background was in-house television, but its methods, in some respects, resembled those of the workshops. Research involved setting up an accessible base where local people could drop in and get involved. So, for *Making Cars*, on the history of car workers in Cowley, the production company opened a shop in Cowley with an exhibition and staff on hand to discuss the project with anyone who was interested.

Much of the innovative work which was not associated with Independent Film and Video came about as a result of fairly organised outside pressures. The relatively high-profile coverage of the third world, for instance, owed much to the International Broadcasting Trust, a consortium of sixty non-profit-making organisations concerned with development, race, international relations and the third world, which set up its own programme-making company and used the programmes after they were broadcast for continuing educational and campaigning work. Two innovative strands in the early news and current affairs schedule reflected arguments made from outside the channel. One was a current affairs series made by women, an idea which had been vigorously canvassed by the Women's Broadcasting and Film Lobby, and although the concept was watered down so that women merely had editorial control, part of the series was commissioned from Broadside, a new company which was wholly owned by women and committed to feminist principles. The second was a news strand, *The Friday Alternative*, 'alternative' because, unlike the rest of the news, which was subcontracted from ITN, it was produced by an independent company. This slot marked a concession to the view expressed by the Campaign for Press and Broadcasting Freedom among others, and supported by the Glasgow Media Group's critique of conventional news values, that all the news should be provided from sources outside the existing framework.

During the run-up to the start of broadcasting, the Channel Four campaigners were preparing for a continuing struggle. Members of the old Channel Four Group reconstituted themselves as a new Channel Four Users' Group, with the aim of bringing together programme-makers and viewers. The book *What's This Channel Fo/ur?*, produced in association with the Group and with a considerable input from the IFA, prepared the ground for continuing debate. In several areas, particularly the plans for *The Friday Alternative*[22] and those for redressing gender and racial imbalance,[23] the authors discuss tokenism and accurately predict controversies which actually arose in the first year.

Given this prognosis, it may seem disingenuous that programme-makers were soon bitterly comparing their actual experience with the initial climate of euphoria. A *Screen* discussion with people who had worked on early commissions contained this exchange between John Ellis, one of the producers of the *Visions* cinema programmes, and Barry Flynn, a journalist on *The Friday Alternative*:

JE: I think there was an absolute belief that you would be able to say on Channel 4 what you could say in the written press – not just the daily and Sunday

newspapers but also in magazines like the *New Statesman*. It's that belief that
has been much eroded over the last year.

BF: But it's my understanding that the people who actually held that belief in the
beginning were people like Jeremy Isaacs and Liz Forgan. The independent
producers who debated this through with them at the beginning of the first
year of Channel 4 said 'Come on, aren't the Independent Broadcasting
Authority (IBA) going to rebel against this notion right from the beginning?'
And Jeremy Isaacs and Liz Forgan were convinced they could get away with
it. So the belief on the left or amongst radical programme-makers that this
would be a genuine opportunity for 'independence' was by and large fostered
by the Channel. It wasn't a naive piece of utopianism ...

JE: But why did we believe it? Why did we fall for it?[24]

Two answers to the question are suggested by another participant in the discussion,
a researcher for Brook Productions:

in the first year the Channel seemed to commission a much broader range of
programmes than we all predicted it would. So that threw us off guard. And then
we all got jobs in it, which did affect for a time our critical faculties.[25]

The discussion reflects a complicated roller coaster of experience, with moments
of unexpected triumph alternating with unpredicted defeats. Oppositional independents at first did unexpectedly well both in selling existing work and in securing
new commissions, but during the year the situation changed. The output of the first
months had attracted a storm of criticism from the press[26] and complaints about
decency and 'balance'. *The Friday Alternative* had reportedly been a target of direct
political pressures.[27] Most importantly, the context in which those conflicts would
be fought in the future had been settled by a second Conservative victory. There was
a rethink within the channel, and the results were most evident in the politically sensitive area of current affairs. *The Friday Alternative* was axed and Broadside's contract was not renewed, two decisions which were widely regarded as signalling a
retreat from the early promise of 'difference'. Meanwhile, many new companies had
entered the field, most of them set up by producers from mainstream television who
had no fundamental quarrel with the values and working methods they were used
to. The meaning of the 'independent sector' was changing, shedding its oppositional
connotations and acquiring a purely commercial significance.

The defeats were not all external. One of the complaints was that, once commissioned, IFA independents had behaved like any mainstream company. But
there is an interesting difference between perceptions, depending on whether the
speaker had come from the IFA culture or from mainstream television. John Ellis
talks about confusion and disappointment, whereas Barry Flynn talks of the sense
of release:

if I compare Diverse Productions to ITN I'd have to say that editorial meetings
were wonderfully free, that jobs are wonderfully flexible. And just that quantum
leap in working conditions made you forget that you could have been so much
more radical about the way you were going to organise practices. It was so
wonderful to be in this dream world of being paid to do what you wanted to do.[28]

The contrast is a reminder of just how wide the gap was between industry norms
and IFA notions of good practice. To take the latter into the mainstream was an
immense challenge. Discussion about this both in the IFA and during negotiations
with the channel had centred round the workshop model, with the intention that,
gradually, more resources would be shifted towards workshop practice. However,
for the moment, most of those who hoped for funding had to apply for ordinary
commissions and there had been little discussion about what these would entail.
Many of the film-makers assumed that Channel Four's acceptance of the Workshop Agreement and the rhetoric about innovation implied a willingness to tolerate
or even encourage methods which differed from industry norms. It only became
apparent slowly, through experience, that these calculations were wrong.

As procedures within the channel became standardised two major difficulties
emerged. The first was that the legal department refused to accept the principle of
collective responsibility and insisted that an individual producer had ultimate editorial and financial control. The second was that financial supervision was stringent
and based on concepts of appropriate costs which reflected mainstream practices.
Disagreements characteristically revolved round schedules (experimental production tends to require extra research and editing time) and outreach work (many
film-makers considered meetings, film shows and public discussions as an integral
part of their project). Behind the disagreements were ethical and aesthetic arguments about what kind of work is necessary or valuable, arguments which
individual film-makers acting in isolation found hard to win.

The contradictions between radical aims, vague expectations and actual experience created a fertile field for rows: rows with the channel and rows within
companies. Broadside was probably the most notorious casualty of these contradictions, starting out as an exciting attempt to put into practice widely debated
feminist ideas, but ending in bitter internecine dispute. An account of their experiences published some time later by two members of the collective shows how,
despite intensive discussions, the group was pushed off course at a very early stage
by requirements imposed on them by the channel:

Our discussions over Broadside's structure were hotly debated. All twelve
founding members wanted to be involved and participate in the company's future.
At the same time we recognised the need to delegate responsibility within the
group. Discussions revolved round how and whether this could be achieved in a
non-hierarchical but accountable way. . . .

> In the end Channel 4 settled this issue for us. It demanded a traditional editorial
> structure with one editor at the top who would make all editorial decisions and
> liaise with the Channel. It transpired in our negotiations with the Commissioning
> Editor for Actuality, that this structure was to be the condition under which the
> commission for the series would be granted.[29]

According to this account most of the tensions which arose during production followed from the group's unwilling compliance with this condition. Broadside's
difficulties were particularly acute, but other production groups who gained early
commissions found that they were also faced with unexpected situations which they
had no time to consider and adjust to. As John Ellis put it: 'we never made the transition to a sense of what would be practical under the circumstances'.[30] Most of
those who started off with radical objectives found themselves drifting towards
industry norms. This widened the gap between the workshops and everyone else,
on the one hand, lent weight to the argument that organising as workshops was the
only way forward, but, on the other, left the workshops isolated. Independent Film
and Video remained the only department to provide workshop funding, but since
it was also, increasingly, the only department interested in unconventional methods of any kind there were many competing pressures on the budget. Eventually,
amid much recrimination, the workshop contracts were phased out.

Rod Stoneman, who worked with Alan Fountain in Independent Film and Video
throughout this period, gives an account of the experience from his point of view
inside the channel in the paper *Sins of Commission*, reproduced in Part II. Among
the many questions he raises is one which was often asked within the sector: why
didn't the oppositional independents mount more of a campaign once the channel
was on the air? Stoneman points to the lack of discussion,[31] and his remarks might
justifiably be coloured by a feeling that the Independent Film and Video Department did its share of trying to stimulate debate: for instance, by organising, with
SEFT, a conference and season of screenings on the *11th Hour* in 1983, by producing publications on the department's work and by taking part in events like the
Screen debate quoted above. He is, however, slightly unfair to *Screen*, which devoted
considerable space to Channel Four during the first years of broadcasting, and not
only to material that voiced the film-makers' views but also critical pieces like Paul
Gilroy's on the black strands[32] or Sue Aspinall's on the recycling of recent independent films by the channel.[33] If theoretical weakness is to blame, the problem has
its roots earlier, in the disjunction between theorists and practitioners discussed in
Chapter 3,[34] which was marked by a tendency for theorists to avoid analysing work
they classified as realist and to support workshops in principle without examining
what the groups actually produced. The legacy of this all-or-nothing approach can
be detected in Stoneman's remarks on the formal project,[35] where he seems to be
justifying the adoption of conventional magazine formats on the grounds that completely radical experiments did not, according to him, connect with audiences

or critics. The attitude had also discouraged the kind of analysis of workshops products and of quality TV documentary which might have provided an answer to complaints against the workshop programmes on the grounds that, in Stoneman's words, 'relatively few could only have been made by long-term funded, co-operatively structured groups'.[36]

The latter assertion is one of a series of challenges which Stoneman throws at the oppositional approach he once shared, and forms part of an explanation for withdrawing workshop funding. The implication is that if workshop programmes were not discernibly different from other forms, then there was no case for the special contract. Later on he chides film-makers for expecting broadcasters to fund work intended primarily for other forms of distribution.[37] His remarks are scattered within a thoughtful and ambivalent reflection but, taken together, they seem to support a thoroughly orthodox view of broadcasting: that the purpose is to put product on television screens, that the preferred product is made specifically for television, and that circumstances of production are irrelevant unless they appear in a very literal and direct way on the screen. This was the position which commissioning editors in other departments had apparently reached by 1983–4 and which clearly conflicted with the independent sector's ideas about changing the structures of control and the context of reception.

Problems of Organisation

The shortcomings of theory were arguably less significant than the increasing practical difficulty of getting theories heard or considered as the Thatcher government entered a third term. The failure of the campaign of solidarity with the miners and the fight to keep the GLC had demonstrated the difficulty of resistance. The abolition of the large local authorities and strict capping of others had removed local strongholds of left culture. Unemployment and years of anti-union legislation, together with declining public services, made it hard for anyone to earn a living from the mixture of odd jobs, part-time teaching and the dole that many film-makers and activists had done in the 60s. Freelancers in the industry faced worsening conditions as the ACTT, like other unions, began losing its ability to enforce agreements.

The independent movement had always been small, at most a few hundred people trying to make and show films, write and publish, raise resources, imagine a new industry and lobby for it. With Channel Four in action, production work claimed a bigger share of time just when the new situation required analysis and response. The sector was over-extended. At the same time alliances were disintegrating. The projected Channel Four Users' Group, bringing together viewers and producers, failed to take off. The commercial independents from the Channel Four Group organised themselves within the trade association, the Independent Programme Producers' Association (IPPA), and the pragmatic business of defending their interests began to take precedence over cultural issues.

As well as becoming more isolated, the independent sector was also more divided internally. The IFVA remained as an umbrella organisation, but the proliferation of interest groups described above provided sections of its constituency with other support structures: the WFTVN for women, NOW for franchised workshops, ABW for black groups. For members who had obtained Channel Four contracts or work on the channel's productions, the IPPA and the ACTT provided relevant services. The advent of NOW was particularly problematic for the IFVA, because the workshops had helped to give coherence to the constituency which could be conceptualised as workshops (which conveniently covered the access kind as well as collectives) and film-makers with allied aims and methods. When NOW took over the job of representing the workshops, the IFA was forced to rethink its role. There were still individuals and groups without representation: those in transition, trying to get grants, jobs, commissions, or producing on too small a scale to make the expensive IPPA membership worthwhile. Many of them gravitated to the IFA for practical support and encouraged the executive to raise funds for an information and advice service. In theory this was intended to supplement the political and cultural role, but in practice the two proved hard to combine. Outsiders saw the IFA, in its trade association capacity, as serving a constituency of near beginners and tended to assume that, as a cultural movement, it also represented newcomers. This attitude obstructed attempts to recruit more experienced radical programme-makers, like those connected with Broadside and Television History Workshop,[38] whose participation might have strengthened the address to Channel Four.

Nevertheless, during the mid-80s the IFVA continued trying to promote oppositional culture. In 1984 it held an event in Birmingham with screenings and discussion to celebrate its tenth anniversary. In 1985 it organised a two-day conference in Manchester on Channel Four, and in 1987 held a big summer school in Llandrindod Wells. Although the last event was well attended and lively, by this time the IFVA was an anomaly and some of its own members thought it should change course. Its activities began to exhibit an increasing ambivalence between resistance and accommodation. It supported the campaign to save the GLC and metropolitan counties,[39] despite the fact that this campaign itself made concessions to the government's agenda by emphasising the local authority's role in stimulating the economy over that of service provider and, in the field of culture, stressing the aim of developing cultural industries rather than promoting the arts.

Initially, the cultural industries strategy exhibited an unmistakable political dimension. An early influence was the experience of the North East region, where workshops had taken the initiative, working in partnership with local authorities to improve the financial performance of the independent audiovisual sector. Tapping into local, national and European funds they set up the North East Media Development Council (NEMDC) supporting a development agency (NEMDA), a regional training centre (NEMTC) and a distribution organisation. Job creation was part of the scheme, but this was linked to the promotion of local/regional media organised on the workshop model. In London a major influence was economic theory and particularly ideas current within the GLC Department of Economic Development about the role of small businesses in the modern economy. Another contribution came from a group of London-based cultural workers and media theorists associated with the publishing company Comedia, including David Morley, who later formed the think-tank Demos, Charles Landry, Geoff Mulgan and Ken Worpole. The group fostered a critique of left cultural practices, identifying administrative inefficiency and weak infrastructure as key failings and attacking funding policy for a bias towards high art, which, they argued, led to the working class subsidising the middle classes. The mix of economic and cultural theory fed into the strategy for cultural industries formulated by the Greater London Enterprise Board (GLEB) and presented in *Altered Images*.[40] Political/cultural considerations were clearly a factor at this stage, as the plan was to target assistance to the small independent enterprises in music, publishing and audiovisual production that offered alternative products to those marketed by the big corporations.

After the abolition of the GLC and the metropolitan counties and when the 1987 election returned yet another Conservative government, a more limited economic agenda began to emerge. In 1988 the NEMDC dropped the special commitment to workshops, and elsewhere, administrators and funding agencies became increasingly ruled by concepts of efficiency borrowed from business, or from business studies rhetoric. These issues were debated at the BFI regional conference of 1988, and a contribution from Marion Doyen, film officer at the City Lights Cinema in Nottingham, describes the dilemma faced by cultural practitioners trying to work within that environment:

> The language of economic development, the language used increasingly by
> funding bodies such as the Institute and the Arts Council is new to many of us and
> rightly elicits concern, which has already been expressed, about the place of
> cultural practice within such discourses. But it is clear that if we in the
> independent subsidised sectors are going to survive we are going to have to learn
> the language and its meaning. I think it is important to add that it should be part
> of our political programme both to use the language literally for all its worth in
> cultural and financial terms and perhaps attempt to inflect it with new meanings
> that are recognised by all its users – not just us, but the funders as well.[41]

One of the features of the new culture which was causing concern was the increasing use by funding agencies of consultants instead of researchers, a process which collapses together the gathering of information and the provision of advice in a way that pre-empts political discussion. Two of the consultancy firms most frequently employed were Comedia and Boyden Southwood Associates, a spin-off from Comedia. It was predictable that the main thrust of their advice would be to cultivate a more businesslike approach, calling for more training in finance, management and marketing. By the late 80s this was interpreted to mean more than just improving administrative techniques. A joint report on the independent sector in London[42] is highly critical of forms of organisation which differ from standard British business practice. Although the authors insist that 'we are not seeking to attack collective or cooperative working practices',[43] they devote two pages to stating the problems specific to this way of working, and none to the advantages of collectivism or the problems associated with small individually owned hierarchical companies. In conclusion, they recommend that 'fuzzy historic notions of collectives and cooperatives ... should not be tolerated' and that 'within a reasonable spread pay differentials should be encouraged'.[44]

A related phenomenon, particularly marked in the BFI's funding policy, was a shift away from supporting outside initiatives – elected associations, independent magazines – in favour of promoting services run by the staff. This was partly, no doubt, a response to declining funds and the wish to protect its own sphere of influence from cuts, but it went along with the preference for a more managerial, less democratic style of work. As a result, funds were withdrawn from SEFT and WFTVN in 1988 and the IFVPA's grant was cut, which led the Association to warn that its future funding was in question.

The IFVPA staff embarked on a review of the Association's work for the BFI which resulted in a downbeat, wordy paper full of phrases like 'proactive marketing plan', 'management systems' and 'project-based initiatives';[45] proposing the professionalisation of information and advice services, it hardly mentioned politics. The document failed in its purpose. At the end of January 1990 the BFI decided that there would be no further grant as from April, leaving the staff and members nine weeks to adjust to the loss of funds. In the event, the Association was wound up.

The fate of the IFVPA illustrates the way that 'the language of economic development' was gaining ground through a mixture of coercion – the wish to placate paymasters and preserve jobs – and consent. The basis for consent was complicated, because the development of business strategies could be seen, not as a denial of the sector's tradition but a return to practices which were very much part of it. Effective distribution had always been seen as a key to success. The older left film distributors, Contemporary and Concord, functioned within the market and survived better than the subsidised The Other Cinema. The early IFA had expressed strong reservations about state subsidy. Some of the first groups, Amber in particular, displayed considerable entrepreneurial skills. But that tradition was misunderstood if it was taken to endorse a retreat from the principles of co-operation and equality. In the 60s and early 70s the ability to deploy certain business techniques and skills coexisted with a well-informed critique of the market and an analysis which stressed the conflict between private and public interest and between employers and employees. In the rhetoric of the late 80s consultancies, cultural politics were attenuated to vague notions of new or under-represented voices.

Nevertheless, the view that there was something wrong with the grant-aided sector other than the shortage of grants was understandable. Levels of funding were far from insignificant. In 1988 in London alone, despite a 10 per cent cut, £2.5 million was still being invested by a combination of BFI, GLAA, LBGC (London Borough Arts Committee), the Arts Council and the Channel Four workshop budget. Comparisons are difficult because of the changing value of money and a changing context, but this was certainly more than was available in 1975 when independent film seemed to have a higher profile. Over the country as a whole in the late 80s there were more film-makers in the sector active in production, turning out between them more films and tapes than in the mid-70s. Yet the work was not conspicuously feeding into political debate and activity. Channel Four was thought by some to have exacerbated the difficulties by seducing film activists into full-time production and by bringing into the home a range of opinion and image that previously had only been available outside. The video revolution was similarly blamed for making the broadcast material conveniently accessible and diminishing the mystique of a film show. Both phenomena, though, in a different climate might have been expected to increase participation at meetings and screenings: television by providing exposure and video by making it easy to put on small shows almost anywhere.

To single out technology or business incompetence was to ignore the underlying problem that there was little political activity with which film-makers could connect. It is significant that one success story was the tape project in support of the miners, whose struggle attracted a massive solidarity movement both at home and abroad. Where there were dynamic political movements, film was a part of them. In the early 80s the women's peace camps generated films like *Carry Greenham Home*, which were widely used within and beyond the support movement. By the end of the decade environmental campaigners were making effective use of video. However, this is not to suggest that political film-makers can only intervene as film-makers in the wake of activism. The total pattern is more complex. In the 30s and the 60s the campaigning activities which accompanied an overtly politicised film culture were preceded by a period of considerable interest in film, and especially in films which were different from those promoted by the dominant commercial interests – films which had the capacity to surprise, to puzzle, to disturb expectations. Although the low-key struggle to make or show such images – images which run counter to current orthodoxies, which contest the received wisdom of the business – does not look or feel as effective as filming political action and screening the results to large enthusiastic audiences, it can create a space, 'an environment for further reflection',[46] and reflection is often a first step towards politicisation.

Notes

1. For examples of these complaints, see John Ellis et al., 'Channel 4 – One Year On', *Screen* vol. 25 no. 2, March/April 1984, pp. 4–25.
2. For instance, Alan Lovell points the finger at the staff of the Independent Film and Video Department in 'That Was the Workshop That Was', *Screen* vol. 31 no. 1, Spring 1990, pp. 102–8.
3. See Rod Stoneman pp. 174–86.
4. This is based on comment from several studies including Sam Aaronovitch, *The Road from Thatcherism* (London: Lawrence and Wishart, 1981); Anthony Giddens, *Beyond Left and Right* (Cambridge: Polity Press, 1994); Will Hutton, *The State We're in* (London: Jonathan Cape, 1995); Lester Freidman (ed.), *British Cinema and Thatcherism* (London: UCL Press, 1993).
5. The Conservative share of the vote was 43.4 in 1964; 42.4 in 1983; 42.3 in 1987; 41.9 in 1992.
6. See Robert Harris, *Gotcha! The Media, the Government and the Falklands Crisis* (London: Faber and Faber, 1983).
7. For a discussion of the effects of the aid regime and its abolition, see Margaret Dickinson, 'We Have Been Here Before', *Vertigo* issue 5, Autumn/Winter 1995, p. 16 and Margaret Dickinson and Sarah Street, *Cinema and State* (London: BFI Publishing, 1985), pp. 246–7.
8. An example of successful collaboration between film-makers and library staff in Sheffield is described in Andy Stamp and Georgia Stone, 'Reasons to Be Cheerful. Part 2 Working in Libraries', *Independent Media* no. 73, January 1988, p. 11.
9. See, for instance, Stuart Marshall, 'Video Technology and Practice', *Screen* vol. 20 no. 1, Spring 1979, pp. 109–19.
10. See, for instance, John Chittock, 'Turning on the TV Tap', *Sight and Sound* vol. 54 no. 1, Winter 1984/5, pp. 20–4.
11. Denis McQuail and Karen Siune, *New Media Politics: Comparative Perspectives in Western Europe* (London: Sage, 1986), p. 89.
12. *Screen Digest*, December 1986, p. 251.
13. See Julia Knight, 'In Search of an Identity: Distribution, Exhibition and the "Process" of Video Art', in Knight (ed.), *Diverse Practices: A Critical Reader on British Video Art* (Luton: Arts Council/John Libby Media, 1996).
14. See interview with Steve Sprung, p. 271.
15. See Simon Blanchard and Sylvia Harvey, 'The Post-War Independent Cinema – Structures and Organisation', in James Curran and Vincent Porter (eds), *British Cinema History* (London: Weidenfeld and Nicolson, 1983), p. 229.
16. For the following account of developments in Scotland I am indebted to Rob MacPherson, who gave me access to his unpublished thesis, *Independent Film and Television in Scotland: A Case of Dependent Cultural Reproduction?* for an M. Litt., University of Sterling, 1991.
17. 'Report on the Funding of Grant-Aided Film and Video in Northern Ireland', in *Fast Forward*, IFVPA North of Ireland, 1988.
18. See Frank Abbott's comments pp. 168–70.

19. IFA Annual Reports; IFA National Executive Report; IFA Financial Statements 14/1/77 to 15/8/77; IFA Accounts 1982/3; IFA Accounts 1987.

20. See, for instance, Rod Stoneman, p. 177, and Sylvia Harvey, 'Channel 4 Television from Annan to Grade' in Stuart Hood (ed.), *Behind the Screens: The Structure of British Television in the Nineties* (London: Lawrence and Wishart, 1994), p. 103.

21. Caroline Spry, introduction to *People to People*, in Alan Fountain, Caroline Spry and Rod Stoneman, *The Work of Channel 4's Independent Film and Video Department* (London: Channel 4, 1986).

22. Simon Blanchard and David Morley (eds), *What's This Channel Fo/ur?* (London: Comedia, 1982), pp. 92, 93.

23. Ibid., pp. 100, 121.

24. Ellis et al., 'One Year On', p. 5.

25. Ibid., p. 6.

26. See Jeremy Isaacs, *Storm Over 4* (London: Weidenfeld and Nicolson, 1989), pp. 51–61.

27. A report in the *Sunday Times*, 28 August 1983, quoted in Glasgow University Media Group, *War and Peace News* (Milton Keynes: Open University Press), 1985, p. 7.

28. Ellis et al., 'One Year On', p. 12.

29. Helen Baehr and Angela Spindler Brown, 'Firing a Broadside: A Feminist Intervention into Mainstream TV', in Helen Baehr and Gillian Dyer (eds), *Boxed in: Women and Television* (London: Pandora, 1987), p 121.

30. Ellis et al., 'One Year On', p. 11.

31. See pp. 184–5.

32. Paul Gilroy, 'Bridgehead or Bantustan', *Screen* vol. 24 nos. 4/5, July/October 1983, pp. 130–6.

33. Sue Aspinall, 'The Space for Innovation and Experiment', *Screen* vol. 25 no. 6, November/December 1984, pp. 73–87.

34. See p. 51.

35. See p. 184.

36. See p. 179.

37. See p. 185.

38. Greg Lanning, one of the producers from Television History Workshop, questioned by me in 1996 said that he kept his distance because he thought IFA policy was extreme and did not relate to his concerns 'as a television professional'.

39. IFVPA, *Strangling the Cities* (London: IFVPA, 1984).

40. GLEB, *Altered Images* (London: GLEB, 1986).

41. Marion Doyen, paper for the BFI Regional Conference Cultural Industries panel, (London, BFI Publishing, 1988), p. 1.

42. Boyden Southwood and Comedia for GLAA, *Developing the Independent Film and Video Sector*, 1988.

43. Ibid., p. 32.

44. Ibid., p. 35.

45. IFVPA, Draft Report for BFI, pp. 19, 22, 24.

46. See Liberation Films, p. 236.

Independent Film: A Chronology

Selected Distributors, Production Companies and Workshops.

1950   Plato Films founded by Stanley Forman. Distributor specialising in documentary and educational films from communist countries.

1951   Contemporary Films founded by Charles Cooper. Distributor specialising in foreign-language theatrical features and political films.

1952   Connoisseur founded by Bill Pollanca. Distributor specialising in foreign-language theatrical features.
Crown Film Unit closed down.
New Era, the production group of Anthony Simmons and other communist supporters, makes *We Who Are Young*.

1956   First Free Cinema programmes at the NFT.

1957   Short Film Service started by Derek Hill.

1959   First film from Derrick Knight and Partners. Documentary production company.
Last Free Cinema programme.

1960   Concord Films Council starts trading. Distributor founded by Eric Walker to distribute films for CND and other campaigns.
Plato forms a second company, ETV, because of a libel case.

1963   Mithras Films founded by Maurice Hatton, John Irvin, Richard De La Mare, Tim Pitt Miller. Production company. In 1968 makes *Praise Marx and Pass the Ammunition*.
Alan King Associates founded by Canadian film-makers. Changes name to AKA in 1970 when Alan King returns to Canada.

1964   First film registered by Lusia Films, a company formed by Richard

Mordaunt and others. After 1968 becomes the support base first for Cinema Action and then Berwick Street Collective.

Dateline founded by John and Marleen Fletcher. Production company and editing service. John is a close associate of Lindsay Anderson and makes *About the White Bus* in 1968.

Document splits off from Alan King Associates.

1965   David Naden Associates formed. Editing services, much associated with development of direct cinema.

1966   London Film-Makers' Co-op formed (LFMC) with temporary headquarters at Better Books. Activities include screenings and publication of magazine, *Cinim*.

1967   The Arts Lab opens in Drury Lane. Centre with gallery theatre, bookshop, cinema and television room. Better Books closes and Co-op screenings transfer to the Arts Lab.

Short Film campaign launched. Evolves into New Cinema Club.

Contemporary open Paris Pullman Cinema.

1968   Amber formed, based in Newcastle.

Cinema Action starts mobile cinema. Based in London.

Angry Arts Cinema Club formed in London. Develops Liberation Films, a distribution and production arm, in 1970.

1970   The Other Cinema (TOC) starts trading. Distributor.

LFMC, New Arts Lab, TOC and other independent distributors organise First International Festival of Underground Cinema held at the NFT.

Berwick Street Collective formed in London by Marc Karlin and others.

TVX video workshop is formed in London by John Hopkins.

1971   LFMC moves to Prince of Wales Crescent. Opens own cinema run by Peter Gidal and receives regular reviews in *Time Out*.

1972   London Women's Film Group formed.

1973   The Other Cinema absorbs Politkino.

A women's film group formed in Sheffield. It will be called Sheffield Co-op in 1975.

Four Corners formed in London.

1974   Association of Independent Film-makers (IFA) founded.
            Newsreel formed in London.
            Albany Video formed in London.
            Chapter Video Workshop formed in Cardiff.

1975   LFMC receives first major revenue grant from public funding.

1976   LFMC becomes a company and an educational charity. Moves to
                Gloucester Avenue.
            IFA first conference.
            Association of Independent Producers (AIP) founded.

1977   Edinburgh Film Workshop Trust formed.
            Cinema of Women (COW) founded. Women's distributor.
            London Video Arts formed.

1978   Leeds Animation formed.

1979   Frontroom formed. Workshop specialising in drama.
            Circles founded. Women's distributor.

1981   LFMC starts to produce the magazine *Undercut.*
            First National Festival of Independent Video, Bracknell.
            Video in Pilton formed in Edinburgh.
            Birmingham Film and Video Workshop formed.
            Ceddo formed. A black workshop.
            Women's Film and Television Network (WFTVN) founded.

1982   Channel Four starts broadcasting.
            Independent Video starts publication.
            Trade Films formed in Newcastle.
            Retake formed in London. An Asian collective.
            Platform Films formed in London.

1983   IFA becomes IFVA.
            Glasgow Film and Video Workshop founded.
            Sankofa formed.
            Black Audio formed.

1984   Derry Film and Video Collective formed.
            Network of Workshops (NOW) formed.
            Association of Black Film and Video Workshops (ABW) formed.

1985   Double Band Film and Video formed in Belfast.
            Red Flannel Films formed in Pontypridd. Women's collective.
            Steele Bank, Sheffield, becomes ACTT-franchised workshop.

1986   Light Years celebration to mark twenty years of the LFMC.
            IFVA becomes IFVPA.
            Independent Video becomes *Independent Media.*

1987   Scrin Cyf formed. Welsh-speaking workshop.

1988   Black Film British Cinema conference held at the ICA.
            Cultural Identities conference held at the Commonwealth Institute.

1989   AIP merges with the British Film and Television Producers'
               Association (BFTPA) to form Producers' Association.
            WFTVN closes London office. Reduced service run from Vera
               Productions, Bradford.

1990   IFVPA closes down.

1991   Independent Programme Producers' Association (IPPA) and the
               Producers' Association merge to form PACT.
            ACTT and the Broadcasting and Entertainment Trades Alliance
               (BETA) merge to become BECTU.

PLATE 1: A 1940s documentary crew. Shooting *The Way We Live* (Jill Craigie, 1946).

PLATE 2: Trade Union enterprise. An ACT Films feature crew shooting *Green Grow the Rushes* (Derek Twist, 1950).

PLATE 3: Independent fiction. Kevin Brownlow shooting a scene with a Bell and Howell for his feature, *It Happened Here* (1956–66).

PLATE 4: *March to Aldermaston* (1959). The CND documentary was released in the Academy Cinema, Oxford Street.

PLATE 5: *Warrendale* (Alan King, Canada, 1966). Spontaneous emotion captured using newly available light-weight 16mm equipment.

PLATE 6: Independent fiction. *Praise Marx and Pass the Ammunition* (Maurice Hatton, 1968).

PLATES 7 & 8: Two of the most influential foreign language features imported by Contemporary Films – (top) *Ashes and Diamonds* (Andrzej Wajda, Poland, 1958) and (above) *Ugetsu Monogatari* (Kenji Mizoguchi, Japan, 1953).

PLATE 9: Felix Green's *Inside North Vietnam* (1967) – a film used prominently in the campaign against the Vietnam War.

PLATE 10: Demonstrators clash with police in Grosvenor Square after the 1967 Vietnam Solidarity Campaign demonstration. Unidentified source re-used in *The People's Flag* (Platform Films, 1987).

PLATE 11: Paris, May 1968. Unidentified source re-used in *The People's Flag* (Platform Films, 1987).

PLATE 12: IRA Guard, Free Derry, 1969. The image may derive originally from Richard Mordaunt's *Ireland Behind the Wire* (1974), although it is taken here from *The Cause of Ireland* (Platform Films, 1983).

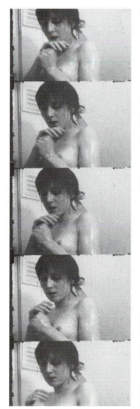

PLATES 13 & 14: Early work from the London Film-makers Co-op. (above) *Vertical* (David Hall, 1970); and (left) *Showerproof* (Fred Drummond, 1968) – the image is transformed by solarisation.

PLATE 15: *The Battle of Algiers* (Gillo Pontecorvo, Italy/Algeria, 1966). One of the most popular films promoted by the Other Cinema.

PLATE 16: Latin American films, released by the Other Cinema and Politkino played an important part in the newly radicaliséd film culture. *Memories of Underdevelopment* (Tomás Gutiérrez Alea, Cuba, 1968).

PLATE 17: *Hour of the Furnaces* (Fernando Solanas, Argentina, 1968).

PLATE 18: (right) Expanded cinema at the LFMC. *2 minutes 45 seconds* (William Raban, 1972). Three successive stages in the filmed performance.

PLATE 19: (below) The LMFC and fine art practice. *Real Time* (Annabel Nicolson, 1973).

PLATE 20: (bottom) *'Something is Going to Disappear'* Serial Interruptions (Annabel Nicolson, 1975). Installation in the artist's studio.

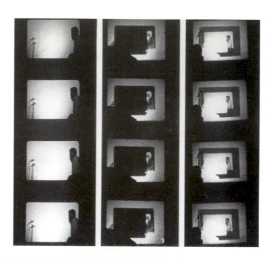

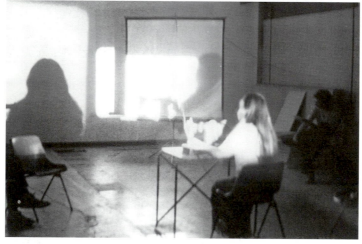

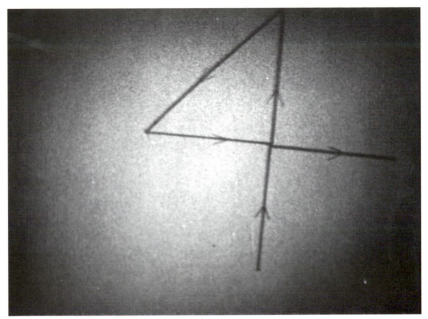

PLATE 21: *Cross* (John Du Cane, 1975). Du Cane exemplifies the versatility of many the Co-op members. While his own work follows in the art tradition, he was also willing to help out on a documentary about community childcare, *One Two, Three* (1975) – see p. 240.

PLATE 22: *Days of Hope* (Ken Loach, BBC TV, 1975).

FILM WITHOUT EDITING / CALL IMAGINARY
WORLD INTO QUESTION. NOT REJECT
FICTION - SITUATE. THEORISTS — FILM
WITHOUT EDITING NATURAL. MONTAGE:
DISCONTINUITIES. NO SINGLE THREAD.
IT IS SOMETHING ELSE: THE
A STORY WHICH IS
AND A HISTORY WHICH
NEVER YET BEEN MADE.

PLATES 23 & 24:
Penthesilea
(Laura Mulvey and
Peter Wollen, 1974).

PLATE 25: *Nightcleaners* (The Berwick St. Collective, 1974).

PLATE 26: *So That You Can Live*, Cinema Action's feature-length documentary, opened the '11th Hour' strand on Channel Four, 8 November 1982.

PLATE 26: Members of The London Women's Film Group shooting *The Amazing Equal Pay Show* (1974). (Left to right) Linda Dove, Barbara Evans and Claire Johnston.

PLATE 28: *On the Air: Workers Playtime* (1982). Frank Abbott's provocative history of broadcasting, financed by the BFI Production Board, broadcast on Channel Four, May 1983.

PLATE 29: *24 Films* (Jeff Keen, 1974). Jeff Keen was among several film artists whose work was featured on Channel Four during early 1983.

PLATE 30: *The Gold Diggers* (Sally Potter, 1983). Feature film financed by the BFI Production Board, broadcast on Channel Four, June 1985.

PLATE 31: *Carry Greenham Home* (Beeban Kidron and Amanda Richardson, 1983) – shot at the Women's Peace Camp at Greenham Common between December 1982 and summer 1983.

Part II

Texts and Documents (1971–92)

Introductory Notes

The papers, articles and extracts in this collection relate to Chapters 2 to 4 of this book, where some are explicitly mentioned and discussed. Written between 1971 and 1992, they are the products of the self-conscious political film culture which evolved from the late 60s. I do not include texts from the previous period covered in Chapter 1 because there is not, in the same sense, a literature of independent film for that time. Political questions were raised from time to time in reviews and articles on particular films or film-makers and in commentaries on film policy and the economics of film business, but in both categories some of the most interesting examples (from Paul Rotha and Lindsay Anderson, for example) are available in other collections.

The oppositional movement, by contrast, was characterised by a continual debate carried on in the major theoretical journal *Screen*, in a variety of less stable magazines and through a stream of ephemeral documents – conference papers, pamphlets, programme notes, festival programmes and film catalogues. The intention of this selection is to reflect debates which were influential across a broad spectrum of makers and users of independent film. So, many of the authors are primarily film-makers rather than theorists, and those who are best known as theorists are represented, not by their most academic work, but by interventions in film politics, polemics and articles for the general reader in publications like *Spare Rib*, and by articles on specific films. Most of the important film magazines are represented, but there are some notable omissions like *Afterimage* and *Independent Media*.

The first texts relate to the politicisation of film theory. Claire Johnston's piece is the second part of an article comparing French and British film criticism and is selected because it provides some background on the previous critical climate in relation to the new critical project launched by that issue of *Screen*. Johnston was one of the most influential activists of the time and someone who made a serious attempt to bring theory and practice together. Involved in the *Screen* project from the beginning, she was a member of the group which prepared the first conference of the IFA and was also a member of the London Women's Film Group.

Just about the time Johnston's article was written, a number of fairly short-lived magazines started up, addressed to political cinephiles rather than film academics, and including *Cinema Rising*, from which 'Notes on Political Cinema' is drawn. The author, Jim Pines, a black American who was on the staff of the BFI throughout the 70s, is one of the theorists who has consistently tried to address the film-makers and the general public as well as academics.

As a retrospective account of the beginnings of the LFMC written two decades later, the next article is a little out of place. However, it is written from memory by someone who was involved at the time and is more thoughtful than strictly contemporary material like the brief news reports which appeared in *Cinim*, the short-lived magazine produced by the Co-op in its early years. The LFMC plays such a central and lasting role in the independent movement that it seemed important to include something about it as an institution, even though I decided, for reasons explained in the introduction, not to try to cover its history in any depth. The article is also interesting because of its author, Malcolm Le Grice, one of the best-known British film artists of his generation and one of those most closely identified with the Co-op.

The placing of the next two pieces underlines the connection between the artistic project of the LFMC and the overtly political project of transforming the mainstream. Simon Hartog, who is mentioned by Le Grice as the co-author of the Co-op's constitution, was one of the first members of the LFMC, but the article included here relates to his work as researcher to the ACTT Freelance Shop Nationalisation Forum. In that capacity he drew substantially on the proposals put forward by the French États Généraux du Cinéma, four of which he translated in their entirety and published in *Screen* (vol. 13 no. 4, Spring 1972/3, p. 58) . The article quoted here is a shorter account of the French project and is followed by an extract from the proposals for the British film industry produced by the Nationalisation Forum.

The following three articles relate to the discussion in Chapter 3 about early attempts by women and black film-makers to confront discrimination in the film industry and establish their own distinctive practices. *Time Out*, the source of Jim Pines' article, was very important at the time as a public platform for political and cultural debate, and frequently carried popular articles about different aspects of independent film. The notes on the London Women's Film Group were produced by the group to serve as a brief introduction to themselves at events and to send out in response to queries. It is characteristic of the practices of the time that the original is just typed and cyclostyled, making for a very rough and ready kind of publicity for a group which, by then, had about eight films in distribution.

The next group of documents relates to the early years of the IFA, and the festivals, debates and campaigns discussed in Chapter 3. The letter announcing the founding meeting is reprinted for its symbolic interest. The paper, *Independent Film-Making in the 70s*, is a key document, the result of intensive discussion by a group including Paul Willemen, Claire Johnston, Marc Karlin, Laura Mulvey and Simon Hartog. There follow two extracts from programmes for the Bristol Festival of Independent Cinema and the Edinburgh Film Festival, both of which had informal links with the IFA. A central element in the IFA's philosophy, the need to relate theory and practice, is the theme linking the next three articles, which are discussed in the 'Theory and Practice' section of Chapter 3. Next come articles which amplify the account given in the history of the IFA campaigns on, respectively, the films' legislation and the fourth television channel. As these campaigns developed, relations with the ACTT became a major preoccupation and Simon Hartog's paper and the extracts from the Workshop Agreement support the discussion in Chapter 3 under the heading 'The IFA and the ACTT'. Simon Hartog had long argued against unionisation, and his brief statement here was a late intervention in the debate when the case in favour had effectively prevailed. The last paper in the series, by Nottingham-based film-maker Frank Abbott, is one of the most coherent interventions in the debate about the role of the IFA after some of its early practical objectives had been realised.

The final documents are concerned, on the one hand, with Channel Four, which in the 80s became the major supporter of film-makers from the 'sector', and on the other, with the development of theory and practice parallel to television. The opening of the Independent Film and Video Department's strand the *11th Hour* with the Cinema Action film, *So That You Can Live* was a pivotal moment in the history, and it is marked by the inclusion here of one of the many reviews which appeared in publications associated with independent film. The reflection on Channel Four by Rod Stoneman, one of the commissioning editors in the Independent Film and Video Department, is longer and weightier than most of the other texts, but its inclusion is justified because of the extreme importance of Channel Four, and that department in particular in the history of the movement. Openly subjective and partisan, several of the points made in it are taken up and contested in Chapter 4.

While Channel Four rapidly became the main outlet for the sector's work, some film-makers recognised the need for other forms of distribution more directly linked with political campaigns. The miners' strike was the major focus for political action in the first half of the 80s, and the *Miners' Tapes* project discussed in the article by Julian Petley was therefore a particularly significant undertaking and important as an example of nationwide co-operation between different workshops. This was, however, one of very few projects of its kind to make an effective intervention through non-broadcast distribution. Film and video art was more successful in maintaining a vibrant presence in a variety of spaces outside television, and this continued momentum is reflected in the leading role played by the magazine *Undercut*, which was based at the LFMC. The two articles from *Undercut* reprinted here illustrate the range of subject matter. The first, by an artist who had long been associated with the Co-op, discusses implications for media artists of the video revolution and the market-oriented culture of the 80s. One of the reasons for selecting it is that, although addressed primarily to media artists, it raises issues of concern to practitioners in all areas of independent practice: namely, the distinction between using the mass media and being used by it, between making work popular by reaching out to a large public and making work popular by adopting mainstream values. The second article, by a critical theorist, is taken from an issue of *Undercut* entirely devoted to the Conference on Cultural Identities at the Com-

monwealth Institute. This conference was held in 1988, the same year as the Black
Film British Cinema conference at the ICA, and the black workshops, Sankofa and
Black Audio, played an important role on both occasions. Developments in the
theoretical and practical address to race, gender and other identity issues represents
one of the major achievements of the movement in the 80s.

Film Journals in Britain and France

Claire Johnston

Screen Vol. 12 No. 1, 1971

Compared with its French counterpart, film criticism in Britain seems almost primitive, and attempts to alleviate the situation have been isolated and spasmodic. The only real school to have emerged in Britain was the 'film grammar' school which had far more influence in the field of film education than elsewhere. Its influence was not undermined so much by the emergence of new aesthetic principles, as was the case with montage theory in France, so much as by educational factors such as developments in the teaching of English. At present, British film criticism largely exists at the pre-Bazin stage. There are a number of factors which have contributed to this situation, not least the firmly entrenched empiricist, anti-intellectual tradition and the way the British Film Institute inadvertently serviced this tendency. This is exemplified in the way film columnists are elevated to the status of critics, and film fans are regarded as historians. This explains why *Sight and Sound*, which is subsidized by the British Film Institute and therefore need not adhere to the demands of the market, chooses to do so, and sees itself as a predominantly journalistically motivated magazine. In this context, the critic is seen as someone of discrimination and taste which cannot really be contested. In Barthes' words, 'the bourgeois ideology ... will state a fact or perceive a value, but will refuse explanation. The order of the world will be self-evident or ineffable; it will never be meaningful'. All the critic is required to give is an impressionistic account of his immediate responses on viewing a film. Subjectivity has always been a crucial part of the bourgeois ideology. This enables the critic to impose his own language on to a work without explaining or justifying the stance to the reader. The critic's interpretation of an image, to take an extreme example, can be cited as the intention of the film-maker. Thus in a review of Oshima's *The Boy* (*Sight and Sound*, Summer 1970) Philip Strick can assert with confidence that the symbol of the Japanese flag in the film 'is intended as an ironic reminder of a militant nationalism'. If the work cannot be assimilated into the critic's own experience, it is written off as exotic, or, if necessary, simply a 'failure'. The extreme 'otherness' of such films as Glauber Rocha's *Black God, White Devil* can lead to the following kind of response: 'the cangaceiro also appears as a kind of samurai figure, in his adherence to extravagant codes as much as in his sudden wild shrieks, flat-footed leaps and wheeling death fall' (*Sight and Sound*, 1970, by Penelope Houston). It is for these reasons that it is regarded as unwise to take the cinema too seriously, which accounts for the obligatory columns such as Arkadin. The bourgeois critic sees his work as a kind of vicarious emotional experience, and his skill lies in the way he puts words together to achieve the impressionistic account he is searching for, rather than in expressing ideas.

However, it is only in the last ten years that *Sight and Sound*'s approach has become so monolithically entrenched; and one of the more depressing aspects of our film culture is that during that time its circulation has risen to over 30,000. The influence of writers like Gavin Lambert and Lindsay Anderson from *Sequence* in the early and middle fifties had much to do with this. Their involvement with the re-discovery of the American cinema and their concern about critical values led to a measure of self-scrutiny. It was in the late fifties and early sixties with the emergence of new magazines like *Movie, Definition* and *Motion* that film criticism as a whole was forced to examine its current assumptions, and it was in the pages of the short-lived magazine *Definition* that the controversy took hold. *Definition* took the position suggested by Lindsay Anderson in his article 'Stand Up! Stand Up!' in *Sight and Sound* in 1956 which was that film criticism should be based on clearly defined social values to which the critic should be totally committed. *Definition*'s search for a normative aesthetic was not simply opposed to the empiricism and superficiality of *Sight and Sound* at that time. Its attacks were aimed with equal force at a group of writers who were later to form *Movie*, then writing in *Oxford Opinion*, whom they regaled as 'right-wing' in their formalist preoccupations and their interest in 'second-rate' directors like Hitchcock and 'fifty-third rate' directors like Fuller. The *Movie* writers (primarily Ian Cameron, Victor Perkins and Robin Wood) in their concern with developing a critical vocabulary took their ideas from the *Cahiers* writers of the middle fifties and Sarris's interpretation of them. The main body of their pantheon consisting of Hitchcock, Hawks, Preminger, Minnelli, Aldrich and Tashlin mirrored that of *Cahiers*, but their originality lay in the discovery of directors like Richard Brooks, Clive Donner, Richard Lester and Michael Powell. Their polemic for an alternative view of the British cinema in the form of Donner, Lester, Powell was a useful corrective to the realist/documentary tradition. *Movie* concentrated on discussing 'mise-en-scène' rather than delineating the thematic structure of the auteur's work. This led to an extremely detailed examination of sequences, and naturally led to the magazine increasingly confining itself to examinations of single films rather than the *oeuvre* as a whole, and extensive interviews were used to examine these questions in more detail. The stated aim of the *Movie* critics was to attempt to achieve an objective description of the film through detailed scrutiny. However, their emphasis on the film as a self-sufficient entity meant that Robin Wood's Leavisian method could be easily accommodated, for once objective description had been achieved, *Movie* critics were as enthusiastic as anyone else in making moral judgements about the film in question. Nevertheless *Movie* is the only magazine to have successfully introduced polemics into British film criticism, and its popular format meant that it reached a much wider audience than the usual 'small magazine', so that it offered a real alternative to the established magazines. Regrettably it is no longer a real force, as it appears extremely spasmodically, though it has been influential in spawning other magazines and through its development into a publishing venture.

The Brighton Film Review has in many ways continued the polemical position of Movie, but it labours under the difficulty of having to restrict itself to films shown at film societies and local cinemas month by month. The critical policy of the magazine was never clearly delineated, though the reviewing of films as self-sufficient entities reflects not only exigencies under which the Review has to operate, but it expresses the policy of its editors. While much of the writing is extremely interesting and reflects a serious involvement with auteur theory, because of the need to publish the magazine monthly, the editors have been forced into the position of printing articles which suggest that the critics as a whole do not share a common approach to the cinema. As a result, the Review never really managed to acquire a distinct personality, which undermined much of its polemical intention. The general impression the magazine conveys is one of imitation (of Cahiers and Movie) rather than of adaptation, which is most evident in the Review's Conseil des Cinq, a slightly modified version of Cahiers' Conseil des Dix, which is quite meaningless in the light of the fact that many of the contributors have not seen the films in question. One has to count the Brighton Film Review as perhaps the major casualty of British film culture; lack of resources and viewing facilities, together with an insufficient number of knowledgeable critics prevented it from reaching the wider audience it deserves.

While eclecticism was forced on the Brighton Film Review, it was one of the expressed aims of Cinema, which in its first editorial stated its policy as 'keeping in contact with contemporary movements in acting, directing and aesthetics'. Its commitment to a series of structural analyses, therefore, did not constitute a polemical position as such. For this reason, Cinema involves itself quite extensively with the underground. Although contributions tend to vary the approach to the cinema, on the whole the concern with adhering to rigorous critical principles became one of its central features. Taking the auteur approach for granted, it is much more concerned with its reformulation in terms of structuralism; in this sense, while the Brighton Film Review reflects the Cahiers of the fifties, Cinema reflects the more recent development in Cahiers. Although some Cinema critics have sacrificed precision for obscurantism and mystification, one can detect a genuine desire to explore new areas of the cinema, such as the Italian western. In general, the assumptions under which Cinema appears to be operating are that Britain already possesses a well-developed film culture. This, of course, is far from the case; its eclecticism and lack of any real polemic about the cinema is unlikely to radically change this situation.

The concern about the role of ideology in film criticism seems to be of fairly recent origin; Cahiers' reformulation of its position and the emergence of

Cinéthique in France were the spearhead of this movement. In Britain, two magazines emerged which set out to follow their example, *Cinemantics* and *Afterimage*.
It is too early yet to assess the influence these magazines will have. *Cinemantics*
seems to have abandoned any serious critical purpose after an extremely interesting first issue which contained a translation of some of a paper given by Umberto
Eco at the Pesaro Festival in 1967.

Afterimage, which grew out of a university film magazine *Platinum*, has only
brought out two issues so far, a special issue on politics in the cinema, and an issue
on the underground. It may be significant that *Afterimage* has not, as yet, been able
to formulate its critical principles, and their second issue contains two totally conflicting editorials on the achievement of the underground. While *Afterimage* is
committed to the growth of an 'independent cinema' to counter capitalism in the
West, and believes that such a cinema is possible, it does not seem to be falling into
the trap of over-simplification which much of the writing in *Cinéthique* does, and
one can only hope that its attempt to create some polemic within its own pages will
be fruitful.

Rather than giving an exhaustive survey of film magazines in Britain, it has been
the intention of this article to suggest some of the critical principles underlying film
magazines in general. For this reason magazines like *Films and Filming*, *Focus on
Film* and *The Monthly Film Bulletin* have been excluded as they appear to be based
on the same critical assumptions which inform the most influential magazine of
this type, *Sight and Sound*. What distinguishes *Films and Filming* and *Sight and
Sound* is a different conception of the market, rather than any critical principles.
Perhaps it should be said here that magazines like *Focus on Film* and *The Monthly
Film Bulletin* nevertheless, as predominantly information magazines, perform an
extremely useful function in providing data for the film historian. A strong argument could be put forward that *The Monthly Film Bulletin* should confine itself
exclusively to this function, and extend it.

The most significant feature to emerge from this survey is that the only real challenge to established critical attitudes in this country has come from student
magazines. *Cinema* began at Cambridge, *Afterimage* (formerly *Platinum*) at Essex,
Brighton Film Review at Sussex; going further back, *Definitions* was founded by
ex-students of the London School of Film Technique, and *Movie* developed out of
the activities of a group of writers for *Oxford Opinion*. (In the case of *Motion*, which
was started in the early sixties by students from LSE and Cambridge, the critics were
much less concerned with challenging current critical assumptions than were the
other magazines; its contribution lay in starting a series of largely informational
monographs which was to develop into the publishing enterprise, the Tantivy
Press.)

As compared with the situation in France there has been a marked resistance to
any challenge to empiricism in the established journals; *auteur* criticism has been
consistently misrepresented and trivialized, and the problems posed by the 'inde-

pendent cinema' have never been considered seriously. For this reason, market factors have played a large part in undermining the impetus of this movement. The
publications in question, even *Movie*, by far the most successful, audacious and
professionally produced magazine, were all sporadically produced and comparatively short-lived. Their influence outside a narrow circle is negligible. The
paperback market has proved less economically formidable and the critical criteria
less entrenched; it is significant that the greatest inroads made by *auteur* criticism
have been made in the paperback market, in the *Movie* and *Cinema One* series.
Quite clearly if any vital film culture is to finally emerge in this country there has
got to be a consolidation of these new approaches in a proliferation of regular film
magazines. The importance for these magazines to publish a detailed account of
the critical principles which inform their writing cannot be emphasized enough,
with the regular reassessment and reformulation of their position as they progress.
The example of *Cahiers du cinéma* in this respect is instructive, and it is only in this
kind of critical climate that genuine polemical criticism can emerge.

Notes on Political Cinema

Jim Pines

Cinema Rising No. 1, April 1972

The need to redefine cinema politically and ideologically germinates from particular social, political and cultural circumstances. Its rationale is to develop a counter-cultural critique for, and a method of, revolutionising society, in which cinema functions as a weapon. The form(s) in which militant cinema develops, however, is determined by the urgency and the quality of the (local) circumstances: functional and aesthetic dissimilarities exist. Therefore, despite their common perspective, their common counterimage of society, etc., militant-political-revolutionary films do not embody a generalized (universal) definition of political cinema. (Cf. Godard, Solanas, US Newsreel, the left-wing of British establishment media, etc.)

Circumstances such as the May 68 events in Europe, the student and anti-Vietnam War protest movements, the ghetto uprisings in the US, and the growing liberation movement throughout the third world, greatly influenced the realization of various forms of militant-political film-making (and film criticism). Although the genre has its roots firmly in the revolutionary Soviet cinema of the 20s: e.g. Eisenstein's montage structure, and the emergence of the proletarian masses as protagonist. Later, film-makers like the international documentarist Joris Ivens and the Cuban socialist Santiago Alvarez expanded the tradition through a militant vein; while the British documentary movements of the 30s–40s and 50s served as the best examples of social cinema/reformism. Also influential in this network were Robert Flaherty, Pare Lorentz, and of course Leni Riefenstahl, whose masterly glorification of Nazi Germany (*Triumph of the Will*) is still considered one of the best propaganda films ever made.

A crucial factor in the development and accessibility of an alternative cinema has undoubtedly been the technical improvements in portable film-making equipment. Independent film-makers (of all persuasions) have been able to harness a great deal of this technology, construct and propagate a sub- (and in some form counter-) cultural film language, and use images against traditional imagery. A natural extension of this has been the emergence of 16mm cinema circuits in Europe and the US, and relatively viable clandestine circuits in parts of the third world. For radicals, etc., this has provided the most effective base to function from; perhaps more conscious of the propagandistic value of media (both sides), they've created countermedia – whose sole intention is to wreck social-political, and in some cases also cinematic-aesthetic, conventions. And added to this, the emergence of revolutionary third world film-makers, which has rendered traditional and/or sympathetic Europeanized images more or less defunct.

Starting from the premise that all films are inherently political by nature of their economic (and therefore ideological) substructure, we can proceed to categorize various forms of politically-orientated (i.e. politicized) cinema – particularly some of those forms that have appeared in Britain.

The traditional cinema audience is defined by a type of collectivism – cultural coexistence – in which otherwise violent social tensions temporarily 'disappear'. To function in such a situation, successfully, militant-political-revolutionary cinema has to be aimed at provoking social contradictions, and to the extent of alienating sectors of the audience from one another. The purpose of the film is then clarified. But in this context the majority of political film shows in Britain have been essentially informational and far from political.

The reasons for this are complicated by several general conditions: (1) Extremely limited outlets. Political films are mainly restricted to 'specialist cinema' outlets like Politkino, which in any case don't survive on political films alone. (2) A non-existent radical film movement that (seriously) deals with situations like Ireland. (3) The lack of a dynamic film culture, which is a reflection of (1) and (2). And (4) lethargy, a terrible disease, which is reflected in the quality of life generally. These conditions are tightly interrelated and operate against all forms of alternative cinema, which in turn are supported by a two-headed monopoly.

The mythical notion of a 'third' circuit presented a vaguely defined solution to the problem. But in real terms it would have developed into yet another chain ... another tentacle. However, the general argument is reasonable; although perhaps less pragmatic in terms of effective political films. This was certainly the case with *Battle of Algiers* which seemed to lose its final battle going through conventional cinema circuits. Its serious attempt to deal with a revolutionary situation was obfuscated by its 'general popularity', until the film finally became a sort of 'moving piece of fictionalized documentary/entertainment'. Moreover, Pontecorvo's very human rendition of the anti-revolutionary army colonel undermined the realities of the revolutionaries: the revolutionary group's decision to use violence, for example, was overly simplified. So that the presentation of events, of the film, etc., made it very difficult to deal with the film other than in *nouvelle vague* terms.

Pontecorvo's later film *Queimada* is basically a Hollywood film with some of the artistic peculiarities shown in *Battle*; it had a very limited life here ... Costa-Gravas' *Z* and *L'Aveu* are also good examples of films with explicit political content but conforming to commercial conventions. These films reveal the importance of defining one's audience.

Hollywood social films, especially the recent ones depicting blacks in various souped-up roles, are political insofar as they are produced to satisfy certain social, economic and psychological needs. They stultify mass cultural consciousness. The newly-arrived black Hollywood director functions as a carrier of black plastic dreams; and under his auspices, numerous minority technicians are given 'opportunities' ... These films function on the same premises as any other Hollywood movie.

In both these definitely commercial categories provocation doesn't arise; the films do not deal with causes, only with vague, palatable effects. However, it doesn't follow that militant films necessarily deal with the causes of social malady. For example, in his highly-charged *Punishment Park*, Peter Watkins concentrated on the effects of social polarity, violence, overt and covert repression. The causes were intertwined with the effects, so that the film's statement became both cause and effect of a generalized condition. Although Watkins defined the film as not being political (nor artistic), but rather 'a film about the condition of people', one nevertheless responds to it in distinct political terms.

The film is intended to provoke general audiences into 'awareness', but doesn't provide alternative frames of reference. Moreover, its emotional impact is so intense and uncompromising that a rational interpretation of the film's images is either suppressed or frankly incensed – in an alienating way.

Punishment Park poses a fundamental question: When dealing with conditions that can only be changed through definite political action, is it enough for a film to simply show the conditions ...? ... however humanistically and sympathetically ...

The authenticity (realism) of *Punishment Park* is conveyed through the film's fictionalized documentary technique. As a form this technique has great potential for militant film-making – because it is the most effective way of overcoming the limitations of conventional dramaturgy and 'live' documentation, and yet remaining controlled. (E.g. *Battle of Algiers* is effectively a documentary film; Sanjines' *Blood of the Condor* and Littin's *The Jackal* work similarly in parts; while Solanas' mammoth historic essay/documentary, *The Hour of the Furnaces*, utilizes some simulated action.

The use of simulated reality is also an essential element in the films of Ken Loach/Tony Garnett. In this respect only, their films are similar to Peter Watkins'. Otherwise the films deal with clearly defined areas of social-psychological conflict, emotionally and intellectually (cf. *Kes, Family Life*). However, these films are presented like any other establishment film, and therefore are accepted or rejected in those terms. In other words, they rely on the liberal-wing of society to the extent of depoliticizing themselves.

During the British documentary movement of the 30s–40s, the late John Grierson defined (and elevated) the social function of the documentary film. He had developed, among other things, the notion of 'universal education', in which documentary film would play a key role in 'deparochializing' individuals and structures, and would liberate society generally. Sponsored by governmental and industrial agencies, the early documentary movement functioned as a viable social force, and was quite successful educationally (propagandistically). But the liberation it was concerned with was in the direction of social reformism. The movement's ideological basis was a reflection of a social democracy (and all its contradictions, e.g. colonialism). So that despite Paul Rotha's insistence that documentary should not be 'defined by the source of its financing', it's quite clear that this aspect was crucial in determining (defining) the movement's frame of reference. (Cf. the nationalized Cuban film/TV industry, ICAIC, which has similar policies relating to education, etc., but functions within a socialist infrastructure.)

In Europe, Jean-Luc Godard's experiences demonstrate the ambiguous role of militant-political film-making working through conventional production/finance methods. Both *British Sounds* and *Le Gai Savoir*, for example, were refused showings by the TV companies involved. On a more important level, however, Godard's later films in particular represent the best examples of militant-political cinema evolving towards revolutionary aestheticism (e.g. *Made in USA, Weekend, Pravda*, etc.).

Because of their intellectual intensity, Godard's films are clearly directed towards radical intellectuals. The films tend to be more concerned with (film) language than with the social situations they're about. In this sense, they reflect the intellectual climate in Europe, particularly as a result of May 68.

The Third World Festival currently running at the NFT and Collegiate Theatre represents an *integrated* system of militant-political-revolutionary cinema – based on (against) the experiences of Latin America. The emergence of third world filmmakers is important, and represents perhaps the most viable model to consider, because they integrate the liberation of historic, cultural and aesthetic conditions, while simultaneously being directed toward the dispossessed.

A Reflection on the History of the London Film-Makers' Co-op

Malcolm Le Grice

From *Light Years*, Catalogue of a Festival, celebrating twenty years of the LFMC, 1 September 1986

In 1967, Simon Hartog and myself were asked by a large open meeting of the year-old London Film-Makers' Co-operative, which he represented, and the Arts Laboratory film workshop group, which I represented, to prepare a joint constitution and development plan for the Co-op, expanded to include a workshop.

This we did, exceeding our brief somewhat in the ambitiousness of the proposals we made. It is extraordinary the extent to which those plans have materialised and how much the fundamental philosophical attitudes of the Co-op, embodied in the original constitution, have remained consistent. What though, with the benefit of hindsight, I now find most extraordinary, is that the Co-op got off the ground at all and that it has survived as successfully as it has.

The idea of the Co-op, though clearly outside the terms of the dominant culture, was timely. The sixties in Britain provided an atmosphere of some optimism for change. The concepts for the Co-op drew variously for their formation and sustenance on a range of diverse influences as wide as that of the hippy movement, Marx, Marcuse and May 68. It drew heavily on the precedent of the New York Film-Makers' Co-operative, but, through the merger with the Arts Laboratory group, took on a much wider set of objectives. Though it was not fully appreciated at the time, even by those of us most involved, as well as having more ambitious aims, it always had a more strongly developed set of social and political objectives than had motivated the New York Co-op.

When the Co-op was formed, there were plenty of great ideas around for radical experiments in life-style and the formation of new organisations, few of which have survived. The gap between an idea and its realisation is wide indeed. 'All You Need Is Love' (or a good idea) is rubbish. Whilst ideas, concepts and enthusiasm were essential you needed at least twice as much, if not more – tenacity, obstinacy, tolerance, patience, the ability to type (two fingers would do), to lay breeze blocks, mend pavements, pull cable through conduit, improvise plumbing and then later, teach people to use somewhat temperamental equipment, plan screening schedules, refuse free entry to screenings even to those good friends who half an hour before were fixing the projection box floor, and even later prepare proposals to con money from individuals or government agencies on the slenderest of arguments which no one else understood.

In spite of having created a production framework particularly suited to film-makers who wished to produce films as individuals, the Co-op remains one of the least individualistic organisations – there are no careers to be made and it has always been too uncomfortable to see working for it as other than a form of 'service', even when paid. However, that the Co-op survived continuous uprooting with the huge problems involved in re-installing the distribution library, the cinema and above all the workshop equipment, in near derelict temporary lease buildings in Robert Street, the Prince of Wales Dairy and Fitzroy Road, before the luxurious stability of Gloucester Avenue, relied heavily on the motivation and commitment of a number of individuals with no outside financial support. During this period, without Fred Drummond, Mike Leggett, David Curtis, Peter Gidal, Annabel Nicholson, Roger Hammond, Lis Rhodes, George Cragie and others, it is probable that the Co-op or at least sections of it would have collapsed.

Together with the enormous input of time and energy given by these individuals, from my perception, one of the most important reasons why the London Film-Makers' Co-op survived, whilst other Film Co-operatives in Europe, and many contemporary experiments in other fields of art in Britain, failed, was its concern with simple practicalities and its genuine openness. Where other similar organisations often tore themselves apart in ideological dispute before a single film was made, even the most theoretically stringent film-makers, like Peter Gidal, clearly recognised that detailed theoretical disputes made little sense if they did not refer to a substantial body of work. Consequently, in the early period, those of us involved with the Co-op made sure that all the collective energies available were concentrated on establishing the facilities and encouraging film-makers to produce work. We frequently helped in the production of films we did not like or agree with and made sure of their presentation in some format or other within the Cinema. Those of us involved in theoretical discussion about the films kept this debate separate from any idea that there should be any common ideological, theoretical or aesthetic basis for films made, distributed or presented through the Co-op. Of course, the more secure the Co-op became and the more numerous the active film-makers, the more theoretical differences could be aired. The role of *Undercut* in this theoretical debate is clear, but it is a demonstration of the consistency of the Co-op's philosophy the way in which there remains a subtle distinction between the editorial policy of *Undercut* and any representation of a collective attitude of the Co-op.

It is perhaps curious that in writing this short reflection on the twenty years of the LFMC, I have concentrated on the institutional issues rather than the films, for whilst there has always been a deliberate resistance to the idea that the Co-op represented a certain style of film-making, I am sure history will show that it provided the framework for a very distinct and special development in film. I am also confident that when the crushing poverty and imperialism of our mass film and television culture is more generally recognised, the work of film-makers associated with the Co-op will be seen as the most important and radical film work of the period. Whether the Co-op has a function in demonstrating or 'preserving' the history of this film practice, in the way in which the Anthology Film Archive works in New York, is a complex question.

Again the balance of attitude must be fine. Another consistent strength of the Co-op has been its concentration on the needs of contemporary practice and its ability to allow younger film-makers to come forward both in the sense of the presentation of their work and in taking initiatives within the organisation. The Co-op has never over-burdened itself with its history and has rightly avoided a sterile and academic attitude to it. This has brought with it its own problems. Successive generations of film-makers have produced work in isolation from the knowledge gained in the previous work of other film-makers. In the absence of a real Film Museum in London, a role the NFT should fulfil but never has, perhaps this is a problem the Co-op will need to take on at some time. However, I am pleased to say, I am not in the least interested in either an academic or nostalgic review of the past work of the Co-op, and any review of its history must serve the needs of the current practice. I hope the Light Years screenings will be viewed in that spirit.

I feel fortunate to have played a part in the establishment of the Co-op, and am similarly glad that, like Peter Gidal, I recognised the point at which to 'hand on' to other people. To date the Co-op has been of enormous importance in providing a framework for an actual practice clearly distinct from that of all the dominant modes of production and meaning in cinema. In the significantly more reactionary politics of Regan and Thatcher and their effect on our cinematic and televisual culture, the existence and survival of the London Film-Makers' Co-operative may be even more crucial now than it was in the somewhat naively optimistic period of its origin.

Les États Généraux du Cinéma:
The Nationalisation of the Cinema

Simon Hartog

Cinema Rising No. 1, 1972

> As for film, I simply wish to emphasise that the shadows we attend to and analyse are only part of the phenomenon called motion pictures. Beyond them, making the shadows possible, are social and industrial mechanisms which reflect certain beliefs and assumptions we have about the best way to organise ourselves to meet our needs.
>
> Thomas H. Guback, quoted in the American magazine *Cineaste,*

If the TUC has not been outlawed by the time this article appears, it is its declared policy that the British film industry be nationalised without compensation to its present owners, under the control of the workers and the community. The Labour Party will be asked to adopt a similar policy at its next annual conference. Sick transit ... The structure and functioning of a nationalised industry has as yet been given very little thought. Strange, that! A variety of existing models present themselves. Yugoslavia, Cuba, Sweden, Russia. There is even the BBC. But information about existing systems is scattered and unreliable. The first meeting of the film technicians' union's Nationalisation Forum is being held this month to discuss the problem, and to take the first steps towards clarifying the aims and outlines of a nationalised film industry. With massive unemployment among film technicians, certain internal strains resulting from the union organisation in television and the Industrial Relations Act as the ACTT's immediate preoccupations, the prospects for a serious, studied and comprehensive approach to the problem are not promising. But similar discussions have been going on in a number of countries.

One of the most significant discussions about the organisation of a national film industry under workers' control took place in France during the May 68 revolt. Film-makers, technicians, critics and students established the Estates General of the French Cinema (Les États Généraux du Cinéma). In a series of open meetings, they set about drawing up plans for the reorganisation of the French film industry. Their meetings were long, stormy and inconclusive. The Estates General did not last long as a forum for radical thought. Its energy was generated by the wider social movement, and when that faded, so did the Estates General.

The plans for reorganising the French film industry were, however, produced, and remain as essential documents for future discussions on the relation of the state to the cinema. Rather than translate the texts of these projects, which are available in their entirety together with considerable background information in the August 68 *Cahiers du cinéma*, I will restrict an analysis of the three major reorganisational projects presented to the Estates General, to stating the major operating principles, since a more detailed analysis requires an intimate knowledge of the complex inter-relationships existing between the French state and cinema.

The three major projects shared a critical attitude to the existing structures. They differed not so much in their view of what should be done, as of how it should be done.

Project 4, which was presented to the conference by Thierry Derocles and written by Michel Demoule, Claude Chabrol and Martin Karmitz, was the most radical of the three proposals. The text of Project 4 ends with the words: 'The authors of this project are aware of this document's utopian appearance. They, nevertheless, certify that this utopia is practically realisable in any economic system, and consider the apparent insanity of the project to be proof of their seriousness.' The project calls for the creation of a national office for all audio-visual media, in immediate terms, meaning cinema and television. This organisation is to be independent of the government, and would be financed by the direct participation of the entire population, a financing system not dissimilar from the television licensing fee. ('The spectators will become producers.') Entrance to films would then be free of any charge. Concomitant with this abolition of entrance charges, the project demands a real decentralisation of audio-visual culture, and the opportunity for all to become professionals.

Since the amount of finance available for film production will be known well in advance, the Office can establish an average budget for films to be made during the financial year. All films with budgets equal to or less than this established amount are automatically approved for production. Any film with a budget which exceeds this amount is submitted to a council of film workers and spectators for discussion. The Office is also responsible for the buying of foreign films and the sale of French films abroad. All cinemas and all distribution of films are to be administered by this Office.

Training for and admission to the profession are to be re-structured, liberalised and de-centralised. 'Genius and talent are not learned. Technique is learned by experience. The traditional idea of film schools must, therefore, be abolished.' Trainees of all grades pass through a series of stages before being admitted to the profession. The stages include practical film-making and discussions with other trainees and professionals. The trainee also has the opportunity of attending an experimental centre (which is also open to professionals) which will 'allow pure research, re-train technicians in new techniques' and function in a way which will avoid excessive specialisation and isolation within the profession.

Once a trainee is admitted to professional status, he is guaranteed a monthly income which is supplemented by additional salaries for work on specific films. Any monies paid to a specific production team as a result of foreign sales are divided equally among all the members of the group. Training, production and exhibition will be organised on a regional basis. 'The cinema must go out in search of its public and its workers where they live.' New cinemas must be built, and mobile projection units must be established to show films in factories and rural communes.

The other two projects, Project 13 and Project 16, were unquestionably less utopian. They were also much more technical and detailed. They both posit a nationalised film industry, the public sector, financed initially from the state treasury, co-existing with a private sector. They both demand the unification of all audio-visual production, free movement of labour within this area, and freedom of expression and abolition of all censorship. Project 13, presented by Pierre l'Homme and written by a group from the CGT's film technicians union, states their commonly-held condemnation of censorship, by proposing that: 'The cinema is a mode of a universal language. As such, it belongs to all men.'

Projects 13 and 16 also placed much more emphasis on the problems of the cinema's relationship with television, and, of necessity, with the private sector. Unlike Project 6, they did consider the functioning of the cinema's industrial superstructure – the laboratories, the filmstock producers etc. They shared with the proposers of Project 4 a belief that the distributors' role and power had grown out of all proportion to the service they provide. Distribution is simply transportation, and it should return to its original function. Publicity for all films should be handled by a single agency. All three projects make production units the cornerstone of public sector production, though none of them is particularly clear about the human composition of these units. The production units are, nevertheless, in the hands of their workers, and representatives of the production units have considerable control over the working of the public sector. These units essentially decide for themselves, within the financial realities, what films they will, or will not, make.

While the advocates of Project 13 placed more emphasis on the relationship between the public and private sectors, Project 16 (entitled 'The General Line – The Old & The New'), written by a group of film-makers that included René Allio, Jean-Louis Comolli, R. Dembo, Jacques Doniol-Valcroze, Robert Lapoujade, Pierre Kast, Louis Malle, Jean-Pierre Mocky, J-D. Pollet, Alain Resnais and Jacques Rivette, concentrated most of its attention on analysis of the existing situation, and on the structuring of the proposed new public sector. The opening paragraphs of this project state the problem as it was seen at the time. It remains an essential point of departure.

The French cinema is today produced, distributed and consumed in conditions of slavery engendered by the capitalist system, which is itself protected by a number of State-controlled organisations. Any liberation of the cinema, any creation of

new structures, must start with the destruction of the old structures. .... The
system is characterised by its constant search for profit. In consequence, films are
reduced to the level of mere merchandise. The manufacture, distribution and
consumption of films gives only subordinate consideration to their artistic, critical
and cultural value.

Nationalising the Film Industry (extract)

Report of the ACTT Nationalisation Forum, August 1973

Why Workers' Control?

13. Public ownership of vital industries and services is hardly controversial. Steel, coal, electricity, gas and transport are publicly owned. Broadcasting and television are public monopolies. The principle of public corporations is well established in this country, but the experience of past nationalisations has taught us some lessons. It has emphasised the errors to be avoided.

14. The Attlee Government of 1945 nationalised certain industries which remain a gain for the working class, but the scope of past nationalisations has always been insufficient at the outset and the industries, once in public hands, have been manipulated so as to serve the needs of the private sector. For instance, coal, electric power and gas are sold at reduced rates to private firms. These basic industries are, in effect, nationalised to assist capitalism rather than to replace it. The nationalised industries have consistently been used as instruments of short-term governmental policy, not as tools for the transformation of society. Pits have been closed. Steel workers are threatened. Railways lines are shut down. Men are made redundant. Wages are kept down in the interest of propping up an ailing capitalism.

15. This partial conception of public ownership has resulted in grave shortcomings in the existing public corporations. The two most serious failures of past nationalisations concern the individual worker's relations to his industry, his working life and conditions, and the failure of existing methods of managerial control. Nationalisation has not sufficiently changed the worker's life. Oligarchical power structures remain both within the industry and outside it. A managerial bureaucracy replaces the private capitalist owners, and some of the inadequacies of both are surprisingly similar.

16. We do not question the fact that the ultimate control and the ultimate responsibility for a publicly owned industry must rest in the hands of the people through its government. We are, however, questioning the existing systems of exercising

that control. Direct state control or indirect bureaucratic control are both socially and administratively unsatisfactory. The dangers of such control are even greater in an industry which daily handles information, images, and ideas. Whitehall is a substitute neither for Wardour Street nor for Hollywood. Our demand is for an industry in which the workers themselves are responsible for the management of the industry. Government appointed boards of management are replaced by elected management committees. The fundamental power within the industry rests with those who know its potential and its limitations. It rests with those who work in the industry and without whom it could not exist.

17. Workers' control of the film industry is not a pretty frill but an essential part of our demand. Without it an unresponsive, inaccessible managerial oligarchy is inevitable. Without it neither the worker's relation to his life nor the industry's relation to the community can change. Although our plan provides for both direct and indirect community participation in the affairs of the industry, not the least advantage of workers' control is that a thousand or ten thousand film workers throughout the country are much more a part of and involved in the daily life of the community and aware of its aspirations than ten or a hundred individuals in plush offices, whoever they might be and whoever owns the offices. In addition, the experience of Trade Union democracy provides the workers with the knowledge and experience to control their own industry. The operation of and the model for workers' control has a firm basis in the Trade Union movement.

Why without Compensation?

18. We are opposed to compensation for a number of reasons. First, the assets of the industry reside in property and in films. The value of both has been created by the workers in the industry. We should not pay for the products of exploitation of the public and the workers in the industry. Second, by far the largest single item in the industry's statement of assets is its exhibition sites. Most, if not all, of the land and buildings were acquired many years ago. In recent years land prices have risen extraordinarily. The great bulk of compensation would, therefore, have to be calculated on the basis of current land prices which are the result of the present criminal property speculation. We categorically refuse such a prospect. The industry's film assets are almost exclusively held by the very domestic and foreign monopolies which have been strangling and squeezing the industry and the public, and the prospect of compensating these monopolies for their exploitation is here again repugnant to us. Thirdly, the experience of past nationalisation demonstrates that the financial burden of compensation and interest repayments hinders the crucial early years of the industry's development though the precise effects of this are difficult to calculate since governments have often been forced to write off

some of the debts of the nationalised industries. Finally, we oppose compensation, because it provides private companies with large capital sums out of public funds which are then used in the private sector, more often than not in ways which undermine the function and development of the public sector. The result of paying such compensation is public subsidy for private dividends, and this we cannot condone.

Black Films in White Britain

Jim Pines

Time Out No. 58, March 7–21, 1971

Black Art concerns black people; it expresses the nuances of black existence and articulates the levels of truths and lies that define black communities. It relates to life, black life, with images of human understanding, self-respect and survival; it is functional. The black artist is not concerned with the flagellation of white people (many of whom have by now either grown used to it or get more turned-on by it), but with the de-mystification of white fantasies: fantasies that the media presents as definitions of blacks and which society uses to humiliate and de-humanize black existence. The black artist, then, whatever his discipline, is engaged in an unyielding battle against mass media mentality.

One of the frightening aspects of the mass media is its ability to appear radically liberal and yet be essentially racist: it has so flagrantly mystified and popularized the Black Liberation Movement and the notion of black consciousness that many people, black and white, take political violence, miscegenation and hipness as the *only* qualities of the black experience. (The black experience has been ingratiated as some kind of avant-garde minstrel show, in which everybody can catch a bit of soul, do a dance/fuck, and prove that we're all alike ... white.) We are now in an era when a great deal of stereotype thinking isn't overtly pernicious: the media has put a shiny gloss on racism, making variations of it the hip thing to do [see 'Putney Swope']. Consequently, black artists are expected to do anything, dance, sing, even shoot people, provided they don't express real frustrations and real anger. Black artists are expected to live in the same white fantasies.

Films in particular have probably done the most damage, projecting as they do numerous sterile characters supposedly representative of black people. Most are overtly racist while a few are apparently liberal. 'Carry On Up The Jungle' and 'Leo The Last' represent the limits of British racism and liberalism respectively, and I doubt that either of them will be modified in the near future.

Clearly there's a desperate need for black film making, and obviously it will have to function outside the system in order to destroy these myths. Therefore, the black film maker is, by definition, an independent film maker. Initially the black film maker is confronted with similar problems as the independent white film maker: having to find especially sympathetic backing for a non-commercial project, producing a good quality picture with limited resources, etc. But at some point the black film maker is confronted with blatant bigotry, and he finds that making the film has very little to do with art, more to do with race. (Some white backers actually invest in black projects just to prove that blacks can't make it.) Every black film maker is fighting to keep what's on his face as well as what's in the script. That's a pretty heavy trip.

There's actually a history of black film making in the US. Several black production companies existed in the late 20's, supplying films to the newly emergent ghettoes in the North. Apparently the films were made with formula scripts, following Hollywood conventions. The contemporary scene is very much on the fringe/u.g. idiom, relying heavily on community/cultural themes [see 'Right On']. Even the black directed Hollywood films are moving in that direction, though they're too polished and white-washed to be considered black films.

The scene here, however, is quite different – partly because of the multifarious structure of the black community and partly because there isn't a significant film culture in Britain. What it amounts to is a handful of artists and technicians.

There have been two significant black films produced here: Frankie Dymon Jnr.'s 'Death May Be Your Santa Claus' and Horace Ové's 'Reggae'. Both concern the black man in England, but in diametrically opposing ways: 'Santa Claus' is an allegory, a pop film with political pretensions; while 'Reggae', on the other hand, deals with a black art form that's had a profound effect on Britain. ('Reggae' is thoroughly in the black film ethos, making a poignant statement about the black experience.) 'Santa Claus' is the first *black-produced* film, while 'Reggae' is the first *black film*, made here.

Despite its strength and technique, many people see 'Reggae' out of liberalism rather than as a technical and artistic achievement: 'The review it had in *New Society* put it on a professional level – because white people couldn't believe that a West Indian could make a film' (Horace Ové). Harcourt Nichols, whose shorts 'Breakfast' and 'The Big Save' – produced through the London Film School and shown recently at the NFT in a programme of shorts, takes the point further by saying that 'one can make films here only if one is interested in making Boulton Bros. laugh-at-yourself films'. Something like 'Leo The Last' is the only type of film that has a relatively wide appeal – that is, a race film that can be made here and have an interest outside England.

The only solution to this dilemma, most film makers feel, is to produce material for African and West Indian audiences. Nichols agrees that serious thought must be given to black film in Britain, but he, like other black artists here, feels that black film makers should exploit the Jamaican market, say, as a group (black companies) rather than as individuals. The issue is confused further by the need *not* to be appreciated as a black film maker in Britain – but as a West Indian or African film maker. Ové made two other black films: 'Baldwin's Nigger', a documentary of James Baldwin talking to a group at the West Indian Student Centre; and a film of Dick Gregory talking to black and white youths in the Grove. He nevertheless feels that, really, it would be better in terms of his acceptance if he returned to the West Indies to work there.

Chris Konyils, theatre agent, actor, and an ex-student of the London Film School, has in fact taken that very step by setting up facilities in Nigeria: one of his primary goals is to counteract the 'Coronation Street' mentality put down there. 'Most of the films there are absolutely rubbish, the worst of the British lot.'

Black film makers here have pretty much the same attitude about working in England and all of them have thought seriously about the validity of black films in this country. In this sense, it's pointless talking about film art here, because most black film makers don't see themselves as black British film makers (and rightfully so).

A film like 'Reggae' works, because it exposes an area that's provocative. A dramatic film would be extremely difficult to produce, because many whites here don't think a black community situation is possible or commercially viable.

The overriding factor in black film making is that white technicians demand that the black director come black – not in-between. White technicians want to experience *black* not white models (which they get every day).

Notes

The London Women's Film Group

Extract from information produced by the group, 1976

Formation of the Group

The London Women's Film Group was formed in January 1972 in response to a notice in the *Women's Liberation Newsletter* and a showing of films dealing with Women's Liberation issues organised by the Belsize Lane Women's Liberation Group/Liberation Films.

The group was initially formed for two basic reasons: to disseminate Women's Liberation ideas, and for women to learn the skills denied them in the industry. The film industry is excessively male-dominated and this is reflected on the screen in terms of portrayal of women and choice of subject matter. For this to change it was obviously essential that women acquire the necessary skills and experience (to make films).

One of the basic precepts of the Women's Liberation Movement was and is that women need to organise separately to develop their own politics. Making films is a highly technical process; in a patriarchal society women lack confidence in technical areas, quite apart from the bias in both formal and informal education and actual discrimination in the industry. We wanted to break down the unnecessary mystification that surrounds technical skills, and to do this we particularly wanted to learn technical skills from other women in a supportive situation.

We aimed to work collectively; those of us who had worked in the industry were particularly frustrated by the existing division of labour and women's place in the hierarchy (at the bottom, in secretarial grades, neg. cutting, continuity jobs, etc.). So our intention was that everybody in the group becomes familiar with all the stages in the process of making a film, both at the level of technology and the level of ideas.

The First Year

The first three months were spent learning to work cameras and tape-recorders. We were working in small groups and produced two short films 'SERVE AND OBEY' and 'BETTSHANGER '72' (which we believe was the first sync sound film made entirely by women in this country).

The group acquired other films made by women in the group before its formation, 'WOMEN AGAINST THE BILL', 'MISS/MRS', and later 'FAKENHAM OCCUPATION', 'WOMEN OF THE RHONDDA' and 'PUT YOURSELF IN MY PLACE'.

These films (with the exception of 'PUT YOURSELF IN MY PLACE' which was the most recent of these, and is a role-reversal comedy) fell loosely into already established black and white documentary traditions. At a time when Women's Liberation was challenging events like the Miss World Contest, and the way in which commercial advertising exploits women, we tended to reject commercial films wholesale as the ideological products of a capitalist, sexist, racist society. We were dissatisfied with the roles offered women in films – sex object, virgin, whore, mother, wife, doormat, as non-assertive, ultimately unhappy creatures. We wanted to counter this by showing women's lives 'as they really are'. We felt that women, and particularly working class women hadn't previously had the chance to express themselves on film. Television documentary manipulated. We thought we could avoid this manipulation by establishing relationships with the women we were filming and therefore make more 'honest' films because we were working outside the industry, with all its restraints. Because we were women filming women we were in a unique position to identify with them.

Women's Cinema Events

A women's event was organised in conjunction with the Edinburgh Film Festival in August 1972, bringing together for the first time in this country a collection of films made by women. (It was there that we filmed a programme for BBC2. A BBC editor cut it with our supervision, it was shown on Film Night, and we earned £70.) In April and May 1973, Claire Johnston organised a season of Women's Cinema at the National Film Theatre. Both these events included films by Maya Daren, Germaine Dulac, Ida Lupino, Dorothy Arzner, Stephanie Rothman and Nelly Kaplan as well as many films made by independent contemporary women film-makers, many of them having their roots in the Women's Movement. The season gave rise to many questions: 'Is a film made by a woman necessarily feminist?' 'Can a film made within the dominant mode of production, i.e. Capitalist Hollywood, do anything other than reflect the values of the society it is made for and comes out of?' 'Is documentary necessarily more useful than fiction, to the Women's Movement?' etc. Looking at films made in Hollywood, we began to challenge the tendency common in the left – and among ourselves at that time – to dismiss Hollywood as a monolithic dream factory, not worth serious examination. The films, especially those by Arzner, showed how women directors, working in Hollywood could, while using the stereotypes and icons of Hollywood itself, subvert the myths surrounding women, and to some extent break with the dominant patriarchal discourse. (See 'DANCE GIRL DANCE' by Dorothy Arzner.) At the very least, a woman's point of view, usually absent from Hollywood films, (we are not including 'weepies' made by men), and set within a conventional Hollywood structure, could be disturbing, (as in Ida Lupino's films.)

The French film-maker Nelly Kaplan, discussed her films, 'LA FIANCÉE DU PIRATE' (DIRTY MARY) and 'PAPA LES PETITS BATEAUX' at the NFT. She emphasised the importance of fantasy in creating new images of women: although the image of a strong woman on the screen might not correspond with reality in patriarchal society, it could help give women strength and confidence by widening their possibilities. Kaplan's heroines aren't punished. The prostitute isn't made to repent and the witch isn't burnt; on the contrary she struggles and wins. To accusations of making men 'ugly' in her films she responded, 'Of course my films are a little misandronous. We live under patriarchal oppression. We have to fight the enemy.' (Interview with Barbara Halpern Martineau, New York City, June 20th, 1972.)

'The Amazing Equal Pay Show'

Our decision to make 'THE AMAZING EQUAL PAY SHOW' was based on our worries about the documentary mode of film-making, and a concern, inspired by the Women's Events, to make a political film which was entertaining. 'WOMEN OF THE RHONDDA' and 'BETTSHANGER '72' worked within a realist naturalistic tradition; the material was intended to speak for itself. Both films asked the audience to make their own deductions, and we hoped or assumed their deductions would be the same as ours. But we learned that audiences weren't necessarily in accord with our views unless they were already previously committed to feminism. 'THE AMAZING EQUAL PAY SHOW' was more overt in its approach. It attempted to be more didactic and to provide an analysis of sexism within capitalist society.

The script was written and performed by the Women's Theatre Group in response to a request from TASS. (The play was also performed at the Acton Women's Liberation Conference in September 1972.) We were very enthusiastic about the play and sympathetic to its political analysis. Throughout the making of the film we collaborated closely with the Theatre Group (who acted in the film as well as the play).

Union Activities

Several of us, already in the union, began raising the issue of discrimination against women in the film industry. Women have always been ghettoised in secretarial jobs in TV and low-grade jobs in the labs.

'In film and TV production, out of over 150 grades covered by ACTT agreements, 60% of the women are concentrated into just three of those grades.' (Patterns of Discrimination Against Women in the Film and Television Industries.)

'In half of the existing ACTT grades there is not a single woman.' (Patterns of Discrimination.)

The excuse used in the camera department is that cameras are too heavy for women. The excuse used in the labs is that it would be impossible for women to work in the dark alongside men.

Eventually the union formed a so-called Anti-Discrimination Committee, later called the Committee on Equality.

A Women's Caucus, independently of the Union Committee, managed to put forward three motions from three different shops at the Annual Conference of 1973, which was unprecedented since women represented about 5% of the 500 delegates. One of these motions demanded that the union appoint and pay a researcher to write a report on the situation of women in the film industry. The resolution was passed, but we heard the union might appoint a male researcher. We picketed the union offices, Sarah Benton was appointed and in 1975 she produced a report 'Patterns of Discrimination Against Women in the Film and Television Industries' and its recommendations were passed by Conference. This was the first project of its kind ever undertaken by a union.

Patterns of Discrimination (extract)

ACTT Report, 1975

The Nature of Discrimination

'We don't discriminate here' was the first response from employers to questions about job segregation in their companies. And shop stewards often confirmed this statement. By this they mean that the most blatant form of prejudice – telling a woman that she cannot have a particular job **because** she is a woman does not exist in their company. In fact, this sort of open discrimination is fairly widespread throughout the industry, but it is by no means the most important cause of women's inequality. The same causes exist throughout the field of employment, though of course they vary in importance according to the type of industry. The most significant ones are:

(i) **Blatant discrimination** against women applying for particular jobs in any firm, or for any jobs in particular firms.

(ii) **The undervaluing of jobs primarily done by women** in terms of pay and respect.

(iii) **Educational and social 'conditioning' and the lack of training facilities**, which deny women the opportunity, both before and after they enter the industry, to work in a wide range of grades.

(iv) **The job structure of the industry**, which makes most women's jobs dead-end jobs, and makes movement across and up from the type of work they normally do extremely difficult.

(v) **Job insecurity and work relationships**, which make men see women (and other minority groups) as a threat not only to the existence of their jobs, but also to the work relationship they have with other men doing the job.

(vi) **The denial of women's 'right to work' by both State and employers**, which exclude many women from various rights and conditions of employment because it is assumed their main responsibility lies in the home.

(vii) **The lack of trade union activity against discrimination**, because women have less time to attend union meetings, and many of their needs and concerns are not regarded as suitable union concerns.

(viii) **The economic and social structure and the inadequacy of legislation**, which force women into certain economic roles which the law does not alter.

Many of these points are clearly connected and themselves create an enormous number of discriminatory attitudes and ideas which are not listed above. They reinforce each other in such a way that progress to equality of rights for women and men involves not only a change of 'male chauvinist' ideas, but also far more wide-reaching changes in both the film and television industry itself, and in the structure of the society in which the industry exists.

Letter

Steve Dwoskin, Peter Gidal, Simon Hartog, Nick Hart-Williams, Marc Karlin, Malcolm Le Grice, Laura Mulvey, James Scott

Film & Television Technician, November 1974

BBC Television is planning to transmit a series of British independent films. While this belated initiative is to be applauded, there is an urgent need for the film-makers themselves to be involved in the planning, organisation and selection of the series. To this end we have taken it upon ourselves to call a one day conference of independent film-makers to discuss the series and, hopefully, to work out a collective strategy for dealing with the corporation.

The Conference will be held on Saturday, November 9th 1974, 10 a.m. to 6 p.m. in the Screening Room, Department of Film and TV, Royal College of Art, Queens Gardens, London SW7.

There is in addition a need for an on-going forum where film-makers can discuss common problems and formulate policy and although the immediate objective of this conference is to draw up a statement of our position on the BBC plan, we hope that it will also lead to the formation of some sort of organisation to represent the views of independent film-makers not only to the BBC but also to such bodies as the British Film Industry and Arts Council.

We hope members will be able to attend. People coming from outside London who need a bed should contact The Other Cinema. ...

Independent Film-Making in the 70s

An introductory discussion paper from the Organising Committee for the
IFA Conference held in May 1976

The Independent Film-Makers' Association was formed in the Autumn of 1974 in
response to a BBC programme on Independent Cinema hosted by Melvyn Bragg.
The programme consisted of a series of 'spots' lasting between 30 seconds and
5 minutes. The nature of the programme was such that it in no way accounted for
the emergence of that very independent cinema which it ostensibly was meant to
represent. Indeed, we discovered later that the producers had censored most of the
independent films suggested by the programmers. As a result of this travesty, a
small group of film-makers decided that they should call a meeting of independent
film-makers, with the aim of making a collective protest to the BBC and demanding another programme – this time with the help and advice of the film-makers
themselves. The response of the BBC to this suggestion was unequivocal. Aubrey
Singer, Director of Programming for BBC2, stated, 'I'm not having that kind of film
on *my* television.' Needless to say, we did not respond by pointing out that the BBC
is a public corporation.

But the outcome of that first meeting of independent film-makers proved to be
of more importance than the simple despatch of a delegation to the BBC. The meeting revealed a need for an organisation that could cope with the years of frustration
imposed on independent film-makers by the monopolies which had for too long
controlled the means of production and distribution, had for too long controlled
access to the cinemas which were quickly becoming mausoleums. The film-makers
at that meeting were certain that an organisation had to be formed to represent our
interests but in the back – the very back – of our minds, certain questions fed our
doubt about the validity of such an organisation in that critical economic climate.
Those questions devolved on whether such an organisation could validly represent
the conflicting interests between those who wanted to keep within the mainstream
of the established film cultures and those who wanted to transform it; we were
aware that any close analysis of the nature and aspirations of independent film-
making would involve a series of value judgements and serious argument, and that
the organisation would become more a forum for debate about film culture than
the guild that the meeting declared the IFA to be.

As a guild it was an abysmal failure. Those dissatisfied with the irregularity of
results in the face of the regularity of meetings soon left, whilst those remaining
continued to meet and eventually to confront the difficulty of fighting for an area

of film-making which is not recognised by even the liberal sector of the industry, having been censored out of existence by the productive and ideological forces of British film culture. Recognising that independent film-making can only develop if the state accepts its responsibility to support this area, we concentrated on the BFI Production Board and, parallel to internal changes within the BFI, we managed to win the right to IFA nomination to the Board in the form of two elected members. At the same time, we started to arrange screenings of independent films so that members could see and discuss each other's work, and thus begin to see the extent to which independent films contradict the established practices of cinema. Through these activities we became conscious of certain common key factors which relegate all independent film-makers to the same 'condition'.

There are at present no means of existence for film-makers and there is no viable economic outlet for their work. The reason for this is that independent film is not seen as important or even necessary. In its aims to restore the present to the past – or rather, history to the present – it cuts right against the prevailing ideology of instant meaning, instant consumption. Time, which is an important element in the work of a writer, scientist or research worker, has to be fought for economically and psychologically, beyond support for actual work produced. For how can the minimal state grants and private subsidies *support* an emerging independent cinema if the returns from their films would not even keep the makers in cigarettes? As inflation makes production costs astronomical, independent film-makers must fight harder and longer against pressures which increasingly force them into an isolated ghetto. Independent cinema cannot afford to be regarded as a cultural oddity, like the Sunday speakers in Hyde Park. The struggle of independent film-makers entails not only a fight for their films, but also a fight for their idea of what an independent cinema could become. It is precisely to discuss both this latent potential and how to make it an actuality that we have called this conference. In order to understand this, we have to analyse why this potential still does not exist – when and where it has shown promise of existence and why none of these promises have been fulfilled.

'Independent' is a term used extensively to lend an assumed dignity to a host of activities which by their very nature can only be dependent. The London telephone directory lists 42 concerns who use the word independent. Among these are television companies, advertising agencies, publishers, newspapers, accountants, temperance societies, petroleum companies, sherry importers, investment companies, and a sausage-casing manufacturing company. The word independent implies both an absence of any higher authority and a certain neutrality within an appointed field; that is, one is 'independent' of any external obligations. So that in speaking of people who have an independent income, we refer to those who do not have to earn a living, though their income is invariably dependent on others; when those who control the means of living use the word independent they mean that they themselves are not controlled, yet their livelihood is in fact ultimately dependent upon those whom they control. Clearly independence is virtual rather than real, but its apparent reality is incessantly reiterated by those people who describe themselves as 'independent'. And since we, too, are using this term in claiming a stake for our association the least we can do is to try to restore some sense to what the word signifies, and by doing so to come to a better understanding of what our association signifies.

For the divergence in the general conception of the term independent is paralleled by a fragmentation within the film world itself; we want to analyse the current implications of this fragmentation and its historical basis. Thus we can see that the newly emergent Association of Independent Producers and the IFA are using the term independence in ways that are only superficially similar. It is true that the use is similar in the financial sense. Both associations seek to organise people working on films that are independent of big private capital. Although AIP is talking about budgets of around £50,000 whereas we are mostly working on films made for far less, the range of budgets of films made by both our memberships differ spectacularly from, say, the £3,000,000 spent last year on the British picture *Shout at the Devil*. The use of 'independent' here is analogous to the way the owners of individual small cinemas are organised into the Association of Independent Cinemas, thus differentiating themselves from the exhibition oligopolists of the Cinematograph Exhibitor's Association.

But there is a second, and important, respect in which the IFA insists on using the term. For we also seek to develop an independence beyond the mere absence of financing by big capital. After all, we are certainly not morally averse to access to extensive material resources for our membership; quite the contrary. What we are all averse to is artistic and political delimitation big capital invariably tends to impose. It imposes this control on two counts: the first is the short-term aim of making unchallenging films to attract large audiences immediately, thereby attracting large and swift profits. The second, closely connected, count is to contribute to the reproduction of this ideology that helps maintain the status quo – a status quo which of course includes the concentration of big capital in the same hands.

Set against this ideology are the films of IFA members, many of whom see their work as aesthetically and politically innovatory in form and content. Thus we have become independent in the sense that we are 'absent'. We are absent because what we have made present in our work has been systematically censored by the established, productive and critical forces. Because our opposition to these forces stems from a sense of absence, it is an opposition which embraces many styles of film-making. But those styles have one thing in common: they extend the language of film by confronting the established forces that so far have stifled all development in British film-making.

Our work together forms an aesthetic and political struggle in the field of cinema – the production of films which made a much more fundamental and far-reaching contribution to the lives of audiences. The ambitiousness of our goals means that these audiences have to be built up more slowly, although we expect this pace to accelerate as the crisis deepens. We have to remain independent of the need to make profits in order to have real artistic independence. Whilst constantly fighting for access to more funds and equipment for its members, the IFA must also defend and develop this political independence and aesthetic independence. For it is in this respect that the work of the IFA members is particularly important, and it is in this respect that we try to use the term independent meaningfully.

To clarify the importance of this definition of independence, we will briefly examine the history of independent film activity in Britain. An understanding of this history should be seen as the basis for our struggle at the present time. Mem- ory – a sense of one's own history – constitutes a vital dynamic for any struggle. The questions we face today relate in a very real way to our struggle for an inde- pendent cinema in the past, dating back to the 1930s when the development of 16mm distribution to avoid the censorship paved the way for the development of an alternative cinema with a politico-aesthetic purpose in the form of Kino and the Progressive Film Institute. It is extraordinary how this period remains largely unex- plored even now. But we can see that in the thirties, as now, the debate centred on the question of whether it was preferable to produce political films in line with Labour Party policy within the context of commercial companies and for conven- tional theatrical showings on a large scale (and with all the compromises this would involve), or whether to make them independently and as cheaply as possible for non-theatrical showings to minority audiences consisting of Labour Party branches, Co-ops, and trade unions (providing the opportunity for discussion). The decision to opt for this second alternative – to see the developments in politi- cal cinema as part of a general ideological struggle, however rudimentary, taking as its focus the anti-fascist front – and the gradual growth of a non-theatrical network showing workers' newsreels and Soviet films was to lead, as early as 1936, to the demand for a nationalised distribution system. In spite of its limitations, the polit- ical film movement of the thirties offered the only real challenge to the assumptions of dominant cinema and the encroachment of American finance. Avant-garde activities in Britain were as yet isolated with no institutional basis. So the only other alternative was being provided by the work of Grierson and the documentary movement. Yet it was the structure for documentary film-making he founded under state sponsorship which was to provide the prevailing model for indepen- dent film-making for the next 30 years. But Grierson's pragmatic stance as a film-maker and producer saw no contradiction involved in making films about social reform within the context of state patronage. In contrast, the work of the Pro- gressive Film Institute, and the union around film-makers like Ivor Montagu, Sidney Cole and Ralph Bond constituted a radical break with these assumptions. From the outset their work was founded on a debate about the problems of realist aesthetics and questions of the nature of the audience in relation to consumption. While many of their ideas may now appear naive or reactionary, they nevertheless represent an important beginning of a struggle for an independent cinema conceived not simply in economic terms but also in terms of the necessity for seeing it in relation to a broader social struggle; they challenged the static situation in which films were simply part of leisure and consumption in capitalist society by setting up different relationships between audiences and films as well as different production relationships, establishing film-activity as part of a struggle in ideology.

Recognising this, we can now see that independent film-making of the 1950s – the 'free cinema' – was effectively no different from Grierson's documentary movement despite the fact that developments in 16mm technology at the time provided a real opportunity to extend the political and aesthetic potential of the cinema. Ultimately anti-theoretical and unable to articulate any class position and concerned with conventional notions of the artist, reworked in terms of a liberal-humanist commitment, the 'free cinema' film-makers' attacks on the film industry were necessarily short-lived and easily assimilated into the industry's political and aesthetic assumptions. The entire concept of independence during this period was elaborated within the basic cultural framework established by the industry. The need felt for this type of independence arose precisely because the industry was clearly degenerating; the 'independent' productions of the 'free cinema' and of Woodfall Productions were construed as regenerative movements – a new wave which would revive an industry-orientated film culture. The young talent which comprised Woodfall and the free cinema recognised the industry's over-dependence on American finance and the subsequent artistic restrictions imposed by demands for a large international market in which to recoup that investment, and they held out the hope of making the British film industry more flexible by accepting a changed status and by developing a changed market through modestly financed films which had a specifically British appeal. But the industry was able to re-incorporate such independent activity into its own strictly defined methods of production, distribution, and exhibition as soon as it perceived the potential millions to be made from a film like *Tom Jones*. And the film-makers lacked both the desire and the ideological consciousness to resist such recuperation.

The general strategy to shift the emphasis in production from studio produced films to 'independently' produced films was roughly paralleled by attempts to open up the distribution/exhibition circuit, then (as now) controlled by Rank and EMI. The Short Film Service began, as early as 1957, to independently distribute short films on the commercial and club circuits, as supplements to the main feature. The establishment of a viable distribution circuit for such films would, of course, have encouraged independent film-makers to initiate such projects without industry backing. The industry, for its part, retained control over its own production of accompanying shorts, limiting the market for the Short Film Service. In opposition, the Short Film-Makers' Campaign in 1967 began to lobby the Cinematography Films Council for a change in the Cinematograph Act which would require that funds from the Eady Levy be channelled into the production of short independently produced films – as was the case in most European countries. The lobby failed to achieve even this modest goal, and even as it was getting under way the Short Film Service's intervention was superseded by the more ambitious New Cinema Club, which shifted emphasis from the promotion of short films to the promotion of shorts and features which otherwise could not find commercial distribution and exhibition, often because of the lack of a censor's certificate. By incorporating itself as a club and holding regular screenings, the New Cinema Club recognised the need to co-ordinate distribution and exhibition activities in establishing an independent film culture.

But the New Cinema Club drew its identity from the exhibition of censored or non-certified films and could challenge industrial hegemony only to the extent that it could exploit the material withheld from the duopoly by censorship practice. With the easing of rigid censorship, the New Cinema Club lost its momentum. It is because independent activities of this type ultimately rested on hopes of reviving or salvaging an altered industry that their progressive aspects could be conveniently co-opted by the industry. The contradiction between the notion of an industry devoted to the efficient marketing of a mass activity within a film culture dominated by that industry was never fully analysed. Thus independence of this sort could be too easily ignored or too easily incorporated into an essentially unchanged industry production situation.

Some of the films championed by the Short Film Service and the New Cinema Club were more completely independent of the industry in the sense of having been primarily financed and executed by one individual. The developments in *cinéma vérité* and the New American Cinema of the '50s demonstrated how 16mm equipment could be utilised by a few individuals to produce very low-budget films, allowing the film-makers to retain complete personal control of subject and style. This led, in the mid-60s – a period combining increased affluence with increased availability of high-quality 16mm equipment – to the apparent emergence of a 'personal cinema' based on individual expression. Films made in this way encompassed the entire range of film-making styles (from documentary to personal drama to avant-garde etc.), but were united in their complete break with the industry and in their aspiration to extend access to the movie-camera as a common instrument of communication. There was little attention paid by these film-makers, however, to the need to alter the distribution and exhibition situation, and there was no systematic attempt to educate a new audience or cultivate a new market for the films; there seemed to be a naive optimism that the intrinsic worth of the work would sustain itself. But economic recession means the end of such activity for all but the hardiest; film-makers were forced into television or attempting to continue working alone on the strength of previous work or personal will.

This independent film-making activity was related to that broad cultural manifestation of the mid-60s known as the 'underground movement'. The underground sought to establish an alternative culture and provided the hope of fundamental social change, a project which engaged independent film-making on two major levels: the radicalisation of film aesthetics and the radicalisation of political film-making. The international nature of the underground and the significance of the role envisaged for film in that underground culture was illustrated on the continent by the Experimental Film Festival held in Knokke-le-Zoute, Belgium, in December 1967. That event demonstrated the dynamism of a new type of film-making and at the same time crystallised political discontent around protests to American involvement in Vietnam.

In Britain, the London Film-Makers' Co-operative, founded in 1966, absorbed new energy from the experience of Knokke. Comprised of film-makers who tend to make films as individuals, the Co-op nevertheless developed from the outset a strong sense of co-operative activity in distributing its members' films and in organising regular screenings at unconventional places like the basement of the Better Books bookshop and the Arts Lab. This meant that when, in 1970, the Co-op made processing and printing equipment easily available, all aspects of film production and distribution and viewing could be integrated into a system independent of established modes. The significant change in the production situation intensified a concomitant change in the films produced; working with processing and printing machinery heightened the sense of the importance of that technology and inscribed it into the films themselves, films which constantly invoke the act of their own production, presentation and perception. The Co-op has been able to continue to expand and develop this aspect of independent film-making by attracting a membership and an audience from the art schools, which produce a steady, if small, number of film-makers who are completely alienated from the social and aesthetic values of the film industry, and who are sympathetic to the aesthetic discourse of modernism.

It was a student constituency which also acted as catalyst to the development in Britain of an explicitly political vanguard in independent film-making. The political events on the continent during May '68 spurred political activity in campuses across Britain, and raised the political consciousness of the notion of 'independence' in all social institutions. For it was the failure of the media in presenting relevant information and in representing these revolts which emphasised the need for a re-evaluation of the entire system of making, distributing and presenting films. The Angry Arts Group, which had been sponsoring shows of the American Newsreels since 1967, deliberately shifted its tactics in 1969 to stress the importance of presenting a film in a way which challenges the existing ideology in addition to simply screening films with the appropriate political content. It did this by involving itself in the distribution and exhibition of films to the extent of co-ordinating small-group discussions after each screening to encourage spectators to consider what they had just seen and its significance to their lives. Angry Arts became Liberation Films in 1970 when the group began to produce its own films in this new production/distribution/exhibition context.

As early as 1968, those film-makers working collectively as Cinema Action began touring the country in a van with their film and projection equipment, creating cinema in factories, in pubs, anywhere that working-class people assembled, following the films with discussion. Again, it was the intention to completely transform film practice at all levels of production and distribution and exhibition which, despite individual differences, motivated Cinema Action and Liberation Films and the Berwick Street Film Collective (formed in 1970), all dedicated to contributing towards the politicisation of film. In the last few years, a variety of film-making groups has emerged which acknowledges the need for group support and encouragement in film-making, and which recognises the pressing need for new models of production and new styles of film-making: Amber Films (1968/69), the London Women's Film Group (1972), Independent Cinema West (1974), the Merseyside Communications Unit (1974), the Newsreel Collective (1975), and the North East Co-op (1976).

Despite a common appreciation for the need to co-ordinate all aspects of film practice in establishing a viable independent film culture, the 'aesthetic avant-garde' and the 'political vanguard' have developed separately. Yet certain conditions have mitigated against a continued ignorance of common interests. These films have a not altogether different audience, generally based among young people and specifically cultivated as a sophisticated film audience through the occasional publication of periodicals such as *Cinim*, *Afterimage*, *Cinemantics* and *Cinema Rising*. All encouraged the growth of a heterogeneous independent film culture, as did the important 'parallel cinema' conference held in May '69 which sought to establish an alternative distribution circuit and which resulted in the organisation of The Other Cinema as a distribution/exhibition alternative for British and foreign films finding no commercial outlet here.

But it was several years before the state would even begin to accept its responsibility to encourage the growth of a broad-based constituency for independent film. A challenge to the BFI's lack of any policy in this direction was made initially in 1968 in the form of an open letter to the Minister Responsible for the Arts in an attempt to open the debate but very little was achieved. In 1970, an 'action committee' of BFI members was set up which included independent film-makers, film critics and lecturers and those involved in alternative distribution and exhibition around The Other Cinema. A central theme behind the action committee's manifesto – which specifically demanded election of BFI governors by the staff and membership, as well as arguing for the development of the BFI as a cultural base for activities like independent film-making, film education and the establishment of regional film centres – was that the BFI should recognise its responsibility to expand and co-ordinate state funding in the face of a failing industry. Although the motion for the dismissal of the entire governing body was initially narrowly defeated, the action committee gradually won considerable support within BFI membership as a whole. And we can now see a resultant shift in the approach to

state funding, signalled by various reforms in the BFI structure such as the institution of the election of two governors, and changes in the production board and
regional policy. A parallel shift – opening new areas of state funding for independent film-makers – occurred in 1972 when the Arts Council Film Panel established
a sub-committee designed to fund small individual films, and when the regional
arts committee began to consider funding local film-makers. Support from all these
bodies has increased slowly but steadily since that time, supplying energy needed
to develop and extend independent film activity.

History reveals the abyss from which independent film-makers have had to
climb. Now the government proposes the establishment of the British Film Authority whose sole function is to reconstruct the British film industry. A look at the
Government White Paper shows that the people who are responsible for drawing
up the proposal for its reconstruction are, in large part, those who have presided
over its decline; thus they affirm their own economic bankruptcy at the same time
that they demand that the government rescue an industry which will remain in
their control. Nor is there, anywhere in the White Paper, an attempt to analyse why,
when the industry did have money, it produced so little of value. Its only explanation for the malaise places the onus on the American majors, failing even to point
out how uncritically this American finance was received when the going was good.
A desperate strategy disguised as nationalism will not suffice when what is needed
is a thorough analysis of the years of inertia. But even the vague reference to US
ownership cease when the White Paper confronts a gap it doesn't quite know how
to fill. We refer to paragraph 108:

Support for the art of the film

Many overseas countries including, for example, France and Sweden, recognise
that films of outstanding merit often fail to reach a wide enough audience to
secure a proper commercial return. They accordingly operate special schemes
providing financial rewards for films considered by an independent body to
possess outstanding artistic qualities, and in some cases support is also given to
exhibitors who show films of this kind. Such schemes have led to the production
of films which have greatly enhanced the international reputations of the film
industries in the countries in which they originated. In Britain, a quality award or
similar system would give recognition to the view that film-making can be an
artistic pursuit in its own right. It would also lead to an enrichment of the variety
of films available and contribute in the long term to the commercial health of the
industry. We therefore recommend that the Authority should study the feasibility
of such a system being established in the United Kingdom.

If the authors of the White Paper were at all serious about this proposal, they would
have developed paragraphs 1–107 to this end – for it is only by transforming the

present means of production, exhibition and distribution that the requirements set out in paragraph 108 can be authentically achieved. As it is, they expect the BFA to culturally guide the shabby mercantile throne in which it will sit. From this position – comfortably ensconced in Mayfair – it allots to 'artistic creation' of a cinematic Speakers' Corner.

In writing this paper, the conference organisers have grappled with the difficulties of defining what constitutes independence in the area of film production. In the present political climate we are witnessing the two-party system's suppression of political dissent in the name of solving the national crisis. We are referring not only to direct political repression – such as the gaoling of pickets, the anti-terrorism act, etc. – but also to an ideological and cultural suppression. The ideological struggle has obvious repercussions in the state's attitude towards the funding of the arts, in the recent *Evening Standard* attacks on the GLAA for the funding of political art, and in the setting off of alarm bells in the Tate brick affair. However limited these particular attacks, we must be aware that the tradition of liberalism in the state's attitudes towards the arts is always on a short fuse. And so, given certain political conditions, we can see some of the advances that we have made quickly eroded. In the light of this, we believe that independence can be defined as the preservation and development of critical thought. Therefore we must resist the notion that the only alternatives for independent film-making are either to accept its milk-crate on Speakers' Corner or to stifle itself by attempting to obey the law of the market. The BFA represents conservative reformism whose sole object is to control and subsidise those who conform to their ideological values. It is with this in mind that we return to the IFA and its obligations to resist those values.

Independence is the bedrock of critical thought; the IFA must fight for the preservation and development of this position, and in doing battle with those who at present legislate film production we have realised that:

1. the struggle for the rights of an independent film culture to exist includes all those who are involved in producing film meaning – that is, it not only involves independent film producers but also distributors, exhibitors, film teachers, critical workers and film technicians;
2. our struggle is both an economic one and a cultural one – economic in the sense that it has to demand an increase in state sponsorship for the making and distribution and exhibition of films, cultural in that it has to fight the isolation that independent film-making can all too easily be forced to accept, and must transform all aspects of dominant film practice;
3. it has to fight for the right of access in both film production and exhibition for those who have neither.

In developing these demands, we came to the realisation that – if our call for the right of independence is not to be a hollow one – we must acknowledge our basic collectivity as opposed to remaining isolated. Thus if the IFA is to develop mean-ingful independence it can afford neither the cost of strident sectarianism nor the luxury of subsuming its critical awareness in liberal inertia. The negation of these two tendencies will, we hope, creatively inform the activities of the IFA.

Lastly, the authors of this paper wish to state that its contents do not represent official IFA policy – that is up to this conference to debate – and that it should be read as simply offering guidelines for that debate.

Polemic

Extract from the Festival Programme of the First Festival of Independent
British Cinema, Bristol 1975

1. The festival has a polemical function. Its main characteristic is the combination
of different combinations of independent film – the avant-garde on the one side,
the overtly political film on the other, plus a lot in the middle. The combination
which we have made is not only an attempt to be comprehensive but is based on
the belief that the development of independent cinema depends on cross fertilisa-
tion between different forms and intentions. The festival represents, we think, not
only what is now the current position of independent film work but also what that
position might generate.

2. Because the festival, in our eyes, represents a specific future of film work, it is
about independent cinema and not about 'the independently produced' film alone.
We think that the inclusive and prospective term 'cinema' (production, distribution and exhibition as one process) is the key to the head start that independent
cinema may have over industrial cinema and TV very soon. The film-maker by having, potentially, control over the whole travel of his film, can respond directly,
unprogrammed by institutional pressures, in his future work. This, to us, constitutes the independence of independent cinema – the individual and collective
responsibility of the film-maker for the whole trajectory of his film. It is the direct
opposite of that translation of responsibility the TV film-maker has to make to the
institutions of State broadcasting and the 'market system' respectively.

3. At present the film-maker is subject to the whims and misfortunes of the
remaining agencies of aristocratic patronage. If independent cinema is to live up to
its name it has to have a direct relationship, both economic and cultural, to its audience. What audience? The audience in the sense still has to be created. We have to
work on our own organisation, anarchic or not.

4. Industrial cinema and TV are losing the capacity to respond to the situation
around them. Their language is neutralised yet continues insistently talking to itself
like a meths drinker in a bad dream. If the will to independent cinema is there then
the fug will evaporate and the real problems of our work emerge – the formation
of a de-industrialised heterogeneous cinema.

Edinburgh 76 Magazine: Introduction
Phil Hardy, Claire Johnston, Paul Willemen

Seven years ago, in 1969, the Edinburgh Film Festival published its first book, *Samuel Fuller*, in conjunction with a retrospective of Fuller's films. The decision to publish books to accompany the festival's major retrospective was not taken in a vacuum. Peter Wollen's *Signs and Meaning in the Cinema*, published earlier that year, set in motion a series of reverberations that ran through British film culture in its attempts to formulate and articulate a theory of authorship and a mode of reading that for the first time took into account recent developments in the related fields of semiotics and structuralism. The publications policy of the festival from 1969 onwards followed up a series of questions which *Signs and Meaning in the Cinema* raised. These books, studies of the work of individual directors, explored the structural configurations providing the coherence of a given director's work. The increasing influence of semiotics, following the publication of Metz's work in English and *Screen*'s post-1971 policy, refocussed, but did not fundamentally alter this auteurist policy.

A second factor shaping both Edinburgh's publications and screening policy was the concern to make an active intervention against the dominant trends within British film culture. This intervention was on two levels. Firstly, Edinburgh, by the choice of films to be screened at the festival, questioned the traditional notions of a festival being either 'the best of the world's cinema' or a market place for the buying and selling of films. Secondly, Edinburgh concentrated on directors whose very neglect exposed the limitations of both progressive (*Movie*) and dominant (*Sight and Sound*) trends in British film criticism. Accordingly, Edinburgh's early books were attempts to pursue simultaneously both theoretical and political/cultural concerns through their analyses of the work of various directors (Fuller, Corman, Sirk and Tashlin). The artificiality of Edinburgh's separating out its concerns in this fashion produced a series of problems which increasingly marked the festival's publications, making the positivist separation between film as an object or study and the politics of film culture progressively untenable. The contradictions contained within the books, particularly the last two on Walsh and Tourneur, though already discernible in earlier publications, forced the realization that the key issue at stake was film as an ideological practice rather than as a predetermined and self-sufficient object of study. This notion of the cultural text, within which both films and readings are embedded, was already present in outline in Wollen's book, but it was not until recently that the question of film as a signifying practice, of film as a process of articulation, tracing relations of subjectivity within film texts which themselves are embedded in the discourse of ideologies present in a given social formation, has been systematically examined. The realization that auteurist studies, linked to the grouping of a series of films merely because they were made by one and the same director, were deeply implicated in the theory of meaning founded on the assumption of the existence of a transcendental ego, as described most clearly by Julia Kristeva:

> The theory of meaning now stands at the cross-roads: either it will remain an attempt at formalising meaning systems by increasing sophistication of the logico-mathematical tools which enable it to formulate models on the basis of a conception (already rather outdated) of meaning as the act of a *transcendental ego*, cut off from its body, its unconscious and also its history; or else it will attune itself to the theory of the speaking subject as a divided subject (conscious/unconscious) and go on to attempt to specify the types of operation characteristic of the two sides of this split: thereby exposing them to those forces extraneous to the logic of the systematic; exposing them, that is to say, on the one hand, to bio-physiological processes (themselves already inescapably part of the signifying processes; what Freud calls 'drives'), and, on the other hand, to social constraints (family structure, modes of production, etc.).
>
> (*Times Literary Supplement*, Oct. 12, 1973)

Such a realisation made it impossible for Edinburgh to continue its screening and publishing policy of the last six years. The main problem of film criticism can no longer be restricted to the object cinema, as opposed to the operation cinema (a specific signifying practice which places the spectator).

The political/ideological ramifications of this shift now constitute the central issues for Edinburgh, and it is in order to explore them that the festival broke with its past last year. The centre of the 1975 Edinburgh Film Festival was the Brecht Event, organised in collaboration with *Screen* magazine (see *Screen*, Winter, 1975/76), which consisted of a number of screenings accompanied by a series of seminars focussing on the idea of the cinema as a political practice. This change of emphasis, from the traditional notion of film as a form of cultural consumption, to one of meaning-production (stressing the practice of reading films) exposes a problem suppressed by the majority of film festivals. It is essential, if the festival is to continue to make a progressive critical intervention in British film culture, to move from a notion of consumption to one of production, with the act of filming and the act of reading being seen as two moments of equal value, neither having priority over the other. This breaking down of the ideological division between work (production) and leisure (consumption) in society challenges, in a fundamental way, traditional ideas about the role of the artist in society and constitutes a radical break with criticism's ideological history. The recognition of this dialectic of making/viewing forms the cornerstone for the developing of a new social practice of the cinema, a social practice based on the notion of struggle in ideology directed towards the building of a vital film culture in which cultural dominance can be displaced and undermined.

These are the main reasons why the festival has abandoned auteur publications and instead opted for a new annual magazine which seeks to provide critical and theoretical work related to the seminars and informing the festival's practice in general. By posing the problematic of reading film texts in general rather than the exigencies of a particular director's work, it is inevitable that the festival will emphasise those films most conducive to the exploration of this problematic, i.e. films which in their own textual strategies raise the problems of ideological transgression. Accordingly, the festival has extended its area of concern to include developments within independent cinema, much of which foregrounds the notion of film as an ideological operation. Concomitant with this, Edinburgh will continue to show those films made within the industry which because of their exploitation of contradictions within the industry's practices and constraints, produce in their texts, often unconsciously, shifts and breaks which open up the very problem of the inscription of the subject constantly elided by mainstream cinema, and which by their transgressive play with conventions, foreground (but no more than that) the problematic of reading.

In this context, the politics of film criticism informing the present publication stems from the premise that what has to be interrogated is the dialectic constituted by the fact that there is a perennial disjuncture between the inscribed reader of the text and the social subject who is invited to take up this position. Although the social subject always exceeds the subject implied by the text, because he/she is also placed by a heterogeneity of other cultural systems and is never co-extensive with the subject placed by a single fragment (i.e. one film) of the overall cultural text, the social subject is also restricted by the positionality which the text offers it. It is this problem of interlocking subjectivities, caught up in a network of symbolic systems, that psychoanalysis (as the theory of the subject developed by Freud and Lacan) addresses itself to.

Accordingly, this year's publication is primarily devoted to the subject of psychoanalysis and the cinema, one of the festival's two events (and also includes texts relating to the other, the avant-garde). Our aim in publishing some of the papers presented at the psychoanalysis event and other key texts is to formulate and clarify some of the important theoretical issues raised by the meeting of film theory and psychoanalysis and to situate the political/ideological implications of this meeting as it relates to avant-gardist/independent film practice and the development of a new social practice of the cinema founded on the dialectic of making/viewing.

Memory, Phantasy, Identity: 'Days of Hope' and the Politics of the Past

Colin MacCabe

Edinburgh 77 Magazine

In the history of philosophy, discussions of memory have always been linked to problems of identity. For Plato, it was the faculty which allowed contact with our divine origin, removing us from the flux of phenomena to take us back to the security of the eternal soul and its ability to contemplate the unchanging forms. For Hume, and for the empiricist tradition, memory has always been the guarantee of identity; of that constancy which provokes the fictitious unit of the self.

The philosophical heritage which links memory so closely to notions of individual origin and personality should sound a caution to those who wish to talk of memory in relation to class. The empiricist tradition denies the term memory to any claim about the past which is not grounded in the individual's experience and this thesis emphasises the sense in which memory presupposes a unified ground for present and past: a subject of experience. To talk of a working-class or popular memory may all too easily lead to talking of class as a collective subject. A class, however, is not a subject, an identity, but rather the ever-changing configuration produced by the forces and relations of production. A set of economic, political and ideological forces constantly constitute classes in struggle and classes can find no definition outside those struggles.

To slip into the use of a class subject will also deflect attention from the serious weakness of any empiricist theory of the past and its relation to consciousness. For if we look at some of the comments and asides of Marx and Freud we can quickly see that they pose a relation between present and past in memory which renders the very concept of subject incoherent. In his earliest writings on memory, Freud postulated memory traces as susceptible to re-articulation under the pressure of events in the present. For Freud the traces that composed memory were always open to a 're-inscription'. Such a re-inscription disturbs the unity and constancy on which the empiricist subject relies.

These problems, however, have received no attention from those theorists on the left who have concerned themselves with popular memory. Rather than seeking to analyse or characterise that relation between past and present which is encapsulated in the term 'memory', those who consider the field have a tendency to content themselves with constantly stating and bemoaning the fact that since the First

World War the working class's memory of its own struggles has grown weaker and weaker. This fading of the past is understood as almost irreversible in the face of an ever-more absolute ruling class control of the means of communication and information.

In response to this state of affairs a great deal of effort of intellectuals on the left has gone into preserving the memory of the people, a memory and memories that the people have consigned to oblivion. Such an effort has not been confined to left-wing academics or to the written word. Within the visual media one need think no further than the Loach-Garnett-Allen *Days of Hope* as recent evidence of a filmic effort to produce a different set of memory images to those usually summoned up in response to 'The Great War', 'The Twenties', 'The General Strike'. What I have to say about *Days of Hope* is specific but there are obvious consequences for a general attitude to the past and its representations.

Days of Hope covers the years 1916–1926 through the lives of three characters: Sarah Hargreaves, her husband Philip and her brother Ben Matthews. The first episode, set in 1916, shows Philip's treatment as a conscientious objector in the army and Ben's experience as a member of the British Army in Ireland at war with the IRA. The second episode portrays a miners' strike in 1921 and the behaviour of the ruling class and the army when vital interests are threatened. In this episode Ben deserts from the army which he had joined as a regular and allies himself with the miners. As a result of his desertion and his support for the miners he is sent to jail for three years. The third episode shows Ben coming out of jail to join the Communist Party and Philip becoming a Labour MP in the 1924 election. This episode covers the period of the General Strike and cuts between the Council of Action in which Ben and Sarah are involved and the machinations within the TUC and Government which Philip observes from the sidelines. The series ends with the TUC's decision to call off the strike.

The films articulate a classic relation between narrative and vision in which what we see is true and this truth confirms what we see. This apparently tautologous statement is one that finds its reality in its distribution through the time of the narrative and across the space of shot and character. The reality of the character is guaranteed by the shot, and the reality of the shot is guaranteed by the character.

This coincidence of truth and vision which is achieved through narrative is accomplished in *Days of Hope* through the different progressions of Ben and Philip. At the beginning of the four films, Ben is a young country lad without any political knowledge and unable to understand why Philip will not fight. Through his experiences with the army, the miners and prison he comes to understand the realities of class society and joins the Communist Party. By 1926, however, he is already beginning to have his doubts about the Party's subservience to Russia and Russia's subservience to Stalin. Ben acts as the major articulation between viewer and screen because what he sees and what we see are the same. Each stage of his political development is a response to what he has seen and what he has seen is what we have

seen. Philip, on the other hand, starts out with a fully fledged commitment to paci-
fism and the Labour Party. The inadequacies of this position before the 'realities of
the class struggle' are stated in the first film by a revolutionary who is only refusing to fight in a capitalist war and they are demonstrated in the third when we are
shown the Labour Party's true relation to the capitalist state. Philip's refusal to
abandon his political beliefs before the evidence of what he has seen leads him to
become more cynical and apathetic about the abilities of the people. He ends up
sneering at the popular enthusiasm in the Council of Action and supporting the
union leaders' handling of the General Strike. Philip's politics are presented without any visual evidence to explain their origin or form. As such, and opposed to
Ben's, they are simply *unrealistic*. The film emphasises Ben's position as true
(co-incident with what we have seen) and Philip's as false (non-coincident) when,
at the end of the film, Sarah sides with Ben against Philip and they declare 'We
could have got what we wanted' and 'The Labour Party and the TUC are there to
deliver the workers to the bosses.'

  In this congruence of realms of truth and of vision, *Days of Hope* adopts an
empiricist attitude to knowledge in which the process of the production of knowledge (a process which constitutes both subject and object) is elided into the
instantaneous moment of sight. This sight places the subject outside any area of
production or process and always already in the position of knowledge. Where *Days
of Hope* differs from the majority of ideologically conventional films is that this subject is posed as collective. Our identification with Ben is marked primarily in terms
of his class-membership; his truth (his view) is not individual but collective. *Days
of Hope* positions a class as viewer, as subject. And it is as subject that the class is
placed in relation to the past. The past is not submitted to re-articulation in terms
of the present (for if it was, any subject would immediately become contradictory)
but it is the constancy of the past that demonstrates identity in the present.

  Marx understood the past as constantly confirming men in an imaginary relation to the present (e.g. *The 18th Brumaire of Louis Bonaparte*). In *Days of Hope* we
can understand that the articulation between the *imaginary* and the *past* confirms
not only Marx but also those philosophers who could find no internal criteria for
distinguishing between memory and phantasy. In both cases the subject finds itself
in a relation of imaginary control. It is only the introduction of the present that can
make those memories and phantasies any more than the constant confirmation of
the subject's position. In analysis, for example, it is the work of interpretation and
the resistances of the analysand which makes both memory and phantasy such a
profitable ground of investigation. Similarly one can argue that the past is only
interesting politically because of something which touches us in the present. Benjamin expressed this position acutely when he wrote: 'To articulate the past
historically does not mean to recognise it "the way it really was" (Rank). It means
to seize hold of a memory as it flashes up at a moment of danger. The danger affects
both the content of the tradition and its receivers. The same danger hangs over

both: that of becoming a tool of the ruling classes. In every era the attempt must be made anew to wrest tradition away from a conformism that is about to over-power it.' (*Illuminations*, p. 257.)

Benjamin's attack on the reality of the past aligns itself with both Marx and Freud. Both the cure and the revolution have the aim of re-articulating the past out of any existence within the present at all. Marx writes: 'The tradition of all dead generations weighs like a nightmare on the brain of the living. And just when they seem engaged in revolutionising themselves and things in creating something that has never yet existed, precisely in such periods of revolutionary crisis, they anx-iously conjure up the spirits of the past to their service and borrow from them names, battle-cries and costumes in order to present the new scene of world his-tory in this time-honoured disguise and this borrowed language.' (*18th Brumaire*, p. 10.) In response to this threat from the past Marx calls for an active process of forgetting: 'The social revolution cannot draw its poetry from the past but only from the future. It cannot begin with itself before it has stripped off all superstition in regard to the past. Earlier revolutions required recollections of past world his-tory in order to drug themselves concerning their own content. In order to arrive at its own content, the revolution of the nineteenth century must let the dead bury their dead. There the phrase went beyond the content; here the content goes beyond the phrase.' (Ibid., pp. 12–13.)

These considerations of Marx and Benjamin demand a relation to the past which attaches a primacy to the present. Only that which has an affectivity in the present is worth considering in terms of the past. What one might then focus on would be the very opposite of the mythical history of the working class which *Days of Hope* offers but rather a history of institutions. *Days of Hope* is concerned with the demonstration of the falseness of institutions (the TUC, the Labour Party) beside the truth of working-class experience. But that notion of class experience postu-lates a class subject and a class memory such that the features and positions of the working class are given for all time. Such a conception has nothing to do with polit-ical perspectives for revolutionary change. What revolutionary change does demand is a transformation of institutions and practices. To change institutions it may be necessary to understand them but simply to condemn them as false is to ignore their reality. In *Days of Hope* institutions have no reality over and above their ability to produce individuals who are betrayers. Instead of an analysis of the Labour Party or the TUC we are treated to the *sight* of the perfidy of a Wedgewood or a Thomas. Whereas in the first two episodes we are shown the reality of state power, the second two episodes concentrate on the individual betrayals involved in the accommodation of the institutions of the working class to that state power. There is thus no possibility of an explanation of the structure and history of those institutions which would make the behaviour of a Thomas or a Wedgewood pos-sible. Such an investigation would, however, have to start not from the past but from the present and the introduction of the present would also subvert the primacy of the visual for the closure on which the guarantee of narrative is predicated would be broken.

It might be argued that to follow this up would be to produce programmes which would be turned down by television on the aesthetic grounds that they would be 'too difficult'. This may well be true but it raises the further question of whether the concept of 'audience' which is used for aesthetic judgements within television may render any political use of television fiction impossible.

All this is not intended as some condemnation of *Days of Hope*: there is much to admire in the first two episodes. But it is intended to indicate that the relationship between sight and story which produces the film is fundamentally inimical to the production of political knowledge. Further that this relation is complicit with an understanding of the working class's relation to its own past which reduces the working class to an identity.

'Penthesilea'

Mary Kelly

Spare Rib No. 30, December 1974

Laura Mulvey and Peter Wollen's first film, *Penthesilea*, recently shown at the 'Edinburgh Film Festival in London', is an attempt to examine, rather than enact, a myth. In this case it is attempt which is well grounded on classical sources, inspired by psychoanalysis and committed to the Women's Liberation Movement.

The film is rigorously structured in five somewhat discordant yet didactic sequences. Each sequence is a continuous, unedited take using direct sound whenever possible. Although this method is stark in conception and demanding in execution, the end result is far less authoritarian than the conventional obsession with technical continuity. Similar to the work of Straub, *Penthesilea* is held together, not by devices, but by an integrity of intention.

In the first sequence, entitled 'Ghost White, Like a Not Yet Written Page', the camera is absolutely still and at a safe distance from the powerful spectacle which unfolds before it. The spectacle is Kleist's 'Penthesilea' (a nineteenth-century German Tragedy), carefully adapted to mime and skilfully performed by the Northwestern University Mime Company. In Kleist's version of the encounter between Achilles and the Amazon Queen, it is she who fells the Greek hero. This is a significant reversal of the usual plot where he kills her, because it reveals a less familiar aspect of male phantasy – the narcissistic and ambivalent man who seeks submission and even death. Inevitably, the reversal only reinforces the threatening yet provocative image of the woman as warrior, insatiable lover and castrating mother. Even as victor, Penthesilea is captured by the vanquished's myth.

A myth could be described as a collective dream. Its raw material is made up of real events in the history of a group and reshaped according to the needs and desires common to that group. In the context of the film, the Amazon myth, like the individual dream, symptom or slip of the tongue, is overdetermined. The excavation of its meaning requires a tool – 'the words'. In the mime, they are conspicuously absent but they emerge with a vengeance in the second sequence.

'Shadow Sprinkled in Black Characters' is a droning but incisive twenty-minute monologue by Peter Wollen. Simultaneous or subsequent narration is a familiar classical technique, but here 'the words' make a significant rupture with the tone and intention of Kleist's drama. They examine the myth. They are both literary and literal. They are spoken by a man in order to show that language itself has been appropriated by men, but in every other respect they are anonymous.

This sequence performs the essential task of providing the premises for the conclusions we see in the first part of the film. For example, Wollen (the words) describes Leni Riefenstal's plan to film Kleist's 'Penthesilea' and carefully points out how the Amazonian superheroine inevitably joins the patriarchal superman. He says, '… their weapons and strategy are men's weapons and strategy. They offer a solution which is magical not political'.

Some form of Amazon myth exists not only in Greece, but also in parts of Asia, Africa and South America. Its appearance seems to coincide with the transition from matrilineality to patriarchy and to be based on the actual or phantasised resistance by women to the consolidation of male hegemony. If a matriarchy did develop during this historical stage, then it would necessarily have been a society based on the exchange of men and probably on their exploitation and oppression as well. Consequently, the Amazons, as an antidote for female subservience, are not as attractive as some feminists have assumed.

The second sequence also functions on another level. It attempts to disengage 'the words' themselves from the very ideology in which the film itself holds them. The camera is constantly in motion. It wanders away from the speaker, explores the room and finds 'the words' in written form, on notecards. By focusing on the cards, the previously spoken words are visually played back against the ongoing monologue which has now come to represent merely the existence of communication. The level of sound is not adjusted to the camera's movements, nor is there any concern over variations in lighting, for instance over-exposure is frequent. The viewer can identify with the cameraman's autonomy and feel almost in control her/himself – a rare experience in the cinema.

Less rare but equally rewarding is the very well-researched slide show which comprises the third sequence, 'Seals of Phobia; Blazons of Self-Punishment'. The blazons are images of Amazons on Greek vases, Roman tombs, Byzantine mosaics, Medieval tapestries, Baroque paintings and contemporary comic strips. Don Lembeck's animation is simple and flawless, and it is riveted to the sense by an intoxicating soundtrack (a vocal composition by Berio which represents the birth of language).

However, the blazons are more than images, they are the signs, the symbols of phobias nurtured by patriarchal dominance; misogyny, incest, necrophilia. In most of the works, Amazons are pursued, abducted, raped, murdered and humiliated by Greek warriors. Sex antagonism is irresolvable in this embattled world. The Penthesilean triad seems inevitable – frustration, aggression, regression. Then a curious intervention is made in Wonderwoman in a cartoon printed in 1972. She joins a consciousness-raising group, and this, in fact, is the point at which the film pivots from the realm of phantasy into the world of 'real' women and everyday struggle.

The fourth sequence, 'Net of Light on Overlight', is like a song in three parts. First soprano is the refilming of a silent film of a fictional play on the Suffragettes made in 1913 and actually starring Emily Pankhurst and Mrs Stanton Blatch.

Second soprano is the reading of Jessie Ashley's letters, published in the *Boston Women's Journal* in 1912, by Grace McKeaney who is being filmed in close-up over the silent film. Alto is a low rumbling of women's voices and machinery which blends the noises of the projector and the narration together into one harmonious entity.

When Laura Mulvey was asked why she chose the particular incidents of 1912–13 to represent the Women's Movement, she replied, 'The Suffragists have also become something of a myth themselves but one which contrasts radically with the Amazons because they are ordinary women concerned with real issues and I feel that the general problematic outlined by Jessie Ashley is still relevant today.'

Jessie Ashley's contribution is essential in two respects; firstly, because 'the words' have finally been appropriated by a woman and secondly, because her testimony bears witness to the fact that in the last instance economy is determinant. However, her loyalty is divided between the working women militants on the one hand, and what she describes as the predominantly middle-class Suffrage Movement on the other. Her letters end on a pessimistic note, '. . . voluntarily I hold my peace'. The Amazons, their strategy, their words, have vanished but there is only self-imposed silence to fill the void.

In the fifth sequence, 'Notes on the Magic Writing Pad', videotapes of the first four sequences are played back simultaneously and refilmed. The four screens are like the analyst/film-maker's memoirs, they take notes on the film/dream as it is recollected: the phantasy, 'the words', the images, the 'real' issues and finally the message. Penthesilea (Debra Dolonsky) takes off her stage make-up and with it the myth, saying, 'Women looked at each other through the eyes of men. Women spoke to each other through the words of men – an alien look, an alien language. We can speak with our own words. We can look with our own eyes and we can fight with our own weapons.' As an answer to the absence in the fourth sequence her words are simply too weak to support the weight of questions it imposes. For example, how has the language of women's liberation changed since 1912?

Perhaps in filming a collective discussion by women about female sexuality the problem could be resolved less dogmatically. This would locate the film itself, historically, within the Movement because it would demonstrate organisational principles like the small group and introduce concepts such as sexism and consciousness-raising. Most importantly it would be women speaking 'in their own words'. But aside from this hypothetical alteration the film as it stands makes an important contribution towards developing a theory of ideology based on the unconscious and it does this in an imaginative way.

'The Nightcleaners Part 1'

Claire Johnston

Spare Rib No. 40, October 1975

It's difficult to think of many films which have elicited the kinds of response *The Nightcleaners* has, both within the Women's Movement and on the Left in general. There have been two dominant types of response to the film, both resulting from a clash between the nature of the film, the sort of expectations people usually take with them to the cinema, and ideas about what 'political cinema' should concern itself with. The first dominant reaction is that the film is 'unwatchable' – in its search for new forms of political cinema, the film loses its coherence. The second aspect of the film which has infuriated many people is that it does not appear to give a blow by blow account of the nightcleaners' campaign itself, and is therefore not a 'useful' film to tell people about these kinds of struggles. However, these reactions mirror people's un-thought-out assumptions about what political film-making is, rather than what the actual film does, and the intentions of the film-makers.

What these reactions demonstrate most clearly is the widely held assumptions about the necessity for political cinema to produce the effect of realism, to show things as they really are. This question of realism in the cinema should not be confused with that of naturalism in other art forms. The central difference between the cinema and other art forms is that the cinema mechanically reproduces reality through the camera. This has led to the widely held belief that reality can be recaptured on film as in no other art form, and in this way, the idea of 'realism' has, throughout the entire history of the cinema, been used as an artistic justification for its existence. Often the term 'realism' is used as a label by film critics as a substitute for 'highly valued' and little more. The argument usually runs – this film is good because it lives up to *my image* of the essence of the medium – that is, the true nature of film is that it impassively reveals the world as it really is. This attitude has been, to a large measure, taken over unquestioned by political film-makers. It is an aesthetic position which is particularly strong in the field of television documentary, where the viewer, through camera style, use of commentary and editing (e.g. the *Man Alive* series) is made to feel that what is being presented to him/her is objective and impartial. The camera is supposed to be a neutral observer on the scene, and what we see is presented as the 'truth' of the situation. Often people see the manipulative aspect of television solely in terms of its political content. In fact, it is in the aesthetics of television forms that television's greatest ideological weapon really lies, a weapon which is used to encourage the passivity of the viewer, to suppress thought and to stress what is, rather than what might be. Political films usually aim at changing the content of the film, using the same mode of film-making as television documentaries. They present the 'correct' position (e.g. The Newsreel Group's new film on abortion) without opening up the contradictions within the situation or encouraging the viewer to think for him/herself. In this aspect they are just as oppressive as the established media.

Too often audiences and people writing about political films elevate their own dominant assumptions and their subjective responses into a way of judging a film without realising that these aesthetic problems should be examined more fully. *The Nightcleaners* is a film which radically challenges such assumptions and the ideology which spawned them, and as such I think it is the most important political film ever to have been made in this country.

The film was begun in December 1972, and Part 1 (Part 2 is not yet completed) took over four years to complete. It was conceived of originally very much in conventional terms, using extensive interviews, a neutral camera and all the other gimmicks characterising TV documentaries, but this time from the nightcleaners' point of view (intended for use in the campaign). However, the film grew into something quite different at the editing stage. Faced with their basically TV-style material, and comparing this with their experience during the shooting of the film, another conception of the film began to emerge, out of discussions and experiments around the editing table. The result is a film which, rather than tracing a series of political events in time, attempts to involve the viewer in a process of consciousness-raising. In this process we (as the film-makers say) 'will come to realise both the poverty of our own consciousness and the real possibilities for enriching it'. Someone I spoke to who saw the film remarked on how the images stayed with her for days (unlike traditional forms of documentary) in a quite disconcerting way. The film questions the traditional passivity of the spectator in the cinema. It attempts to create a situation whereby the viewer is not only able to participate, but is in fact required to do so – to make his/her contribution to the process of meaning-production which is the film. (By this I mean that a film of this kind makes a break with the idea of art as self-expression, which is essentially a bourgeois idea. Instead it poses the idea of film as a product where the act of filming and the act of viewing comprise two moments of equal value, neither having priority over the other. In this way the traditional division between work and leisure in capitalist society, with the viewer as passive consumer of the film, is broken down. The film is a material object in which meanings are produced, not by the film-maker alone, but by the film-maker and the viewer together.)

The film-makers also reject the widely held assumption that it is possible to give a report of such a struggle, no matter how committed one may be as a film-maker, without intervening in that event in some way. As a result, the film contains within itself a reflection of its own involvement in the history of the events being filmed, an involvement which necessarily re-stated and re-defined the events themselves. This aspect marks the film off from almost all political films which take their form from television. It does not attempt to document events as they happen. All we see are fragments from these events, often cut off quite arbitrarily, or frozen for us on the screen, sometimes repeated again and again. But, gradually, the systems which order and unite the various political, ideological and cultural events and processes become apparent as the film progresses, *if*, we, the viewers, are prepared to try and become aware of them. All the contradictory elements in the struggle (e.g. working-class consciousness together with traditional ideas about the family; internal stresses between the cleaners and union representatives; class differences between the leafletters and the nightcleaners) are brought to the fore and examined in the film. Simultaneously, the film incorporates various aesthetic devices (e.g. slow motion) to describe the nature of the work in great detail, and not least the devastating isolation, soul-destroying boredom and exhaustion.

One of the questions posed by the film, and perhaps its most important question for all of us, is what is a photographic image? Is it transparent and self-evident in its meaning, or is the question a more complex one? Can one just go somewhere and rely on the camera to record mechanically the real social processes at work? How is meaning produced in an image or a series of images edited together?

The Nightcleaners isolates images, reframes them, replaces the synchronised soundtrack with different sounds. It uses black leader, inserted in between shots, so that the screen goes black and we have time to think about the image we have just seen. The film scrutinises the kinds of images we are bombarded with daily in the media so that we see them afresh, the process by which they produce meaning is brought to the fore. We are made conscious of the way in which images, while appearing natural and obvious to the spectator, through their connotations, produce other meanings relating to the dominant ideology of the society in which we live. Conventional documentary techniques of editing have been developed which gloss over and disguise these aspects of the image. Their aim is to confirm the naturalness of the dominant ideology by which we live. Despite certain shortcomings in this respect (e.g. sometimes the demands put on the spectator are too great) *The Nightcleaners* could provide the basis – if critics and other political film-makers are prepared to abandon their reactionary TV ideologies – for a new direction in British political film-making. Approaching the film is rather like approaching a book. With a book the reader always has the opportunity to go back and reread some point which he/she has not been able to understand at the first reading. With most films, this is not the case – the viewer is trapped. One of the most innovatory aspects of *The Nightcleaners* is that it attempts to trace this process of rereading. We are no longer consumers of the film, we become part of a learning process.

Finally, something must be said about the central theme of the film which is the distance between the lived experience of the middle-class Movement women involved in the struggle and the cleaners themselves. The point is made visually near

the beginning of the film when we hear Movement women on the soundtrack discussing the notion of female sexuality while we see an image of a cleaner working
alone in a high office block shot at a distance and from below. The incongruity of
sound and image make their point which is returned to again and again in the film
to be amplified, re-examined and explored further. The problem of class differences
and the divisions within the socialist movement are rarely dealt with in political
films. Too often these contradictions are repressed by film-makers in favour of a
cosy romanticism. *The Nightcleaners* presents an honest vision of what such political work really entails. As Sally Alexander in her excellent article in *Red Rag* No. 6
about the campaign points out, 'the women's movement, like the rest of the left,
still has to learn how to popularise its ideas and politics successfully'. As the film-
makers themselves say, if one were making a film about any other struggle it would
not be possible to talk about such things. 'Women's Liberation has taught all of us.'
As the Women's Movement is redefining the class struggle, so is *The Nightcleaners*
redefining the struggle for revolutionary cinema.

The Perils of Film Policy

Simon Hartog

Independent Film Workshops in Britain, ed. Rod Stoneman (1979)

A personal view by Simon Hartog, convenor of the IFA London Region Film Policy Group

Abbreviations:

IFA – Independent Filmmakers' Association (founded in 1974, not to be confused with the organisation of the same name founded in 1934, with advisors such as John Grierson, Anthony Asquith, Paul Rotha and Basil Wright); AIP – Association of Independent Producers (founded in 1976 to represent the commercial producers, mainly those backed by the British duopoly of Rank and EMI and the American 'majors'); KRS – Kinematograph Renters' Association (trade association of major distributors, dominated by American companies); IFDA – Independent Film Distributors' Association (combining some of the older small private 'art' distributors with non-commercial radical groups such as Cinema Action and The Other Cinema); CEA – Cinematograph Exhibitors' Association (trade association of commercial exhibitors, mainly Rank, EMI, Classic, Granada, Star circuits); AIC – Association of Independent Cinemas (commercial 'independent' exhibitors); DTI – Department of Trade & Industry; DES – Department of Education and Science; NFFC – National Film Finance Corporation (set up in 1949 by Harold Wilson to provide loan capital for commercial production); BFFA – British Film Fund Agency (set up in 1957 to collect and pay out 'Eady' Levy to producers of registered British films); CFC – Cinematograph Films Council (trade dominated advisory committee to Department of Trade); NFDF – National Film Development Fund (set up in 1976 to provide national loans of up to £10,000 for the development of projects for commercial films); Terry Report (1976, Prime Minister's Working Party report, chairperson John Terry, '*On the Future of the British Film Industry*'); IAC Report (1978, report of the Interim Action Committee, chairperson, Harold Wilson, on proposals for establishing a BFA); BFA – British Film Authority (proposed body to amalgamate CFC, NFFC, BFFA and films division of Department of Trade).

Fact – Government Legislation for the Film Industry Expires in 1980

In response to the Terry and the IAC reports, and particularly to the complete ignorance of the existence and the character of the British independent cinema manifest in both official reports and the strategy adopted in them of merely providing a new umbrella, the BFA, for the same policy of State support for commercial production, the London Region of the IFA set up the Film Policy Group in the spring of 1978. The Government had yet to respond to the proposals and policies put forward in the Terry and Wilson committee reports, and it was felt that, although it was late and we had no experience of dealing with 'the commanding heights' of the State, we could not let the opportunity for an IFA intervention in the policy-making process pass, particularly since if we let the case for the British independent cinema go by default, by remaining unspoken, that would be it for at least ten years. (The Films Acts generally run for ten years.) After a long series of discussions, the Film Policy Group produced a draft submission to the Parliamentary Under-Secretary of State for Trade (Michael Meacher, junior minister in the Department of Trade, responsible for publishing, tourism and films) on the 'future of the British Film Industry'. The draft was circulated, discussed and amended at regional level, and after national approval sent to Michael Meacher in early July of 1978. The document was the first attempt by the IFA to agree a general analysis of Government film policy and define the demands of independent filmmakers in this country. Apart from the inherent difficulty of the task, there were a number of major external confusions. Both Terry and Wilson had recommended that the existing division of Government responsibilities for film between the DTI (commerce) and the DES (culture) should end and that responsibility for film be given to a single Government department and a single Minister of Arts who would have Cabinet rank. But for this to happen, the Prime Minister must decide it when s/he hands out and divides ministerial responsibilities. The attitude of the top civil servants in the DTI was also a factor, since Departments often resist such changes. The future of the BFI was also unclear. The Terry committee had recommended that the BFI should come under the BFA, but the Wilson committee had recommended that it should not. And the DES (responsible for the BFI) was letting the DTI (responsible for the Films Acts) handle the consultation with interested parties although there was an interministerial committee sitting to consider the matter with civil servants from both departments on it. In addition, the BFI's position on support for independent film was unclear.

Finally, while the Trade Minister (then E. Dell) had announced the Government's support in principle for the BFA in Parliament, it was clear that the support was not enthusiastic and that nobody seemed to have a clear idea of what the BFA was to be or to do. So we were trying to throw darts at a moving target in the dark while hoping that we would not do ourselves a grave injury in the process. Our initial submission received a moderate amount of press coverage (*Screen, Screen International, Financial Times, Variety* and *Sight and Sound*). Press comments were generally favourable, but our 'press campaign' was certainly too modest to have any major impact. A few weeks later the AIP published its proposals with much press fanfare. Basing their case for the need for State support for the commercial industry on cultural grounds, the AIP's proposals differed only slightly from those of the Terry and Wilson committees. They wanted the NFFC's terms of reference to be made less commercial/more cultural. They were very much in favour of the establishment of a BFA, and they called for the income from the Eady Levy to be distributed on a wholly selective basis instead of the current automatic distribution to the most commercially successful films. The IFA's position on these points was different with the exception of Eady distribution. We made the case for State support of films on cultural and social grounds, but, we argued, the way to do this was not to continue to prop up the commercial industry with public money. Instead, we proposed the extension and further development of the existing independent sector. On the BFA, we were somewhat ambiguous since in light of the Terry and Wilson proposals (and the membership of the two committees) we saw the BFA as a trade-dominated body. The first indication we had that our initial submission had made some impact came in a speech delivered at last year's Edinburgh Film Festival which was written by Michael Meacher. (A somewhat abridged version was published by *The Guardian.*) Broadly speaking, Meacher adopted our analysis and critique of Government film policy, while hinting at changes along the lines suggested by the AIP. The IFA and the AIP were of course not the only groups putting forward proposals and suggestions to Meacher, but the vested interests, the FPA, the KRS and the CEA were not saying anything in public about the contents of their representations to the Government. As far as one can tell they supported the creation of the BFA provided that there were no changes in the NFFC and Eady distribution policy and that, of course, the BFA had no powers to deal with the alliance of British and American multi-national monopolies which control the British film industry. The ACTT's position was somewhere between that of the FPA and the AIP, so the union was in no sense adopting a radical line. An IFA delegation met with Michael Meacher on September 19th to discuss our initial submission. (The full text has been re-printed in the current issues of *Film and Video Extra* which is available from the Film and Video Officer of the Greater London Arts Association.) It was clear that there was still a considerable gap between the Department of Trade's conceptions and mechanisms and our understanding of the situation and proposals for changing it. The 'Films Minister' nonetheless asked us to prepare a supplementary memorandum which would outline in greater detail the model and the cost of our proposals and to submit this to him as soon as possible, since the Government was planning to issue a White Paper in January 1979.

The process of drafting, discussion and amendment was completed at a meeting of the IFA's national committee in Nottingham on the 2nd and 3rd December. Basically, the document called for a new level of State support for film funded through the BFA on a grant rather than a loan basis. Building on the structure and practices developed by the British independent cinema during the last decade, we proposed a publicly funded independent sector, independent that is of commercial industry and, as far as possible given the source of the money, of the State. The sector which would include production, distribution and exhibition would be adequately funded and coherently structured. It would 'fit' between the commercial industry and the existing DES aid systems (BFI Production Board, RAAs etc.) and grew out of a critique of them. The existing aid to production, whether through the DTI or the DES, has, in our view, two crucial failings. First, it took no account of distribution and exhibition, and secondly, it was project based, consequently discontinuous. We proposed, therefore, a structure of production units with small permanent staffs which would be funded on the basis of a production programme over a number of years instead of funding for one-off projects. The definition of the unit's production programme and the decisions about which projects to produce would be the responsibility of the filmmakers in the unit rather than the committees of independent 'experts'. The range of production envisaged was determined by the range of practices manifest within independent filmmaking in this country. Funds for distribution would be included in production budgets, and the utilisation of the distribution funds would be decided by a council of the production units.

The production units would grow from 5 in the first year to 25 in the fifth year of the development programme. Each unit would have between 5 and 10 members, and there would be a policy of positive discrimination in favour of units outside London. To deal with exhibition we propose a circuit of 25 small cinemas throughout the country run, where possible, in conjunction with local production units, by exhibition co-operatives. These cinemas would receive capital and revenue grants for showing primarily British independent films. Apart from a capital fund of £1.5 million for these cinemas, we estimated that, at current prices, revenue grants for the sector would need to be about £1 million in the first year rising to about £3 million in the fifth year. That, in the broadest of terms and avoiding major economic and political problems, is the model and costing we submitted to Michael Meacher early in December. We had a second meeting with him to discuss our second paper on the 1st February, 1979. In correspondence with us prior to the meeting, he had indicated two major stumbling blocks to our detailed proposals. Firstly, the proper location of the IFA project in relation to the likely division of responsibilities for film between the BFI and the BFA, and secondly, the high rate of subsidy involved which the Department had, somewhat generously, calculated to be about £1 per seat. At our meeting with the Minister we argued that our model did not fit comfortably under either the BFI or a BFA but that if there was to be a real shift in government policy, this needed to be put into practice within the proposed Authority while continuing and increasing the resources available for production from the DES. At the request of Michael Meacher, we agreed to provide the Department with an estimate of the income from the sector to go with the costing in our supplementary paper and a definition of the independent sector 'for the layman' and to deliver these as soon as possible since the White Paper was to be published very soon. Although by then it was clear that legislation to establish the BFA (if it was to be established) was not going to be introduced before the 1980–1 session of Parliament, we had some hope that the White Paper and the planned short Bill to refund the NFFC might contain at least some of the things we had been pressing for, even though we had no direct or definite confirmation of this from Meacher. Neither the White Paper nor the Bill appeared before Parliament was dissolved.

The Independent Film-makers' Association and the Fourth Channel

John Ellis

Screen Vol. 21 No. 4, 1980

Introduction

A fourth national broadcast television channel is to begin transmission in Britain in Autumn 1982. Over the past year, the necessary legislation and basic organisation of the Fourth Channel have been produced. We publish here two related papers that have formed the basis of the Independent Film-makers' Association's campaigning and lobbying during this process.

The idea of a fourth channel has been debated for several years. The Annan Committee on the Future of Broadcasting recommended in 1977 that the new channel should be operated by an Open Broadcasting Authority, separate from both the BBC and the Independent Broadcasting Authority, and acting as a publisher rather than a producer of programmes. The eventual legislation introduced into Parliament by a Conservative government in 1979 is much less radical. It proposes that the new channel should be under the control of the Independent Broadcasting Authority, and should have close ties with the existing commercial television companies which operate the present ITV franchises. Indeed, the designation originally proposed for the new channel was 'ITV 2', the title 'The Fourth Channel' being the government's sole concession to the Labour opposition during the course of the bill through Parliament. The exact mechanism for the Fourth Channel is that it should be financed from the excess profits levy currently paid by ITV franchise-holders to the Treasury. This will be diverted to form an initial 'contribution' which will fund the first five years of the channel's operation, after which its own advertising income is expected to be enough to fund it. In return, the existing ITV companies will manage the channel's advertising, and provide a large proportion of its programmes, thus making use of their excess studio space.

The channel itself is to be organised as a company which does not produce any of its own material for broadcasting, but buys it from various sources. One major source will obviously be the existing ITV companies; the other is an amorphous sector known as the 'independents'. This definition covers both major multi-national operators like Lorimar (the producers of *Dallas*) or the Robert Stigwood Organisation, as well as radical innovators. News coverage will be provided by ITN (Independent Television News), which services the ITV companies. Overall, very little money will be available: if the channel is to provide about 35 hours per week when it begins transmission, it is estimated that it will have an average of £30,000 to pay for each hour of material: roughly the cost of a chat-show on the existing channels. The situation, then, is one in which the channel's options are extremely restricted, and there would appear to be little chance that any genuinely radical work could appear.

However, the debates that have taken place around the character of the new channel had at least one important effect. The legislation setting up the channel stipulates that it should encourage 'innovation and experiment in form and content'. These few words are perhaps the closest that legislation has ever come to specifying aesthetic criteria for television. They have provided the basis for the IFA's campaign to ensure that genuinely independent film and video workers will provide a significant proportion of the Fourth Channel's output. Several papers have been published stating the views of the IFA, and these have gained wide support from other groups (e.g. the Women's Film and Broadcasting Lobby, the Channel Four Group), from Labour, Liberal and *Plaid Cymru* parliamentarians, and from some members of the Fourth Channel Board. Of these papers, we publish two. 'Channel Four and Innovation – The Foundation' (February 1980) details the IFA proposal for an organisational mechanism which can provide a 'catalyst and guarantee for innovation and experiment for the Fourth Channel', a proposal that is currently under active consideration. The second is a discussion document 'British TV Today' (November 1980), which attempts to characterise current television output and the points at which innovation and experiment are both possible and highly necessary.

Major organisational decisions about the Fourth Channel are being made at considerable speed. As soon as the legislation had been passed through the Commons, the IBA appointed a 'shadow' Board for the new Fourth Channel Company*. They in turn have appointed their Chief Executive, Jeremy Isaacs, and Programme Controller, Paul Bonner. By the beginning of 1981, it is expected that the precise mechanics of the channel will have been decided, including whether it is to have a Foundation along the lines proposed by the IFA.

---

* The Board of the Fourth Channel: Chair, Edmund Dell (former Labour Trade & Industry Minister, now with Guinness Peat merchant bankers); Vice-Chair, Sir Richard Attenborough (film director); representatives of ITV companies, Brian Tesler (London Weekend TV), David McCall (Anglia), William Brown (Scottish TV); other members, Roger Graef (documentarist), Dr Glyn Tegai-Hughes (University of Wales), Hon Mrs Sara Morrison (former chairman, Conservative Party), Anthony Smith (Director, British Film Institute), Ann Sofer (Camden Labour councillor), Joy Whitby (children's programmes, Yorkshire TV).

Channel Four: Innovation or ITV2?

IFA Documents, 1980

In his key speech to the Royal Television Society in Cambridge guiding the IBA's deliberations on the Fourth Channel, the Home Secretary clearly stressed demands that the service should:

- be distinctive
- give new opportunities to creative people
- extend the range of programmes available to the public
- find new ways of servicing minority and specialised audiences
- give due place to innovation

This emphasis, together with the clear intention that TV4 should not become ITV2 pleased and stimulated a wide range of independent media interests.

In spite of consultation between the IBA and representatives from this extensive sector of groups, individuals and companies who have the capacity to produce material for the channel, the IBA have produced a report extraordinary in its capacity to misconstrue, dilute and simply ignore their suggestions. By delivering the channel into the hands of the ITV programme contractors the IBA's proposals even reverse the Home Secretary's intentions, providing a virtual blue-print for the ultimate and inevitable emergence of ITV2.

Whilst some large and small production companies whose interests are commercial rather than cultural might expect to gain access, the majority of independents who reasonably expected the report to respond to their proposals are united in their disappointment and condemnation.

... Where is the structure which would ensure real distinctiveness, a real extension of the range of programmes?
... Where is there a genuine concern for minority and special interests?
... Where are the new opportunities for creative people and the framework for innovation?
... Where are the ideas for the new structures of access?
... Where is the positive policy to redress television's shameful record in the employment of women?

The failure by the IBA to take any account of the views of the very sector from which real innovations would emerge indicates that a special mechanism must be established to implement and formalise the access of this creative sector to the Fourth Channel. The mechanism that we propose is a Foundation in close contact with its constituency and shielded from overriding commercial interests. This is the only way of achieving the cultural aims expressed in the Cambridge speech. Such a Foundation would have the primary function of funding groups, organisations and individuals for the production of genuinely innovative programmes to be transmitted on the new channel.

The basis of such production exists in the already extensive, but under-funded independent film and video movement widespread throughout Britain and organised in the Independent Film Makers' Association (IFA). Its range extends from creative works of fiction through newsreel and documentary. It is innovative in subject matter, form and methods of production. Unlike mainstream television it is in close touch with the needs and aspirations of social, ethnic, regional, educational and cultural minorities. The existing network of regional film and video workshops provides an obvious basis for expansion and development.

The Foundation should have an independent legal existence with a governing body responsible for major funding and policy decisions with members nominated by the Board of the Fourth Channel, film and video makers' organisations and other cultural bodies.

It would also be concerned to develop communication with viewers through complementary publications and events, perhaps similar to those developed by the Open University.

While its first function would be the funding of individual projects for transmission, the Foundation would also of necessity concern itself with developing innovatory approaches to scheduling which challenge existing practice. The Foundation would be funded from a small percentage of the channel's annual budget.

An adequately funded Foundation is the only means of ensuring that the new channel's cultural and social obligations will be, at least in part, fulfilled.

The IFA and the ACTT: A Piece of Paper

Simon Hartog

Paper circulated at the IFA Annual Conference, 1981

Since the ACTT decided to involve itself in independent production by agreeing codes of practice with the Production Board and the RAAs, by setting up a sub-committee of its Films Branch to deal with independent films, and by promising tickets to eligible members of the IFA who do not have them, there has been much discussion about the union's initiative within the IFA. As a long-time member of both the ACTT and the IFA, I am concerned that little of this discussion in the IFA has concentrated on the question of the impact the union's initiative will have on the IFA. Assuming that the ACTT acts on its promise about tickets and that there is a reasonably democratic structure for independent film makers within the union, there will be two organisations (with overlapping membership) with defensible claims to speak for independent cinema. The consequences of a major difference of policy could be dire, particularly for the IFA. Avoiding damaging differences between the IFA and the ACTT independents must be a priority. In any case the process of adjustment to the new position is, for the IFA at least, not likely to be either quick or simple.

In the short term, membership problems are the most pressing. The union is selective and the IFA is not. Not all IFA members work in grades organised by the ACTT, and, hence, not all IFA members are eligible to join the union. Those in the IFA who are eligible and who wish to join the union will have to apply. On what basis the decisions on the applications will be taken and who will take them are still unclear. One way for the IFA to combat a murky, arbitrary application process would be to suggest a concrete set of guidelines for the use of the union committee or committees that make the initial recommendation on membership applications. Even if only to be able to deal with applications from film makers who are not members of the IFA, the union will itself probably feel the need for a set of guidelines. If that does happen, the IFA will have to make suggestions about the contents of the guidelines, either formally or informally, but before doing that the IFA's attitude to the principle of guidelines needs to be decided. In any case, the IFA must do all it can to ensure that the process of applying for union membership as an independent film maker is both clear and fair.

Grant-Aided Workshop Production Declaration (Abridged)
ACTT

Promulgated by the ACTT in consultation with the representatives of the English Regional Arts Associations and the Welsh Arts Council, the Channel Four Television Company and the British Film Institute. (Revised March 1984.)

1. The English Regional Arts Associations, the Welsh Arts Council, Channel Four Television and the British Film Institute undertake to make the terms and conditions of employment contained in this Declaration, reached after full consultation and discussion between them and the Union, a condition of grant-aid to such Workshops or other organisations recognised by the Union under the provisions of this Declaration and to observe and promote the principles contained in the Declaration.

2. Workshops and other organisations eligible for accreditation under this Declaration shall be exclusively those whose sources of revenue funding are derived from public bodies, charities and other organisations and individuals, where it is explicitly stated and understood that funding is provided on a totally non-commercial and non-profit distributing basis. Disputes on the definition of eligibility in individual cases shall be adjudged by a National Committee of representatives of the organisations named in the preamble to this Declaration, whose majority decision shall be given serious weight by the ACTT, with whom the responsibility of a final decision will lie. The funding bodies shall derive no commercial or other monetary entitlements in any of the productions emanating from any Workshop or other organisation operating under the provisions of this Declaration. Specifically no funding body shall demand, expect or be granted any rights in the commercial exhibition or distribution of any production made under this Declaration, or any similar subsidiary rights relating to activities supplementary to that production. Revenue and capital funding bodies shall however reserve the right to reclaim up to the level of each grant in each case where the need for such a grant cannot be demonstrated.

3. The Union and the other parties consulted in drawing up this Declaration do so in the explicit belief and with the explicit intention of encouraging the cultural, social and political contribution made to society by the grant-aided and

non-commercial production activities historically undertaken by persons and organisations in this sector. In recognition of the specifically non-commercial character of the work undertaken in this sector no Workshop or organisation shall be eligible to operate under the provisions of this Declaration unless they are able to satisfy the Union that they are non-profit distributing and that any surpluses generated by their production activities shall be wholly reinvested in the activities and infrastructure of the Workshop or organisation and shall not be distributed to persons or organisations in the form of dividends, gratuities or other supplementary payments not related to the payments specified under the provisions of this Declaration. Funds remaining upon the dissolution of any recognised Workshop or other organisation once members' legitimate claims have been met shall be used to benefit only non-profit distributing organisations of the same or similar aims and objectives. Any Workshop or organisation fulfilling these basic conditions, which may not be varied, and properly able to observe the other provisions in this Declaration to the satisfaction of the Union, may apply to the Union for recognition as a proper Workshop or organisation under this Declaration.

4. Further to the foregoing provisions, all rights in productions originated by the permanently employed staffs within a Workshop or other organisation recognised under this Declaration shall be held collectively by those staffs and all contractual arrangements shall be approved collectively by the staffs employed under the terms of this Declaration within any Workshop or other organisation. At the discretion of the recognised Workshop or other organisation this provision may apply to ancillary staff members who may, subject to the agreement of the Union, be members of other appropriate trade unions.

5. Notwithstanding the foregoing provisions, where a production by any recognised Workshop or other organisation is subsequently considered for commercial exhibition or distribution by any person or company or other body, the Workshop or other organisation shall first obtain the approval of the Union for such use of a production which shall not be granted unless and until a sum of money is paid to the Union equivalent to the difference in cost of production under the provisions of this Declaration and the cost of production under the full terms and conditions of the appropriate ACTT Agreement.

6. After consultation with those organisations integral to the formulation of this Declaration, the Union shall at its own discretion, grant the right to operate under this Declaration. Recognising the diverse character of public and other funding arrangements in the grant-aided sector, the Union shall recognise the Workshop or other organisation for a period of one year, two years or three years. Prior to the expiry of these periods, a Workshop or organisation may re-apply to operate for a further fixed term under this Declaration which shall normally be granted where

the financial, organisational and other circumstances of the Workshop or other organisation remain substantially unchanged.

7. Further to the above conditions for recognition under this Declaration, where the Union deems this necessary, any Workshop or organisation so recognised shall agree to provide to a properly qualified person or persons nominated by the Union a proper balance sheet and audited statement of accounts in order to demonstrate that the conditions specified in the preamble to this Declaration are fully and properly adhered to. Any Workshop or other organisation shall be asked to contribute an agreed sum in order to finance this necessary service. The Union undertakes to make such audited accounts and any written assessments of them available to the other organisations named in the preamble to this Declaration.

8. Any Workshop or other organisation shall provide the Union with a written undertaking, see appendix A, committing themselves to accept, without exception the above provisions and those which follow. All permanently employed staffs within a Workshop or other organisation shall be held individually and jointly responsible as members of the Union for the proper observation of the provisions of this Declaration. Failure to honour the terms of that written undertaking shall result in the withdrawal of Union recognition from any such Workshop or other organisation.

9. Recognising that this Declaration makes special and beneficial provisions for permanently employed staffs in the cultural and grant-aided sector, and further recognising the 'special' status of productions by Workshops and other organisations recognised under this Declaration, the Union has established through agreement with Channel Four Television, Quota arrangements limiting the number of hours of grant-aided regional production which may be screened by the Fourth Channel each year. Production by recognised Workshops or other organisations are covered by these Quota arrangements.

10. No less than four members of ACTT shall normally be regularly employed in a recognised Workshop or other organisation under this Declaration. Regular employment shall be on the basis of one, two and three year contracts in accordance with the arrangements specified earlier in this Declaration. The terms and conditions of employment of these ACTT members shall be no less favourable than the provisions stated in this Declaration and shall cover salary, insurance, holiday entitlements and such other matters as are specified subsequently.

11. Where a Workshop or other organisation is still engaged in generating sufficient funding, in accordance with Clause 2 above, but is otherwise able to satisfy all other provisions of this Declaration required for recognition by the Union, that

Workshop or other organisation shall be entitled to apply to the Union for *provisional franchising* which constitutes interim recognition by the Union which the Union may grant at its discretion. In the event that the provisionally franchised Workshop or other organisation subsequently succeeds in developing a level of funding appropriate to the fulfilment of the obligations given to the Union when provisional franchising was obtained, they shall inform the Union who, in the event of funding, shall grant the Workshop or other organisation *full recognition*. No Workshop or other organisation may engage in any production or related activity under the provisions of this Declaration until they have received full recognition under this Declaration.

12. Where a Workshop or other organisation seeking recognition under this Declaration includes among its proposed regularly employed staff individuals who are not members of the Union, those persons shall be required to obtain Union membership under such terms as the Union's rules and membership shall determine. The Union undertakes not to withhold such membership.

13. Recognising the cultural nature of the work undertaken under this Declaration, the Union may at its discretion permit a Workshop or other organisation to employ non-members on certain projects or programmes of work, who shall be employed on a non-regular basis in accordance with the salary schedule contained in this Declaration.

14. Workshops and other organisations recognised under this Declaration shall be production-oriented, i.e. they shall be organisations expressly constituted for the purpose of engaging in production. It is, however, recognised that in the cultural and grant-aided sector a range of other activities have and will continue to constitute important elements in the practices characteristic of the sector. These supplementary activities may include exhibition, education, distribution, administration, research or any other activity seen as necessary but supplementary to the central activity of production. Union members engaged under the provisions of this Declaration may continue to engage in these activities in addition to engaging in production, except where inter-Union relationships may require consultation with other bodies.

15. Recognition under this Declaration shall, in addition to all other provisions specified in this Declaration, require any Workshop or other organisation seeking recognition to demonstrate to the satisfaction of the Union a record of past production and supplementary activities in the grant-aided and cultural sector which indicate a genuine and ongoing commitment to the specific objectives, practices and output of the sector.

16. In recognition of the integrated nature of the activities specified in Clause 14 above, the Union recognises that it is necessary and proper that any regularly employed staff member operating within a recognised Workshop or other organisation shall be free to engage in any of these activities and may perform with the agreement of the member and the consent of the other regularly employed members within the recognised Workshop or other organisation, any role in relation to the pre-production, production, and post-production activity.

The IFA: Film Club/Trade Association
Frank Abbott

New Cinema Workshop Bulletin, 1983

I am writing about the Independent Filmmakers Association in the light of discussions that have been going on within the East Midlands.

While what I say comes partly out of the situation we find ourselves to be in here, it may well relate to other workshops in a similar position. This leads on to some thoughts about the IFA nationally.

In the East Midlands, we have seen the IFA develop from a small pressure group of film activists to a much larger group of mainly filmmakers concerned generally with all aspects of film culture in the region. Whereas the initial group was able to unite on a fairly basic level in terms of demands for equipment, screening facilities, production funding, film education, etc., etc., and to provide a cohesive and coherent voice in relation to the region's film institutions, we find a very different situation today.

With many of the IFA's *basic* demands in Nottingham fulfilled, there is a production workshop, a reasonable RAA production budget, a cinema that screens independent work, IFA members active in education work, day schools, writing, etc.; we find that the local IFA group, the largest it has ever been, is casting around for a role for itself. The cinema is programmed by a full-time programmer – with IFA input – the workshop is run by an underpaid staff, who submit equipment applications and manage it – with IFA support – much integrated programming and production initiatives are carried on by liaison between individual IFA members and the different institutions – with IFA support. But all this activity goes on outside of the organisation of the IFA. The IFA itself is the site of debate around financial/structural/contractual aspects of film production (ACTT, Channel 4, BFI, ACGB, RAA), the point for debating detailed strategies, approaches, applications – almost like the debates of a professional association over lobby politics. These debates oscillate between the region and the National Executive of the IFA and are obviously of great importance in developing and maintaining independent film as an establishment, an establishment we have worked long and hard to establish.

However, counter to this debate in the local IFA, there is another debate which says that these issues do not concern many new members – that they joined to develop their confidence, make films and establish their practice. At the stage they are working at, the most important thing for them is film cultural debate – discussion of their work, screenings and education in film production, distribution and exhibition. The IFA is alienating these people by not providing them with what they require by its obsession with the minutiae of lobby politics.

The way this debate falls out in practice has, in the East Midlands, been roughly along two lines: both of which I feel are inadequate.

The first line argues that the IFA must continue to pursue its 'lobby politics' but must also engage in a process of education of its membership and maintain its organised education, discussions, screenings, debates, etc., to develop this – thus politically educating the new membership in the importance of obscure seeming institutions like the BFI, ACTT, etc., in the long run. I find this position idealist in that it is based on the false premise that the new membership of the IFA would adopt the same political stance as the old members if they were educated about it. Because of the established nature of the IFA we are now attracting a new membership, many of which do not share the activist, campaigning political thrust of the original membership – they merely want to make films and membership to the IFA is one pre-requisite for doing that.

The second line is that the IFA should return to its 'origins' – base its work around screenings and discussions – cultivate an open educational atmosphere in which films, and what we do with them, are the thing – and if anyone is interested in Channel 4 or the ACTT, well, let them discuss it amongst themselves. This position seems to me to betray all the IFA ever was, since it ignores the notion of film culture as a political entity and tries to turn the IFA into a finishing school for ex-art students and reduces film work to hobbyism. It does nothing in terms of the political transformation of film practice which, if you look back to the first IFA conference, was embodied in the papers and discussions.

Both these positions seem to me to be flawed because they place the development of the IFA within the context of film culture, in splendid isolation from the rest of left culture in this country. The IFA East Midlands, a voluntary organisation of 50 people, cannot run film culture in the region and should not wish to. To do so would place it in an institutional role which would preclude its more important task of evolving and developing a specifically radical Left cultural practice in the region. It should work and pressure in every way to establish institutions which give the opportunity for Left cultural work to take place, and seek to transform the reactionary ideas of the institutions it comes into contact with. It should also fight for the opportunity for new sectors to enter the field of film production, discussion and viewing, if those new sectors bring a progressive approach to that area. It cannot, however, be a step on the ladder towards film production for anyone who wishes to take part, whether they want to grapple with the genuine political problems or not.

Finding unity around a programme of aims like the above is, however, problematic. When the IFA was formed, the current theory of the two avant-gardes, developed by Peter Wollen, exemplified a theoretical rule-of-thumb which enabled the IFA to contain within it the most incredible diversity of practices defined in some way as oppositional. Since then, the IFA has held together under 'cinema of social practice' and the current definition 'the grant aided sector'. However, with the current mixed economy of production, with public and commercial finance, Channel 4, co-productions, the rock/video industry, the information market and the prospect of profits looming at some point, the sector has outgrown its own self-definitions. In the East Midlands the label is degenerating into 'anyone interested in film & video'. This is a worrying development since it could presage the IFA settling into the niche of defending the interest of filmmakers whose practice has been defined as 'independent' within the context of the present definitions of film culture. It moves away from any notion of analysing or challenging the present structure, since its role is safely defined within that structure and becomes what might be termed a trade association campaigning on behalf of its own member-ship.

The question then becomes, 'is the IFA the kind of organisation now which can work to reflect a left political stance in film and left culture generally?' Or does a new organisation need to be set up to raise and carry forward the very real ques-tions of how oppositional filmmakers relate to the newly emergent mixed economy of production and distribution, re-raise the question of the state and independence, look at film culture and mass culture, look at the relations of how professionalism and the 'community', democracy and access, politics and form – all questions which cannot be restricted to discussion and practice within the context of film cul-ture – they need to be addressed to a wider arena – the Labour party and the Left, the trade unions, the newly emergent socialist society of the Left publications, com-munity and ethnic groups and other cultural workers in theatre, television, writing, music, etc. Would a large body of filmmakers in the IFA even recognise these ques-tions as relevant to their practice?

While it is important to maintain, within our area of practice, a clear cultural specificity – film and television is what we know and are concerned about – this is different to insularity – and the extent to which we progressively appear to be a trade association looking after its own interests, the less we will be able to make credible contacts with other groups, the more suspicious will people be of our wider cultural and political concerns.

I hope that the AGM of the IFA will enable us to debate these issues out and enable the organisation to move forward with an outward looking political dynamic that will enable us to attract and work with a wider politicised member-ship through a series of concrete public alliances and shared platforms with other sectors of the Left.

'So That You Can Live (For Shirley)'

Michael Chanan

Framework No. 18, 1982 (expanded from *Tribune*, 20 November 1981)

The most important British independent film since Berwick Street Film Collective's *Nightcleaners*, Cinema Action's *So That You Can Live (For Shirley)* is in many ways a very simple film, about a family in a South Wales valley community which has been struck down in the last five years – the period over which the film was made – by the socially destructive consequences of pit and factory closures and the result-ing unemployment. The opening moments introduce us to the Family, Shirley and Roy Butts and their children, Diane and Royston; then to the themes of the film presented through titles and readings ('Seeing the history of the country in the shapes of the land. A collective reflection on change and relationship') and in the shape of Diane in London reflecting on her inadequate education, and then a man surveying the South Wales landscape in which the processes of capitalism have become ingrained, with the comment, 'Had I known I would be as interested as this at my age I would have known a lot more about it because I'd have asked ques-tions ...' We see a small group of people examining an old photo ('Oh, it used to be a pretty place') and after a brief shot of a children's band of drummers rehears-ing on a hillside ('March up to the camera and then turn round') which carries echoes of a previous culture and returns several times during the film like a *leit-motiv*, we then find ourselves on a picket line outside the GEC factory on the Treeforest Industrial Estate a few years back, with Shirley as AUEW convenor at the head of a mass of women who've been locked out in the course of an equal pay struggle. A speaker (Hywel Francis) then reads to camera an account of the libraries in the Miners' Institutes which were established around the turn of the century ('There was no comparable educational institution generated entirely by a prole-tarian culture existing anywhere else in the world during this period'). Then we accompany Shirley on a bus ride as she talks about her working life. Apart from a motor cycle race meeting and an evening sing-song at the local club, these are vir-tually all the elements of this 85 minute film: family, the inscription of history in the landscape over which the camera is constantly and searchingly panning, and the remnants of history in artefacts like photos and books; education and learning; work, and struggle in the workplace; community and culture.

The simplicity of the basic elements is important to observe: they are fewer than would be typically employed in a conventional TV documentary on the same sub-ject of even merely a third of the length. In contrast to the nervous rapid movement from one sequence to another by which such films try to give the impression that everything has been covered, when actually we're never given time to reflect on what is shown, *So That You Can Live* represents a kind of minimal film making. To my mind it's an example of what the Cuban film maker Julio Garcia Espinosa advocated in his seminal essay 'For An Imperfect Cinema'. This extends to the camerawork, which isn't, to be honest, particularly artistic, like that of the television documentary – but then the beautiful but unimaginative framing of the classic television image encloses it in a way that resists the viewer's entry into the world. Here the slow pacing of the film ensures that we have plenty of time for reflection as the elements I've just listed unfold and we learn how the Butts family have had to struggle to survive.

I don't want to say that the simplicity of the film is illusory. It isn't. Yet the way these elements are montaged establishes a relationship between them which gives us access to the real complexity of the subject. This is also a function of two other factors: the relationship of the film makers to the family, and the incorporation of texts by Raymond Williams, himself a South Wales man. These texts come from a variety of sources: *The Country and the City*, the novel *The Fight for Manod*, and *Politics and Letters*, which Cinema Action used while making the film to develop their understanding of the chosen subject. There are also some texts which Williams wrote specially for the film after seeing the rough cut. These texts are both read out by Diane and appear in the form of titles. They are nothing like an exterior commentary. They are like a voice from deep within the film, and never do we get the idea that they are words which the film makers have put into Diane's mouth. The way the film represents the film makers' relationship to the family forbids this. Following Shirley's bus ride, for example, we come to Diane recalling the first time she met Cinema Action: 'I was at my gran's and my mother was late coming to pick us up from work so I went down the house myself, and my father answered the door, and there were all these strange people there, and lights – 'cause I didn't know you then – so I just walked straight through into the back because I was really shy, and my father came out after a while and told me that Mam had invited you in, and what you was doing. So I just went in then and sat down and listened ...'

Now in this and other ways, not only do the subjects of the film get drawn into Cinema Action's quest to understand their subjects' situation, but the film also fulfils precisely one of the criteria of imperfect cinema, which is 'to show the process which generates the problems'. I prefer this reference to the idea of imperfect cinema rather than relating the film to theories of structuralist film making, with the typical obligation they impose upon the film to employ self-reference or some other display of theoretical self-awareness, because the method the film employs is no mere abstract exercise; it goes far beyond theoreticist stipulations. The film is not at all anti-theoretical – witness the pleasure it takes in showing us an old copy of *Capital* from an Institute library with its pencilled notes: 'First read pages 364 to 387 ... Secondly skip everything to conclusion of book and observe how the plot turns out ...' (So much for Althusser.) But it is not, in the normal sense, an ana-lytic film. As Garcia Espinosa explained: 'To analyse, in the traditional sense of the word, always implies a closed prior judgement. To analyse a problem is to show the problem – not the process – permeated with judgements which the analysis itself generates a priori. To analyse is to block off from the outset any possibility for analysis on the part of the interlocutor.' Instead of analysis, the process of trying to understand: Diane reading the texts and struggling to make them intelligible. Or the camera trying to read the landscape.

In this sense, simple as it is, the film presents difficulties. The non-analytic approach gives the film an intense lyricism, but there are already reports that some people – middle class, to be sure – are disturbed by the sense of loss which it pro-jects, which is also expressed through the film's simple and direct music. Yet the film is correct to insist on the cultural loss that has taken place, the demise, for example, of the Institutes and their libraries, which Hywel Francis explains as the combined effect of the growth of secondary education and what he calls the 'recre-ational revolution' of television and bingo and club life – or presumably, more accurately, the commercialization of the clubs. It is true that there are problems here, and this is the area to which I myself would direct such criticisms as I have of the film. The club where we see Shirley singing is not a commercialized one, but if it suggests the struggle to retain a sense of community it is nonetheless a pathetic scene – in the best sense of the word, the sense Tchaikovsky meant in the title of his *Pathetic Symphony*. There is something awkward about this, perhaps a certain evasiveness. But it's wrong to suppose that the film falls into sentimentality. In the final sequence Diane reads out questions from an O-level economics paper – 'What factors influenced the location of manufacturing industry?', 'Discuss the likely eco-nomic effects of the long-term closure of the Severn Bridge' – in a way that shows she has acquired an understanding of the difference between the two kinds of his-tory: the school kind she gave up when she was 13, and the kind she learned from her gran's.

Slow and beautifully controlled, a poetry unfolds in this film of enormous depth of feeling and lucid intelligence, and in this way it becomes a passionate plea for the voice of conscience to be heard again in the labour movement. For the word and the idea to become once again part of our vocabulary, as it was for previous generations. For us all to look around and see, in the shapes and forms of our envi-ronment, what parents and grandparents tell to those who ask of what is only recently past, the history of living memory.

This is a film which should be seen, not on television but in live gatherings, in factories and schools and halls in every community up and down the country where a sense of community can still be found. For wherever that may be, I cannot imag-ine that it won't be felt as a film of great strengthening quality.

Sins of Commission

Rod Stoneman

Abbreviated from *Screen* Vol. 33 No. 2, Summer 1992
(by permission of Oxford University Press)

> An oblique encounter with television, the provenance of independents, the role of
> chance, the passage of workshops and diverse other stories ...

This article attempts to chart a particular encounter with television across a decade
and is articulated from inside one of the broadcasting institutions. It has its origins
in a rather specific personal trajectory stretching from involvement in para-*Screen*
theory of the late seventies,[1] via some independent programme production[2] to
work as an apparatchik of Channel Four almost from its conception in the early
eighties. As Consultant, then Assistant Commissioning Editor, and Deputy Commissioning Editor, this work has developed as part of a project for radical television
that started inside an institution (soon calling itself The Company) itself taking
shape in the dawning of more optimistic aspirations.

The image of Channel Four often encountered abroad as an inspiring beacon, an
exemplary model of a new generation of publisher-broadcasters is projected as myth,
nature or fetish. From afar, an imaginary unity is often imposed on the divergences
and differences which fissure any organization. The Independent Film and Video
Department has contributed significantly to Channel Four's image through commissioning and buying a range of political and personal-documentary, experiment,
access and community programmes, low-budget fiction and third-world cinema.
The department's annual budget has risen from about £1.5 million in 1981/2 to a
peak of £10 million in 1990; adding up to perhaps £50 million and around a thousand hours of programmes passing through the department in the last ten years.

The '*d'ou je parle*'

Outside, inside, elsewhere – the position from which one speaks inevitably under-
lies what is said and how it is said, perhaps not as a sole determination but certainly
as a considerable factor in this discourse, these explanations ... Whatever the connection with and concern for the independent sector, there are different agendas
and time scales for someone working inside Channel Four – it is sometimes an
unbridgeable gap. It is never easy to live one thing and think another. These views
may draw fire as a great deal is at stake in this outline of unsteady perceptions, partial analyses and fallible decisions. Unlike other semi-academic interventions too
many livelihoods have been affected by these arguable tendencies.

Carrying the unwieldy framework of seventies *Screen* theory into the practice of British broadcasting has involved a curious journey leading to some strange connections – manifest, for example, in the unlikely experience of reading two magazines entitled *Iris*: one a scholarly journal of film theory published in French and English by Bordwell and Thompson, the other an irregularly published Irish Republican magazine featuring a section entitled 'War News' – the direct speech of the IRA. The unusual intersection of otherwise discrete discourses leads to an ironic and relativist distance between the various 'worlds' at play and a momentary displacement of the self from the actual field of engagement.

Any self-examination in terms of class, gender and race raises the questions of who ends up in television? Whatever the identity people initially bring to television, the work and its context eventually have an effect: gradual implicit institutional repositioning.

Clearly there are disproportionately low numbers of women, non-white or working-class people in positions of power in British television. Three of the thirteen Channel Four Board members were women in 1983, in 1991 the numbers remain the same. Perhaps more significantly there were four women among the original thirteen commissioning editors, while almost a decade later it is only two out of sixteen. But of those from such groups that have 'got through', unless they strive to remain consciously connected to their communities of interest and their original imaginary identities, they can become displaced, deflected and repositioned. There is something sad in the spectacle of disavowal as powerful individuals, recently confirmed in position, distance themselves from their constituencies in an exaggerated way, pulling the ladder up behind them.

One correlative gauge of the change in Channel Four over the years is that the initial, brave tendency to draw in editorial people from outside television has been gradually eroded as recruitment became increasingly oriented towards taking other 'professionals' from within television with prealigned and compatible ideologies. The original incorporation of someone like myself from the co-op end of the Independent Filmmakers' Association into the Channel Four Trojan horse seems rather less likely now.

In these curious and puzzling times when a number of dramatic historical shifts are taking place, when so many received ideas and values are challenged, a heightened degree of openness and self-questioning seems necessary. Despite the theoretical reflexivity of Marxism which (like psychoanalysis) should constantly re-examine its own project, discourses and determinations, left positions have too often been characterized by an inadequate grasp of the complexities of reality. The subtle dialectics of the original thought system can easily calcify into rather manichean understandings of the world.

Whilst restraining the dangers of introversion it seems relevant to refer to the hitherto unspeakable terrain of the autobiographical. Unspeakable in the sense that seventies *Screen* theory, like other forms of ultra-rationalist discourse traditionally inhibited the self (that which thinks it is 'I'), preferring forms of enunciation which avoided the personal pronoun.

Many factors determine the changes in perspective which distance this article, for instance (written in late 1991), from the last article I wrote on independent film published in *Screen* at the end of 1979.[3] Not least that the energy and focus of every-day life has shifted in a decade with the accretion of some more age/history, not to mention History itself . . .

The passage of workshops

This wider ranging article originated from an invitation to respond to Alan Lovell's 'That was the workshops that was'[4] which mounted several partial arguments seem-ingly at cross purposes with one another. It expounded an almost *ad hominem* employee/employer register of complaint, combined with imprecise (self-)criti-cism of workshop-sector programme-making, described as the 'degree zero of documentary' and finally drifted into an irrelevant restatement of cultural pop-ulism. For a historical materialist, albeit of an anarchist tendency, the critique is remarkably devoid of any sense of history or the dynamic of change, rather it dis-plays the small-business mentality that many in the workshop sector inexorably fell into.

Considerations of the provenance of the workshop movement begin from the base of the political possibilities of the late seventies; although there existed a longer preformulation of co-operative filmmaking aspirations amongst groups such as Cinema Action, the Berwick Street Collective, and Amber Films in Newcastle from the early seventies.

Many individual filmmakers and a few of the groups were drawn together at the First Festival of Independent British Cinema held in Bristol in February 1975. The rapid expansion of independent film workshops is indicated a few years later by at least twenty groups being represented at the Bristol conference held in May 1979[5] (a flurry of London groups declined to attend because they had not organized it and were predictably suspicious of a non-metropolitan initiative). Other, looser, umbrella organizations such as the London Filmmakers' Co-op, London Video Arts[6] and the idiosyncratic Fantasy Factory were creating and positioning them-selves at this time. The Sector, as it came to call itself, was increasingly self-identified and organized.

Part of the adjacent history of these movements was an earlier initiative to nationalize the entire British film industry; the ACTT published a report (that might fairly be characterized as ultra-left in origin and strategy) in the early seven-ties which proposed that the entire British industry should come into public ownership under workers' control as 'only public ownership can meet the creative, democratic and economic challenge of the years until the end of the century'.[7] This vanguardist initiative received little support among the wider membership and was quietly and quickly dropped.

By the late seventies echelons from the proto-workshop movement made direct and potentially fertile contact with the last Labour government. A little to everyone's surprise, discussions with Michael Meacher, then junior minister in the Department of Trade, led to the concrete proposal that a structure of small production units with permanent staffs be funded on the basis of a programme of work that would be carried out over a number of years instead of funding for one-off projects. Funds for distribution would be included in production budgets and a circuit of twenty-five small cinemas would be run by exhibition co-operatives. The definition of each unit's production programme and decisions about which projects it produced would be the responsibility of the filmmakers in the unit itself. The development programme proposed that five new workshops would be financed each year for five years (four of each five to be outside London).[8] It seemed as if the workshop sector's self-development might be expanded and sustained by substantial state funding. Enormous energy, potential and optimism pervaded discussions at this time as the conception was developed in a rapid and agile fashion and the infrastructure of innovative audiovisual co-operative units spread regionally.

The abrupt fall of that Labour administration initiated the epoch of Thatcher's conservatism and the end of the proposal. But within two years Channel Four, in partnership with the British Film Institute and other bodies, began to realize a scaled-down version of the same workshop strategy. Inevitably elements of this opportunistic transposition were problematic from the start – the attempt to place a large-scale long-term structure in a commercially funded, albeit public-service, television station.

The overall context of this period involved the movement of some sections of a dissident cultural intelligentsia into television (several from the *Screen*/BFI penumbra), carrying the values of late sixties radicalism into the broadcasting of the Thatcher years. Indeed the Annan Committee's 1977 recommendations can be seen as the last document of the benign post-war settlement, and Channel Four as its delayed and overdue progeny. It is a relevant irony that by the time the seventies lobbying was eventually effective, the television station it had created was based on the ideas and values from a previous epoch – belatedly launched into a rather new situation.

The nascent Channel Four had another ambiguity at its centre from its inception. Initiating a new generation of publisher-broadcasters, it opened the progressively pluralist possibilities of programming from a wide range of autonomous independents with variegated views. But this possibility was built upon the uninhibited choice of short-term insecure engagements from a pool of increasingly desperate semi-dependents competing in a 'free' market. Inevitably it involved the destruction of existing broadcasting infrastructures and of the continuity and security of employment in large broadcasting organizations. *Gauchiste* colleagues in the Channel Four Lobby Group and in the IPPA consistently disavowed the problem-

atic effect of imposing independent quotas on the political and employment structures of the television industry. Unfortunately, this – the central contradiction of
the Channel Four model and the dilemmas it poses – has rarely been discussed or
confronted.

The formulation of the much quoted remit within the 1980 Act: 'to innovate and
experiment in the form and content of programmes, cater for interests that ITV
does not, to provide a distinctive service …' was of course never unassailable. But
however vague or fragile, the notion of innovation is proving more durable and
graspable than the current fetishism of an ineffable 'quality'.

For the workshops the important thing to remember is that they, and (to some
extent) the unlikely bedfellows ITN, Diverse and Mersey Television (which makes
Brookside), were the only exceptions to the standard short-term relationship with
independents in that they were contracted for medium-term output (one to three
years) rather than programme by programme.

At its height a budget of about £2 million from Channel Four contributed to a
network of twelve to fifteen workshops each year. The original centrifugal aims
were manifest in the regional/national spread; two groups in Northern Ireland, one
in Scotland and two in Wales gave emphasis to non-British cultural and national
identities. Other specific priorities led to the support of four black and Asian workshops and three women's groups over the years, a considerable strengthening of the
production capacity of these sections of the independent sector and the representation of the communities of interest they connect with. The instigation of the
Workshop Declaration by the ACTT in 1984 involved a close and formalized role
for the film and television union in all discussions. Inevitably there were some frictions, part of a healthy syndicalist dynamic between the workshop committee and
Channel Four apparatchiks, but in general a workable relationship pertained.
Normally Channel Four was only interested in rights for British television and so
uncertainty, impatience and sometimes hostility grew around the special negotiations that were necessary to shift the balance of rights towards the Channel before
it would agree to provide the higher levels of finance involved in each low-budget
fiction film. There were also problems around the abstruse and obscure calculations necessary to operate the 'buy-back' formula – the fee payable on transmission
of a workshop programme.

Creative release occurred as archaic industrial craft demarcation lines were
successfully dissolved and workshop members could move flexibly between production roles – researcher one day, sound recordist the next, editor the day after.
Although understandably created as a syndicalist counteraction to unrestrained
employer exploitation and surplus value accumulation, these restrictions were
notoriously clumsy and ineffective in the production situation and, seen in an
international perspective, bizarre. There were some inevitable problems with the
relation between the co-operative/democratic impulse and creative processes of
production. For many groups the sensitive choice involved in prioritizing compet-

ing projects developed by different individuals within a non-hierarchic group was externalized – left to the broadcaster to select via its Commissioning Editors.

At a political and cultural level, with the exception of the connected and militant work done during the miners' strike, the regional infrastructure rarely came into productive relationship or realized its full potential. A network of autonomous groups owning and controlling their own means of production should surely have led to more energetic exchange and experiment, higher cultural profile, a profusion of video newsletters, pilots, polemics, poems and provocations.

Any fuller assessment and analysis of workshop programme-making should take place elsewhere but, in brief, the system produced in ten years many good, some extraordinary, and a few brilliant programmes. Certainly, many groups and individuals strengthened and developed their work in the looser space offered by a workshop contract and regional development. The examples of the much vaunted 'integrated practice', combining production with exhibition, distribution and training, working well in workshop structures were rarer. The balanced relation of production to the other connected activities was undermined and distorted by Channel Four's intervention itself. Quite quickly funded groups prioritized production for television and neglected their training and resource commitments.

Relatively few finished programmes (documentary or fiction) were characterized by the specifics of workshop production – that is to say relatively few could only have been made by long-term funded, co-operatively structured groups. From the viewer's perspective, which must weigh heavily, it is only that which is manifest in the text/on screen that counts. And despite the relative stability of continuity funding and closer relations with the communities in which they were situated, there were very few films or tapes which showed this in discernibly different ways from those of other independent production companies.

Although much was made of the workshops' relative autonomy enshrined in the contract, perhaps one can note that, from a perspective inside the Independent Film and Video Department, the experience of working with workshops was not very different from commissioning – in either the process or the cost of a production, or the aesthetics or politics of the result.

As part of the historical background of this period the TV AM lockout initiated the equivalent of a post-Wapping era in television industrial relations. Also the formal role that the ACTT had found was increasingly uncomfortable and anachronistic within Channel Four. In tandem with the Conservative government's changes in employment law, minor alterations in the formulation of production contracts at about this time betray a small but significant change of verb: from the original formulation 'Channel Four *requires* producers to work with relevant union agreements' to 'Channel Four *advises* …'.

As the decade wore on, the economics of this enterprise began to deteriorate. By the later eighties, as national and local state support receded, Channel Four was funding the majority of groups to between eighty and ninety per cent of their total income. This created an effective dependency and began to pull each group into a commissioning relationship, each producing a single project for transmission every year. From the broadcaster's point of view the original relationship only made sense if it were a co-partner with other state funders supporting a critical mass of workshops. If, say, twenty-five workshops were producing forty pieces of various shapes and sizes each year, a looser and less dependent relationship might have pertained.

The original concept, formulated in the discussions with the Labour Party and the BFI, was for an open system which ingested new, young filmmakers and embodied an element of fluidity and change within a network based on continuity. As the Channel Four-funded workshops became more entrenched, the need for new groups and individuals to enter the workshop formation and break into what was increasingly seen as a closed cartel became acute. Seen as much 'easier to stay in than to get out', the acronym of the National Organization of Workshops was satirically inverted to WON – expressing the closed, remote and introverted nature of the workshop sector when seen from the more precarious perspective of many other independents and community media activists.

Awareness of the stasis of the sector in the Channel as a whole was probably a small determinant; the built-in novelty factor at Channel Four (demanding a kind of premature obsolescence in many strands of production and programming) was a dangerous predisposition which was bound to counter the notion of continuity. The Independent Film and Video Department's own version of television executive instincts came to the fore as enthusiasm for the 'difference' of the workshop system was gradually replaced by scepticism. It should also be said that, in general, with one or two exceptions, the workshops never managed to connect with other commissioning areas in the Channel or indeed with other British broadcasters or funders.

The whole enterprise ended with something less than a bang as the Department decided to open out the £2 million budget previously reserved exclusively for official workshops into the 'Television With A Difference' scheme, a two-year transition supposedly extending the workshop-funding basis to any individual or group (including those not franchised by the union). It became difficult to reserve a budget of this scale for the production of a set of programmes that were not linked to a specific slot in the schedule. Although this scheme enabled many producers to shoot and edit over an extended period and some strong pieces emerged from it, in the context of diminishing departmental finance this halfway stage became untenable and the separate budget was finally abandoned in 1991.

When Mao Tse Tung was asked if the French Revolution of 1789 had been successful he apparently replied 'It's too early to tell': the same could be said of the workshop movement. Its significant achievements will doubtless be reassessed and chronicled eventually; but it can already be asserted that any future attempt to build a regional structure of independent producers to challenge the centripetal forces of the metropolis will have to refer again to the workshop experience in Britain 1980–90.

The provenance of (some) independents

As described in the previous section, the cultural origin of many of the individuals and groups who fed into Channel Four through the early *Eleventh Hour* was rooted in a lively pre-existent film culture — part of the discursive superstructure of a sector which included the emergent workshops, though the nexus for most individuals and some groups was the Independent Filmmakers' Association. The IFA was a loose alliance of the widest range of culturally and politically motivated independent practices, which included not only filmmakers but also critics, distributors, exhibitors and teachers. It is difficult to underestimate the interactivity during the 'moment' of *Screen*; BFI, SEFT and the Edinburgh events all provided foci of related activity and discussion (within shared assumptions).

However, *Screen* seemed to cast a rather intimidating and inhibiting shadow and its formidable theoretical explorations were interpreted mainly as a limitation or constraint on independent filmmakers. The configuration of Marx, Saussure and Freud and their progeny Althusser, Metz and Lacan provoked furious intellectual debate but also posed significant problems of interpretation and application. The British version of this continental discourse seemed impossible to square with the 'normal' creative and imaginative processes of audiovisual production. In so far as the *Weltanschauung* of *Screen* penetrated the independent sector, it had a rather uneven and constraining effect.

Part of the problem was that, initially at least, *Screen* was looking to classical Hollywood and only gradually connected with modern cinema and television at all; and even then felt unsure and uncomfortable relating to indigenous independent product. Some seminal analyses of independent film were published[9] but they were few and far between. One can interpret the rare inclusion of these occasional articles in terms of the *Screen* board's reluctant solidarity with progressive production and a politically motivated form of guilt did seem to underlie the magazine's belated address to the independent sector. But the maelstrom of theoretical (theological) disputes on *Screen* boards and sectarian bloodletting on SEFT executives largely passed the production sector by and in contrast, perhaps, *Framework*, with its combination of reviews, attention to third-world cinema and international independents, seemed to offer a looser and more productive relationship (although this underfunded magazine was never able to carry its precarious project through in a sustained way).

The contemporary models offered to practitioners interested in progressive and theoretically informed creative work seemed merely to encompass the short span from Godard to Straub/Huillet and back again. Unfortunately, even figures such as Kluge, Makavejev or Oshima stayed at the edge of the debate and hardly widened the spectrum of non-naturalistic form. Noël Burch's notable attempt to extend the frame of reference to Japanese cinema, Dreyer and others remained peripheral.

The legacy of this schooling was that many filmmakers had minimal knowledge, experience or interest in continuity cutting or directing actors or achieving narrative rhythm. The old adage about acquiring the discipline and precision of traditional methods of working (say figurative painting) being a necessary precursor for departure towards experiment (say abstraction) seems pertinent.

The independent sector produced several examples of the 'textual film': an eventual legacy of this formative genre for many filmmakers was that when television offered new budgets and the possibilities of wider audiences they were initially struggling to find appropriate forms either to utilize mainstream 'grammar' with adequate control and precision or even to counter the dominant mode of representation in a conscious, elegant and successful way. Ideologues of the television industry constantly utilize a concept of professionalism to justify exclusion, but the term could be redefined as 'serious in intent and deliberate in realization'. To shoot a scene hand-held, 'badly' or edit it with jump cuts should then be the result of a determined strategy rather than incidental ineptitude.

There were recurrent examples of 'roughness' in early *Eleventh Hour* documentary work: the placing of captions in a subtitled interview, the calculated use of voice over, the construction of an ending (not to be mistaken as the battle of polysemy against closure!). In fiction there were particularly serious problems with the consistency of acting codes (often given away through the voice/soundtrack), writing and script construction, and the speed and the rhythm of a narrative.

Before these would-be constructive criticisms turn into a litany of complaint or a threnody of lamentation, a rational contextual explanation may be available. Replacing previous understandings of the creative process as purely romantic/ inspired self-expression is overdue. With a Constructivist concept of art as 'just' another form of work (mere meaning-making) the underlying problems of training[10] and practice begin to emerge. Skill in handling the plasticity of sound and image is built from *work* and, as Godard remarked, 'taxi drivers get to take their cars out every day, I only get to make a film once a year . . .' – and this from Europe's most successful experimentalist. Perhaps the recent convergence of broadcast and domestic/leisure video equipment, and the easy availability of the latter, will help to supersede this problem in the longer term.

The middle of the road is a very dead end

Over a number of years the effect of the magnetic forces that pulled independent film practices towards dominant modes of representation became increasingly clear. They were driven both by the political and social imperative, but also the underlying economics – the need for constant sources of work. One can point to the continued existence and marginal resistance of some rare operatives who are still concerned to explore the politics of form but for a sizeable proportion of the sector even in the seventies concerns with communicating political content led to standard documentary formats. Many who had originally followed an inclination to experiment with form made an uninhibited move towards an audience's pre-existent position and expectations.

These differences can be clearly seen in the comparison between an early *Eleventh Hour* series like *Pictures of Women – Sexuality* (1984) and *Out* (1989–). The latter is certainly much more 'well-formed' and stylish, succeeding in reaching a wide audience beyond its primary concern with gay and lesbian politics and culture, but making little challenge to standard television form. In contrast, it often seemed that uneven experimentation in *Pictures of Women* undermined its avowedly political project.

Also the range of independents producing for the Department widened significantly across the years – this has led inexorably to a smaller and smaller proportion having the origins detailed above or carrying with them the burden of such ancient cultural histories. The slow dissolution of an independent community such as the IFA represented in the seventies must be, at least in part, also a result of the reconstruction of the sector as a profusion of small businesses, isolated and competitive.

A shift towards magazine programmes located in accessible parts of the schedule took place in the late eighties. *Visions* (1982–5) was replaced by the *Media Show* in 1987. *Critical Eye* (1990–), a highly controversial and successful series connects single polemical and analytical documentaries. Magazine shows like *Out*, the world's first networked gay and lesbian series, and *South* (1991), made by creative documentary filmmakers from Africa, Asia and Latin America, have all found mid-evening scheduling. Building on the earlier *People to People* (1983–7), a series of separately produced access programmes, a half-hour magazine programme of 'people's investigations' called *Free for All* was launched in 1991. Over a period of time the inevitable movement away from formal/representational difference took place as independent producers made shorter pieces for the new magazine formats.

Clearly this historical compromise carried the *Eleventh Hour* away from its origins (adjacent to ZDF's earlier *Das Kleine Fernsehspiel*[11]) where it was programming late-night weekly singles in the tundra of the schedule. The slot title was dropped in 1988 as the enormously diverse range of material meant it retained little identifying meaning for most of the audience; however this also marked the erosion of any residual sense of collective identity for the sector itself. A gradual conceptual change took place as the idea of independent cinema on television merged into the idea of new television itself. In distinction to the ZDF example the *Eleventh Hour* programming had been more television oriented and connected from the start: working with clusters, seasons and groups of programmes.

This is not the place for a full assessment but some of the effects of this shift in commissioning strategy towards television formats can be weighed against others: on the one hand, the new series connect with wider audiences and hopefully challenge them, extending their contact with effective contents and (relatively) creative forms; on the other hand, their populist compromise is part of a shift to the shorter attention span of television culture in general – aesthetically weaker material, and shorter-term aspirations for each individual work. There is little expectation that each item in a magazine programme will be viewed more than once, circulated in cinemas or achieve posterity in the archives. Of course one can question why the aspiration to the condition of longevity should be confined to cinema rather than television production. Certainly the magazines stop short of full integration in a consumable disposable culture, but – put crudely – any notion of the dialectic of form and content is eschewed for radicalized content utilizing close relatives of mainstream television forms.

A strong factor in this turn from earlier preoccupations with formal difference was that there had been no discernible resonance or support for the radical formal project from either audience or critics. This is not stated as a question of moralism or betrayal but objectively: this dimension of independent practice would not have become so weak and assailable if there had been evidence that it could connect with anyone at all.

The myth of the debate-based film culture

The original concentration on discussion as a necessary and interactive context for film/tape viewing[12] led to tentative experiments with placing a discursive frame around the programmes when screened on television: the first *Eleventh Hour* series, *Ireland: The Silent Voices* (1983) and *Women on Film* (1983). These gestural film intros and outros were soon abandoned as too clumsy, pedagogic and seemingly ineffective, although there has been occasional retention when necessary with difficult or distant material: *Video 1–5* (1985), *Dazzling Image* (1990) and *Vietnam Cinema* (1991) for instance.

Given its discursive origins one would have expected the independent sector's transition into television to be accompanied by intense and open cultural debate. In fact there has been minimal public argument. I know of no articles addressing the overall project of British independent film on/in television – describing the scope of it, dissecting the material, analysing or criticizing even. Instead, over the years there has merely been a plethora of quickly produced interviews, which have been useful for the exposition of information perhaps, but with the rare exception of Alan Lovell's piece and Jez Welsh's short article 'Resigning not resigned'[13] there has been no published critical engagement with this version of the project of radical television. Indeed it is only when funding is finally withdrawn that a workshop member engages in debate.

There is some irony in this state of things, given the genesis of this area of production within a self-proclaimed 'debate-based film culture' – perhaps too much was made of this at the time and, in retrospect, it can be seen to have been overstated. Furthermore there is sad continuity from the original lack of debate in the sector to its new situation. Theoretical discourse did not strengthen and consolidate practice. One would have thought that a lively critical film culture would have developed as especially essential in the transition to the new challenges of television.[14]

But 'the Sector' has never found a way to debate or criticize its own production (perhaps a recurrent symptom of this is the sense that a high proportion of programmes, from shorter avant-garde pieces to full-length feature films, are loose and over-extended). Although the term indulgent is perhaps too quickly used, the recurrent pattern is material edited too long. It is indeed rare to encounter work truncated and compressed into too tight a shape. The familiar anachronistic notion of the Artist interposes itself unhelpfully here and can be easily exacerbated by the Oedipal relation of oppositional independents to the institution of television.

Too often the angle of approach is that of a filmmaker using television money to make his or her next film rather than an engagement with the opportunity to extend their work to the specifics of a television space and ensure that the programme functions in that context. Different answers to the same question will be reached if thought through from the perspective of the audience. Of course there are endemic problems involved in the hypothetical and abstract projection of the idea of an audience but for any socially engaged audiovisual producer this consideration should be paramount.

The problem of independent *cinema* on *television* is revealed in the articulation of its distribution and exhibition. The specifics of separate traditions, of the cinema and television documentary, as well as fiction film, must not obscure the way in which cinema lives in, on and through television in the late twentieth century. Whatever our vestigial affections for the focused experience, public space and higher resolution images of cinema, the social experience of the audiovisual is now overwhelmingly in the home. After all, this is the reach and specificity of television: a subtitled, intellectually opaque series of interviews with Jacques Lacan transmitted at midnight is watched by 250,000 people while the most successful art-house cinema release is unlikely to reach more than 50,000.

Without an environment of dialectical discourse, discussions of audience and arguments about cinema and the balance between Politics and the Other (culture/imagination/desire) are either dominated by purely political criteria or drift off elsewhere. Once politics is introduced it can assume an ethical dominance over all the other dimensions of creative practice. The resolute hegemony of political criteria for a large proportion of the Independent Film and Video Department's output (the *Eleventh Hour* was once satirically dubbed The God Slot) stands in stark defiance of the general cultural shifts in Britain which, by the mid-eighties, had developed a mannerist, fashion-based and depoliticized culture with little sign of navigation by any political co-ordinates. Certainly the lack of debate about forms and strategies confirmed the lost chance to establish the necessary political/artistic equilibria. A culture of open discussion and self-reflexive argument is central to the project of developing imaginative and transformatory cultural forms and renewing 'old' agendas.

Horizons/orisons

This article articulates a partial vision of recent histories available from a personal position inside 'fortress television' and attempts to chart a phase of independent film that has flowed through a precarious set of broadcast opportunities. Standing back, one is struck by the considerable and extraordinary achievements of the decade. One of the pleasures of this area of audiovisual production is working intensely with images and sounds, films and programmes that are powerful, beautiful, moving. Necessarily, this article based as it is upon a critique of structures rather than a celebration of the pleasures of the text, takes a more derogatory and negative tone.

What new generations of work exist beyond the edges of that vision, what are the possibilities of renewal at grassroots? Against the pessimistic mood of a debilitated *fin de millennium*, reeling from rapid shifts in the axes of politics and power, it seems necessary to reassert that the motor of change, social and audiovisual, is not the calcified tradition of received socialist dogma but the continuing perceived disparities of material conditions. There will be constant renewed contention over wealth and power, representation and control, as emancipatory forces persist and metamorphose in a landscape of change.

This article is not a recalcitrant apologia or a valediction – the process of renewal continues. The entry into television inevitably involves the erratic rhythm of the rise and fall of institutions and individuals. Nothing should be taken for granted; as Mikhail Gorbachev indicated in a reference to Heraclitus: 'as the ancient Greeks say, "everything flows, everything changes" '.[15]

Perhaps there will be a temporary reduction of scale of well-financed radical work as a result of the climactic changes taking place in European public-service television. In 1991 TVE in Spain reduced its workforce by ten per cent and its coproduction budget with Latin America by two thirds; *Das Kleine Fernsehspiel* was reduced from fifty to thirty-seven slots; the *Carre Noir* series on the French-Belgian station RTBF was discontinued; a financial crisis in Greek television temporarily suspended work with independent producers. Meanwhile the British government has constructed haphazard legislation designed to release market forces which themselves, in the longer term, will lead to new, more congenial and conservative configurations. This is a subtle, British way of reshaping broadcasting in an ideologically more amenable form. The relative balance of factual and entertainment programming on European television is shifting. The whole ecology of public-service television is threatened as a widespread process of global warming occurs!

It may be diminished and uneven, but there will still be significant scope for the renewal of innovative film and television making: imaginatively, politically and formally in whatever the institutional spaces that prevail. The most likely scenario is one in which transformation is uneven and diverse, continually modified by local conditions, local demands, expectations, resistances and compromises, the future still bearing the residual traces of the way it always was.

The Channel Four experience has barely scratched the surface of the possibilities of progressive and creative audiovisual production, of television programming, of democratic potential. 'Veniamo da lontano e andiamo lontano ...'[16]

Notes

1. *Screen* board 1980–5, SEFT Education Officer 1982–3, WEA and university extramural courses in Plymouth and Bristol, Art College teaching in Exeter and Falmouth.

2. *Photomontage Today: Peter Kennard*, Arts Council of Great Britain, 1983, not broadcast; *Ireland: The Silent Voices*, Channel Four, 1983; *Italy: The Image Business*, Channel Four, 1984; *Between Object and Image*, British Council/TVE (Spain), 1986.

3. Rod Stoneman, 'Film-related practice and the avant-garde', *Screen*, vol. 20, nos. 3–4 (1979–80), pp. 40–57.

4. Alan Lovell, 'That was the workshops that was', *Screen*, vol. 31, no. 1 (1990), pp. 102–8.

5. *Independent Film Workshops in Britain*, Torquay, 1979.

6. London Video Access since 1988.

7. Alan Sapper quoted in Simon Hartog (ed.), *Nationalising the Film Industry* (London: ACTT, 1973).

8. Simon Hartog, 'The perils of film policy', in Rod Stoneman (ed.), *Independent Film Workshops in Britain*.

9. For example: Claire Johnston and Paul Willemen, 'Brecht in Britain: the independent political film', *Screen*, vol. 16, no. 4 (1975–6), pp. 101–18; Peter Gidal, 'The antinarrative', *Screen*, vol. 20, no. 2 (1979), pp. 73–93; John Ellis, 'The BFI production board', *Screen*, vol. 17, no. 4 (1976–7), pp. 9–23, with letters in response by Peter Wollen and Jane Clarke in vol. 18, no. 1 (1987), pp. 119–22.

10. This is an area where I agree with Lovell's analysis: cf. for example an early panel discussion of the question: 'Training the independents', *Screen*, vol. 25, no. 6 (1984), pp. 5–16.

11. Created in 1962 by Hajo Schedlich and continued from 1975 with Eckart Stein.

12. Stoneman, 'Film-related practice and the avant-garde'; 'South West Independent Film Tour' in *South West Film Directory* (Exeter: South West Arts, 1980); *The New Social Function of Cinema. Catalogue: BFI Productions '79/80*.

13. Jez Welsh, 'Resigning not resigned', *Independent Media*, no. 103 (1990), pp. 12–13.

14. The ICA day conference on the *Eleventh Hour* held in July 1983 was an early attempt to focus this interaction.

15. Mikhail Gorbachev, *The Observer*, 5 June 1988. Cf. Charles H. Kahn (ed.), *The Art and Thought of Heraclitus* (Cambridge: Cambridge University Press, 1977; reprinted 1987).

16. Palmiro Togliatti, 'We've come a long way and we've a long way to go ...', in *Geschichte der Nacht* (*Histories of the Night*, ZDF, 1979).

Doing without the Broadcast Media

Julian Petley

Broadcast, **28 June 1985** (by permission of *Broadcast*)

This week the Mobil/BFI John Grierson Award goes to the Miners' Campaign Tape Project. Julian Petley, co-author of the Campaign for Press and Broadcasting Freedom's booklet 'Media Hits the Pits', commends the decision.

Most media awards are pretty predictable ... *The Jewel in the Crown, Amadeus, A Passage to India* – no surprises there. How gratifying, then, at this week's Mobil/British Film Institute's Awards to find the prestigious John Grierson Award going to the Miners' Campaign Tape Project.

This consists of six videos made during the coal dispute to promote the NUM's cause and, more importantly, to draw attention to aspects of the dispute ignored or distorted by the mainstream media.

Although some will doubtless object to the 'political' nature of the award's recipients the tapes stand, in fact, fairly and squarely in the tradition established in Britain by John Grierson, the founding father of the British documentary.

Though one of Grierson's major achievements was the establishment of a framework of State sponsorship for the documentary in the Thirties he was only too well aware of the limitations of such an arrangement.

As he put it after the last war, if the documentarist 'wants to pursue the more difficult and controversial themes, I am afraid he must look elsewhere than to governments, and here I think it will be well to examine in future years the sponsorship potential of authorities and associations who are less hamstrung than governments necessarily are. In particular, one expects much from the trade unions and co-operative movements.' Precisely.

Nor was Grierson himself any stranger to political controversy. 'Enough to Eat', a ground-breaking Thirties documentary about malnutrition, was, as he points out, 'branded by political busybodies as "subversive". Silly enough it sounds, but obstacle after obstacle was put in the way of the documentary film whenever it set itself to the adult task of performing a public service. Sometimes it came in the cry of the censor that the screen was to be kept free of what was called "controversy". More often it was in the whispered obstruction emanating from Conservative Party politicians.'

Though written several decades ago, and about film, Grierson's words are highly relevant to broadcasting today. Though not guilty of the deliberate bias of most of

Fleet Street, British television (with a few honourable exceptions such as *Channel 4 News* and the *People to People* slot) hardly comes out of the coal dispute untarnished.

Whether through uncritical acceptance of agendas set by the politically motivated press, intellectual laziness, moral cowardice or simple toadying to the establishment, television as a whole can hardly be said to have covered the dispute fairly or adequately. In particular the subjects tackled by the campaign tapes were notable largely by their absence – hence, of course, the need for the project in the first place.

What these tapes, and Grierson's own words, drive home so forcefully, is that it is the duty of broadcasting which is *truly* a public service to reveal precisely those matters which those in authority *do not* want the public to know about.

Fleet Street may have become a mere recycler of official hand-outs, but that is no reason for the broadcasting authorities to follow suit. Indeed, the need for fair-minded, decent and, where necessary, investigative, journalism on television and radio has never been greater – and yet never so under threat.

Recent events around Stonehenge, and the threat of new 'public order' legislation, show just how much the State has learned from the coal dispute – media coverage of both shows just how little notice has been taken of criticism of television's coverage of that dispute. What the Miners' Campaign Video Tapes show, however, is just how much can be achieved without the conventional broadcast media at all.

If television consistently ignores or misrepresents those in conflict with the State in one way or another (an ever increasing number given the State's growing authoritarian stance) then they in turn will increasingly ignore and distrust mainstream television and start looking to the alternatives offered by the new technology.

When television, like the BBC at the present moment, comes under renewed attack from the Right it will look to those who, traditionally, might be expected to support the 'public service' ethos – only to find it's got no friends left.

Post-Modernism and the Populist Tendency

Jez Welsh

Undercut No. 12, 1984

In this essay on current issues informing much video art production in Britain, I shall first reflect on some general issues raised principally by the parallel situation in the US and elsewhere, and in the light of this I will then look at some of the more particular concerns and attributes of work being produced in Britain. The point of departure is in itself problematic; while in many ways it is now desirable to dispense with the term, 'Video Art', it is nonetheless a fact that the impetus for this enquiry springs essentially from the historical process of twentieth-century art, and that the work under consideration is mainly produced by individuals who, in the absence of a better description, term themselves video artists. It has been argued, particularly by the American John Sanborn, that 'Media Artist' becomes a more apt title for the video user who begins to situate her/his activity within the context of mass culture; in describing the works of several artists including Tony Ousler and Gary Hill he writes: 'These quirky examples simply illustrate the growth of what I feel is a group of misleading media artists who do not make art as much as they make, well ... media. The material is so strongly spelled PRODUCT that the process oriented world cringes.' However, this is an artist talking about other artists, and I have no doubt that the media world itself would have no doubt but that such PRODUCT is art since it is clearly not MEDIA in its terms, as it originated somewhere 'outside'.

Undoubtedly, there are still those within traditionalist pockets of resistance in the art world who would argue the validity of video, or any popular cultural form, as art, but when considering the issue of the proposed new genre 'media artist' any such argument is irrelevant on two counts: firstly, it is historically untenable in its own terms, and secondly, whatever frame of reference is used to describe such individuals, as far as the media world itself is concerned, they are still basically UFOs, and 'video artist' is as good a bracket as any to put them in. The media world cares little about what artists call themselves, nor does it concern itself with whether or not one group of artists is considered to be art by another group of artists. The media can always find somebody to trot out a definition of art should the need arise.

However, the point of this preamble is not to become embroiled in a fruitless area of discussion, but to establish the point that one is accepting as given the term 'video artist' for better or worse in order to avoid confusion.

Is that all there is?

Populism in contemporary British art is not so much a consciously defined issue, as a tendency which has evolved over the past few years. It first became apparent in the late 70s, alongside the concept of Post-Modernism, and while some early attempts were made to launch Post-Modernism as a new canon (notably in a 1978 *Artscribe* appraisal of a number of painters including Duggie Fields), the idea and the attendant concern with populism have largely taken root outside of the kind of rigorous debate that typified the preceding eras of minimalism, conceptualism and formalism. Whereas in the US populism is being heralded in a rather naive and inappropriate manner as the force that simultaneously puts the lid on the formalist avant-garde, and allows artists to penetrate the mainstream of media culture, here it is seen either as a stage in an ongoing process of development, perhaps a cause for cautious optimism, or simply as an opportunity, particularly when manifested through painting and sculpture, to pull bigger crowds into the galleries, thus validating their existence within a Thatcherite economy, and enabling dealers to sell more art.

The uncritical acceptance in the US of the inevitability of significant 'crossover' into the mainstream looks suspiciously like a reiteration of the 'more = better' equation that lies at the heart of imperialism, monetary or cultural. There is an assumption that making art available to a mass audience is an act of democratization in itself, regardless of content, regardless of the consumerist connotations, regardless of the political position into which the artist must of necessity have been forced by the communications industry. This is not to suggest that an oppositional stance is irrevocably debarred from a mass context, but the dynamics of that context inevitably dictate a rigid, unilinear flow between producer and consumer. There is no doubt that the crossover from minority interest to mass culture will increasingly take place; as the industry's hunger for new material grows, more artists will find their work reaching a mass audience, and they will gain expertise and not inconsiderable stimulation from their relationships with the entertainment industry. But it will not make their art either better or worse ultimately, and it will probably not make any real difference to the industry itself or to the behaviour and attitudes of the recipients, other than extending the range of what they are prepared to accept as entertainment. The overriding effect of television – a kind of tautological democracy – is a process of evening out. Everything comes across, within a limited range, as more or less level, as a unitary measurement in the ongoing flow of TV time. Although it is possible to intervene, to introduce new ideas or alternative viewpoints, the context somehow militates against the efficacy of content. The radical is generally assimilated instead of being defined or directed; the uniform quality of television is an affirmation of dominant values. The recent British election was won in the media because the Conservative political machine ruthlessly exploited the ability of the media to confirm suspicions, fears and prejudices by postulating them as inherently laudable national characteristics, which, if held firm, would deliver us ultimately to the gates of a consumer paradise. Political debate was reduced to the status of soap opera, which itself inadvertently took on the heroic characteristics of classical tragedy.

And so it is against this background of what mass media actually does or does not do that we must consider the issue of populism as a viable cause for the artist to embrace. Inserting 'alternatives' into the dominant stream does not subvert it and does not create access in any generalized sense. In fact, if one were to espouse a 'conspiracy theory' approach to the whole issue, it would be tempting to think that the real motive for allowing access to alternative viewpoints is simply to posit the inviability of such viewpoints in relation to the dominant norm. Utopianism is a tolerable deviation.

A recent issue of the American magazine *Art Com* devoted much space to the populist issue. Amidst a plethora of fashionable rhetoric, polemical platitudes and indigestible terminology, the apotheosis of the buzz-word mentality, there was little evidence that anyone had much idea what was going on, other than that a number of artists had broadened the scope of their work to embrace popular culture and would therefore address a wider audience, thus escaping from the cultural ghetto to which twentieth-century history had hitherto confined them. It seems the assumption had been made somewhere along the line that because these artists had been 'liberated' and cut loose in the mass market of popular culture, they would immediately start in on the heroic task of liberating everyone else, armed with their sharp sensibilities, their intuitive grasp of the new technology, their phrase books in media-speak and their pretence to the status of Businessmen. The real issue behind it all is whether the advocates of populism will win the battle for art world supremacy, so that they can call the shots, define the context, refine the codes, dismantle the nexus of economic relations within the art world to institute a system more appropriate to their particular aspirations. (It is apparent that selling a lot of cars to a lot of people at the lowest possible price is a more effective strategy than selling a few cars to a few people at a high price, and subsidizing this endeavour by trafficking in cocaine.)

Of the many views expressed in the *Art Com* survey, the most realistic in broad terms was that of Canadian artist Tom Sherman, who is worth quoting at some length: 'Let's face it, artists choose to work within the mass media context for a couple of pretty good reasons. What better place is there for indulging in or criticizing mass media than the mass media itself? What better place could anyone suggest for finding an audience interested in indulging in or criticizing mass media?' Sherman's statement can be contrasted with the contention of editor Carl Loeffler that 'The "cross over" tendency creates an expanded arena or context for the expression of ideas by visual artists. The "new" arena for art involves radical changes toward the perception and definition of art.'

To determine 'new' perceptions and 'new' definitions for art, on behalf of the world at large, and to dump these into the context of popular culture, is not popularization through mass engagement, it is simply elitism on an extended scale. The issue of populism is not unique to American and British art, it crops up everywhere that an established avant-garde practice exists. It is probably more highly developed in America due to the sheer scale of the media industry there, and the comparative accessibility that artists enjoy. In Britain, it is a comparatively new issue, and one which is barely documented. There is the ongoing cable debate in Britain, but few now believe that there is any provision for truly democratic public access, and even if this were not the case, the question of art is not especially 'hot'. It would be pointless to make any claims on behalf of populist artists in Britain or to assume that the dawn of a new age of mass creativity or mass aesthetic involvement will be the inevitable result of a broadening of the art context.

Populism as reaction

In beginning to look at the implications of populism within contemporary British art, and video in particular, we must first ask what it was that caused the idea to develop. It is apparent in the first instance that it was, in art terms, a reaction to the formalism which preceded it. For many young artists in the late seventies, there seemed nowhere to go. Many retreated into a romantic rerun of some era or other from art history, others reached the conclusion that the whole issue was arid territory and turned, as had happened in the sixties, to popular culture. The violent energy of new wave culture quickly penetrated every level of creative activity in Britain, throwing up a whole new generation of musicians, graphic artists, fashion designers, poets, performance artists and writers. By the eighties, most of the early energy had dissipated, but by then certain ideas had firmly taken root in the art schools and in the minds of young artists trying to define a context for their own activities. And at the same time, cheap colour video was becoming a reality, video games were becoming a national obsession, home computers were becoming commonplace, and home recording technology to cater for the independent musician was invented. In the late seventies, Post-Modernism was declared as the point after the end point in the modernist process. Painting started to come back, artists' film abandoned structuralism in favour of a vocabulary that drew a direct line of descent from punk, but that also had all the right art-historical references. By the time punk had been declared officially dead, popular culture and high art alike had fractured into a million cults, trends, revivals and reruns. The era of New Romanticism introduced a note of self-conscious pomposity perfectly attuned to the emerging national philosophy of Thatcherism.

Within art schools, the great revival of painting, the noises coming from Berlin and New York, the reaction against all the avant-garde strategies of the seventies, created an opportunity for video to come into its own. Video provided a refuge for those unwilling to take up the task of re-establishing painting and sculpture. It also provided a language that was rapidly becoming universally regarded as the authentic expression of the media-dense times, and it provided a direct point of access to the whole field of popular culture.

A new generation of video artists emerged at the beginning of the decade. With scant regard for the process-oriented video of the seventies, they set about their task of synthesizing; anything could be incorporated, TV commercials, soap opera, pop music, literature, art history, fashion, performance, dance, computer graphics, video games.

Video in Britain is, all things considered, remarkably healthy now. Its roots lie in the development of video access facilities, such as that operated by London Video Arts, which came about in the seventies in response to demands from avant-garde artists and community activists alike for the opportunity to explore and exploit the medium of video. We have now reached a position where such access facilities, in Britain at least, are becoming more widespread through the infusion of public money and more recently through the support of Channel Four television. Alongside this move towards an open access to video facilities has been the massive explosion in sales and rentals of domestic video equipment. At a grass roots level, video production is mushrooming, not only in terms of the obvious examples of domestic pornography and home movie-making, but also in terms of a video subculture that is analogous to the opening up of musical production initiated by the new wave phenomenon in the late seventies. This inherently anti-consumerist trend embodies the assumption that instead of paying to see a high-tech multimedia extravaganza, you can do it yourself, albeit crudely, with whatever tools are at your disposal. The audience will inevitably be smaller, but a context exists, an exchange of ideas is integral to it.

Against this background of developing guerrilla activity, it is possible for the video artist to embrace populist concerns, to gradually reach out to a broader audience, without having to bow to the demands of the media industry. Through a network of alternative venues ranging from small galleries to clubs, cafes and discos, to community-based arts centres and video workshops and to private homes, a more critical media consciousness may develop, based not on the assumption that acceptance into the mainstream of media culture will automatically open up new horizons, but on the assumption that the media mainstream is not the only alternative. And the most vital element of this tendency is the fact that it operates on the principle of engagement and involvement rather than that of exclusion; it is still about communication, social interaction, all of the things that the immobilized television (or domestic video) viewer is denied. And populism in this sense does not simply mean the espousal of the style or imagery of dominant popular/cultural trends; it allows an engagement with issues of mass concern; sexual politics; the nuclear arms race; race relations; community politics.

Having illustrated the naiveté of assuming that intrusion into the processes of mass culture will ultimately be the saviour of art, or that such intrusion will have any quantifiable effect upon the mass media itself, the mistake should be avoided of assuming that an emerging subculture based on video and other electronic processes will in itself make any noticeable impact upon dominant cultural forms.

Certain elements will inevitably filter through and become assimilated; various individuals will make the transformation from 'alternative' to 'mainstream'; but a living oppositional culture will at least provide a spur to creative experiment and radical intervention which are difficult if not impossible within the dominant form.

Image, music, text

The contemporary cultural project, and the video tape in particular, exists within a matrix of references, historical, cultural, linguistic and social, which has multiple points of access, drawing as it does upon an extensive pool of information that is generally available through the media of mass communication. Yet it is dense in so far as the extent of comprehension is determined by the ability of the viewer to decode and isolate particular strands, and to extrapolate constructs based on the interrelations and connections between these strands, a process that may in one case be based upon an established theoretical methodology, and in another, be entirely intuitive. This disjuncture between the analytical and the instinctual exists as much in the makers of the texts as in those who endeavour to interpret or simply comprehend them. While some artists, commencing from a position of acquired theoretical methodology, translated into informed practice, pursue a deliberate process of deconstruction/reconstruction, others operate instinctively in a field, drawing upon a wide net of inputs, and employing techniques of deconstruction/reconstruction as learned responses rather than developed techniques. The text is the direct reverse of the formalist work, whose reductive purity sought scrupulously to eradicate all reference to anything beyond the blunt reality of the object itself. The text is an admission of the relationship of itself to everything else, it desires to merge with the context surrounding it, accepts that it would be irrelevant in isolation: the individual video production as text is essentially a part of a wider text whose parameters are delineated only by the range of contributory cultural/linguistic threads.

Thus, for video, the context may shift from gallery to cafe to discotheque to specialist festival to television to community centre, and may ultimately mutate into a form that owes something to all of these, whilst being a response to a new set of imperatives. If the video production is itself a text, or part of a text, then the situation in which it is experienced and commented upon is also part of that text on a broader scale. If video continues to attempt to engage a wider and less specialized (fragmented) audience, then the dialogue between that audience and the art/artist will contribute to the growth of the form through the development of a shared cultural syntax. One area in which this process can already be seen is in the work of various artists who are currently concentrating on image/music relationships, and on the relationships between sounds/words/images. Such projects can clearly be seen to relate to and to be influenced by mainstream tendencies in pop video and commercial television, but they differ essentially in orientation. Whereas in the instance of the commercial pop video, the image, the narrative, is subordinated to the primary function of selling a separate product, artists, image/music tapes are aimed at creating a synthesis, a form in which neither part would be effective in the absence of the other. In this area there exist both great potential for the development of a truly populist cultural form, and the risk of rapid assimilation into the machinations of the consumer industries. A conscious decision by practitioners and enthusiasts of video art to encourage active participation in the production and dissemination of video through independently controlled channels, for the purpose of a broad and engaging dialogue, could create a strength that would allow for (potentially) mass exposure without massive dilution.

The most interesting aspect, perhaps, of the whole populist development in video, is that it is no one individual's sovereign province; it arises from a broader cultural concern. Although, like any other form, it produces both 'good' and 'bad' or 'successful' and 'unsuccessful' art, the individual work or the individual producer is not the main point; the fact that it is happening and that a vital and energetic cultural endeavour may result, is the main point. For this reason, I have avoided the consideration of particular video tapes and individual artists. Another piece of writing setting up another new genre with its attendant personality cult of 'key' figures is not what we need at this point in time. What we do need is a sense of responsibility, a commitment to maintain an openness to new possibilities and a confirmed suspicion of anything that appears to be the easy option. The Post-Modernist ideal of Populism will either result in a further de-specialization of cultural production, or it will simply deliver up another load of willing compliants to the waiting arms of the media industry.

Sexual Identities: Questions of Difference

Kobena Mercer

Undercut No. 17

The debate presented here must be one of the most intense, frustrating, exciting and open-ended dialogues in film criticism that I can remember. It was an important event, bringing to light the sheer scale of the complexity that characterises cultural politics today. As such, the debate dramatises a convergence of ethnic and feminist political perspectives around the question of 'cultural identity' in film and cinema. With questions of sexuality, in the foreground, the common concern with 'difference' in the debate also underlines the transformative impact which sexual politics and psychoanalytic theory have had on the way we talk about films. The outcome of this convergence has produced a discourse on cinema made all the more compelling by the uncertainty or impossibility of any consensus.

I want to try to tease some of the recurring themes which emerged in the 'crowded space' of this dialogue, not so as to reduce the complexity of the issues under discussion, as much as to figure out some of its implications in a context where independent cinema is in a state of crisis, where 'the old is dying and the new cannot be born'. Inevitably this will be a partial and provisional point of view, aiming to do no more than indicate some possible directions in which the conversation which began at *Cultural Identities* might continue. There seem to me to be three key issues involved: reassessing the meaning of cinematic 'independence', re-thinking the relations between film practice and theory, and re-appraising the problematic issue of the politics of pleasure with regards to film and cinema as institutions of popular culture.

The need to recognise inflections among different traditions of 'independent' film-making is a current that runs across all four of these *Cultural Identities* debates. It may be agreed that the term usefully distinguishes film practices that are critical or 'oppositional' in relation to the politics, ideology and aesthetics of the dominant commercial film culture. But it cannot be taken for granted that this same term adequately articulates the strategic choices and conditions that inflect different meanings of cinematic 'independence' between films made in Europe and America and those made in the Third World.

In the case of the former, the centralisation of the film industry as an apparatus of capitalist entertainment in the 1920s and '30s created spaces on the margins for alternative practices which became institutionally accommodated as 'art-cinema', with its own 'avant-garde' and its own canon of 'auteurs'. In the latter, however,

independent film in Latin America, India and Africa developed at a later historical
point (during the 1960s and '70s) and the orientation of counter-hegemonic film
culture in these contexts has aligned itself with notions of 'agitation' or 'education'
rather than 'art'. The salience of the documentary genre in this tradition emphasises this inflection. My remarks on 'combined and uneven development' in the
debate allude to the need to make these distinctions, particularly as the new black
independent productions in Britain draw critically from both traditions.

These inflections also underpin the discussion of didacticism, an issue brought
into focus by the way some of the films shown seemed to aspire to a transparent
relation of theory and practice. Gayatri Spivak diagnoses this as a 'globalising desire
to save the world' with an aesthetically, politically and theoretically 'correct' film
practice, and Angela McRobbie emphasises how much the 'precious' desire for
'purity' evoked by some of the films sidesteps the political problem of popular pleasures. What emerges is a feeling that the Leninist desire for 'correctness' now seems
somehow archaic, or at least outmoded as a political ideal. The debate around
didacticism presents an opportunity to re-evaluate the inheritance of the theoretical frameworks that characterised the 'ascetic aesthetic' of independent practices in
the '70s (in England, at least).

Informed by the Brechtian critique of realism and the Althusserian analysis of
ideology, film criticism and theory formed in the moment of the new left after 1968
encouraged avant-garde practices that sought to disturb or dislocate the viewer,
inscribing an 'alienation-effect' or modernist 'shock' to effect a critical, reflexive
attitude towards the cinematic apparatus, where it was argued that the very technology of the camera (based on Renaissance linear perspective) was 'contaminated'
with the ideological effects of bourgeois hegemony, 'structural-materialist' film-
makers, for example, outlawed the representational image.[1] It was as if the films
wanted to 'teach' their audience a thing or two about cinema and in this way to
decontaminate hegemonised subjects out of their ideological illusions, as in Plato's
cave. As an aesthetic strategy this appropriated Althusser's epistemological opposition of science and ideology, seeking 'scientific' guarantees at the level of theory
for practices that ruled pleasure out of the question.

Today that positivist relation of theory and practice has collapsed: it no longer
has the same kind of political credibility it once claimed. The '80s have seen a reaction against asceticism, demonstrated in the opulent excess of 'new romantics' and
more generally by the return to narrative. Jacqueline Rose's defence of the texts
whose didactic qualities elicited impatience amongst the audience accurately
observes that, 'These films have not won out institutionally.' But this could also be
interpreted as a criticism of a strategy which is now exhausted, ghettoised in art
schools and academia and unable or unwilling to engage with the contaminating
and contaminated question of pleasure.

The pleasure principle of popular cinema was identified as a key political problem by Laura Mulvey's epochal analysis of narrative structures of spectatorship

which showed how deeply the traditional psychic, sexual and political economy of the Hollywood movie reproduced and conserved the hegemony of patriarchal ideology, centrally and crucially dependent on the endless erotic objectification and exploitation of women's image.[2] This framework underpins the intense discussion of two salient moments from *Territories* and *Un chant d'amour*. The ensuing exchange emphasises the value of psychoanalytic concepts in film analysis, but the critical voices emanating from black, gay and lesbian perspectives also focused on the limitations of an aesthetic of 'passionate detachment' prescribed as the antidote to the sordid filigree of voyeurism, fetishism and scopophilia inscribed in the dominant construction of white male heterosexual identity.

The black man in Genet's film, like the representation of the 'native' in ethnographic documentary, is fixed like a stereotype in the fetishistic axis of the look. In both instances, the black subject is subjected to a 'pornographic' exercise of colonial power, endlessly returning it to the position as the 'other' whose 'difference' is subordinated to the construction of a European identity. But this is a profoundly ambivalent process; as Gayatri Spivak says, 'the movie moved me', raising the question: can we still say that Genet made an exquisite and beautiful film if it is so imprisoned by a desire which reproduces colonial fantasy?

As with the image of the white old lady in *Territories*, it is impossible to contain or articulate the admixture of emotions aroused by talking in theoretical stereotypes that label this as 'sexist', that as 'racist'. As Rose argues, the question raised by the hierarchical ordering of sexual, ethnic, national differences in the construction of identity is whether or not we want 'identity' as a political category in the first place. Neither feminism, ethnic politics nor independent film-making can embrace a simple logic of 'opposition' – radical feminism or anti-racism often collude with the categorical essentialism they seek to overturn – but a deconstructive affirmation of 'difference' is equally problematic as it often implies a politics of indifference where 'anything goes' (as in the neo-conservative response to postmodernism).

But this is not an either/or issue. Rose cites Black Audio Film Collective's *Signs of Empire* as a text that refuses identification for the spectator, in this way attempting to 'undo' the barrage of colonial discourse through an aesthetic of 'terror', likened by Rose to the logic of psychoanalytic inquiry, but equally identifiable within the ascetic emphasis on displeasure. This is not the only strategy because texts such as *Illusions*, adopting certain narrative conventions fully aware of the risk of ideological contamination, offer access to positions of pleasure and identification which, for black spectators, have not always been available in mainstream movies. As Spivak points out elsewhere,[3] sometimes a little bit of essentialism is a strategically necessary choice. For me, the representation of the two black men in *Territories* offers an image of identity denied and excluded in a political sense by the image in Genet's film. It seems to me that it is not a question of the marginal particularism of homosexuality transcended by 'the human' (a globalising view that

could be recruited for powerfully homophobic ends), but of how the same or similar elements are always open to antagonistic discursive articulations.

Indeed, what seems to be absent from the debate is a sense of cultural politics as
a practice of articulation[4] in a historical situation which demands that we think a
multiplicity of differences at one and the same time. An impossible demand perhaps, but the doubts expressed as to the adequacy of psychoanalysis in dealing with
the specificity of ethnicity revolved around the concern that it subordinates all
other differences to 'sexual difference', which thus becomes a hypostatized absolute
as *the* critical difference, not just one among many.[5]

If anything, these are two of the key issues at stake in the way the debate returns
to the notion of a diaspora in trying to designate the effects produced by black
British independent films. Spivak's term, 'hybridisation', is one worth extending as
it connects the post-colonial problematic of 'identity' (not more complex than
either the chromatic metaphors of black and white or the neo-colonial emblem of
nationality can allow) with the post-modernist problematic of 'difference', where
binary contrasts collapse into the flux of a heterogenous intertextuality.

Spivak's comments in an Australian radio interview, however, are more
confusing:[6]

> I'll tell you a story. I was at the Commonwealth Institute in London to discuss
> some films made by black independent film-makers ... and one of the points I
> made to them was (in fact I am a bit of a broken record on this issue), you are
> diasporic blacks in Britain, and you are connecting to the local lines of resistance
> in Britain, and you are therefore able to produce a certain idiom of resistance; but
> don't forget the Third World at large, where you won't be able to dissolve
> everything into Black against White, as there is also Black against Black, Brown
> against Brown, and so on.

I don't remember it in quite the same way. Unlike earlier generations of black
film-makers rooted in a 'monologic' single-issue discourse on ethnic politics, I feel
the younger workshops fully accept and engage in the hybridised space of being
black and British, which in a society that predominantly regards these two terms as
mutually exclusive,[7] entails a logic of resistance that must be 'dialogic'. Texts such
as *The Passion of Remembrance* and *Handsworth Songs* have defied attempts at neat
categorisation precisely because they recruit a dialogic perspective on ethnic politics, moving in nomadic lines of force not to find a 'home' or some finalising conclusion to their stories, but to articulate a diasporean aesthetic that moves among
the differences *within* black identities as much as those *between* the plural ethnici-
ties that make up England's post-imperial national identity.

These issues were followed up at the conference on *Third Cinema* in the 1986
Edinburgh Film Festival, another event in which consensus seemed to be out of the
question.[8] One thing at least is clear: that we have to deal with the paradox in which

traditional sources of cultural identity and authority are becoming decentred (post-modernism), while questions of 'race' become increasingly central to culture and politics in the way the society represents its experience of crisis (post-colonialism). The popular appeal of a film like *My Beautiful Laundrette* would seem to emphasise that.

This paradox was also a precondition for the debate which took place at the Commonwealth Institute, an unlikely venue, which opened its doors in a wave of 'benevolence', as did other institutions – the Greater London Council, Channel Four, the local state – as part of the response to the 'riots' in 1981. Many of these spaces are no longer available, many have closed down or are now squeezing out the possibility of 'independence' and freezing out 'opposition' in the cold winds of the marketplace. Important as it was, it is an open question as to whether the conversation which took place can continue in the face of a conservatism that would have us believe that our cultural identity has overcome those contradictions and that 'it's great to be great again'.

References

1. See Jean-Louis Baudry, 'Ideological Effects of the Basic Cinematographic Apparatus', *Film Quarterly* Winter 1974 and 'The Apparatus', *Camera Obscura* No. 1, 1976. On independent cinema in Britain see Peter Gidal (ed.), *Structural/Materialist Film*, British Film Institute, 1975.

2. Laura Mulvey, 'Visual Pleasure and Narrative Cinema', *Screen* Vol. 16, No. 3, 1975. See also, for her reflections on the impact of that article, 'Changes: Thoughts on Myth, Narrative and Historical Experience', *History Workshop Journal* No. 25, 1987.

3. See interview with Angela McRobbie, 'Strategies of Vigilance', *Block* No. 10, 1985, and Gayatri Spivak, *In Other Worlds*, Methuen, 1987.

4. In the sense that Mouffe and Laclau 'call articulation any practice establishing a relation among elements such that their identity is modified as a result of the articulatory practice', *Hegemony and Socialist Strategy*, Verso, 1985, p. 105.

5. A concern expressed by Mandy Merck, 'Difference and its Discontents', Introduction to *Screen* Vol. 28, No. 1, 1987, on 'Deconstructing Difference'.

6. From 'Questions of Multiculturalism', an interview with Sneja Gnew, *Hecate* Spring 1987 (Sydney), p. 141.

7. On this issue, see Paul Gilroy, *There Ain't No Black in the Union Jack*, Hutchinson, 1987, especially Chapter 2 on 'Race, Nation and Ethnic Absolutism'.

8. See my report, 'Third Cinema at Edinburgh', *Screen* Vol. 27, No. 4, and for an alternative (outrageously ethnocentric) view see David Will's report in *Framework* 32/33.

Part III

Oral Histories

Introductory Notes and Comment

The two distributors covered here have been selected because they form a link between the left film networks of the 30s and the oppositional movement which began in the late 60s. Charles Cooper, who set up Contemporary Films, had worked with Kino; Stanley Forman was in close contact with Ivor Montagu and took over the archive of the Progressive Film Institute for Plato Films. Both were carrying on that tradition of renting and showing progressive films, although, unlike their predecessors, they were only very occasionally involved in production. Another difference is that these were professional enterprises based on paid rather than voluntary labour, although the difference is one of degree, since Kino eventually took on a paid worker.

The practice of integrating production with distribution and exhibition was re-established in the late 60s by groups which had no direct links to the 30s, although some soon developed a relationship with Contemporary and Plato. Detailed histories of five of these groups explore the circumstances of their formation and their politics, aesthetics and methods of organisation. The five are selected first, because they illustrate between them a wide range of political influences, organisational structures and film practices; and second, because they were early and influential players in their particular fields. Considerable attention is paid to internal dynamics, because it is in its structure that a workshop can be expected to differ most obviously from a conventional company. In devising their own constitutions and working methods, group members confronted, in a very practical way, problems which, as activists, preoccupied them in a wider context: how to organise social relations in a way which is satisfying for the individuals involved, efficient enough to achieve objectives, tenable within a given external environment and allows for continuity and growth.

Drawing conclusions from these histories requires caution, since the groups differ in too many respects to be directly comparable, the accounts are largely subjective and the circumstances of recording varied. For instance, I knew some of the interviewees well, some only slightly and some not at all; some were talking about a group they had left long ago, while others discussed the background to their current working relationships. This is not to suggest that the latter were less frank but that the perspective is different. The dossier on Liberation Films, for instance, examines structural problems which are not even hinted at in an account researched in 1977 (Heinz Nigg and Graham Wade, 'Liberation Films', in *Community Media*). This is probably because the structure was not perceived as problematic at the time, rather than because the interviewees were being discreet.

One reasonably safe observation we can make from the material is that most gen-eralisations about workshops are misleading. Nevertheless, there are patterns of similarity and difference which invite comment. A common feature is that they all coalesced initially around shared political concerns with a commitment to using media for a political purpose rather than to film-making as such, although in the case of Amber, film-making was *one* of the initial objectives. A second feature com-mon to four of the groups is an international dimension in the early membership: of the three key members in Cinema Action, one was from Germany and one from Portugal; in Angry Arts/Liberation Films a Canadian, an American and an Aus-tralian played key roles; one of the Amber members is originally from Finland and one of Black Audio's from Ghana. Even in the context of the British media and art world, which tend to be relatively cosmopolitan in their recruitment, the compo-sition of these groups is atypical, suggesting that sharing different experiences is an important stimulus both to creative activity and to political analysis. However, Dave Douglass from Cinema Action is the only interviewee to make a point about the advantage of such contacts.

In terms of class and regional origins within Britain, the groups present no com-mon pattern. Cinema Action contained an extreme range from different geographical areas, some drawn from a moneyed, public-school-educated elite and some from the industrial working class. At the other end of the spectrum, the mem-bers of Black Audio present themselves as coming from essentially the same world: black, London and working class (although parents include school and college teachers, occupations not normally classified as working class). Data for Sheffield Co-op and Liberation Films from unpublished sections of interview show both groups as moderately mixed, with members from working-class and not particu-larly wealthy middle-class backgrounds. Taking the five groups together it emerges that a decisive majority of their members are either of working-class origin or from middle-class families with a strong left tradition, a finding which has some bearing on those critics of the collective movement who imply that they represent an 'unnatural' form of economic organisation, adopted in conformity to abstract theory. In these case studies it would seem that, on the contrary, the decision to work collectively was inspired less by theory than by inclination, influenced by a culture in which co-operation is valued; it is the working relations of competitive capitalism which are felt, not just theorised, to be 'unnatural'. Murray Martin makes this point very clearly in relation to his own commitment to the workshop concept and, although some interviewees are critical of particular experiences of collective working, the criticisms are mostly that collective principles were not properly adhered to.

The histories do not suggest any neat conclusions as to the most successful meth-ods of organisation, partly because of the difficulty of defining 'success', but also because the most measurable, objective criterion, durability, does not correlate strongly with one kind of structure over another. The longest lasting of the groups, Amber, has operated for twenty-nine years at the time of writing. Cinema Action comes next with twenty-one or twenty-five years of active life (depending on whether the last production or the closure of the premises is taken as the end of activity). Both represent fairly extreme applications of the collective principle, but otherwise were very different. Cinema Action was open and unstructured, while Amber early on had a defined membership, a structure and agreed policies on pay and working methods. Black Audio is thirteen years old at the time of writing and has been very successful in surviving the withdrawal of workshop funding and remaining consistently in production. Its formal structure and patterns of work are more those of a co-operative of producer/directors than a collective. Liberation Films had the shortest lifespan, operating for between ten and thirteen years (depending on how the group is defined), and it had the most orthodox formal structure of any of the five – namely, that of a non-profit-making limited company. But there is not enough evidence to suggest that the tensions referred to were *caused* by that structure, although they were certainly aggravated by a lack of clarity about it. Clear structures and procedures can help to overt problems, as Jenny Woodley points out, but they would seem to be neither sufficient nor necessary for survival: Cinema Action was effective for many years without them and, despite a well thought-out constitution, the Sheffield Co-op failed to prosper after the withdrawal of workshop funding. Even before the formal structure of Liberation Films had been determined, it is notable that, unlike Black Audio and Cinema Action, the group apparently could not deal with changes in relationships between its members, so that the ending of the personal partnership between Sue Crockford and Tony Wickert resulted in the former leaving. However, the problems leading to the winding-up of Liberation Films were not only internal. The difficulty of funding the kind of educational/community work the group specialised in was an important factor, and one which also affected the development of Sheffield Co-op, where it helped determine a shift away from a community-based practice towards producing for television.

Great variety in professional background and training exists both within and between the groups, but none conform completely to the notion promoted by some of the funders in the 80s that workshops are a kind of nursery for the inexperienced. Key people in Liberation Films and Cinema Action had considerable industry experience. Tony Wickert had worked in one of the most prestigious niches in television, as one of the BBC *Play for Today* team. Even Black Audio, formed by recent graduates with minimal training or experience in film-making, included one member who had worked at the BBC and, although she was not employed in programme-making, no doubt she could have progressed within the organisation had she not found its culture so antipathetic.

All the groups were committed to reaching an audience beyond that of a film intelligentsia associated with *Screen*, *Afterimage* and the IFA, and to some extent

succeeded. The arguments between film academics and film activists about audience and address, as articulated in the interviews, tend to pose the question as a
conflict between, on the one hand, engaging an audience of intellectuals in theoretical debate and, on the other, supporting working-class action. But some of the
comments, particularly those of Jenny Woodley, herself a teacher, are a reminder
that the struggle for cultural/political influence takes place in a complex arena
which is not neatly divided between an intelligentsia and a proletariat, and that, in
Britain, film theory and film art had a rather limited following even within the culture of the liberal professions. In this respect the strategy of Liberation Films is
interesting in that it included targeting particular professional groups like teachers,
health workers and social workers, encouraging them to re-examine, in the context
of their own use of the media, their assumptions about the way films transmit information or influence attitudes. While this work received little recognition from film
academics, it did raise questions about the relationship between texts and readers,
while the resistance the group met to a quite straightforward critique of the
authoritative, instructional documentary suggests they were proselytising in circles
which were unfamiliar with the debates of the 60s around *cinéma vérité* and had
remained quite untouched by concepts like 'dominant narrative discourse'. It is
also worth noting that Liberation Film's *Fly a Flag for Poplar* attracted the attention of one of the very few academics outside the world of film studies to have
written on workshop productions (see Gillian Rose, 'The Cultural Politics of Place:
Local Representation and Oppositional Discourse in Two Films').

Liberation Films closed down too soon to respond to the challenge of Channel
Four, which gave the other workshops the chance to address larger and less specialised audiences. However, looking at the development of the other four it is
doubtful how far, by itself, access to television translated into better opportunities
to change audience tastes and attitudes. A public completely satisfied by *World in
Action* or *Horizon* and unfamiliar with other documentary traditions was likely to
find a film like Cinema Action's *Rocking the Boat* over long and short on facts. Cinema Action and Amber continued to give a high priority to working directly with
audiences, but in the case of Sheffield Co-op, TV production began to take precedence over other work and the productions started to look more like conventional
television programmes. Black Audio was differently placed in that it was formed
after Channel Four had begun broadcasting and only made one film before receiv-
ing funds from it. Nevertheless, the group paid considerable attention to promoting
their work through other channels, writing, speaking at events, sending their films
to festivals, trying to obtain theatric releases for some productions and distributing non-theatrically, mainly to colleges and universities. As with all broadcast work
it is difficult to establish who the main audience is, but the group has certainly been
successful in gaining attention in professional and academic circles, particularly,
but by no means exclusively, among a black intelligentsia. *Handsworth Songs*, for
instance, ignited a controversy in the press, including a high-profile exchange in

the *Guardian* in which the principal participants, Salman Rushdie and Darcus Howe attacking, Stuart Hall defending, were well-known literary and intellectual figures. (The correspondence is reproduced in *Black Film British Cinema*, edited by Kobena Mercer.) At the same time the audiences reached through non-theatric distribution include a significant contingent of young black people from the world the group members themselves grew up in, and it would seem reasonable to assume that the films also interest this audience when broadcast. Success in reaching these two key kinds of audience was, no doubt, helped by favourable timing: they were one of the first black media groups and were raising issues of race when race was much in the news. But it was also the result of a determined programme of co-operative work involving a coherent strategy for getting the films noticed and discussed.

Apart from the self-evident difference that the members of Black Audio are black, while those of the other groups were and are, with one or two exceptions, white, Black Audio also stands out from the other groups in having been well received in the world of film theory and treated as relevant to discussions of film art. Two of its members are included in David Curtis's *Directory of British Film and Video Artists*, and the group features in Michael O'Pray's recent collection, *The British Avant-Garde Film*. The rationale behind inclusion and exclusion is intriguing. Unlike most film-makers classified as film-artists Black Audio (so far) produces primarily for television and, up to a point, use the audiovisual vocabulary of mainstream television. Some of the possible reasons for inclusion – namely, that some of the film-makers in the group have a fine arts background, that the films are distinctive and have an aesthetic consistency – are clearly not sufficient, as these would apply to both Amber and Cinema Action. One very obvious way that Black Audio's work differs from, for instance, Amber's output is in the degree to which it is reflexive and overtly concerned with questions about representation. But if this quality helped to earn them critical respect, it was initially perceived by the group to work against them by puzzling or alienating potential funders. Yet these funders were known to support other work precisely for such qualities. This apparently arbitrary way in which the workshops and their films have been classified, praised, dismissed or ignored by arts administrators and critics is a reminder that the process of inclusion/exclusion is highly complex and driven by political and social agendas as well as critical ones. The advantage of the workshop methods – collective or co-operative working and direct contact with audiences – is that it provides a base of strength from which those agendas can be questioned and challenged. The difficulty which all the groups encountered was how to sustain that base financially and with a reasonable degree of autonomy for long enough to make the challenge effective.

Contemporary Films

Interview recorded in 1995 with Charles Cooper, director of
Contemporary Films.

Kino, the War and Un-American Activities

MD—Let's go back briefly to your involvement with Kino in the 30s. Could you explain the background to why you appear in the Kino records under a different name?

CC—The name was Gralnick. I changed it when I was in New York.

My family came from Russia, from near Kiev, and my parents had come over to England in about 1895–6 with 2 young children – there were seven more born in England and I was the last. My father was a ritual kosher butcher.

MD—Was the family orthodox?

CC—Moderately. I went to *heder*. I translate from Hebrew into Yiddish. In our home our parents spoke to us in Yiddish, although we spoke to them in English.

MD—What brought you into politics?

CC—I must have been about twenty and I was in a socialist direction already. Then I met a friend I hadn't seen for quite a time and my friend told me how he was in love with a cousin of his who had come over from Russia and had just gone back. Over a period of about six months he converted me to what communism was all about. Also, returning to my own history, I had an elder brother whom I loved very dearly who had been in the First World War and had been gassed and shell shocked. He came back and lived for a year and a half and died. All these things had an effect. I felt one had to do something positive and I joined the party, a group in Hendon.

MD—And why did you get involved in the film side?

CC—I was already interested in films and I'd been doing a lot of photography. My whole generation learned from films and I know they had a terrific effect on me – films like *Battleship Potemkin* – seeing the sailors refusing to shoot on their fellow men, throwing the officers overboard. We'd never seen anything like that!

In the setting up and running of Kino I was secretary of the group. We worked on a voluntary basis, about eight of us. Then in 1935 we decided to take on a manager to take the pressure off us. They asked me if I would do the job, but I couldn't because I had just opened a butcher's shop in Wembley. I got married in 1935 – that was my first wife, Celia.

I didn't want to stay in the butcher business. I wanted to work with films full time. So, after about three years I sold the business, and my wife and I decided we would do a cycling tour in America. With the political situation as it was then we didn't know if England would go on the side of Germany or whatever. Another factor was that in 1938–9 there was a progressive President of Mexico – Cárdenas – and we were going to make a documentary of the Cárdenas administration. So I sold the business and got a little money, which enabled us to go to America.

We left England in June 1939, went to New York and cycled south as far as New Orleans, where my wife had an aunt. While we were there the war broke out and as citizens of a belligerent country we could no longer be allowed into Mexico. So we returned to New York. At that stage it was difficult to go back, so we decided to stay on, and that stay on took us to the end of 1950.

I was due to be called up into the American army in 1942 but the call-up was cancelled because my wife had just had a baby. So, I found work. Through friends I started working in a labour organisation, the International Workers' Order, where I was in charge of starting a film department.

The idea was to keep up the culture of the minorities, that America should not be the melting pot where you forget whether you came from Italy or Russia or wherever.

MD–I thought at that time the radical idea was integration?

CC–No. On the one hand, you integrate gradually, on the other hand, the idea was that if people come from Italy or Romania – and especially with black people, if they feel that the only thing is to be American it creates an alienation.

The International Workers' Order was doing a lot of good work, it had crèches, it was fighting for a national health plan, but it was considered a communist organisation. At the end of the war, in 1946–7, Attorney-General Clark, I think, brought out a list of about a hundred organisations that were considered un-American, and this was one of them. The state was out to smash it. So the organisation allowed me to buy the film department and I carried on with it as a commercial thing but along the same lines as we'd always done. A year later I wanted to make a trip back to England, but first I had to sort out my resident's status. Something was holding it up and my lawyer told me, 'They've issued a deportation order. They've got on your record that you showed a Russian film in Pennsylvania in 1945' – when Russia was their ally!

In the end we decided not to stay on. We came back at the end of 1950 and I knew exactly what I wanted to do. I set up the film library in Frith Street and registered the name as Contemporary Films. This was February 1951.

Contemporary Films – The Distribution

CC–I had a house in London that we'd been paying for on the HP while we were away, so I was able to take a loan on that – about £4,000, which was a lot of money then – and bought some prints and made sure I had the rights for 16mm.

I started off with 16mm and the thing that encouraged me was that there was a big film society movement with 700 groups round the country. They provided an

Children of Hiroshima (Kaneto Shindo, Japan, 1952).

audience and we used to have a kickback from them as to how they felt about the films. It was a whole culture that has largely disappeared.

Then I met George Hollering who ran the Academy Cinema. I'd been told he'd be a difficult person to work with, and we didn't agree politically, but we accepted each other's viewpoint. He liked quality films and I knew that if I bought particular films he'd be pleased to open them. The way the business was then, you wanted to have a long run. A number of films ran for a year and this was good publicity and you knew you had a steady income from it. We would release films on 35mm with a theatrical opening and then on 16mm for the film societies.

The other thing that was happening was that we were taking a lot of Soviet and Eastern European films, and at that time the British major companies were not supplying films to Eastern Europe. So, we began sending over these British films. Then the British companies saw this and started dealing directly. They came to the Moscow film festival for the first time in 1959.

MD–Why did you set up your own company rather than working as part of the Party?

CC–Had the Party set it up and said, 'you run it', I'd have done that. But I couldn't see that coming. The other thing was that I did have a disagreement with the Party, with certain people who suggested that I run the organisation handling only Russian or East European films, but I said, 'nothing doing', because I wanted to release worthwhile films from wherever they were made. We were releasing films from thirty-five different countries.

MD–What films do you remember as particularly important?

CC–*Children of Hiroshima* was one. About 1954 someone in the Esperanto Association told me that this film had come out in Japan, made with support from the teachers' union. We couldn't get a good enough print for Hollering, who was a

Pather Panchali (Satyajit Ray, India, 1955).

stickler for quality, and we opened it in the Marble Arch Cinema. We got a very good response and it started the ball rolling, that you could take a political film and open it in a cinema.

Later there were the Wajda films, Resnais – *Last Year in Marienbad* – the Satyajit Ray films.

MD–How did you first hear about Ray?

CC–This was when Ray was making his first film, *Pather Panchali*, and it was through Marie Seton, who was an old friend. I didn't support the Empire. Because of the way I grew up and my influences, I felt we needed to have relationships with people from other countries based on mutual respect. The basis of the distribution library was to find films from other parts of the world which had something to say.

MD–Were you worried about taking *Pather Panchali* when Indian films were virtually unkown in Britain and the director was new to films even in India?

CC–There were always risks in opening films. For instance, with *La Règle du jeu* – Renoir – we never thought it would work We put it on late nights at the Academy and it ran for a year. Then we put it on in the day time – it ran for three months.

MD–Do you still feel you can't predict what will go down and what won't?

CC–You need to work on your own reactions. During your stay at the festival you will bump into film critics of the national press and have the opportunity to obtain their reactions. It becomes a summing-up job. We could never have distributed these films if we hadn't had the support of the critics.

Difficulties with Production

MD–At the time you set up in distribution, why do you think there was no revival of the kind of production work that groups like Kino had done in the 30s?

CC–Well, there was the war. People were still in the process of coming back. Then you had to ask for money. I thought myself, first of all, that I would produce and make films, but I found it so terribly difficult. You had to raise money and you spend half your life doing this. People want to see guaranteed results. We've never had any finance put into the company from outside, and I couldn't have a situation with someone breathing down my neck saying, 'This is not making enough money'. Whereas with distribution we could do the things we wanted to do.

MD–I was thinking more of the kind of political films made with almost no money. Some individual films of this kind were made in the 50s but it wasn't as organised as before the war, was it?

CC–It was a matter of a few people getting together and paying for film stock.

MD–A bit later there was the CND film and you were involved as the distributor, weren't you?

CC–This was *March to Aldermaston*. In 1958 there was a group who got together to make a film of the march. We assured them it would be distributed and people from ACTT came in and filmed without making any charge. One of the people working with the group was Lindsay Anderson. He was going to do the editing and finishing off. Being the sort of person he was, he put himself up and then rushed off somewhere. So, the filming was finished and Lindsay was not around and we arranged for somebody else to do the editing. After some weeks Lindsay shows up, and I was one of those who said we should let him do it because he's got talent. So he did the editing and narration and made a first-class film of it.

Another film we involved Lindsay in was the *Adventures of Private Pooley*, from a book published in the late 50s and serialised in the *Evening Standard*. It was based on a true story about a British regiment which surrendered, after the fall of France, to a German regiment under two Nazi officers, who marched the prisoners into a field and shot them. A director came over from East German TV and said he'd like to make a film about it and would I help him? So I arranged with Actors' Equity and sent over eleven actors, and we asked Lindsay Anderson to go and edit our version of it.

MD–You and Lindsay wouldn't have seen eye to eye politically?

CC–To me Lindsay was a great humanist. He had the talent and I wouldn't take any notice of what he thought about communists. He could be destructive, but the point is he could take material and had the ability to make something out of it. And he wasn't controlled by money.

The Cinemas

CC–I was also interested in developing our own cinemas. There weren't enough independent cinemas, and if you wanted to release quality films you had to have your own. In 1967 we bought the first cinema, the Paris Pullman in Kensington. I took it with two other people: one was an accountant at the BFI and one was James Quinn, who was Director of the BFI. So we opened our films at the Academy and the Paris Pullman.

MD–But a place like that in Kensington was quite far from the original objectives of Kino wasn't it? It was a very upmarket district.

CC–I have to say I'd have been afraid of taking the risk of going into many working-class areas with a foreign-language film with subtitles. It took a certain degree of education to take a film with subtitles.

MD–Was this a drawback to the whole objective of propagating political ideas through films?

CC–I don't know. Certainly there was a class thing that kept a lot of people out, but you'd hope that somewhere along the line people coming from a lower income level would come in and see a film and get caught up in it. I mean, I got caught up in quality films in the early days.

MD–How did you see the cinemas developing?

CC–We started with the Paris Pullman in 1967 and we had that for about seventeen years. Then we had the Phoenix in East Finchley for about twelve years and a twin cinema in Oxford for about twelve years. It was a question of doing them up and then making sure that they were doing something for the area, that people could come along and discuss the films. You'd be able to bring in the director. You'd have a restaurant. So the cinema becomes a centre. People paid an annual membership and got a percent off the seat prices. Then there were free screenings on Sunday afternoon, so that if someone had made a political documentary there was a chance show it.

We developed the three cinemas on our own and we thought if we go ahead and have twenty or thirty then it would be self-sustaining. But we needed to finance it, and in that period – this was about 1985 – for an overdraft from the bank we were paying 19 or 20 per cent interest. I remember I called in someone from Hambros Bank and said we'd like to extend and buy other cinemas, and he said, 'What do you think you can make in the cinemas?' and I said, 'I suppose about 10 per cent' and he said, 'That's not good for us. It's got to be 30 to 40 per cent.' But if we'd had a sympathetic government they could have lent money at 5 per cent, as it was for cultural purposes. This would have made sense. So from our part there's a frustration that we weren't able to do the job we wanted to do.

The cinemas paid their way, but I felt it needed to be done on a bigger scale.

MD–So you sold the cinemas?

CC–We sold the Paris Pullman first in 1983; the one in East Finchley in 1985 and Oxford about five or six years ago.

Now, even the few film societies that are left are showing just popular English-speaking films. A whole culture of quality foreign films is not happening and the films are not being made as well, because people can't see the outlets. It goes round in a circle.

Plato Films

Interview recorded in 1995 with Stanley Forman, director of Plato Films.

From Anti-Fascism to Plato Films

MD—How did you become involved with political film?

SF—The politics certainly came first. It began at school, and the year is 1936, when I would have been fifteen. I had the good fortune to be at a school in the East End – coming from lower-middle-class East End Jewish origins – and among the people that taught me was Michael Stewart, who subsequently became Foreign Secretary in Harold Wilson's government. Remember, the Spanish Civil War was on, and there was a ferment of discussion among my group of friends, and very quickly we were all in the Labour Party League of Youth. That was run – at least in the London area – by Ted Willis, who subsequently became Lord Ted Willis, and he persuaded a group of us to join the Young Communist League. So, from 1937, within a year, I was incredibly active in the YCL, to the detriment of what academic studies one did in those days, and became involved with cultural things including films, but not obsessed with films. I was more into music, and taking groups of people to the opera and ballet. But there was a cinema in Villiers Street, called the Forum, which was so close to Charing Cross Station that you got the noise of the trains at various moments through the film ...

MD—Like the fleapit in *The Smallest Show on Earth*?

SF—Yes. Exactly. And we went to everything that we could possibly afford, and they were showing Soviet films at the time, and that's really where my interest in Soviet culture began.

Then the war came and before I knew where I was I was doing a political job in Yorkshire in Leeds, where I met Hilda. But after about a year I was called up and we're into the war and we can skip that.

MD—You weren't doing anything to do with film?

SF—Not at all. I was something called a gun-position officer's assistant in the Essex Yeomanry. So, I had a hard war, I was in D-Day, the beaches, Arramanches and all that. I was just a gunner until the war ended, and then I got promoted because I had German, and I had two quite fascinating years in Kiel, as interpeter in a big prisoner of war camp and as a de-nazification officer. I got out of the army eventually in February 1947. By now I have married Hilda, another communist – in those days you never considered the field any further than the party. Hilda Forman was then a civil servant, working for the Ministry of Supply in Leeds.

What happened next was I was persuaded by the Party to become the General Secretary of the British-Soviet Friendship Society – British-Soviet Society, as it was then called. In 1947, 1948 this was quite a well-heeled organisation, because we were only a couple of years removed from the war, and even though the 'Grand Alliance' with the Red Army was over and Churchill had made his cold war Fulton speech in 1946, the old ideological superstructure spun on. There were still illustrious people on the executive – not just J. D. Bernal, but people like D. M. Pritt KC, the distinguished anti-fascist lawyer, Hewlett Johnson, the Dean of Canterbury, Professor Gordon Childe, the archaeologist, J. B. S. Haldane and a whole clutch of professors who were involved with Soviet affairs in their particular fields. It had a lot of members, and branches throughout the country, and a large staff.

This was when films entered my life, because we began to organise film shows. We ran them at what became 60 Charlotte Street, the first headquarters of Channel Four, in a theatre called the Scala. We would hire the theatre, and the films were loaned free by the Soviet Embassy: we showed them every month and it was a big theatre, holding, I should think, about 1,500, and it would be packed to capacity irrespective of whether the film was a great Soviet classic or junk.

It was good fun, and that went on until I decided I'd had enough of the British-Soviet Friendship Society. This was because I kept being elected to take delegations to Russia, but at the last moment, I'd be rung by the office to be told, 'I'm very sorry, but your visa hasn't come through.' You see, my full name on my passport was *Israel* Stanley Forman.

MD–Did you realise that's what was going on?

SF–I became growingly aware that the reason why I wasn't going on these trips – which after all were the perks of the job – was the fact that I was Jewish. As simple as that. So I left the job, but not in a hostile way. I was still on the executive of the British-Soviet Friendship movement. Then through a friend – in those days, I'm afraid, the appointment of union officials in small unions was ...

MD–Nepotistic?

SF–Indeed! – I became national organiser of the Civil Service Union (CSU). And that's when Ivor Montagu entered my life. Because every time I would go to the TUC or a trade union conference, Ivor, who was one of the key activists of the ACT, was there. So, I got to know Ivor well and some other party people who did not quite know what to do with a load of films which were now coming not just from the Soviet Union but from Eastern Europe and China. So, I had a discusssion with Ivor and one or two others and Bill Wainwright, who had taken my job with the BSFS, and became Deputy General Secretary of the party. He said, 'We've got all these 16mm films arriving, cluttering up the office of the BSFS, and we haven't got the resources to do anything with them but we *do* have a bit of money from BSFH Ltd' – British-Soviet Friendship Houses Limited was a bizarre organisation established during the war to buy houses where Britains and Russians could meet. With the cold war happening it never got off the ground, but the money was there and

I was given very quickly £500 pounds and some personal donations to form a company. So we were able to set up Plato Films.

In 1950 it was seen purely as a political venture. We started very modestly. We produced our first catalogues and got films reviewed in journals like *Film User*. Of course, we had an enthusiastic clientele – not so many schools and churches but all the BSFS branches wanted Soviet films and all the branches of the Britain-China Friendship Association wanted Chinese films. We acted as the distribution centre for these Friendship organisations, which were all to a degree subsidised. One must be truthful about this: essentially they were all part of the long arm of the various embassies, who didn't pour in money but gave enough to keep them going.

MD–This must also have been about the time that Charles Cooper was setting up Contemporary?

SF–Exactly when we were formed. But there wasn't embarrassment that Charles wanted to set up Contemporary Films. We never fell out. Charles and I have never to this day had a quarrel, but there was a real difference of opinion. There were two views: ours, which wasn't followed, and Ivor Montagu's. Our view was that there should be one organisation, because Jack Gaster, the lawyer who helped us set up Plato Films, felt that with two we'd never be strong enough to survive. Ivor Montagu felt that two organisations would be better than one, providing that Charlie stuck to feature films and we stuck to documentaries. Ivor's view prevailed because Charles had the right to form a company. He didn't have to obey party discipline. We were never a Party institution, never part of the Party machinery like Central Books or like Lawrence and Wishart, the publishers. We were always a private limited company. That was the pattern that Jack Gaster decided for us, very wisely. It gave us a degree of independence which we would never have had had we been part of the King Street set-up.

Charles went out to get really worthwhile feature films; we never had Charles's financial resources So, there was a *modus vivendi*.

MD–And when did Concord start?

SF–Much later. It was started by Eric Walker, who used to work for us as our 'rewind boy'. He helped rewind films, drove our projection service.

Audiences, Finance and the Cold War

SF–Every night the projection service would go out with a film, and a portable screen to wherever – trade union halls, church halls, school halls, the small Conway Hall.

We're talking about the mid-50s, and the Friendship Societies were still going strong, but we had churches who were interested in Russia, or China. We had schools, we had film societies, we had the growing peace movement.

MD–You weren't too tainted politically for schools?

SF–No, we had a terrific advantage, in that we practically gave the films away for nothing, and if you look through our old catalogues, you'll find that side by side with the overtly political documentaries, there were films on geography, nature study, animal life, architecture, medical films. We did specialised mail-outs.

The best client we had was the army: the Joint Services School for Linguists. Then there were nunneries – odd, quirky things like that. We never succeeded in getting the Labour Party to show films seriously. The Communist Party branches and the Young Communist League did but very rarely did we get a Labour Party branch.

MD–Did you get many trade unions?

SF–A few, not a lot …

MD–That's always been a problem. Left film-makers have endlessly tried to get something going with trade unions, and it never went far.

SF–Over and over again we tried. We circularised, we went to meetings with shop stewards, we arranged regional conferences on film and the labour movement which were well attended. We did everything that could be done within the limits of what was possible.

By the way, the Party didn't bother much about us – by 'us' I mean Charles Cooper and I – they very rarely asked what we were up to – except when there were general elections, and the party had to make an election broadcast film. Then they got very excited indeed and were round here every half-hour. These broadcasts were made on 35mm film and the Party was allowed four minutes, forty seconds, based on the number of candidates standing. We did some good things, by the way: we were voted the 'best election film' in 1963.

MD–How did your finances work? Did the distribution make money?

SF–We were afloat. We never made a profit, although it wasn't a charity. The arrangement we'd made with the Russians was, if we were given a serious film which had commercial possibilities on television – a major Bolshoi opera, or a ballet, and we sold it to the BBC – we would split the proceeds.

MD–When did you start to break even?

SF–I would think that began during the 60s, except that you have to remember that we always reflected the ups and downs of politics, so 1956, during the Soviet invasion of Hungary, we were broke.

MD–This was because everyone suddenly stopped hiring from you?

SF–Yes! Everyone! Including the left, including the labour movement. Then it got better but when the Soviet invasion of Czechoslovakia happened in 1968, we took another dive.

MD–But in the normal way, the charges that you were making for hire would keep you ticking over without a subsidy?

SF–We never had a subsidy. All we had was the money we were given at the start. The money we charged for film hire, and putting on film shows, would just keep our noses above water.

MD–But you got these films free, or very cheap. So in a sense you were subsidised by the stock coming in?

SF—In a sense this is true. But remember, we had to print catalogues, advertise, publicise, pay our overheads ...

MD—Did you pay this out of the hire charges?

SF—Yes. Absolutely. And we broke even. And we gave ourselves a pittance – what was then called 'the party wage'. But we were never able to go to a film festival and offer real money for films which we knew were good, and which had a future.

The Speidel Affair

SF—After we got the distribution going, the next big moment was the relationship with East Germany, the GDR. Because of UFA and the whole pre-Hitler back-ground, the East German film industry was always sophisticated and intelligent in the way they handled their foreign partners. They very quickly discovered my exis-tence, and I got invited to see some awful stuff, but some good stuff as well. They started producing remarkable documentaries like the films made by the Thorndikes. From the mid-50s there was a big campaign against Nazis in high places in West German society, and the Thorndikes made a film about Heinz Rheinefath, who had been responsible for the putting down of the resistance in the Warsaw Ghetto, and was then the mayor of the German holiday town of Sylt.

There was a series of films called *The Archives Testify*, and one was about Hans Speidel, who was allegedly involved in the assassination of Monsieur Barthou and King Alexander of Yugoslavia in Marseilles in 1934 – a very big moment in politi-cal history It was clear that apart from the people who were actually paid to do the job, the German Embassy had a lot to do with it. The man who was running it at the time was Hans Speidel, who was then, in 1959, Commander of Nato Central European Land Forces.

MD—Why did these films not make more of a splash?

SF—There was a tremendous splash at the time about the Speidel film, *Operation Teutonic Sword*. We could not get a censor's certificate and there was a long battle with the censor, John Trevelyan, who subsequently wrote in his autobiography that the only errors he made were in relation to Stanley Forman's documentaries from East Germany.

Anyway, the Speidel film changed everything, because it meant we had to shut up shop as Plato Films. We were sued for libel by Speidel ... well, by the West German government, really. They provided the money.

MD—The case was that Speidel had not really had anything to do with ...

SF—No, he limited his case to the things which he knew we couldn't prove in a British court, because the documents used in the film were photocopies.

MD—So, in terms of how this case would have been viewed by a non-communist who looked at it carefully, would they have concluded that Speidel did have a sinister Nazi past?

SF—Oh yes.

MD—In that case why ...

Operation Teutonic Sword, in the series *The Archives Testify* (Annelie Thorndike, East Germany, 1959)

SF—...Why was he a Nato commander?

MD—Yes, and why was it not seen as a major scandal?

SF—It almost took off. As far as the London *Evening Standard* was concerned, we were banner headlines, night after night, because when you can't get a censor's certificate, you can submit the film to your local authority; and so we submitted it to the London County Council, the LCC. And there were great debates, a special meeting was convened just to consider this business of *Teutonic Sword*, and we won by one vote – the casting vote of the chairman! Remember, the LCC in those days was not the GLC under Ken Livingstone.

MD—So, there was conflict about censorship at the national and local level, and on top of that there was a libel case?

SF—The libel case came some days after the LCC had granted the certificate. It followed hot on the heels of that.

We were assured by our East German producers, DEFA, that 'We will provide the money to fight the case.' It wasn't a secret. Everyone knew we wouldn't have the money to fight a Nazi general in the High Court. But we received no more than was necessary: one had to produce the bills.

But the first bit of advice I got from our QCs was, 'You must form another company.' So, in 1960–1 we formed ETV. But we were also advised to keep Plato going. So, we've had this curious thing of having two companies, but one real organisation.

The Leipzig Festival

SF—I was a founder – together with Joris Ivens, Vladimir Pozner, John Grierson, all sorts of East Germans and others – of the Leipzig International Film Festival, which was first held in 1959. I had the job of bringing a bunch of British documentary film-makers plus what I thought were among the best British documentary films to Leipzig each year. I already knew Grierson because of his programme *This Wonderful World*, but through Leipzig I got to know Edgar Anstey, Basil Wright, Arthur Elton. Arthur Elton became a great friend, because we were together on the committee of the SFA, the Scientific Film Association. He worked with Klingender and all sorts of good Marxists. He wasn't afraid of the word.

You remember Peter Watkins and *The War Game*? We took the film to Leipzig, with Peter Watkins, and it was banned by the stupid people who did the selection. I had to fight like a tiger to get that film shown fairly secretly, in the basement of the cinema.

Production

MD–The Progressive Film Institute (PFI) and Kino came to an end with the war, didn't they? I'm puzzled by why, when there was all this activity before the war, and many of those involved were still around after the war, why it took so long before there was a concerted attempt to make films?

SF–It took a long time because, alas, people tended to plough their own furrows. I don't think anyone was big enough – in the best sense of that word – to say, 'Well, we ought to get together more.' There was a Party film-makers' group, but it all withered away. There was a very good guy called Anthony Simmons who was involved, and there was Ralph Bond in ACT Films. But after the war, the co-operative movement was a bit half-hearted. Then there was the cold war, the anti-Sovietism, Korea, Stalin, Hungary and all the rest of it. It was never the same after 1956.

MD–How far was it the cold war fragmenting the left, and how far was it that, with the establishment of things like the Arts Council ...

SF–And the development of the British Film Institute ...

MD–... it wasn't thought necessary to do things on your own, without state funding?

 SF–I think it's a mixture. There was a lot of fragmentation. People wanted to do their own things.

MD–Were you involved in the CND film?

SF–Aldermaston and Lindsay Anderson. I knew Lindsay rather well, and we didn't really go for each other. He saw me as a communist *apparatchik*, and I saw him as a difficult intellectual. I realise he was a terrific asset, but we really would never hit it off together, even in his most progressive phase.

MD–Anti-Apartheid was another issue the left was fairly united on. Do you remember much related film activity?

SF–There was a film group formed by the International Defence and Aid Foundation, run by Barry Feinberg, and we helped him a great deal.

A lot of these people were lovely people, but not particularly talented film-makers. We didn't produce many geniuses like Joris Ivens, a director with fantasy, with imagination, who could make a film which was really an interesting thing to look at, and to enjoy. So much of our stuff is boring. I loved Ralph Bond, but if you look at all his work in documentaries ...

MD—There was a lack of sparkle?

SF—Yes. I became slowly convinced that we would only get somewhere if we made films on British subjects which were of concern to people. Films about unemployment, housing, and so on, not just the old Kino-type May Day demonstrations. So we began very painfully to make our own films, but only very, very modestly.

We managed this because we were shooting certain things for East German Television – they had no diplomatic relations and therefore used us as the cultural department of a non-existent embassy. But this gave us the equipment and the crew, so we were able to make the odd thing for ourselves. It was a distinguished crew, with wonderful people like Wolf Schuchitsky, Walter Lassally.

We made *The History of Labour Monthly* in 1971 about the Marxist journal, *Labour Monthly*, and the *Unveiling of the Karl Marx Memorial*, when there was a new statue of Karl Marx put up in Highgate Cemetery.

MD—Did you not think about making your own films earlier on, in the 50 or 60s?

SF—Yes. We were always being asked, 'Can't you persuade the Transport and General, the major unions, to make films?' But, with a few exceptions, we never got anywhere.

MD—I suppose the restricted resources you had for acquiring films limited the degree to which you could help other film-makers?

SF—Yes, but we always tried. We got to know Liberation Films, Tony Wickert and Sue Crockford. We also got to know Schlacke and Cinema Action, and we just opened our arms to them, because they were clearly doing the right thing, and our only problem was that we never had financial resources to give them. We tried to help where we could. Like with the films on the miners' struggle.

MD—The films on the 1984 strike? Were you involved in that?

SF—Yes, we were. We even scraped the bottom of our financial barrel to help. Then there was Chris Reeves from Platform Films who did *The People's Flag* and got it on Channel Four. I know he interviewed everyone I suggested, and he ended up using a tremendous amount of our footage. Remember that Ivor bequeathed to us – during his lifetime – almost every foot of film that he had ever shot for the Progressive Film Institute.

We always weigh up who is a friend, who's doing a really worthwhile job, and if they can afford to pay the going rate, that's fine, and if they can't, okay, one negotiates. We don't like to turn people away.

Angry Arts Film Society and Liberation Films

The justification for running these groups together is that their membership and activities overlapped and they were, for a time, so closely associated that outsiders, and even members, talked as if they were the same organisation under different names.

The political focus for both was the Camden group of the Vietnam Solidarity Campaign which became Camden Movement for People's Power (CMPP).

The retrospective accounts are from interviews recorded in 1995 and 1996 with: Tony Wickert, Secretary and principal worker of Liberation Films, 1970–81; Sue Crockford, active in the group from 1969 to 1971; Geoff Richman, member of the Council of Management of Liberation Films from 1972 to 1981, and active in the group from 1969; Ron Orders, employee of Liberation Films, 1970–8; and from a letter of 1996 from Ellen Adams, co-founder of the Angry Arts Film Society. At the time, all the above except Geoff Richman worked, or aimed to work, in the media. Geoff was, and remained, a GP, whose involvement in film was on an entirely voluntary basis.

Backgrounds

Ellen Adams

EA–I was what the Americans call a red diaper baby, born to parents with distinctly socialist leanings. I grew up (in Canada) absorbing their attitudes and beliefs as though they were the most obvious and natural ones to hold. Since I hadn't acquired them later in life via a more intellectual or rebellious route, I often lacked facts and figures in the debating arsenal, and consequently didn't feel I was a very effective defender of my beliefs.

My father was one of the fourteen people arrested and charged with espionage in the wake of Igor Gouzenko's defection from the Soviet Embassy in Ottawa in 1946. He has a degree in electrical engineering and a Master of Business Administration, and had been summoned to Ottawa in 1940 to join the wartime civil service. Although he was acquitted on the charges laid against him, the publicity and newly emerging cold war hysteria surrounding these trials had the effect of ruining his career. After a few years of working at various odd jobs (and some of them were pretty odd), he decided it would be best to leave the country until things calmed down. Being an economist he was curious to see how Eastern Europe was developing. So, my parents, older sister and I set sail in 1950 and, after visiting England and Czechoslovakia, settled in Warsaw, Poland, for six years, returning home in the spring of 1957.

Sue Crockford

SC—I grew up in what is now a suburb of South London, but it was countryside then. My dad was a self-made professional from working-class origins, so panicked by the poverty of the Depression that he had rejected a place at art school, although he was a talented artist, in return for the 'safe' professional civil service. He married above himself – my mum's father worked in a bank – and cut himself off from his family. Politically, he gradually moved to the right, especially when the death of the *News Chronicle* meant there was no middlebrow paper with independent leanings, so we were left with *Daily Mail* views which, without my being aware of it, helped shape my early opinions. I remember writing an essay about the fear of being taken over by the Chinese creeping quietly across several oceans undetected! While well versed in the graphic style of many artists, I was politically pretty naive. At one point I thought the world was divided into Christians and Catholics, and up to the sixth form I had no idea that Jews also shared the Old Testament. This may sound incredible in an age of information overload (we were too poor to have a television when I was growing up), but that experience was useful in two ways: I have such powerful memories of experiencing and sharing a right-wing belief system that I don't have any simple dislike of people who remain so; it also has helped me not confuse ignorance with lack of intelligence.

MD—What was your first involvement with politics?

SC—A friend showed me pictures of the police shooting people at Sharpeville. At first I didn't believe them. And part of the horror was that before that I'd only really seen violence at the movies (a rare treat), where the film's construction built you up to expect a killing, while this was so ordinary, matter of fact – midday and these white South African policemen so unemotional at what they were doing – ordinary poorly dressed people crumpled on the ground. I have never forgotten it, and it was the end of childhood in a way. From that moment on I realised that if you once know something and do nothing about it you are complicit.

Geoff Richman

GR—I joined the Young Communist League in 1953, having come at it through starting to write poetry and reading Mayakovsky. I was then a student at the medical school in Hampstead, but I was born in Leeds where my father had ended up working as a time keeper in a little engineering factory. He voted Labour. But I wanted something more than being just Labour.

I went to a YCL meeting and at the end, in proper revivalist fashion, the man who was running the meeting asked for people who wanted to join to come forward and I joined, and my life was never the same again.

MD—Why?

GR—I could never afterwards rest content with any ordinary sort of existence. To become a revolutionary, even for people who go in for quite light-hearted reasons, marks you. It's a complete system that you embrace. It's a way of thinking about everyone, how you deal with marriage and family and occupation.

MD—Was Marie a communist? [Marie is Geoff's wife, also a member of the Council of Management of Liberation Films. Ed.]

GR—Not then. She joined before we married. Afterwards, we moved to Tufnell Park and joined the local branch (Stanley Forman's branch), and were active in the YCL and the branch. I got involved in the student branch and then I joined the Socialist Medical Association. That had begun, under another name, in 1912, and was the body that persuaded the Labour Party to embrace the idea of a National Health Service. It was federated to the Labour Party but was one of the few bodies that didn't operate the ban against communists. I was put on the executive and this enabled me to go and talk on SMA policy to trade unions, co-operatives, women's organisations.

Tony Wickert

TW—I left Australia in 1961 to pursue a career as an actor. I tried to get to the States because of Hollywood, obviously, but that was ruled out, because they accept very few immigrants. So, I went to London and worked in the theatre and on feature films, and then there came a crisis. In Sydney, in the company, The Ensemble, that I was a founder member of, we used acting techniques that were traced back from Stanislavsky and the Moscow Arts Theatre through to the Actors' Studio. In Britain it was text based. To be an actor was to come on stage, to adopt certain mannerisms of an actor which were linked to the character, wear the costumes, say the lines and get off the stage without falling over. I was in a play, called *Naked Island,* and I hated the way it was being rehearsed. In the end I walked out. I'd never done anything like that before.

I had been a stage manager and directed in Australia, and decided to have a go here and to aim for television. There was only one way in – the holiday relief system at the BBC.

MD—BBC drama then was more theatre than film oriented, wasn't it?

TW—Yes. They weren't interested that I had film experience. But I got the job and I loved it and they loved me, and it was a romance from then on. And then there was BBC2 starting, and I was in the right place at the right time. [BBC2 began transmitting in 1964. Ed.]

MD—Had you been to college or university?

TW—No. I learned about literature, about drama, on the job.

MD—Wasn't that a bit unusual then in the BBC, to be of working-class origin and without a degree? How did you find it?

TW—It was fine. I didn't present myself as an Australian. I detected quite a deep racism towards anyone who wasn't one of them – a middle-class, middle-English-speaking person. So, I quickly became a Londoner. But I got on well with all my colleagues.

There was a floor devoted to drama and everybody came to work at the same time as if it was an office job, so we all knew each other. There was Chris Morahan, who was a consummate craftsman in multi-camera television; Ron Eyre; James Ferman … What was going on then was that the *Wednesday Play* was a big hit and Ken Loach had just finished *Cathy Come Home* when I joined the team. Later on he did *The Big Flame* and I was assistant director on that.

MD—It sounds a wonderful situation. What made you leave?

TW—The first thing is there was a change in the political environment in TV, because Hugh Carleton-Greene [DG 1960–9] was either sacked or moved on as the Director-General, and as a result the climate in drama began to change.

Then the BBC were hiring people from a pool of freelance directors, rather than taking on staff directors, and it looked as if one of the best ways to get work was to become a freelancer. So, my reason for leaving in 1967 was more professional than political.

The Vietnam Solidarity Campaign and Angry Arts

Geoff Richman

GR—In 1956 nearly all the intelligentsia left the Party, but we stayed in because we couldn't see an alternative. Then we got involved with a Maoist opposition within the Party and I wrote and circulated a paper saying that the Party wasn't addressing the real issues in society. I was breaking a Party rule by circulating this, and it was like being caught speeding: you receive a missive saying, 'It appears you have infringed rule 15e. Would you like to come and discuss this at the district?' And we went and they said, 'Are you willing to recant?'

MD—Did they do this completely straight-faced?

GR—They didn't find it a comedy at all. And we were very distressed, because the Party was the centre of our lives. We were expelled in 1966.

We were already involved with these Maoists and out of that we developed what we called the Friday Group, meant to be non-hierarchical and not rule bound. There were a couple of Americans in it, Henry and Sheli Wortis, and that is very significant, because they were the link to Vietnam. They joined the Stop It Committee [Americans in Britain for US withdrawal from Vietnam. Ed.]. During 1967 the Vietnam Solidarity Campaign, which had been created by the IMG (International Marxist Group), began to attract larger numbers of people and some of us in the Friday Group went along to the organising meetings for 1967. October 1967 was a surprisingly large demonstration and very militant, and after that we started a local VSC. I chaired all the national meetings of VSC through 1968, and I argued that what is important about a demonstration is its internal organisation and that it's only a tactic, not a strategy. If a demonstration is a way that people speak to each other, recognise their own strength, get to know each other, then it must be organised by communities, because that's where people get together. The focus had to be on developing communities.

Ellen Adams

[Since returning to Canada Ellen had studied zoology and had subsequently taken a laboratory job in Boston, where she married Richard Hamerschlag, a biochemist. Just before leaving to accompany Richard, who was to take up a research post in England, she worked on a voluntary basis at WGBH, the educational television station, and acquired her first experience with 16mm film. In London she started working professionally as an assistant film editor. Ed.]

EA–Shortly after our arrival in London Richard and I joined the Stop It Committee. He had become politicised over the war in Vietnam and although not a draft resister (he had an academic deferment) he became quite active during the years in London.

Early on in the Stop It Committee meetings we learned that the group had a debt to pay off that had been incurred as a result of events the group had held during the summer under the general heading Angry Arts Week. These included some film showings among other activities. Richard and I volunteered to revitalise the film showings and organised the Angry Arts Film Society, to raise money to pay off the debt. We launched our first season of four programmes in the spring of 1968.

By the autumn of 1968 we were including many films made by Newsreel, a group founded in New York in the mid-60s by several radical independent film-makers like Norm Fruchter and Robert Kramer. Richard and I became the distributors in the UK for Newsreel films.

The big demonstration against the war in Vietnam that took place in London on 27 October 1968, organised by the VSC, became a focal point from which several other events spun off. One was the making of the film *End of a Tactic?* by me and Richard. Most of the analytical comments on it were made by members of Camden Movement for People's Power: Geoff and Marie Richman, Geoff Crossick (all subsequently members of the Management Council of Liberation Films) and Henry Wortis (a member of the Stop It Committee, doing medical research in London). As a result of making *End of a Tactic?* and, through it, getting to know the CMPP people, I began attending their meetings and participating in their activities. Richard didn't.

Tony Wickert

TW–It wasn't until the middle of 1968 that Sue and I, reading about Vietnam and the London demonstrations, felt that we too should be active and decided to find out what it would be like to be in a group. So we went along to Camden VSC, and once immersed, of course, your consciousness is raised. I had met

Sue before through some BBC friends and, as I remember it, we grew together politically.

Sue Crockford

sc–The Vietnam group was very interested in mixed media. We were doing plays, leafleting and sticking up posters. For instance, a factory in Kentish Town was a subsidiary of Dow Chemicals which made napalm, and we produced a little play and a leaflet which made the links with napalm. It was basic. We had a Gestetner and Roneoed out these leaflets one after another. Poster Workshop produced the posters one at a time. It was all our own money.

At about this time Tony and I were living in a semi-commune and Ellen was living next door, and I remember seeing some of the New York Newsreel films. Then there was a meeting [this was probably in 1969, when Ellen and Richard were expecting to leave London. Ed.] and Ellen was saying, 'We have these films from Newsreel New York, and they are a donation, but someone's got to organise them and do something with them.' There was silence around the room, and I've always been someone that's felt embarrassed and personally responsible for any silences, so I said, 'I'll do it.' Tony and other members of the Vietnam group were soon involved.

We wanted to share the awakening these films had given us. We saw films about, for instance, the Detroit car workers' strike, where a striker was mown down by a huge lorry at the picket and killed. These films were often grainy and not brilliantly shot – worse, the sound was often naff – but they were so real, so unlike anything on the BBC news – above all with a point of view which thought it was important to ask questions about why a strike or demonstration was happening in the first place – that we weren't surprised people wanted to see them. There was a real hunger for such a passionate viewpoint – people forgave the poor filmic qualities.

We had regular screenings at Camden Studios. A strong part of our philosophy was wanting films to be a spark or trigger for interaction between people. A shared viewing experience meant that when we had discussions afterwards people who'd never met each other before suddenly opened up to share their opinions or learn from others. Often people arrived who knew more about a subject than we did. Because our experience was that in a large group a couple of people tend to dominate, we deliberately broke the discussion into smaller groups with one of us in each to get the ball rolling.

We started by showing American Newsreels, but soon opened up to showing documentaries from all over the place. We showed a film about Castro once, and a policeman came in as I was selling tickets and asked, 'Have you got a licence for this film?' 'No,' I gulped, 'the film-maker has only just got off the plane with it.' 'Good, is it?' he asked. 'Oh yes,' I said, 'and we've only got it for two days. What can we do?' 'Well,' he said, 'you can't sell tickets without a licence. So why don't you sell the sugar lumps and let them into the film for free?' There was a collective sigh of relief. No one refused to buy sugar lumps and the policeman even stayed to watch the film.

We showed features too and often rediscovered ones whose distributors had lost heart in being able to interest people in them. The one we became most identified with was *Salt of the Earth* [Herbert Biberman, 1953. A feature made under extremely difficult conditions about a real-life strike by Mexican zinc miners in New Mexico. Ed.]. The Women's Liberation Movement was just beginning and we found it fascinating to see how the miners' wives helped to win the strike despite their husbands' fear of losing status by accepting their help. This was the first time we went into discussion groups with men separate from women, and when we came back together to pool our thoughts (as we usually did) it was one of the longest and liveliest discussions we ever had!

I remember showing Mai Zetterling's *The Girls*. Three women are rehearsing *Lysistrata* and are sitting in a restaurant chatting, when a a bottle of wine is sent over to their table. They politely return it to the man who sent it and equally politely rebuff him when he comes over himself. When he realises they are serious in not wanting to be disturbed, his smile turns to a snarl and he calls them a load of ugly cows. At this there was a collective intake of breath in the audience, because we had all been through something similar but hadn't realised it happened to other people.

Around the same time we showed a film with Kate Millet about rape and abuse, and when we talked afterwards we discovered that almost every woman in that audience had either been raped, or abused, or grossly fondled in some way by some man that they, on the whole, knew. It took one or two brave people to say that they'd been through the thing being discussed in the film and then the lid was off. This was the first time for almost everyone in the audience that we'd even discussed such matters, and in my case I'd not even acknowledged what happened. I knew the smell of putty curdled my stomach, but I'd refused to remember the local builder who rubbed me all over with his erection when I was a four-year-old.

Not all film showings had this sense of collective experience, obviously, but occasions like it certainly convinced us that film could unlock deep and sometimes unknown feelings, as well as inform or inspire and – it has to be admitted – sometimes bore. They also confirmed our belief that cinemas on the whole do not help the audience to benefit from a shared experience and that, given a chance, people want to meet, to communicate and to do something with the energy and the feelings released.

The Women's Movement

Sue Crockford

sc–Some of the women in Angry Arts had formed one of the first women's groups – which, though attracted to, I resisted at the beginning, thinking surely anti-apartheid and Vietnam and miners' struggles are more important than anything domestic could be. But already our Vietnam group had realised that how you act personally is a political statement. In fact the Women's Movement had – and still has – more influence on my life than anything else apart from my kids and people I love and care for. It was the first time when you felt you could make sense of everything around you without having to divide life into public and private, political and personal – it all related. And what became clearer as time went on was a growing ability to work out what belonged to you alone and what was part of society, which you could do something about with other people.

The Oxford conference, in March 1970, brought together those of us who had been meeting in smallish groups, and though we expected about three hundred people we had no idea how many would be there. Well, that weekend sang – over six hundred people came. We had decided to film the process, and I remember being scared witless having to ask permission of the whole gathering and also to say it was a mixed crew – men and women. In those days there were few women with technical training or experience in film, but there were always thoughtful men who helped. There was of course some resentment by some men at the idea of a Women's Movement at all, but most of the men who were either our partners or our political colleagues understood and supported us. The final film was called *A Woman's Place* and included the first big march we all organised in March 1971 through the snow in Central London.

People from the industry came in and helped, people who didn't get a chance to put their ideas into practice at work and who were therefore very generous with time and access to equipment. Apart from Ellen, of course, there was Esther Ronay – she was an assistant editor but could do other jobs – there was also a cameraman, Andy Carchrae, who shot the Oxford conference for nothing, and Richard Broad, a director from Thames, did the sound recording, also for nothing. Everyone knew we weren't making any money at it. There was a generosity of sharing.

Liberation Films

Tony Wickert

MD–How did Liberation Films evolve from Angry Arts?

TW–What we were largely doing at Angry Arts was exhibition and distribution, and I felt it was ironic that I didn't know much about these but was learning, and I was frustrated because I couldn't do what I was well equipped to do. And so that was a main reason for getting production going, and we started with tape and slides.

MD–When you started working full time with Angry Arts/Liberation Films, how did you survive financially?

TW–I think I must have lived off the dole and I did odd jobs, even as handyman, that kind of thing.

MD–Presumably, gradually, the distribution produced some money?

TW—Yes it did, and there were funds handed over from Richard and Ellen, who, as I remember, both had full-time jobs.

MD—So, there was a significant change when you decided to try to treat it as a professional activity?

TW—Yes, and try to envisage the potential that it would be showing films on a regular basis and trying to derive an income from the money that was gathered and possibly generate more income with which to produce things.

Sue Crockford

SC—Again, the support we got from left-wing people in the film business was important. There was a cinema, the Venus, in Kentish Town, run by Frixos Constantine, who now runs Poseidon Films. He was a radical and used to let us have the cinema on a Sunday night for our own screenings. Charles Cooper of Contemporary Films, Stanley Forman of ETV and Eric Walker of Concord would sometimes lend us films for nothing, for a special event.

Sometimes we organised weekend workshops around themes like radical concepts of education or social work. And we were eclectic. We looked at films about schools like Summerhill as well as Hungarian films that showed children being taught by different methods, including the most draconian where intimidated children curtailed their artistic abilities and withdrew. We worried about the production methods of films like that, but they raised questions that teachers said were

Liberation Films perform street theatre, Queen's Crescent market, 1970. Far Left: Geoff Richman (back to camera) and Tony Wickert. Sue Crockford is in the audience (first woman on the right).

not explored yet in their training. People were beginning to question the under-pinning of their professions and eager to meet with others who were like-minded.

MD—Education was quite a conservative world then, wasn't it?

SC—Yes, the radical image of the 60s is that of the media which showed the demonstrations but not what provoked them.

Tony Wickert

MD—Liberation Films wasn't a company to begin with, was it?

TW—No. The formal structure came in 1972. It was a non-profit distributing company limited by guarantee. We had a council, not to run the organisation but to oversee it like the trustees of a charity, and the members were chosen because they were professionally respectable, they had letters after their names and held certain positions in the community. Geoff Richman was a GP. Geoff Crossick was a lecturer in history. Aubrey (Shayam) was a teacher of dentistry.

MD—Legally they were the directors of the company?

TW—In the formal sense they were directors. I was the secretary.

MD—Was it ever discussed as a problem that the people who weren't the full-time workers had the legal power? Did you think that, if they wanted to, the Council could sack you?

TW—I never thought about it like that and I don't think they did. I felt the group who were the workers ran it as a workers' co-operative.

MD—First of all you were the only employee, weren't you? What enabled you to take on other people?

TW—I think then it was only the proceeds of distribution. The grants came later.

MD—So you took on Ron (Orders) and then later on Caroline (Goldie)?

Ron Orders

RO—I met Tony Wickert at a meeting at the International Film School which was about film, the relationship between production and distribution and taking it out of the hands of the Rank/ABC duopoly, a weekend of wide-ranging discussion which was the foundation of The Other Cinema.

MD—And what happened next with regard to you?

RO—I joined The Other Cinema. It was in the very early formative days, with Peter Sainsbury and Nick Hart Williams. The idea of The Other Cinema at that time was that it would develop the Newsreel Collective idea, would distribute feature films and make short documentaries that were relevant to our situation here. That's why I joined it.

In fact, it didn't. Pete and Nick were really only concerned with showing features and maybe one day making features, and so I got, not disillusioned – I stayed very close friends with them – but I realised this was going to go in another direction.

Tony Wickert then was looking for someone to work for him. So, that's how I started with Tony.

MD–What kind of job was it?

RO–Rewinding and cleaning films and taking them down to the post office, organising the distribution and helping in the production.

MD–And what sort of organisation did you understand Liberation Films to be then? Did you think of it as joining a company or joining a political group?

RO–It was a political group. It felt like an extension of a political group.

MD–Who was the group at that time?

RO–It was really only Tony and myself. We were the only people who worked every day at Bramshill Gardens. [Tony's house and the office of Liberation Films. Ed.] The work was primarily for distribution, but also he had already made, or supervised the making of, *A Woman's Place*.

MD–Hadn't there been a larger group involved in making that film and also in the Angry Arts screenings?

RO–The Belsize Lane Women's Group was active in the making of *A Woman's Place*. And we used to have evening meetings with Geoff and Marie, and with people like Richard Broad, Tony Garnett, Roger Graef, people who, like Tony, had become dissatisfied with working inside television.

MD–Were these policy meetings for Liberation Films?

RO–No. They were cultural, political discussions. We would look at a film and discuss it, and the discussions were as much about the nature of film and about the way to use them as about the political message: how do you use film? How do you use a film like *Salt of the Earth*? What's the point of making a film like that unless you can use it effectively? That was the thing that drew me to Liberation Films, because my interest was in how you use films as a trigger, as a stimulus for discussion in changing attitudes. I had been doing that myself in an educational context while Tony had been doing it in Angry Arts with Geoff and Marie and Sue Crockford.

MD–That had been voluntary work, hadn't it? When you began working with Tony did such voluntary activists still have an important role?

RO–Geoff and Marie were the only ones I was conscious of. Aubrey, the dentist, and Helena were involved but mostly in the making of the first trigger films about dental health.

Activities

Ron Orders

RO–We started to show films in local community centres. There was a shift in emphasis in the whole Vietnam movement. Community action was being taken up after the American model, after the model of the events shown in *People's Park*. [Newsreel, 1969. Documentary about events in Berkeley, California, when a community group, including many students, tried to turn an unused lot near the university into a park, an initiative which led to conflict with the university authorities and violent confrontation with the police. Ed.]

MD–Why were you showing the films yourselves? Why couldn't you just send the films off to the people who wanted to show them?

RO–Mostly we did. We sent them out to a lot of women's groups and to schools. The main users were schools, because schools had the structure, they were used to hiring and had a budget for films. But also we'd liaise with a community group. Someone might phone up and say, 'What films have you got?', and I'd say, 'What are you trying to do with it?', and we would talk about the films, whether something like *People's Park* would be a good film to get people talking. And sometimes we'd rent out the projector and sometimes we'd go with it and show films and talk to people.

I think *All You Need Is an Excuse*, which had its genesis before I joined, came out of doing this and the recognition that American films didn't really work too well here and that films based on England would be better. That's why Tony and Geoff started to make *All You Need Is an Excuse*.

And we were doing tape/slide shows. At that time, with Geoff and Marie, we made *People's War* on tape/slide, which was about memories of people's experience of the war on the home front in their community. We got quite sophisticated and were going into communities saying, 'If you can't afford to make a film, here's the kind of thing you can do.'

MD–How did the work change during the years you were there?

RO–We became more production based. We got a grant to buy a portapack and that gave us a different tool. So, we went out with it to work in communities.

Caroline and I then started to do a lot of that independently.

MD–How did Caroline become involved?

RO–She came in because she saw the first thing we did with the portapack, *Starting to Happen*. We had got a grant from the Greater London Arts Association to do a project – Project Octopus – in three communities, Balham, Poplar and Plumstead. We took the Balham programme, *Starting to Happen*, to the BBC and showed it in the *Open Door* series with a studio discussion afterwards. Caroline saw the programme and came round to see us. We were starting then to do a lot more work, both production and distribution, and we offered her a job. I think I'd already organised a grant from Gulbenkian at that time, so I split my grant with her.

MD–Was that a grant to make specific films?

RO–No. It was a grant to do the work we were doing around distribution and exhibition.

MD–So that was a very early example of recognition for integrated practice?

RO–Yes, absolutely. But at that time it was foundations like Roundtree and Gulbenkian which were putting up money.

MD–Later on, as you moved more into production, did working there still feel different from working with an ordinary production company?

RO–I didn't know then what an ordinary production company was like, but yes, it was different, because we were still spending a lot of energy distributing films and in the evenings going out with a projector and showing them. And training people how to make films, talking to people about how to use them. For instance, we used *Morgan's Wall* a lot, taking it around, stimulating local community art.

Politics

Tony Wickert

MD–Your company in Australia now does quite a lot of work for trade unions, but am I right in thinking that in the 70s, the unions didn't form any part of your thinking?

TW–None. I saw unions then as being politically stigmatised. Their view of what you could do about the situation in which workers found themselves seemed to me to be inappropriate.

MD–What would you say were the politics behind *Fly a Flag for Poplar*? [Liberation Film's most ambitious production, described under 'Productions', below. Ed.]

TW–What I think was being promoted was the notion that you could begin to organise at a local level and you could start to tackle some of the bigger issues that were impinging on people, certainly, quality of life issues; that there is a link between the past and the present and that you can learn from the past and organise in the present to have a future that keeps the best of the values from the past and the present and discards others. There's that wonderful story of the councillors going to prison, and they had a victory that was acknowledged around the world because people stood up for their rights ...

MD–But the organisation which achieved that was the Labour Party, which was very much linked with the trade unions. Isn't there an irony about celebrating that victory while denying the relevance of such national organisations?

TW–I didn't see it that way myself. There seemed to be a populist strand to it that the film was celebrating.

Of course, the film was a catalyst too. When we finished it we took it around in the community where it was made and led people into an examination and a reflection on their lives and whether they might want to intervene in the future to change them.

MD–That was very much part of the theory wasn't it – films as catalysts? Very expensive catalysts! Was there any reason why film is more significant than cheaper methods like speakers, slides, leaflets?

TW–I don't think you could get one which is more powerful. Films have an enormous potential to be able to awaken and arouse and create an environment for further reflection. The medium is particularly good for its enormous ambivalence, the way ten people can see the same filmic events and interpret them in ten different ways. The value doesn't lie, as most theorists have come to acknowledge, only in the process of watching a movie and deconstructing it while you watch it; it comes much more over an extended period of time when you go on and discuss with other people the experience, and extrapolate meanings afterwards, and so the film's potential to do this is something that you have to calculate from the very beginning.

[From 1973 to 1981 Geoff Richman kept a diary of Liberation Films' activities. It notes successful screenings and disastrous ones, invitations to international events and many, often frustrating, meetings with the sponsors of the educational trigger films. Two entries in late 1978 hint at impending problems.

> *September 19th 1978*. The main changes are organisational. Ron and Caroline have left to work for West German Television.

> *November 11th 1978*. Exhausted by the making of trigger tapes ... I cannot suppress a sneaking resentment that after eight years of work in L. F. and after a fair amount of production which has been recognised, we are still working in exactly the same way on shoe-string budgets and without any proper technical resources.

Reading on, it becomes apparent that the departure of Ron and Caroline was surrounded by tension. New employees were taken on but do not last. Tony takes a full-time job teaching film and in 1981 returns to Australia. The company is wound up. Ed.]

Hindsight

Geoff Richman

GR—We weren't aware that there was a crisis looming until a fortuitous event precipitated it, in that against our better judgment and bowing to what you might call glamour we allowed a West German company to come and make a documentary about us. We set it all up and did one of our projects and they made their film, but it precipitated, very suddenly, a break which was bound to cause some bad blood. Because Ron and Caroline were seduced away, Caroline literally and Ron filmicly, and they went away to Afghanistan for six months. Tony felt differently about it from Marie and myself, because he had more in common with them. He was struggling with this difficulty of trying to make a living and be a film-maker and be a revolutionary, and because the three of us were divided we were unable to take any action, and then when Ron and Caroline returned to England it became impossible to go on in the old way and it became evident that Ron was bitterly resentful towards us, which came as a surprise. He regarded us as dictatorial.

Ron Orders

RO—I didn't have a very clear head for organisations. I think I thought of the Council of Management as being a kind of advisory body to Tony and I who did the work

– and later Caroline. So, I think I thought of Liberation Films as being us, although in fact it turned out to be them.

MD—Why did you leave?

RO—I didn't leave. I took six months off – Caroline and I both did – to go and make a film. While we were away Tony, Geoff and Marie decided that they didn't want us to come back and so basically sacked us.

MD—But why did the Council of Management have this power?

RO—It had been structured in that way, because they were directors of the company, in effect.

MD—Had you ever thought that you and Caroline should be made directors?

RO—Oh yes. In the summer of 1978 we argued, Caroline much more than me, for broadening the group. I'd always imagined it should have been bigger, with more production and a broader base. I was getting more interested in the idea of films that could be shown on television, to a wider audience.

Geoff Richman

GR—There is a difference in perspective between people who are trying to make a living working within an off-beat group and people who are dedicating themselves to it out of a lifetime's commitment. Marie and I didn't need to make a living out of film and wouldn't have wanted to. We thought that you might as well earn your living in some way that doesn't take your heart's blood.

MD—Was the issue at stake the question of how far the group should move into other kinds of film-making, like producing for television?

GR—I don't remember that it was raised like that. There was never a time when there was a series of policy meetings when it might have emerged. Had we sat back and thought, we might have resolved things differently, but we weren't thinking in that sort of way and then it was too late.

MD—Your position is hard to argue for isn't it, that showing films to groups of twenty or a hundred odd can be as valuable as getting them on TV?

GR—You can only see it if you had a perspective of keeping alive ideas in people's working practice. There is a ferment in society that people don't believe is there until it's given an environment. What sustained us was the idea that those people who have been in those little groups will do something that otherwise couldn't be done.

Tony Wickert

TW—What makes it difficult to remember is that the past is littered with a learning process.

One can look at what happened another way. Without grant aid and operating as a self-financing unit Liberation Films was effective. When it got grant aid it tended to be not so successful and when that grant aid was taken away it became very unsuccessful.

MD—But it was after you got grant aid that the production side developed. So, do you mean that was a mistake?

TW—No. I just think that becoming dependent on seeking grant aid to make your programmes, which we started to do, means you spend your time making submissions and writing them up.

MD—Liberation Films is the only group I know of in which non-film-makers played such a central role. It's obvious that it became a source of tension, but were there also advantages?

TW—What is interesting is that at different times I think we all helped each other in the best ways we could. Geoff and Marie were very supportive and they helped in a variety of ways. They had ideas, they made contacts, they had a political viewpoint, and early on without that kind of benefactor in the background I don't know that it would have survived.

After Liberation Films

Tony Wickert

TW—I went back to Australia mainly for personal reasons, not to form a film-making group. I had a job at the film school and one of the things I did with the students was to take them into a town and we would use the techniques of Liberation Films or Challenge for Change. There was nothing like it in Australia. So, I formed Summer Hill Films.

I knew I wasn't going to have anything like the structure we had for Liberation Films, because I'd seen it as being cumbersome. Summer Hill was a straightforward company with me and Rosie [Tony's wife. Ed.] as directors, and Rosie was a quiet one as she didn't know anything about film-making. So, off I went and hired people.

The structure has been modified from time to time. I devised a variety of profit-sharing schemes, but none of them were felt to be satisfactory. So, the company was subdivided and the two key employees were sold a share – but only 30 per cent. We have two kinds of meetings to run the place. We have the shareholders' meetings where we develop a strategy as long term as possible. I take a senior position in that so it operates in a very transparent way. The other kind of meetings are for the teams. These operate on a multiskill basis and a distinctive aspect is that training is embedded in the practice. We do between forty and fifty small productions a year and it's growing.

MD—Are these similar to the productions you did with Liberation Films?

TW—The kinds of projects are different. They're much more promotional. They don't question. We never had a grant at Summer Hill. They are all straightforward commissions. A client says, 'I want you to produce this to do that.' It is driven by the client.

MD—Presumably, these are not quite the films you would make by choice?

TW—How I would like to operate now would be alongside a university. I'd like to embed the film practice that I think worthwhile in an organised form of research, and I'd require that the people who supervised the allocation of the money were immersed to some extent in both and rigorously dedicated to film use and film practice.

Ron Orders

MD—When you left you started a company?

RO—Cinecontact, very deliberately – it's just me, trading as Cinecontact. I felt the collective ideal had been betrayed.

I carried on making the same kind of films. First of all I got an Arts Council grant to make a film called *Somewhere in Hackney*, which was about arts projects in Hackney, and then when Channel Four came along, obviously, I did what everybody else did and turned to them.

MD—Did you do anything with these films, apart from getting them on television?

RO—The first of those, the Hackney film, certainly I did, but without the structure of a group, some kind of collective, I think it's quite demanding. And the atmosphere was changing. I think it's very difficult now to make films and use them in the kind of way we used to.

Sue Crockford

SC—I left in 1971 after I broke up with Tony. But I went on making political films. The first was *One Two Three* about a radical alternative childcare centre that I'd set up with a group of people, called the Children's Community Centre, in Dartmouth Park Hill.

I went into television deliberately, but that didn't mean I lost interest in community film. I still get involved helping people with no-budget productions! And I've tried to do television work with a spin-off beyond transmission.

MD—What do you think now about the politics of working with TV or outside?

SC—When Channel Four first arrived many of us saw it as the beginning of wider access for radical programmes to people all over the country. It was all very well for us to go round in our van and tie sheets to apple trees to show films to people in camp sites, but most people never got to see our shows. And certainly at the beginning, with Alan Fountain commissioning alternative programming from all over the world and especially with the whole workshop scene in the UK, there was a surge of different programmes. That breadth of access has narrowed, as we all know, so now we see far fewer films made from within struggles around the world – much more likely to see a conscience-stricken news reporter prodding the viewers into donating money for famine relief. But I think another aspect of wall-to-wall television is overload – people can feel less empowered, because the prevailing culture says watch but don't do anything, and anyway the world is full of people better than you at running a country/playing football/cooking pasta and there's no point in getting up and doing anything, because it won't make any difference. That sounds a harsh thing to say and I don't completely believe I just said it, because I know there are a thousand flowers blooming in local community activity, but because I've experienced life where television did not dominate as it now does, I can see that it can sap people's confidence in a quite insidious way.

Instead of over-valuing the achievements of a few, I'd like to go back to valuing people's experience with each other – not in a Jerry Springer way, which wants people to emote unrestrainedly for the greater financial glory of the studio. On another level, the docu-soaps are very interesting, since, yes, it is aspects of real lives we're sharing, but when there's little long-term thought or social consciousness involved either on the part of programme-makers or participants it's the equivalent of muzak. And I think the numbers game is scary – x million people watched this funeral or that sporting event – though I don't deny it's an amazing feeling to think you are part of some great public event. In the end I reckon E. M. Forster's 'only connect' is a pretty good shorthand philosophy, but it makes more sense when it values the connection at the smallest, quietest level first.

Chronology: organisation and funding

Angry Arts

1967   Summer – Angry Arts Week event organised by Stop it Committee (Americans in Britain for US withdrawal from Vietnam).

1968   Angry Arts Film Society formed and run, as a spare-time commitment, by two members of the Stop It Committee. Organises two seasons of film shows with discussion. Distributes American Newsreel films.
Makes short film, *End of a Tactic?*, involving members of the Camden Vietnam Solidarity Campaign group, which becomes Camden Movement for People's Power (CMPP).

1969   Film shows reorganised by group from CMPP. They introduce practice of small group discussions.
Newsreel distribution handed over to an individual outside CMPP.

Liberation Films

1970   Screenings renamed Counter Act.
Liberation Films set up with aim of developing distribution and production. Starts with one full-time unpaid worker (Tony Wickert) with the screenings group working in spare time. By end of year, first wages paid from distribution revenue.
Newsreel films taken back into distribution.
Start of first production as Liberation Films: *A Woman's Place*.

1971   Production of first trigger films (on dental health).
        Second paid worker, Ron Orders, employed.
        First project grant from public funds: £200 from London Borough of
            Camden for *People's War*, a mixed-media event.
        First weekend workshops organised around themes.
        Counter Act screenings discontinued between 1971 and 1972.

1972   Liberation Films officially registered as non-profit distributing
            limited company. Legal control vested in voluntary Management
            Council of Four, which does not include Company Secretary and
            principal worker, Tony Wickert.
        Starts research project on community film shows.

1973   Second project grant from public funds: £2,500 from GLAA for
            Project Octopus.
        First substantial sponsorship: £3,000 from Health Education Council
            (HEC) for three trigger films on sexually transmitted diseases.

1974   First revenue funding: £8,000, to be spread over three years, from
            Gulbenkian Foundation.
        Project funding: £6,000 completion grant from the BFI for *Fly a Flag
            for Poplar* (a development from Project Octopus).
        Makes programme for BBC *Open Door*.

Fly a Flag for Poplar (Roger Buck, 1976).

Third paid worker, Caroline Goldie, employed.

1976   First public revenue funding: £5,000 from Arts Council. over one year.

1977   Revenue funding: Arts Council and Gulbenkian Foundation pays
        three full-time workers £50 per week each.
        Sponsorship: HEC agrees £12,000 for trigger films on smoking.

1978   Arts Council funds *Morgan's Wall.*
        Brings out new distribution catalogue. About eighty films in
        distribution.
        Ron Orders and Caroline Goldie leave; two new full-time workers
        employed.

1979   Turnover approximately £19,000.
        Income: £3,800 net (£6,805 gross) from distribution.
        Miscellaneous project grants: £2,330.
        Arts Council (Film Panel) project grant: £2,000.
        Arts Council (Community Arts Panel) revenue funding: £8,000
        (figures from application to Arts Council 30 November 1979).
        Tony Wickert reduces involvement to take a full-time teaching job.
        Continues to manage Liberation Films on a voluntary basis.

1980   Revenue funding: £7,000 from Arts Council.
        Two employees earn £80 per week.
        Employees leave after dispute with Management Council. Replaced
        by two part-time employees.

1981   Last of Arts Council revenue funding.
        May – gives up office and employees.
        December – Tony Wickert returns to Australia. He later sets up
        Summer Hill Films, a small production company.
        Distribution is handed over to Concord.

Productions

Based on the 1978 catalogue, and supplemented by information from Geoff Richman. None of these films is currently in distribution. Copies are located with Geoff Richman, 138 Fordwych Road, London NW2. The location of other copies or reference material is indicated.

1969   *End of a Tactic?* 16mm. B/W. 15 mins.
        In October 1968, 100,000 people marched through the streets of

London on what was to be the last of the big Vietnam
demonstrations. Six months later only 4,000 turned out. Using the
comments of participants and organisers and some exciting shots
of what took place, the film explores the significance of the big
demonstration as a tactic and why it failed in this case to live up to
expectations.

1971   *A Woman's Place* 16mm. B/W. 32 mins.
One of the most important reasons for making this film was to show
    Women's Liberation not as a bunch of bra-burning heavies but as
    real people seeking to liberate themselves from a male-oriented
    society, and with creative concepts for its eventual change.
Filming began at the Women's Liberation conference in Oxford
    February 1970. A year later we filmed the Women's Liberation
    demonstration of 6 March on its way through London.
Location of archive material: NFA.

1971   *Trigger Films on Teeth* 16mm. B/W. Series of three. Total length 9
mins.
Trigger films represent a new approach to the use of film in
    education. They are non-didactic, designed to provoke discussion
    rather than provide information. Above all they seek to avoid
    presenting a problem from any position of pre-given moral
    attitude, so that they provide students with a chance of exploring
    their own preconceptions.
The films are short open-ended narratives, often ending before the
    problem reaches its climax, rather than concluding as films usually
    do with the solution of a problem.
This series raises questions about dental behaviour and attitudes, and
    is most suitable for use with children from nine to sixteen years old.

1972   *All You Need Is an Excuse* 16mm. B/W and Col. 10 mins.
A community-action programme in North London, occupying
    unused private land for conversion to playspace. Opens with a
    sympathetic interview with a woman who isn't involved,
    explaining some of the problems of the area. The film contrasts her
    feelings with those of the minority, who are involved.

1973   *Starting to Happen* 16mm. B/W. 42 mins.
An exploration of the potential of portable video and film to
    stimulate community action. Shot in Balham, South London, this
    was part of a bigger project – Project Octopus – funded by a GLAA

grant and carried out in three areas – Balham, Poplar, Plumstead. There were several elements: first Liberation Films made a trigger film on 16mm, designed to get people talking. The audience was then shown a Sony Rover portapack (½ inch high-density portable video) and invited to come and learn how to use it. The idea was that they would then record their own programme, present it to the community and finally, the communities would present their work to one another.

1973 *Something to Talk About* 16mm. B/W. 35 mins.
   Made for teacher training colleges, and itself a trigger for discussion, the film is a record of a teacher's presentation of the trigger films on 'Teeth' to two classes of twelve- to sixteen-year-olds.
   Location of reference material: NFA.

1974 *Trigger Films on Sexually Transmitted Diseases* 16mm. Col. Series of three. Total length 21 mins.
   Naturalistic drama.

1975 *Wallingford Community Hospital* Video. B/W. 25 mins.
   A look at an experimental community hospital in Oxfordshire.

1976 *Fly a Flag for Poplar* 16mm. B/W and Col. 77 mins.
   A development from the Poplar part of Project Octopus. In the summer of 1973 a committee in Teviot Street had decided to put on a festival, partly so that people could just have a good time, partly in an attempt to recapture a sense of community which seemed to have disappeared. In the mind of the Chairman, Bill Pyne, and perhaps others, there was a hope that the festival might provoke the local people into involving themselves with the running of their community.
   At the centre of the film are the events of 1921 when the council, lead by George Landsbury, went to prison for six weeks for withholding the metropolitan rate – an action which forced a change in the law over poor law provision. Their victory introduced the word – 'poplarism' – into the dictionary, meaning the 'habit of giving out extravagant poor relief', but for working-class people it was a symbol of a fight for improved conditions and equality.
   Location of reference material: NFA.

1976 *Trigger Films on Mental Health* 16mm. Col. Two films, each 15 mins.
   Naturalistic drama intended to help the audience share feelings and

attitudes on what is often a difficult subject.
Location of reference material: NFA.

1976   *Trigger Films: Living Standards* 16mm. Col. 20 mins.
            A son is helping his father move house. It seems they haven't talked
                much to each other for years. During the story they come closer
                together and the question is raised, 'What standards do we live by?'

1977   *Peterhead Project* Video. B/W. 50 mins.
            Record of a Liberation Films video project in Peterhead, Scotland.

1978   *Morgan's Wall* 16mm. Col. 50 mins.
            Why do some artists choose to come out of their studios and paint
                on walls, bridges and public buildings, rather than confine
                themselves to easel paintings to be exhibited in galleries and, if they
                are lucky, sold to an individual owner?
            Silver Hugo, Chicago Film Festival 1978.
            Location of reference material: NFA.

1978   *Trigger Films on Smoking* 16mm. Col.
            (i) *I Think It's Time* 10 mins.
            Short drama.
            (ii) *The School* Series of six, each film approximately 10 mins.
            Issues seen through the eyes of fourteen- to seventeen-year-olds and
                through their concern about becoming adults and being allowed to
                decide for themselves what to do – or not to do.
            (iii) *Forever Is a Long Time* 30 mins.
            Documentary on a group of people who have decided to give up
                smoking.
            Location of reference material: NFA.

1979   *National Uprising of Public Employees* Video. B/W. 30 mins.
            NUPE strike at the Central Middlesex Hospital.
1981   *Toy What?* Video. B/W.
            On Hackney Toy Library.

1982   *You Can Still Be Beautiful* Video. B/W.
            Documentary looking at old age, made with members of Willesden
                Pensioners' Club.

1986   *You Can't Be Told* Video. B/W.
            Exercises in helping a nurse tutor teach communication skills.

Amber

Interview recorded in 1995 with Murray Martin, founder member of Amber

Before Amber

MM–I came from a conventional working-class background in Stoke-on-Trent and I came to university, to do a fine arts degree in Newcastle, and that's where I became politicised.

MD–Were your parents Labour?

MM–Yes, staunch Labour. But not political, they were, like most Labour people conservative Labour.

So, I came to university and that was for me a great freedom. We're talking about 1961 and there was a political feeling in the period. Newcastle Fine Art was a very free place, with Richard Hamilton and Victor Pasmore. They were in conflict with each other because Pasmore was on his way out and we were in a very peculiar position as a year to watch that, and I think we became radical partly because of that schism. When you can see that one year everybody paints like Victor Pasmore and gets first-class degrees and the next they all get third-class degrees, you suddenly see those contradictions.

MD–What about art in the community?

MM–Well, at that time all my paintings personally had been documenting working-class life, streets, factories and the people. When I came to university I was suddenly told to forget that: we've selected you because that shows ability, but now art is about colour and shape and it's an abstract thing. You learn the language.

Now I was fairly sharp, and I realised that there was a sort of exclusion system going on within the department on the basis that if you learned this new language quickly, you were accepted, you were taken on the inside. I suppose I was on the inside, but I felt this was wrong. There were kids who painted passionately and whose work was rejected. So, I organised a criticism of the department, and out of a hundred students I reckon I got something like eighty to eighty-four essays and stories. So, I handed them in and then something very strange began to happen. Those people who were in the final year were called in and told if they didn't withdraw their criticism they wouldn't get a degree.

Later on, two boys in our year (who knew because their brothers were lecturers in the same course) told me that after the trouble I had caused, they made a ruling in the fine art department saying no working-class kids again, and I think they didn't take any for ten years.

MD—One forgets how reactionary the early 60s were.

MM—Yes, and there is the idea that it was a great liberal period. It was not true. It was a very oppressive period.

So, I was politicised through that action, and I and a lot of other people began to question what we'd been taught and there was a movement among the group that I was in, about five or six people, to go back to your own roots, your own childhood and reconnect with your interests there. I began to document the working-class life that interested me, but using Tyneside as the base. So I began to go to North Shields and record things. I got an 8mm camera and started doing it with that or a stills camera.

MD—Were you already interested in film?

MM—Only in the sense that I was a film freak. Where I was brought up in a suburb of one of the Stoke towns there were, within a mile, six cinemas, changing programmes twice a week, and I remember double bills. I remember going to see *Serpent of the Nile* with Raymond Burr and that was double-billed with Delmer Daves's *Broken Arrow* at the Alambra. I liked *Broken Arrow*, I remember. I suspect it was the fact that it was one of the few films that took the position of the Indian – if I remember correctly.

MD—Anything else you particularly liked – or hated?

MM—If you take, first of all, the Saturday matinee, the things we really liked were all the conventional things: *Batman, Nyoka, Jungle Girl*. You loved those, and then you graduated to the bigger cinema and even there on a Monday night they had family night, where you went to see *Superman* as a second feature.

I remember seeing *The Third Man* and being very impressed, but generally speaking it was the American films, adventure movies, that we were encouraged to see, because most of the cinemas showed American films.

But in Newcastle we had a cinema club, run by the fine art department, and we saw all the French films there – *La Jetée*, Jean Vigo's *L'Atalante, Zéro de conduite* – Polish films, Wajda, as well as American films – *Kiss Me Deadly*, I remember particularly.

MD—So did these films strike you as strange when, in your childhood, you'd seen mainly the American films of the time?

MM— I think you tried to pretend you liked them more than you did. You're talking about eighteen-year-olds who are trying to be sophisticated. But there were some films that were quite marvellous there, like *L'Atalante*, and it was a big event, a big social do. You went every Wednesday night and it was full.

Of course we saw the neo-realists which were a big influence on Amber – *Rome, Open City, Bicycle Thieves*, in particular. Subsequently they're the sort of films we showed here at the Side Cinema. So, those influences were there from a very early period.

MD–If we go back to the films you were making, did you see them as related to art or to politics, or both?

MM–It becomes very merged in my own memory.

I got myself a 16mm camera and began to record my experience. For a long time I used to do a regular weekend trip, to get a bus to North Shields, to get on a ferry which took me to South Shields, to go to the second-hand market, which was every Saturday. So the first film I began to make seriously was about that ferry. I began to shoot that and then I decided to go back to learn the craft of film, because my technique was too limited. I went to London, to what was then the Regent Street Poly.

Beginnings of Amber

MD–Who were the other people that you met in London who became members of Amber?

MM–Graham Denman was one. He was a technical genius relative to me. Sirkka [Sirkka Liisa Konttinen. Ed.] was another. She's a photogapher/film-maker.

We made a couple of films there which are relevant. We completed the ferry film and the other was a film called *All You Need Is Dynamite*, which was banned for being an incitement to violence. Even students would not show this film. It came out of the Dialectics of Liberation conference in 1967, which was attended by Stokely Carmichael, David Cooper, R.D. Laing, all those sort of people. That was at the Roundhouse, a very influential conference.

All You Need Is Dynamite was basically the dialectic argument that apathy and violence are the same thing. If you control people, if you feed them bingo, if you put them in high-rise flats, you get a violent reaction. By chance, Grosvenor Square happened in the middle of a shooting and we managed to film it from a flat overlooking the square. We followed the court cases after the Grosvenor Square riots, and the interesting thing is that all the publicity was about 'anarchists', whatever that means, but the fact was that many people arrested were unemployed labourers. And that's why we pursued this apathy and violence theme. It was a very crude, inadequate film, but the reaction to it was amazing.

Suddenly we had on the one hand the ferry film, which is a nostalgic, romantic vision, and on the other hand this other picture. People couldn't match the two at all, and we've often found that within Amber's work there are these different strands.

MD–So, what was Amber before you went to Newcastle and why did you go there?

MM–At that time we opened ourselves up to anybody who was prepared to join the group and there were maybe six or seven people interested.

We didn't decide at once to go to Newcastle, but we came to the conclusion very quickly that we were not going to stay in London. We looked at Bristol, Liverpool, Glasgow and Newcastle and I was the one probably most in favour of Newcastle. So I elected to go to Newcastle and about five other people came.

But the group quickly changed. Within eighteen months it was reduced to myself, Sirkka and Graham and we were looking for other people. We quickly recruited Peter Roberts, an animator whose work we'd seen – very abstract films but I just recognised an empathy. I wrote to Peter, who was in Manchester, and he gave up his job and joined the group straightaway. Lorna Powell was from Newcastle. I'd known her as a student. Peter and Lorna were from working-class backgrounds, so the real basis of Amber's future was laid by four people of working-class origin and one Finn who was enthralled by the richness of working-class culture. Lorna had administrative skills and we decided very quickly on a structure, so that the administrator was at the centre and the other four people rotated. There would be one person waged, while the others would have to forage for the money.

MD–You mean even if you worked outside you shared the pay?

MM–All our money has always come back into the company. Nobody's allowed to have outside money. You can go out and earn as much as you want, but you've got to bring it back here. So if Peter went and worked as a cameraman for the BBC, he gets paid, it comes into the company.

MD–And has it sometimes caused tension?

MM–Yes, but not very often. I think it was a factor in Graham Denman leaving ten years later. When you leave groups like this, it's a bit like a break-up of a marriage: it creates sadness, but I don't think there was a big angst about it.

I think we've lasted better than other groups: we've lasted twenty-five years, so you can hardly say it's problematic in that sense. Of the five people I mentioned only Graham Denman left.

MD–But doesn't it make relationships more difficult when you're cutting against the grain of what society expects?

MM–Yes, that's right. But I think it's more problematic to have a hierarchical structure. I suppose I come from an egalitarian, socialist tradition which can't understand why a film director should get paid more than a dustbin man, and even more so, why the person directing the film should get paid more than the person doing the clapper loading, because I'd rather be a director than a clapper loader.

Of course, you have that debate in a group and people won't join unless they agree with that.

Another point is we've always argued for professionalism, we've always argued that you're only a film-maker if you live off film-making, an artist if you live off your art. What we did here was all the money came into the pot, we took a percentage of that away and we took a percentage for work. Now I think the first wage was about £5 a week.

MD–That was a pittance even in 1970.

MM–It wasn't. You see, we were paying 15 shillings which was 75p a fortnight rent in Byker. We're talking about a very cheap sort of existence. Compared with the average wage, it was low. We did that for years, but I don't think we felt it was a hardship. One thing was that our leisure and our work were very much intertwined.

We would socially work together. Sirrka and Peter, for instance, met in the group and are now married.

Most people spend their lives earning money in order to go and do what they want to do. We started with the premise that our activities were what we wanted to do and that we had to generate enough money to maintain that. We've never earned big money. Now at the age of fifty-two, I take out £10,000 a year, which is not big money. But we've had turnovers up to £500,000 a year and from 1982 we have been seriously waged. So we wouldn't cry poverty.

Now, obviously you've got to decide what you want out of life, that's important, and it seems to me that after having a reasonable place to live, after healthcare and education, the rest is a dialogue. I have enough money to indulge: I have racehorses, I train them, and that doesn't make me poor.

We have thirty acres of land. The group has always invested and reinvested. We've owned pubs, fishing boats, we have another place beside this chapel, we own the building here. This is not a poor operation.

Philosophically, we've always believed that there's an equation between cheapness and freedom and that if you don't take too much out of the system, you'll reinvest in it and that gives you a freedom, and I think that philosophy has served us well.

Group Dynamics

MD–Do you think the way you work together has been affected by there being couples within the group?

MM–You have to be aware of it. In the discussions you don't want someone coming to the defence of someone else because they are spouses. When there are couples you have to be more conscious of the group dynamics.

MD–What about domestic relationships and children? Often egalitarian arrangements begin to founder when people's needs change because some have children and others don't.

MM–I'd be dishonest if I said there haven't been occasional problems. I think it was recognised in Amber in the early days that commitment to work was so intense that children were not an easy option. It wasn't particularly encouraged and although I personally don't remember that, I know people who've had children who've said they found that difficult.

We would say, if you wanted to have a child, that's a choice. We have been through the debates, and they've been long debates, about how much does somebody need and how much should they earn. But the fact is, if I want a Jaguar car, why is that less desirable to me than a child? We've agreed that there are choices that you make in your life. So the question is, what is the level of pay? The debate is not about what you do with that money. We don't want to tell you what to do with the money.

With children, I think sometimes the dilemma's been a different one, with somebody wanting to have children but not wanting to give up the work.

MD—But what about part-time work?

MM— We have created that possibility, but it makes your communication and your role in the group difficult, because how the group's survived is to do with the day-to-day communication. It's a design problem.

MD—Another potential source of conflict in a group like yours is ability or perceived ability. We all feel that we've got creative potential, but sometimes somebody is stuck being an administrator.

MM—Well, I think that's right and in our history there have been moments of tension but never long-standing, because I think once it's brought to somebody's attention that they are disrespecting somebody's skills, it's usually been recognised as the fault of the people who've been elitist. Administration is an easy area to take for granted, because it is perceived as non-creative. Lorna Powell, who accepted the role as administrator, was sometimes exasperated by our lack of understanding of what was involved in her area of work. Nevertheless, Lorna has developed her film skills and, as well as assistant director, is the central writer on our current production, *The Scar*. I do think our process offers opportunities outside the scope of the conventional system.

MD—You don't think that some people are just better at some things?

MM—When we constructed the group I had looked at collectives. I'd thought about the group, I recognised that when people come to join the group, one thing that was important was that they had their own skill and they were respected for that skill. We constructed the group so that most people in this building who are members of Amber have specialist areas for which they are respected and which they are good at, and if they're not respected for it I think they wouldn't survive.

MD—When you're working on a film, you allocate roles?

MM—Oh totally, yes, specialist roles.

MD—So you have a conventional breakdown?

MM—Absolutely, except that we work with much smaller crews and if I'm director it doesn't mean I don't carry the bags.

We have roles and we have a departmental structure here, so that Ellie [Ellie Hare, member of the Amber production team and director of *The Scar*], is seen as the editor, Peter as the camera person. I'm seen as producer/director, but it doesn't mean I do that. It means that the department is your domain and you have to organise it. Now within this group currently, out of seven partners, five have directed films. The Workshop Declaration, with its recognition of cross-grade working, allows people to avoid getting stuck in a single discipline. Because you have directed the last film does not mean that there is not merit and satisfaction in being assisant editor on the next one.

MD—It can take a lot of regular talking, negotiating all these things.

MM— I've constantly said that my experience with the group was that if an individual wants to do something, it usually doesn't get done, but if two people want to do it, it does. You don't have to all agree, but you've got to carry somebody with you in order for it to become a collaborative, collective affair.

Cinema and Gallery

MM—We have a small 53-seat cinema designed when, through the influence of the IFA and others, a debate-based film culture was fashionable. It was designed around that idea, as was Four Corners and the one in Nottingham.

We ran it full time from about 1977 till about 1983–4, and all sorts of debates took place there, both with film-makers and political groups, and there were tangential debates on the work that was on in the cinema.

When the Tyneside Cinema was being pressured to become more and more commercially orientated, as all the cinemas were in the early 80s and onwards, we went in a different direction. We went for what we considered specialist films, so we would show *Man of Aran* and we'd have to turn people away.

MD—And that was just from advertising in the paper?

MM—We also had a huge poster campaign and fly-posting. Roger Buck, who ran the cinema, would go round all the Poly dining rooms and put a piece of paper out saying *Man of Aran* this week. Roger Buck's worked with Liberation Films and was a visionary cinema programmer as well as a very good film editor.

The other thing that really built an audience was the interface between the gallery and the cinema. We have a photography gallery which was very popular, especially on a Sunday when there's a huge market here. We'd get several thousand people a week coming through. So, a film programme would have some purchase on the gallery or vice versa. For example, we would have the 30s dust-bowl photographs and show John Ford's *Grapes of Wrath*, but not just films on the 30s but radical television programmes as well.

One thing we found which I don't think is surprising is that the exotic – Nicaragua or El Salvador – was always more attractive to people, than, say, unemployment. People wanted issues that they felt they could be inspired by.

MD—You'd have a film show and then a debate?

MM—Yes, and we developed the idea in many ways, like short trigger films. We realised if you had a very long film the debate tended to be stunted, but if you had a 15–20 minute film there was much more discussion. And we would research people from the area. If we did a thing, say, on mining, as we did when we showed Ken Loach's *Days of Hope*, we would have three old miners who would have a discussion about their lives.

MD—It's a lot of work isn't it, this kind of exhibition?

MM—Oh, a huge amount of work. The first couple of years we ran seven days a week. But increasingly, we decided to focus down and eventually we reduced it to four days a week, of which Tuesday night was always a debate night and was known for that.

MD—What about the revenue for running the cinema, because a cinema that size doesn't make profits?

MM—The argument for the cinema was that although it would always need a subsidy its subsidy would be limited, because the rest of the infrastructure supported it. Don't forget, we had bought these buildings, we owned them. So we've never charged the cinema rent. What we needed to run the cinema was a budget to pay one person.

The Aesthetic

MM–We haven't wanted to talk over people's heads, so you look for a language which is comfortable and accessible, and I think realism is something we feel comfortable with. But there are different strands within our work. Some of it is quite abstract, especially the animation. A film like *Jellyfish* is a million miles away from being realist. And there've been various formal experiments. I don't think *T. Dan Smith* would be seen as realist.

MD–Did *T. Dan Smith* have a more difficult reception?

MM–Not really. I went round with the film to Labour Party groups in places like Sterling, Billingham, and it was very well received and there was a lot of debate generated from it.

The way we distribute is often part of the process of making a film. We make something and then spend a lot of energy distributing it and working with it.

We made a little local soap which was made not for television but issue-based. The idea was that we'd set it up to show in places like DHSS waiting rooms and things like that. The local authority would invest in a video circuit and we would supply it. What stunted that development was that the Tories brought in a law which says local authorities couldn't engage in political activity, and the films were political. But there was quite a large distribution, with workplace showings organised by Pat and Richard through the trade unions.

We ran our own theatre group here for years, a group called Live Theatre, which played four nights a week in working men's clubs.

We took a decision very early on that we would make things that were accessible, and so both in theatre and film that's what we try to do and I think that led to a certain dismissal of Amber by the people like Paul Willemen, who saw us as being too simplistic.

MD–There's a nostalgic strand in your work as well as a fighting strand, isn't there?

MM–Yes, and we wouldn't apologise for that, because we would say that nostalgia is experiences held in affection and we think there's nothing wrong with that. If people say we're romantic, fine.

Peter Sainsbury, who was then head of the BFI Production Board, was critical of a film we made called *High Row* (about miners), because he said it was totally romantic. Now when we – that's myself and Eric Nowley – researched the film, we wrote a much harsher script, but when we showed it to the workers they said, 'If you think that you wouldn't work down the mine.' So, we let the men direct the vision. They didn't see it as romantic.

Finance

MD—What kind of budgets do you work with?

MM—The biggest budget we've ever worked with has been £350,000 and *Eden Valley* was £200,000.

MD—Before Channel Four came into the picture, what sort of proportion of income was from commercial work?

MM—It varied from year to year. Depending on how much public money we had, we reduced the amount of commercial money we needed to make. Our aim would have been for fifty-two weeks of the year to pursue what we believed in. Obviously, in order to do that there were times when we had to go out and earn money and that money meant selling our skills. For example, we had the contract for documenting the development of the metro system in Newcastle, which was a straight competition between our company and Turner Films, which was a commercial company.

MD—How did you buy the buildings here?

MM—We borrowed the money from the Lombard and a little bit – £500 – from my mother and a bit from a friend called Tom Hadaway, who's a writer. We negotiated for them and they cost £12,000, the whole building, both sides of the alleyway. It's a big space and once we got the buildings that attracted certain grants.

A large chunk of our money since 1982 has come from television, almost exclusively with Channel Four. Up to *Eden Valley* almost all our money was given under the Workshop Declaration to do as we wished. Most was from Alan Fountain's department, but we occasionally had hits with other departments, from drama for *In Fading Light* and for *Dream On*.

Now we've got our first major amount of money from the BBC under the Workshop Declaration.

MD—And have you had anything from Tyne Tees?

MM—No, Tyne Tees is largely antagonistic.

MD—Foreign television?

MM—Oh yes, NDR in Hamburg put money into *Eden Valley*. We've had our work shown extensively in Scandinavia, particularly *Dream On*. We've been fairly popular in Australia and New Zealand. We've had French television but not French cinema. We've had some interest in Italy.

Since Pat McCarthy joined us, maybe twelve years ago, and focused on the distribution side, our distribution took off. You need somebody who looks after it. When a film suddenly emerges we are directed by the distribution department as much as we are by production.

The other thing is, since we own the films we direct – because the Workshop Declaration ensures we always own our own films – we make constant monies from sales.

MD—How far ahead do you plan?

MM—We tend to work on five-year plans as a group.

MD—Is that a business plan or a political plan, or a mixture?

MM—Ideological/political and cultural/political I would say, yes, not business. You can't be sure where you are going to be with money, but we'll make a decision to work in an area and we would say we'll have to work there five years to build relationships and do serious work. So, when we went back into North Tyneside we looked for a community base which was in addition to this place here and we bought a pub, which we thought made sense. If you look at the films like *T. Dan Smith*, *In Fading Light* and particularly *Dream On*, they're set in that location, as are the soaps I mentioned. We made three feature films in that period set partly in that location.

Chronology: Organisation and Funding

1968   Formed as a limited company.
            Completion of first short films, *Maybe* and *All You Need Is Dynamite*.
            First application to Northern Arts for funding for *Maybe*. Turned down.

1969   Lambton Visual Aids formed, a company making slides for educational use. Developed into an independent visual aids company.

1970   Group restructured as a partnership.
            First wage structure.

1971–2   Rented Quayside premises.

1972   First public funding: a Northern Arts photography grant of approximately £150.
            Involvement with Live Theatre starts.

1975   First revenue funding from Northern Arts.
            Bought premises.

1975–6   BFI Capital Grant for cinema: £10,000.

1977   Opens Side Gallery and Side Cinema.

            First Arts Council grant for photography. Since then received regular support for photography from the Arts Council in the form of capital and revenue funding.

1978   Northern Arts revenue funding: £30,000. Continued annually at approximately the same level up to 1996.

1981   First drama film – *The Filleting Machine.*

1981–2   Became ACTT-franchised workshop.

1982   First Channel Four revenue funding: £48,000.

1983   Established current affairs unit.

            Side Cinema changes from full-time to part-time working.
            First major sale to foreign TV.

1989   Side Cinema closes.
            Sideshows touring exhibitions introduced as development of the Side
                Gallery's touring policy of the early 80s.

1992   *Dream On* at the Odeon. First cinema release in mainstream cinema.

1994   Last Channel Four revenue funding.

1995   First BBC revenue funding.

Channel Four funding: revenue between £48,000 and £90,000 p.a. In addition
received £200,000 from drama for *In Fading Light.* In all received £1.2 million from
Channel Four and produced four feature-length and two shorter dramas, a total of
500 minutes of drama.

Productions Up to 1997

Descriptions are based on the much more comprehensive information in *Amber/
Side Catalogue and History of Work Since 1968.* All the films are held by Amber and
are available on VHS tape as well as in their original format.

1969   *Maybe* 16mm. B/W. 10 mins.
            A gentle, reflective film about the *Northumbria,* the ferry that runs
                between North Shields and South Shields, and the engine man who
                works on it.

1969   *A Film* 16mm. B/W mag. 8 mins.

1973   *Jellyfish* 16mm. B/W. 7ž mins.
            Two animation films employing a range of experimental
                photomontage techniques.
            Silver Hugo, Chicago Film Festival 1975.

Launch (Murray Martin, 1973)

1973   *Launch* 16mm. Col. 10 mins.
              The gradual emergence of a ship at the end of the street and its
                 sudden subsequent disappearance was part of the annual cycle in
                 Wallsend. The film is a response to the special atmosphere in the
                 yard a few days before the launch.

1974   *High Row* 16mm. Col. 33 mins.
              In Cumbria, near Alston, a small drift mine was licensed from the
                 Coal Board and worked by seven men, who had given up a variety
                 of better-paid jobs in exchange for a more independent working
                 life. The film observes a day in the life of the mine.

1974   *Mai* 16mm. Col. 30 mins.
              Born in India around 1890 from Irish-Persian parents, as a young
                 woman Mai Finglass taught on the Himalayan mountains and was
                 influenced by such radical educationalists as Annie Besant,
                 Madame Blavatsky, Madame Montessori and Ghandi. A film
                 portrait.

1975   *Bowes Line* 16mm. Col. 28 mins.
              One of Amber's documents of working life in the North East,
                 concerning the line from Kibblesworth Colliery to the ships at the
                 Jarrow Staithes and the men who worked the line.

1976   *Last Shift* 16mm. Col. 17 mins.
            The closure of Swalwell Brick factory.

1977   *Glassworks* 16mm. Col. 20 mins.
            The production of handmade glass.

1978   *Laurie* 16mm. Col. 25 mins.
            Laurie Wheatley, plasterer and self-taught sculptor, painter and
            photographer.

1978   *That's Not Me* 16mm. Col. 33 mins.
            Tim Healey, actor turned stand-up comedian, working the rounds of
                the North East's working men's clubs.

1979   *Quayside* 16mm. B/W. 10 mins.
            Campaign film about Newcastle Quayside, made when the area was
                threatened with demolition.

1980   *Tyne Lives* 16mm. Col. 60 mins.
            A retired fish-quay worker, a union activist and a housewife talk
                about their experiences and commitments.

1981   *The Filleting Machine* 16mm. Col. 41 mins.
            The first wholly fictional film, scripted by Tom Hadaway.
                Conflict between husband and wife. The husband, working in the
                fishing industry, disagrees with his wife's idea that education will
                provide a better life for their children.

1983   *Byker* 16mm. Col. 35 mins.
            Based on Sirkka-Liisa Konttinen's photographs and tapes recording
                the transformation of this district over twelve years from a closely
                knit working-class community of terrace streets to a modern
                housing estate.
            Three awards including International Critics Award and Special
                Town of Leipzig Award, 1984.

1983   *Keeping Time* 16mm. Col. 57 mins.
            The dancing school in North Shields has become a symbol, a meeting
                place for dreams and aspirations. Through a mixture of drama and
                documentary the film follows a young dancer from the age of
                seven to seventeen.

1985   *Seacoal* 16mm. Col. 82 mins.
A story about the community who live by gathering coal off the beach at Lynemouth, told through a mix of documentary and dramatisation. Two awards including European Film Award, Munich 1985.

1986   *Double Vision* 16mm. Col. 60 mins.
A mixture of documentary and drama, about a former boxer and the gym where he trains young boxers.

1986   *The Box* 35mm. Col. 101–4 mins.
Animated film expressing the feelings of fear and isolation created by the new urban environment.

1987   *T. Dan Smith* 16mm. Col. 85 mins.
T. Dan Smith was a working-class lad who became the 'City Boss' in the 60s. But in 1971 this visionary politician was sentenced to five years' imprisonment. As public relations man for the infamous architect, John Poulson, who won contracts by bribing city councillors, Smith was trapped in a web of corruption.
Royal Television Best Network Programme, 1988.

1988   *From Marx and Engels to Marx and Spencer* 16mm. Col. 75 mins.
Documentary co-operation with DEFA, the East German film organisation. Amber filmed in Rostock and the DEFA team filmed in Newcastle.

1989   *In Fading Light* 16mm. Col. 103 mins.
The upheaval caused in a traditional fishing village by the arrival of a young woman. Documentary-style drama scripted by Tom Hadaway.
Silver Medal, New York 1990.
Silver Anchor, Toulon 1991.

1991   *Dream On* 35mm. Col. 115 mins.
A blend of magic, fantasy, dreams and the hard-hitting realism Amber is reknown for, the film treads a knife-edge between humour and tragedy. Set in North Shields, the story follows the impact on some of the customers of a community pub of the arrival, on her ramshackle motorbike, of the publican's irreverent and bossy mother.
Six awards including Public Prize, Creteil, Paris, 1991;
Prix Futura Berlin, Television Fiction, 1993.

In Fading Light (Murray Martin, 1989)

1991   *Writing in the Sand.* 16mm. Col. 43 mins.
              Evokes the magic of an urban family's day out on the windswept
                  beaches of North East England.
              Three awards including Le Prix du Documentaire 'Cinéma du Reel',
                  Paris 1992.

1994   *Letters to Katja* 57 mins.
              Documentary.

1995   *Eden Valley* 16mm. Col. 100 mins.
              Naturalistic drama set within a harness racing fraternity and
                  exploring the conflict between urban and rural values through the
                  medium of an evolving relationship between father and son.
              Jury Prize, Creteil, Paris, 1995.
              Best British Independent Feature, North West Film Festival,
                  Stockport, 1995.

1995   *It's the Pits* 32 mins.
              Documentary.

1997   *The Scar* 95–114 mins.
              Feature film.
              Four awards including Prix Europa Special Prize, Television Fiction,
                  1998.

Tapes

1983   *News from Durham* U Matic. 12 mins.
            The Durham miners' gala.

1983   *Where Are We Going?* U Matic. 35 mins.
            Centred round a miners' weekend school, the tape provides an
                insight into the state of the NUM prior to the 1984 strike.

1984   *Why Support the Miners?* U Matic. 8 mins.
            Arguments around the miners' strike.

1984   *Behind the Vote* U Matic. 31 mins.
            An introduction to election campaigning. Based on Chesterfield by-
                election.

1984   *Beyond the Vote.* U Matic. 22 mins.
            Based on Chesterfield by-election, programme for Channel Four
                about the Labour Party and its supporters.

1985   *Can't Beat It Alone* U Matic. 45 mins.
            On the campaign against nuclear energy.

1985   *The Sadler Story* U Matic. 23 mins.
            The life of John Sadler, a pacifist through two world wars.

1986   *Who's Next for Privatisation?* U Matic. Six tapes, between 8 and 20
            mins. each.
            Issues to do with privatisation in the specific context of North
                Tyneside.

1988   *Shields Stories* U Matic. Ten tapes, approximately 10 mins. each.
            Ten short dramas in soap form highlighting a variety of social issues.
            Royal Television Special Award, 1987.
            Silver Medal, Film & Television Festival, New York.

Cinema Action

Beginnings

Gustav (Schlacke) Lamche's account is drawn from three interviews conducted in 1996. Ann Guedes (formerly Lamche) now lives in Portugal and her account was taken from telephone conversations at the end of 1996 and the beginning of 1997.

Before Ann and Schlacke arrived in England in 1968 they had lived in France for four years and before that in Germany. Schlacke is German, Ann is British but with a French mother.

Schlacke

SL–Ann started Cinema Action when we were barely in Britain. We had a small family, three children, and we had been thrown out of Paris by the French government, lost of course our jobs in Paris – Ann had a responsible position at the ORTF, the French radio and television station, doing news bulletins in the English section, and I had various freelancing jobs.

MD–Why were you thrown out?

SL–The French government thought our further presence in France was not conducive to the welfare of the French nation!

They appointed a new Interior Minister and his first act was to throw Ann and me out of France. Twenty people came to our flat and interrogated us, broke the floorboards open with crowbars and threatened, intimidated our family out of their wits – our eldest boy was about eight years old.

I was writing poetry at the time and, to know where to put the stress when I was reciting it, I made a little mark underneath the vowels. So, these policemen, twenty of them with six or seven who spoke fluent English, fluent German, were absolutely startled by my poems – I had them hung in long reams from the ceiling on telex paper. They saw this as some amazing form of global communication, because I had some marks there which didn't correspond to the usual conventions of language. God knows what little theories they had!

We were brought to the Interior Ministry and next day we were transported to the German border in two armoured cars. We later learned that we were the avant-garde of 500 people which they had thrown out of France. It was on the 9 June 1968.

Ann

AG–I knew people in the SDF, the German Student Movement, and in French revolutionary groups, but I was not an organiser. Daniel Cohn-Bendit was a friend and used to come to our flat, but that was before he was a political figure.

I was working at the ORTF in 1968, and when the attempt was made to assassinate Rudi Dutschke I was on duty the night the news came through and I passed it on directly. The German group got hold of the French groups and there was a meeting in our flat, when they all agreed to appear together for the first time. (Before, even on Vietnam, they would not come out together.) When May came I was on strike and involved with what the ORTF workers were doing. So, I took part in the events but was not a leader.

The police arrested me. Then they arrested Schlacke and took away all his work – not just poetry but plays, two novels, short stories, something he was working on with John Cage – and never gave it back. The loss affected him deeply.

Schlacke

MD–Had you been politically involved before, in Germany?

SL–The question is interesting, because for me life is politics. So, I was, of course, very intensely living. I think every person is politically involved from birth.

MD–What kind of work had you been doing in Germany?

SL–I had my architectural practice in Frankfurt. My first commission was a student house and after that there was a factory, a couple of gas stations, the headquarters of Telefunken in Frankfurt. Our collective was called *gruppe bau* and was similar to Cinema Action but for building.

I met Ann at university, at the *hochschule fur gestaltung*, which was the continuation of the Bauhaus after the Second World War. She was part of *gruppe bau*, responsible for the two-dimensional work – posters, letterheads, book covers.

MD–*Gruppe bau* was a collective?

SL–But it carried my name, because, at that time, I had overall control.

MD–In what sense was it collective?

SL–Because there was a cash box and everybody took out what they needed and wrote in the book what they took out. That's the way we handled the rewards and salaries.

MD–So, it was quite extraordinarily different from a normal company?

SL–Yes. I had never heard of this method, but I thought it was a very successful one, because people knew how much cash had been generated collectively and could determine their own income needs. There were, of course, also extraordinary things. For instance, we had a number of living-in artists who did not contribute to the product output at all but perhaps contributed to the lifestyle: say, for instance, playing the guitar at appropriate or inappropriate moments. And they also went to the cash box and took their cash.

MD–Surely, the fact that you were doing business in that way was significant?

SL–No, not at all. That is traditional where I come from. I come from a peasant background in Silesia and that's the way I remember my grandparents were. We would eat out of one big bowl there. My grandfather, the farmer, the main man, gets first place and then the people who work with him in the fields, in most cases Polish prisoners of war, would each take their spoon and eat the same thing. So, when we went to my grandparents, my brother and I, and got our spoons and ate out of that big bowl it was always a very great experience. I think my notion of civilisation, the need to work together and to enjoy yourself in a more than individualistic way, has a lot to do with the way I learned to eat at my grandfather's house.

MD–What happened about your architectural practice when you went to France?

SL–I finished those contracts which I had already and then stayed in Paris and focused more on writing. I saw that I could do more with words and then, when I was relating to film-makers in Paris, with images, and that it was more effective in improving people's lot than building houses.

MD–Did you start making films in Paris?

SL–I got a commission to start research on a series with the Beatles in India which, in the end, didn't come off. I also made the acquaintance of Richard Leacock, who invited me to start a project with him, which also was never made, but we spent a lot of time travelling together. So, my first influence in terms of film-making comes from Richard Leacock.

Cinema Action: The First Phase

Schlacke

SL–Ann wanted to raise money to import a French student film on the events of May 1968. It was about 90 minutes of married print, of which perhaps half an hour were debates on the film industry, but the other parts showed the debates among students and the street action, battles with police and some detailed studies of the occupation of factories. So, Ann started looking for support.

Richard Mordaunt was a crucial person. He had a film company in Mayfair called Lusia and he arranged a party for the purpose of raising funds for the import of the student film. £30 was raised and Ann sent the money to France for a print. Richard lent his projector, and that was the beginning of the mobile cinema activity of Cinema Action.

MD–Ann was working on her own for a while, with only Richard's support, and then other people began to join. Who was in that early group?

SL–There was Humphrey Trevelyan who bought the truck we used for the mobile projector. Marc Karlin was there and there was also a strong American contingent – people who had dodged the draft or were frightened they would be drafted. There was Dana Purvis and Jane Grant, who had a negative cutting service in Covent Garden. But I did not take part at first.

MD–Who saw the films?

SL–It was multiplying. For example, we showed the French film in Dagenham at Ford's and there were about four people looking and three of them were thinking about how to get to the pub – four workers looking at a French film in French and three of them not interested in the film! But one of the four was able to arrange a big showing at one of their main meetings. So, we had all of a sudden 2,000 people looking at that film, in French – unheard of in Britain!

MD–So, the work started by showing films and then you began to make your own?

SL–A couple of very short cine tracts were made: for instance, one about London transport. These were requests from people who came to the meetings. By now the first workers who had been at shows began to come to meetings.

Ann

AG–When we were making the cine tracts we were only getting very small donations from workers. It was a matter of taking collections. We were helped to make the films, because some people who had money were paying for things. They did it quietly and it was never really discussed. I felt it ought to be discussed. It was part of the reality of how we worked at that time and it meant we never knew exactly what the cine tracts cost.

Later on we started to get substantial donations from the workers. After *UCS1* that really took off. Then, for some films, we received contributions of one or two thousand pounds. We were also given support in other ways. For instance, when we were filming at UCS [Upper Clyde Shipyard] we were sleeping on someone's floor and we didn't have a car but were transporting the double-headed projector by bus. When the shop stewards found out they arranged a car for us and paid for us to stay in a hotel.

MD–Eduardo Guedes was one of the UCS team, wasn't he? How did he come to join?

AG–Eduardo was a draft dodger. [From the Portuguese colonial wars. Ed.] He had come to Britain and gone to the London International Film School, and then was asked to stay on as a tutor. He was already a brilliant editor and had made three films in Brazil. He was working on the steenbeck in Cinema Action on something of his own when I heard the workers were going to occupy the Upper Clyde Shipyards. I asked him if he would go up to Scotland with me to film the occupation. He said 'yes' and he filmed *UCS1*, and from then onwards he was part of Cinema Action.

Schlacke

MD–How did you and Richard come to film in Free Derry?

SL–We were a year into the practice of showing films. So, the word has spread and an activist in Derry phoned that we should come and bring some entertainment films for children. Derry was barricaded and had been cut off from the administration of the UK government.

This was when I met the Coopers. I had previously bought bulbs for our projector in Frith Street [At Contemporary Films. Ed.], and had chatted to the person who sold them and noted that he thought what we were doing was interesting. So, I spoke to him about our need for entertainment films and he said I should go upstairs to see Charlie. Charlie wasn't there but I saw his wife, Kitty Cooper, who said, 'Yes, we are throwing away these piles of films because the sprockets are damaged', and she gave me about sixteen feature films. So, I mended the sprockets and with these films and Richard's projector and camera and Nagra we turned up in Derry.

Everything there was done with votes and motions. So, there was a motion and we were allowed to bring the camera in and we produced an amazing record.

MD–You and Richard didn't finish the film together, did you?

SL–About a year after shooting, for family reasons, Richard had to leave the UK. When he came back our ways separated. He looked at the film, which in the meantime I had continued, and he didn't dislike it but it was not the film that he was going to make. So, we agreed that he would make a dupe negative and from the same material we would make two films. Richard's was called *Ireland Behind the Wire*, Cinema Action's had the title *People of Ireland!*

MD–By the time Richard came back and you parted company, other changes had taken place at Cinema Action, hadn't they?

SL–The studio in Mayfair had been given up and the equipment now was with us and we had moved to rented accommodation in Kilburn, which was where the meetings took place. There were also a number of people living with us who had nowhere else to live, so the place was like *gruppe bau* again. The only thing was that there was no space. We had a small flat with about eight people living there, all to do with the mobile cinema, and the gear right in the middle of it, the children of course being very elbowed, because they were basically living in a film studio. So, it was difficult.

Marc had left Cinema Action while Richard was away. Humphrey was also away. Then, when he and Richard returned, they formed Berwick Street Collective with Marc. So that was a split-off from Cinema Action but with mutual adoration, because I liked Humphrey very much and Richard, I thought, was an important British film-maker.

Some Other Early Members

Humphrey Trevelyan

Cameraman and lecturer and a member of Cinema Action from 1969 to 1970. From an interview recorded in 1996.

HT–I had been in South America for two years up until the Christmas of 1968. I came back to London and a Latin American contact there was in touch with Ann Lamche. So, we went round together to meet up with Ann, probably in February or March 1969.

MD—Did you have a long-standing interest in politics or film, or both?

HT—I had become interested in film-making in South America, although I had done quite a lot of photography before and some 8mm filming on personal projects. It had no political content at all then, but there was an aesthetic search.

I don't think I was very politicised before I went out to South America. I'd done a degree in social anthropology at Cambridge and a sociology MA at the University of Essex. I initially went to Buenos Aires to do some sociology research. Then that rather fizzled out and I did some theatre with an Argentinian group – it was living theatre, anti-imperialist stuff.

When I got back to the UK my ideas for film projects were based on working with anthropologists I had met in Peru, in the Amazon jungle, but I was aware that great revolutions had occurred while I was away and all of a sudden England seemed to be transformed, and I jumped into political film-making very enthusiastically.

At that time Cinema Action, to my knowledge, consisted of Ann Lamche and Richard Mordaunt, a 16mm projector and a copy of a film of May/June 1968. My friend and I joined and within a few weeks another three or four people came.

MD—What was Richard Mordaunt's role?

HT—He had set up a production company called Lusia Films with a couple of rather upper-class friends of his – one of them was Lord Henry Herbert – and they had made quite high-class corporate films for big people like BOAC, and Richard particularly had concentrated on music films. He'd just finished a film on Otis Redding. They were quite successful and Richard himself was a very, very accomplished film-maker. I don't think he ever went to film school but he just had a fantastic feel for the medium. He had celluloid fingers.

The company was in Mayfair, in Shepherds Market, a small but quite luxuriously appointed production house, and I do not know still to this day quite what moved Richard towards taking a very radical position in relation to film. But in quite an extraordinary way he completely opened up all the facilities of Lusia Films to Cinema Action.

At that point the work consisted of showing the French film and one or two other films to shop-stewards' committees, and one of the first things I did was to go up to a British Leyland factory which had gone on strike for the first time in thirty years.

MD—How did the film go down?

HT—I think there were mixed reactions. You tended to find in those days in shop-stewards' committees a left Labour/Communist Party majority and then quite a large Trotskyist minority. This film that we showed is heavily critical of the French Communist Party. So, obviously, that didn't go down too well, but they were terribly polite about it. That's what really struck me, how polite they were.

One of the reasons for going round doing the projections and the talks with shop-stewards' committees was to get them interested in collaborating on film projects, because at that time the British shop stewards' movement appeared to be very militant and the idea was that Cinema Action was going to be a servicing agency for it.

This was very much influenced by the Continental experience. Although Schlacke at that time was not directly involved in Cinema Action, clearly he and Ann thought very similarly and, if anything, the approach was syndicalist but with this strong, rather complex German imposition which came from Schlacke and the various German friends that they had. I'd be hard put to define it now. The German SDF movement, Rudi Dutschke and people like that were prominent, because Rudi Dutschke was a very close friend of Schlacke. Later on it became influenced also by the beginnings of the Women's Movement brought over by a couple of American members later on in 1969.

MD–How were decisions taken about what films to make and how to make them?

HT–We used to have general meetings which would take an exceedingly long time – I think the record was twelve hours – and I think people were fairly autonomous. So, people proposed something and if there were enough people who supported it and there seemed to be the finance to do it, it was agreed.

MD–You were, presumably, only having to pay for film stock and processing?

HT–And transport. I, for instance, bought an old transit van which became the Cinema Action van and had a very honourable and chequered history in radical British politics.

MD–What about paying for the film stock?

HT–I think Lusia Films bore the brunt. Richard continued to do commercial work. So, he was able to make bits of money here and there. But certainly, what did happen after a while was that Lusia Films ran up huge accounts all round Soho and it all came to quite a crisis.

MD–And then what happened?

HT–That was later on, I think in 1970–1 and that really was one of the things that fuelled the mistrust and the aggravation, particularly between Richard and Cinema Action.

I left because I wanted to go on a photographic, ethnographic trip with a Peruvian friend of mine to India. I think things had got very tense in Cinema Action, but that was not the overt reason for me leaving.

Steve Sprung

Freelance film editor and independent film-maker, and a member of Cinema Action from 1970 to 1976. From an interview recorded on 25 June 1996.

SS–I got involved with Cinema Action because I went to a showing of *Fighting the Bill* at a large political meeting against the Industrial Relations Act. I was at art college in London by then, but my father was a Marxist–Leninist and I'd gone to the meeting with a bunch of people from Coventry, from the political group he was part of.

Seeing that film was revelatory. It wasn't that it was a great film as a film. But it was direct and talked to working-class people about things which were theirs. The people who spoke in it were very powerful speakers and that was one thing that the working-class movement had going for it: a strong tradition of oratory.

At the time I was trying to make a film about the Shrewsbury building workers who'd been charged with conspiracy for trying to cause an affray. So, I went to talk to Schlacke, and in the process got involved with working with Cinema Action. Probably the reason I was accepted straight away was that I came from Coventry, from a working-class background, and very few of the people connected with Cinema Action then were from working-class backgrounds.

MD–Did you find that odd?

SS–No. What I did find odd was that when I went to art college (St Martin's) most people were ex-public school.

MD–Some of the people at Cinema Action had been to public school. Did you find their perception of working-class life a bit abstract?

SS–No, I found them very straightforward. They were very committed to what they were doing and very down to earth. Ann was a member of the same trade union, the AEU, which I joined, because, when I left art college, I went to work in a car factory. She spent her time among working-class people or people who were political revolutionaries. The people at Cinema Action didn't have dinner parties with middle-class people at night and then mix with working-class people in the day. It wasn't like that. They were squatters. Also among them there were a lot of foreigners. I didn't see them like the public school people at college, who did seem to come from an alien class.

MD–At the time you were in Cinema Action, how frequent were the showings?

SS–In the early period we were showing films a couple of times a week, mainly in the evenings but also in the day, lunch-hour screenings. With the Shrewsbury building workers' campaign we did a lot of showings on building sites organised through shop stewards.

MD–Were the films adding anything beyond getting people together in a situation in which there could be a debate?

SS–They were adding in something to do with the history which people who weren't active in it at the time wouldn't necessarily have known about, and they were adding in other themes. If you take *Fighting the Bill*, it talked about the relationship between two ideals of democracy, working-class democratic practices as opposed to bourgeois democratic practices, and raised those ideas for discussion.

MD–If they were shown where people were militant, wouldn't the audience already be familiar with the arguments?

SS–No. When a film was shown on a building site everyone who was on the building site would be there. The people who organised the show would already be aware of those ideas, but there were people on the building site who had not thought about them. They were also bringing new things, in that, for instance, the Clyde film brings experiences of an occupation, something which no one would have been able to experience without seeing that film.

MD—But you don't see what is really happening from a film – you only see a representation of it.

SS—Of course, but the representation is that of, say, one of the shop stewards who ran the occupation. So, even if you went to the occupation, that is what you would see. It's not just film that does that. It happens in real life. You get a representation of something in the way that people articulate it.

MD—In a case like the Clyde, where the people engaged in the occupation were from various political parties, would Cinema Action be more reliant on one group than another?

SS—No, Cinema Action was more interested in an enabling action rather than in giving a particular line.

MD—But how was the enabling process seen, because by filming some things and not others you are making judgments?

SS—Of course.

MD—Was that acknowledged?

SS—It was acknowledged within Cinema Action. You were doing research, you saw yourself as active. But when films were shown it was represented as if the workers had made them, which I felt was a misrepresentation, because it denies that active element, that there is something coming from outside which acts as a catalyst.

MD—Given that there was so little money and film is an expensive process, why didn't they move to video?

SS—I suspect there were two reasons for this: one is the power of film that you don't get with a small screen, and the other is that you have a large screen and you draw a large group of people.

MD—Now you could show video on a large screen.

SS—Now you could but then you couldn't. It also had something to do with the discipline of a film-making practice, that you work with small amounts of footage. If you look at the Cinema Action films they are conceived as filmic as opposed to being like a TV programme; they are conceived of as almost epic: with *The Miners' Film* this is a film to represent the story of the miners, of their traditions and aspirations. It goes back to the Joris Ivens tradition of film-making.

MD—What did you do after you left the group?

SS—I went to the Poster Collective and then we made *Year of the Beaver*, about the Grunwick strike which took place in 1977, looking back on it from the 80s.

MD—You have said it couldn't have been made within Cinema Action. Why?

SS—The strength of Cinema Action films is that they are made very much from within the situation, whereas *Year of the Beaver* is made in a situation which is being represented by the people involved in a way which was totally at odds with the reality. So I had to take a much more independent position. But it couldn't have been made by someone who hadn't worked with Cinema Action. Because people who worked with Cinema Action went through a whole experience and a whole practice over a lengthy period of time where they became educated and became able to relate to working-class struggles, be part of them, be able to film them. It's not the kind of thing you can read about. It only comes out of the experience of working in a situation, of being engaged in it.

Dave Douglass

Miner and NUM activist, and a member of Cinema Action from 1971. From an interview recorded on 23 November 1996. Dave Douglass was one of about twenty trade unionists who worked closely with Cinema Action. Others include Mike Cooley of DATA, Don Cook and Dick Jones, Jimmy Reed and Jimmie Airlie of the AUEW.

MD–When was your first contact with Cinema Action?

DD–It was the time of the UCS occupation. A lot of other things were going on then and, in Doncaster, our house often had people from different revolutionary organisations staying en route. Cinema Action came on their way back down from Clydeside, and after that we became lifelong comrades with frequent exchanges of people. When we went to London we would stay in the Cinema Action centre and before that in the houses that they squatted – 'we' being members of the various socialist organisations I belonged to.

MD–What organisations?

DD–At that time I was on the fringes of the Revolutionary Workers' Party (not to be confused with the Workers' Revolutionary Party), but we had a miners' organisation, the Mineworkers' Internationale, which brought together people from different positions: Maoists and Trotskyists and members of the Communist Party. There was cross-involvement with all kinds of organisations, like the Agitprop Bookshop, which was in Gower Street and later moved to Bethnal Green, and the History Workshop. A lot of us thought the revolution was round the corner and it was time to start arming the masses, and Cinema Action was part of that arming.

MD–Which of the Cinema Action films were you involved in?

DD–The student film, *The Miners' Film, Fighting the Bill*.

MD–What was your role – or roles?

DD–Advising, helping to plan, working on policy. We set up a lot of the places where the workers were interviewed and scenes were shot. I was part of the discussions, part of the team.

MD–How did you and your comrades in the union see film contributing?

DD–People like Lawrence Daly, who was General Secretary of the NUM at that time, and Mick McGaghey saw films as being very important. You couldn't attend a world conference or a demonstration every week but a film could show you what was happening. That slogan, 'Dare to struggle, we shall win – London, Paris and Berlin' really struck a chord with my generation of young workers. We felt part of

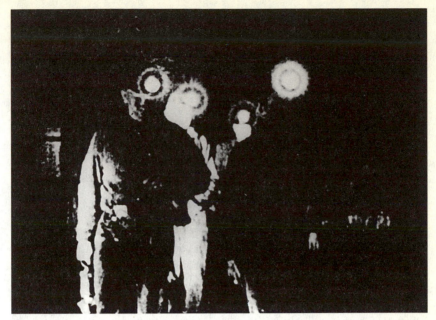

The Miners' Film (1974/5).

a whole European and world process, and Cinema Action was able to give you a window onto that and could introduce you to people who spoke French and Ger-man and took us away from the Little-England attitude which existed round trade union circles.

Cinema Action were making films and showing films on the hoof. The people who were making the films were presenting them. It was a very exciting thing. They'd put films on in factory canteens, in bus depots, in dock areas, in shipyard assembly areas, in locations where there were masses of workers. The UCS film was shown at Plessey's during the occupation there. It's very evocative when you've got films thrown as a huge projection against a big factory wall showing images of workers in struggle!

The films were essentially made by the workers, particularly the UCS film, where they had complete editorial control.

MD—You mean the Shop-Stewards' Committee had control?

DD—Yes, and and there were criticisms of the way the occupation was run which could have been made in the film but weren't. There were arguments between those who wanted to take the struggle out and those who wanted to keep it a parochial fight. But overall, that was a film that everybody could live with.

MD—With hindsight wouldn't it have been more interesting if the film had articu-lated those differences?

DD—Well, it wasn't something that was put on and then people went home to bed. It was put on and engendered a discussion with the audience. So, all these argu-ments came out anyway.

MD—Did you see some of the films made at the time by other groups?

DD—If you got Cinema Action to come along, you got other films as well, like *Rosie the Riveter*.

MD—Did you see *Nightcleaners*?

DD—Yes. That was going around and was played to large audiences of working-class women in Doncaster.

MD—That film could be quite surprising if you were expecting something more like *Rosie the Riveter*. How did your audience in Doncaster respond to it?

DD—They responded very well.

MD—They weren't worried by the repetition of certain images or the bits of black spacing?

DD—No. But then again no one else was dealing with the subject. The very fact that it was being dealt with, on the screen in a debate situation, was important. You were being presented with political questions about your own working life in the images of other workers. It wasn't expected that watching it would be like watching a cartoon. There was a lot of interaction then with the professional film-makers like Phillip Donnellan at the BBC, who was making a series called *Where Do I Stand*. These were four films around particular individuals, and they did one with me.

MD—At the time, if people like Donnellan were getting political programmes on TV, was there any reason for working outside as Cinema Action did?

DD—I don't think they were trying to work on the outside. Some of their material did go on television. But you could wait for ever for the BBC to accept a film you were making, whereas you needed the camera to be hot. It needed to be wild footage. You needed to be there on the spot. It wasn't a documentary you were try-ing to make. You weren't trying to record history. You were trying to make history. And it was set in a context as part of a debate – not entertainment, not an illustra-tion, not a portrayal of the struggle – but part of the struggle.

The whole point of revolutionary film was to make the struggle. There's also a place for a documentary socio-historical piece, and I use a lot of those films today, like the film about Grunwick. But essentially, the work that Cinema Action was doing was different. The films weren't meant to be there for ever, to win an Oscar. They were meant to be a tool in the struggle at the time.

MD—Cinema Action changed in the late 70s towards making more reflective films which did begin to win prizes.

DD—Yes, because the whole revolutionary movement was changing. We lost many people when the revolutionary time we thought was imminent started to retreat. The Agitprop Bookshop closed down. In a sense, Cinema Action's change was part of that. The tide was starting to withdraw.

MD—There was a certain revival of effort around the 1984 miners' strike, which included the making of the 'Miners' Tapes'. But Cinema Action didn't play a big part in that, did they?

DD—No, but Chris Reeves, who co-ordinated the work, had trained with Cinema Action and some people from Cinema Action did bits of shooting. Some interviews were recorded at Cinema Action.

MD—Ann said that when you were working with them she valued your political knowledge, your analytical understanding of a situation. Where had you acquired those skills?

DD—My dad and my grandad had been trade union activists in the mining industry on Tyneside. It was a very cosmopolitan area next to South Shields, where you had a massive influx of ships, foreign sailors, foreign influences, a tradition of political involvement in foreign causes from the Spanish Civil War on. My mother was from Kells, County Meath, in Ireland, and some of her relatives had been active in the IRA.

MD—That has to do with the politics, but I was asking more about the intellectual approach.

DD—I think that was the influence of anarchism in the city – free verse, poetry, the development of music in the city at the time, folk music and the rock music – not having a fear of poetry and art as I should have had.

MD—Why should you have that fear?

DD—Because it was considered middle class, soft. There was a generational input which took us away from narrow parochialism.

MD—Did you do any formal academic study?

DD—Yes, under Ralph Samuels with the History Workshop, which published my work, *Pit Life in County Durham*.

MD—I meant much earlier, in Newcastle, did you go to formal classes in politics or Marxism?

DD—Only in the YCL. I joined the YCL when I was fourteen, but I was only in for about six months and was then expelled for being too left.

We had been excluded from any intellectual practice at school. We were told we were thick and we'd failed the eleven-plus. I was in a secondary modern in a C class, which was the lowest, and we were treated as thick proles. We were given a football to play with and I've hated football every since, because we regarded it as collaboration. I got the cane every single day, generally once, sometimes three times, for wild extravagances like talking, looking defiant.

MD—How was it that this didn't put you off anything connected with learning?

DD—It was a matter of resistance. Knowing a different intellectualism was a defiance.

We used to have open-air meetings in the middle of Newcastle and I used to go along and hear shipyard workers talking, and it struck me that there was a way of using education as a weapon. I remember marching into the local library and asking for *Capital* and the librarian said, 'Would that be *Das Kapital*?', and got me down the three volumes in German. So, I sat there pretending to read it, nodding sagely!

MD–Later on did you ever read it, in translation, all the way through?
DD–I did.

Organisation of the Group

Schlacke

MD–What did it mean to join Cinema Action – was there any kind of constitution?
SL–We tried to have membership fees but we had no structure. So, there was an informality centred on the meetings. We had open meetings, which were very difficult, as students and political activists from various formations could all come. If someone was not run out of the meetings they were a member.
MD–When people work intensely together there are often conflicts. Was this complicated for you by the fact that many of you were living as well as working together?
SL–There were, of course, tensions and conflicts, but the question of how you resolved them took place in a context of knowing that our opposition was very serious, that our achievements were only a dent. So we had a discipline of trying to ensure that conflict was not too intense. We were aware that what we were doing was very important, so that you sometimes had to make compromises in terms of your principles.

Theory and Politics

Schlacke

SL–The core of our strategy was to bring about better solidarisation – improved solidarisation of the dispossessed.
MD–How did you conceive of the relationship with the people you were filming?
SL–For instance, with *Hands Off Student Unions*, the student union approached us to make a film. The film was needed very soon and three autonomous groups were formed to shoot and edit different sections. But the important thing was how, during the making of the film, the editorial line of the three components emerged from discussions in the places where it was shot. The people whose activity was being filmed would decide what should be filmed. So it was very anti-authoritarian.
MD–There was a rather ambivalent article about Cinema Action by David Glynn and Paul Marris in *Afterimage* which questions this anti-authoritarian approach ...
SL–We were personally very critical of Glynn's article. They could never discern that there were intellectuals among Cinema Action. We followed *Framework* and *Afterimage* and understood their preoccupations. We had a close relationship with French thought. *Cahiers* and the French post-modernists were read here and debated. We were relating to movements in France and in Germany. We were developing notions of criticism in film language and supported the notion of critical reflection which was around, for instance, in the *Screen* project. Some people were intensely critical of *Screen*. We never were. We saw how important its contribution was.

MD–In the context of those debates, how would you have described your work?

SL–Our critical project was to work with audiences to counter political and academic simplifications. This means bringing about a discussion after the film – not having an abstract notion of discourse but implementing discourse.

With this work we could hear whether our films were working or not directly, and this would be brought back into the film-making.

MD–There are different meanings of 'working'. Did you want people to agree with the films or to argue with them?

SL–The more intense the argument the better the show. Among our audiences you had not just progressive people but also people who were quite reactionary or brought reactionary ideas.

MD–How did you relate to the established left groupings?

SL–I made sure that there was never a projection of a particular party. For instance, if we were at a meeting organised by Trotskyists and I noticed that some CP people wanted to know what was going on, I would bring them in.

I'm not against structures, I'm against structures excluding each other. It is totally idiotic when people who are in an impossibly weak situation, in terms of bargaining or negotiation, start rowing among themselves. I noticed that in France, you had about fifty revolutionary parties – fantastic! This is the recipe for letting the police run the show!

MD–And what was your position in relation to the arguments within the independent sector, about the IFA, for instance?

SL–There were, within the IFA, very few people who had that notion of pooling resources. The majority of IFA members were individualists. We knew that within an IFA context you could not articulate the demands of the collective.

MD–Were your conclusions from that, that the IFA was not a useful organisation?

SL–Oh no, it was crucial. IFA was not only a crucial organisation, it was us. What was much more developed in the IFA was a cultural criticism and an onslaught on the inadequacy of the media industry.

Amber had a personal vendetta against the IFA, which was a problem for us, because we tried to point out that in this small contingent of *aufrechters* – people who walk straight, who don't allow themselves to be bent by ideology nor by repression – you don't start artificial rows when it is more important to be united.

A Resource and an Influence

Steve Sprung

SS–As an organisation Cinema Action bumped into a big group of people, people who didn't necessarily adhere to their practice but passed through there or were encouraged. A lot of people I know who now work with film first came into either politics or film through Cinema Action. Lots of people came into contact with them and would be encouraged to try to make films, to see that it's possible.

Schlacke

SL—Nick Broomfield is an example. He finished his first film on our machine. Kwate [Nii Kwate Owoo, now director of the Pan-African Federation of Cineastes. Ed.] who had been at the London Film School, made a film, *You Hide Me*, about the African treasures in the British Museum, and edited it at Cinema Action – another no-budget film! Altogether there are about 250 or more people who are now in the industry who went through. For instance, Julien Temple who made *Absolute Beginners*.

MD—Were you worried that some people who came to you were simply seeking entry to the industry?

SL—We were giving people a chance, that's all, a chance which is usually not there. Or if an organisation like the BFI does this work, they go about it in a bureaucratic way.

The Second Phase

This includes extracts from two accounts written at the end of 1996, one from Pascale Lamche, daughter of Ann and Schlacke, the other by Dennis Collum, a member from 1978. Pascale works in the French film industry. Dennis is a freelance cameraman and works with Platform Films.

'The Social Contract' and So 'That You Can Live'

Ann

AG—For *The Social Contract* we went to a factory in South Wales. As we were leaving I overheard a shop steward saying to one of the other workers, 'Are you going over to give those women some support?' I asked what it was about and he said there was a strike by women about equal pay. I said, 'Let's go over!'

MD—That was beginning of *So That You Can Live*?

AG—From the start I was making a different film. I suggested we should go home with the convener. It was something Cinema Action had never done before.

Pascale

PL—The turning point came with the production of *So That You Can Live*. History had moved on and, as film-makers, Cinema Action's analysis of how best to 'continue the struggle' was evolving. Cinema Action still lived and worked as a socialist collective.

So That You Can Live was made over a period of five years. This reflected a change in methodology with respect to how one can be most effective politically when one is working with film. The old forms of direct action, i.e. campaign films associated with particular trade union or social struggles, had been appropriate for their time, but a more sophisticated and analytical approach now evolved which also began to take aesthetics and narrative evolution into consideration.

A Pilot Workshop

Schlacke

MD—Eventually you had proper premises in Winchester Road with cutting rooms and a small cinema. How did that happen?

SL—For ten years we were skipping from one squat to the next. We were squatting a different building in Winchester Road and we were under pressure to move out. As it was a council house, Camden couldn't just throw us on the street. So, together with the BFI, they agreed that somehow a modus should be found in which way we could continue, and the modus was a pilot workshop.

Ann

AG—Ken Livingstone was head of Camden Housing then and I asked him if he would come and look. I worked with a bureaucrat with Camden and wrote something and presented it to the full council. The full council agreed and gave us a grant to convert two new shops into a film centre. Almost simultaneously Ken Livingstone agreed that we should not be pushed out until the two new shops were ready.

Dennis Collum

Member of Cinema Action from 1978.

DC—I first became involved with Cinema Action during 1978 after meeting Schlacke at a screening of *Class Struggle: Film from the Clyde*. I had just left Leeds Polytechnic where I'd studied fine art, but my time there had intensified key interests in film and politics.

At that time Cinema Action was housed in a squat at 35 Winchester Road in Swiss Cottage. However, eviction threatened as the whole terrace was due for rehabilitation by Camden Council. Developing the idea of 'integrated practice' alongside the existence of a remodelled 'film workshop' or 'film centre', Camden Council, the British Film Institute and, at a later stage, Channel Four were successfully lobbied to provide financial support. After a year or so of painstaking negotiations and careful timetabling, Cinema Action was able to move out of No. 35 and into the newly built Nos. 25 and 27 Winchester Road. After eighteen months or so, during 1982 Cinema Action relinquished No. 25 and took over the purpose-built No. 29.

Rocinante (Ann Guedes, 1986)

'Rocinante'

Ann

AG–*Rocinante* was originally presented for funding to the BFI as a mixture of documentary and fiction. It was a development of the work we had done with *So That You Can Live*. There was one fictional character who later evolved into the John Hurt character. There was also a real family we were working with. The man was a forestry worker and that linked with the myth of the English countryside.

When we went to a meeting with the production board there was a feature producer who said, 'What's the matter? Are you scared to do a feature?' We explained that we weren't in the least bit scared of fiction but that we specifically wanted the mixture, that we were interested in the question of what is fiction and what is documentary. But the board took the position that it should either be fiction or documentary, and while we were arguing with them the circumstances of the family changed.

It was unfortunate that we had to change our plan and I think it affected the whole direction of Cinema Action. But *Rocinante* was made completely in the context of our normal working methods. Every idea, every bit of script went through the mill of collective discussion.

The Mid-80s

Pascale

PL–One must never forget that Cinema Action was a political group (it came into existence as such and continued to identify itself almost conceptually as such, much like the Bauhaus defined a sensibility and a design aesthetic that was deeply political – and remember that Ann and Schlacke were trained at Ulm), one which defined its politics independently of all political parties. Schlacke was the political philosopher; Ann was the energetic organiser, the trade unionist and the generator of most ideas; Eduardo was the professional film-maker. These three people constituted the core group.

Dennis

DC–The Channel Four workshop money paid the market rent for the new premises and allowed the pool of labour to be expanded. The wage element (ACTT/Channel Four agreed rate × four) was pooled and divided among the workshop members.

In the distribution area there was still a great deal of interest – political and theoretical – in Cinema Action's earlier black-and-white films of the 70s and these were still being shown regularly at trade union conferences, media studies courses, regional film theatres, etc. The cinema was difficult to make work as a commercial proposition, as programming was very much a hit-and-miss affair. Sometimes queues would stretch round the block to see films, especially ones that were connected to a specific political campaign or movement, e.g. Nicaragua. At other times screenings would not be so successful in terms of audience numbers.

Pascale

PL–The younger generation of Cinema Action members spent most of their time running and organising the film centre. Individual projects were researched and written and received some interest from Channel Four's Alan Fountain, who would have liked to encourage the emergence of production ideas from the younger members. *More Bass*, an experimental fiction about music, was made by them (directed by Tag Lamche) and was well received by Rod Stoneman, although never transmitted, as certain editorial changes suggested by Channel Four led to a collapse in confidence by the film-maker. This interest in film forms (fiction) and music was also reflected in *Sister Suzi Cinema*, an a cappella opera which was shot and produced by Schlacke but then fell into rights difficulties. Cinema Action was learning about practices in the commercial world – collective work was difficult to maintain.

Schlacke

SL–Amber is brilliant, because they at the same time can run a pub. I think that's something we were always short of in Cinema Action – someone who can also run a pub.

The Late 80s/Early 90s

Pascale
PL–The group began to drift apart as individuals members sought their own individual ways and production. This was partly economic – it became difficult to sustain a living organising facilities for other film-makers; partly political – it was difficult to retain a coherent political core around a younger generation that were keen to find their way as film producers, writers, cameramen or actresses rather than militants, and around forms of production that required an entirely different set of priorities (i.e. feature films require an identifiable director, good marketing and exhibition strategies, etc.); partly personal – Ann and Eduardo had by now moved to Portugal and were increasingly interested in feature film-making.

Cinema Action continued as a facility for independent film-makers on a skeleton staff and with dwindling means.

Dennis
DC–Alan Fountain's workshop money dried up and the last BFI cheque arrived in 1990. Everybody had left apart from Schlacke and myself. For the next three years we struggled, in the face of the general recession, to keep the doors of Cinema Action open, until June 1993 when Camden Council appointed bailiffs arrived to nail the doors of 27 and 29 Winchester Road.

Pascale
PL–Had it ever been an enterprise run along capitalist lines rather than as a socialist collective which eschewed all forms of accumulation for individual gain or security, it would have survived and devolved into a production company and facilities house. But Cinema Action's (Schlacke's) politics were too uncompromising in the face of Thatcher's savage onslaught on Britain.

Chronology: Organisation and Funding
Information on funding comprises selected examples. The sources are Cinema Action papers in the BFI special collection and BFI accounts.

1968   Cinema Action mobile cinema started by Ann Lamche with support
            of Richard Mordaunt. First screenings of French film.

1969   Develops into an informal group with a growing membership and
            regular meetings. Production based at Lusia Films. All work
            unwaged.
            Mobile Cinema showings include Ford Dagenham, Ford Halewood,
            Vauxhall Ellesmere Port and a British Leyland factory.
            Production of first cine tracts.

Richard Mordaunt and Schlacke Lamche film in Free Derry.

1970–1   Moves to Alexandra Road.

1971   Police raid premises after a showing of *Fighting the Bill* outside the
           Albert Hall.
           Richard Mordaunt, Marc Karlin and Humphrey Trevelyan split off to
           form Berwick Street Collective.
           Films the occupation of the Upper Clyde Shipyards (UCS).
           First substantial donation from trades unions.

1973   Have completed at least twelve films since work began in 1968.

1974   First public project funding: £900 completion grant from BFI
           Production Board for *The Miners' Film*.

1975   Moves to 35a Winchester Road squat.
           The Miners' Film wins International Film Critics' Award,
           Oberhausen.
           First revenue funding, from GLAA.

1976   First major public project funding: £20,000 from BFI Production
           Board for *The Social Contract*. This film is never completed,
           although shown unfinished at several events. Out of the project a
           different film develops: *So That You Can Live*.
           Applied for ACTT membership.

1978   In danger of eviction from squatted premises. Successful application
           to Camden Council for alternative premises.
           Grants: £16,500 revenue funding from BFI direct grant; £38,080
           capital funding from BFI Housing the Cinema Fund (HCF) (for
           renovating premises).

1979   Grants: £19,000 from BFI HCF; £8,500 from GLAA.

1980   Moves into part-rehabilitated premises, 25–27 Winchester Road.
           Work on offices/cutting rooms completed.

1981   Opens cinema at 29 Winchester Road.

1982   Franchised as ACTT workshop.
           So That You Can Live completed and opens *Independent Film and*

Video strand on Channel Four.

Filming of *Sister Suzi Cinema*. Project not completed owing to rights problems.

Capital funding: £12,178 from BFI; £22,500 from GLA.

1983 First Channel Four workshop funding: £85,482.
Other funding: £25, 700 revenue funding from GLA; £9,189 from GLC.

1986 First drama feature, *Rocinante*.

1985–7 Channel Four provides £270,000 for *Rocinante*; £92,250 for workshop.

1987 *Rocinante* opens at Renoir Cinema. Six-week run.
Cinema Action writes its constitution.

1988 Last Channel Four Workshop money.
Whitechapel (computer firm) goes bankrupt owing Cinema Action approximately £10,000.

1990 Last grant from public funds: £28,500 direct grant from BFI.
Ann and Eduardo leave for Portugal.

1993 Premises closed.

Productions

Where descriptions are taken verbatim from Cinema Action publicity they are marked '[CA]'. Otherwise they are based on a mixture of Cinema Action materials, articles, reviews and the author's viewing.

The list is not comprehensive, because Cinema Action sometimes shot material for campaigns which was screened in rough-cut state and not made into a finished film.

Copies of most of the films listed are held by former Cinema Action members. The references under 'Location of archive material' refer to material in archives or in distribution.

Unless otherwise stated films have optical soundtracks.

1969 *White Paper* 16mm. B/W silent. 5 mins.
Made for the campaign against the Labour government's Industrial Relations Bill, *In Place of Strife*, using drawings, stills, titles and simple animation.

1969   *Not a Penny on the Rent* 16mm. B/W. 22 mins.
            Documentary supporting the campaign against the attempt by the
               GLC, under Conservative leader Horace Cutler, to raise council
               rents.
            Location of archive material: NFA.

1969   *London Transport* 16mm. B/W. 6 mins.
            Documentary supporting strikers at Acton tube depot.

1969   *GEC 1* 16mm. B/W. 8 mins.
            Animation and graphics on the call by the GEC Merseyside shop
               stewards for factory occupation to oppose closures and redundancies.

1969   *GEC 2* 16mm. B/W sep. mag.
            Reflections by shop stewards on lessons of the failure of the campaign
               seen in *GEC 1*.
            Location of archive material: NFA.

1969/70   *Squatters* 16mm. B/W opt. 18 mins.
            Documentary on the early squatters' movement. Homeless families
               occupy empty properties and resist eviction by private landlords
               and the GLC.
            Location of archive material: NFA.

1970   *Vauxhalls* 16mm. B/W. Part silent, part opt. 8 mins.
            Animation, stills and documentary opposing measured day work at
               the Vauxhall factory.

1970   *Us All* 16mm. B/W. 12 mins.
            Documentary on a wages dispute by members of the draughtsmans'
               union, DATA, at Rolls Royce, Coventry.

1970   *Fighting the Bill* 16mm. B/W. 36 mins.
            Documentary for the campaign against the Conservative
               government's Industrial Relations Bill. Shows meetings and
               demonstrations and uses graphics, stills and library film to set the
               conflict in the context of an international struggle against
               capitalism and a long history of trade union struggle in Britain.
               The case against the bill is put by shop stewards Mike Cooley and
               Dick Jones from DATA, May Hobbs from T&GWU, Don Cook,
               Kevin Halpin and Tom Langan from AUEW.
            Location of archive material: NFA.

1971   *The UCS Struggle/UCS1* 16mm. B/W. 23 mins.
            Documentary supporting the occupation of Upper Clyde Shipyards.
            Includes speech by Jimmy Reid.
            Location of archive material: NFA.
            Location of viewing material: ETV.

1972   *Hands Off Student Unions* 16mm. B/W. 33 mins.
            Documentary for the National Union of Students' campaign against
               proposals put forward by Margaret Thatcher when Minister for
               Education. Includes speech from Clive Jenkins of ASTMS and an
               interview with the French student leader, Alan Krevine.

1973   *People of Ireland!* 16mm. B/W. 95 mins.
            Documentary. An analysis and chronicle of the instance of dual
               power in the north of Ireland: we see the barricaded resistance
               zone of Free Derry in August 1969, the struggle for democracy, the
               right to assemble and for free expression, the contradiction
               between labour and capital, the struggle against imperialism, the
               demands: a socialist workers' republic. [CA 1980]
            Location of archive material: NFA.

1973   *Arise Ye Workers* 16mm. B/W. 25 mins.
            Documentary supporting dockers' fight against the effects of
               containerisation. 'The London dockers' struggle to preserve their
               jobs against ruthless rationalisation; profiteering and land
               speculation, police harassment of pickets and finally the
               enforcement of the Industrial Relations Act with the arrest of the
               Pentonville 5.' [CA 1975]
            Silver Dove Award, Leipzig Film festival.
            Location of archive material: NFA.

1974–5   *The Miners' Film* 16mm. B/W. 49 mins.
            Documents – from the inside and for the labour movement – the
               events of the miners' strike in 1974, as part of the successful
               opposition against Phase 3 of the Conservative government's
               incomes policy. [CA 9 April 1975] Industrial action by miners in
               the winter of 1973–4 helped to bring down Edward Heath's
               government. The film covers this crisis but reflects the miners'
               historical and political understanding of it, informed by memories
               of the 1926 General Strike and analysis of the failures of
               nationalisation and more recent energy and employment policies.

International Film Critics' award, Oberhausen 1975.
Jury Award for Documentary, Moscow.

1977   *Class Struggle: Film from the Clyde* 16mm. B/W. 83 mins.
              Documentary made with shipyard workers during the occupation
                  and work-in at the Upper Clyde Shipbuilders, July 1971 to October
                  1972. The yards were occupied and managed by a joint shop
                  stewards' committee after the government had announced the
                  decision to liquidate the company. Scenes of organising, work,
                  discussion, high-level negotiations, relations between the shop
                  stewards and union officials, dealings with the press, all with a
                  strong sense of being seen from 'inside'. Music by 7:84 and The
                  Laggan.

1981   *So That You Can Live* 16mm. Col. 85 mins. Screened on Channel
              Four, 1982.
              Documentary filmed over five years showing the impact on one
                  family in South Wales of developments in the national and global
                  political economy. (See article p. 171–3)

1983   *Rocking the Boat* 16mm. B/W. 63 mins.
              A reflection on the UCS occupation and subsequent political events
                  centred round a group of workers/pensioners on a boat trip.

1984   *The Miners' Film* 16mm. B/W. 65 mins.
              The 1975 *Miners' Film* with a new introduction.

1986   *Rocinante* Super 16mm. Col. 93 mins.
              Feature drama with Ian Dury, John Hurt and Maureen Douglass.
              We went in search of England and found a 'garden of secrets' full of
                  tradition and myth, violence and cover-up. So, drawing on many
                  types of narrative – traditions of the tale, the romance and the
                  novel, and using different cinematic genres, we tried to tell a story
                  about the common ordinary world and the world we have in
                  common.
              We borrowed our title – *Rocinante* – from Cervantes and equipped
                  with Don Quixote's horse set out to tilt at reality. [CA 1986]
              Awards from Berlin, Madrid and Troia film festivals.
              Location of archive material: NFA.

1989   *Bearskin. An Urban Fairytale* 35mm. Col. 95 mins.
              Feature drama with Ian Dury. 'On the run from a couple of hit-men,

young Johnny Fortune escapes from a life in basement poolrooms
to become a dancing bear with the strangest Punch and Judy man
in the business. ...' [Film Four International]
Location of archive and viewing material: NFA.

Sheffield Film Co-op

The interview with Christine Bellamy was recorded in 1995; Jenny
Woodley was interviewed 1996.

The Development of the Group

Jenny Woodley

JW—We all met in the Women's Group in Sheffield, which was one of the very early
groups when the Women's Liberation Movement first got off the ground. Christine Bellamy was from Sheffield. Gill Booth was a Northerner, from Bradford.
Barbara Fowkes and I were from London.

I had a young baby and was teaching part time in a college of technology. Gill
was a careers officer in education. Barbara was a teacher and was pregnant with her
first child. Christine had two under-school-age children and wasn't working at that
time. She'd left school at sixteen and had been a laboratory assistant. So, the four
of us who were the founder members in 1973 all had one or two small children
under school age.

MD—So, three of you were working in education. Were you yourselves from that
kind of professional milieu?

JW—I think Christine's family was middle class. Barbara's mother was an infant
school headmistress. My background was working class. My father was a Ford factory worker in Dagenham and I'd left school before the age of seventeen when my
father died. I'd always wanted to go to university, but I was the oldest of five girls
and after my father died there was no question about me being able to stay on at
school. After one or two jobs I started unqualified supply teaching, which you could
do in those days, and then after three years of that, I was qualified to go to teacher
training college, although not to university.

MD—What brought you to Sheffield?

JW—My partner was also a teacher and we moved up here for political reasons, educational political reasons. Sir Alec Cleg was one of the progressive chief education
officers in the country and he administered the West Riding where all the developments in comprehensive education were going on.

Christine Bellamy

MD—Had you come to the Women's Movement through an existing interest in
politics, or did you come to politics through the Women's Movement?

CB–It was a mixture. Jenny had been involved in International Socialism (IS). Gill was interested in certain things to do with pregnancy, and issues of childcare, but I don't think she was in a political organisation as such. Barbara was interested in politics and her partner had translated Karl Marx's *Grundrisse*. I wasn't involved in anything. I had just had a baby, and I thought, 'There's sum'at funny with this.' So, I decided to go to women's meetings and thought, 'Now I know why I'm a bit dissatisfied' – the Betty Friedan angle, if you like, the problem without a name.

MD–How did you get involved in film?

CB–We got into the whole business through the Women's Movement. We thought we should be talking to more women and decided to see how we could reach a wider audience. The opportunity came to do some programmes for BBC Radio Sheffield. In those days local radio was very different and there were people dedicated to getting the community more involved and doing educational programmes as well. So, quite a large group of us did six programmes called *Not Just a Pretty Face*, taking different aspects of what we saw as important in women's lives at the time.

After that a group of us started thinking about how important the media is in this field, and how we should be doing more. Sheffield was one of the places where there was a new kind of cable television and they were inviting people to go in and make programmes. We wanted to make programmes about women.

We all had kids – we weren't necessarily all married, but we all had kids and part-time jobs sometimes, and we were juggling one or two things at once. So it seemed, if we were juggling two things, why not juggle three things? So we got involved down there, in the television. It was all organised by men, of course. There was a man in charge and two or three other men, technical types. And we were known as, 'Ah … here come our four local housewifes. What are we going to do today, ladies?' We grimaced a bit, and thought, 'If we want to get in there, I suppose we'll have to put up with that for a bit.' The technical people were quite helpful, except that there was a limit as to how helpful they could be, because the equipment was so damn heavy! It was called 'portable', but we could no more lift it than we could lift a studio camera. It was really, really heavy stuff, massive cameras on wheels and the reel-to-reel machine.

But we went out and did a couple of programmes. One was about getting around town with pushchairs, because at that time Sheffield was being quite radically altered by the planners and they were looking at underpasses and trying to get the traffic round the city. The underpasses nearly all had steps, or there were some ramps, but you had to go further round to find the ramps. There was also a bit of an argument about buses then, because these 'one-man' buses, as they were called, were difficult with a pushchair. We demonstrated the problems by making a film in town with me and my two kids trying to get around. It was quite terrible really, because I didn't know anything about technique. There was Jenny at one point asking people what they thought of going into shops with children and she got obsessed about whether there were toilets. And she's there in the bottom of the frame, shooting this microphone at passers-by, saying, 'What about the toilets?'

The next film for the cable television was about provision for the under-fives in Sheffield, which was just starting to move ahead. Our programme looked at child minders and how they should be registered.

Jenny

JW—We got hooked, both by the technology and by the ability to use the media to construct our point of view at a time when the media was almost universally ridiculing Women's Liberation (with the honourable exception of the *Guardian*'s women's page, Jill Tweedy, people like that).

To begin with we didn't need funding, because we were making programmes using Sheffield Cable Vision's equipment and resources. When we came to make our third programme for them about abortion they began to get hot around the collar about the subject. It was the time of the James White back-bencher's Amendment Bill to reverse the advances of the abortion law and there was a big campaign against it, the National Abortion Campaign formed within the Women's Movement. But the programme manager suddenly started muttering about his Home Office licence. I think he said something like, 'That might be a bit difficult, Jenny, I'd have to think about that.'

It was suggested to us then by Barry Callaghan that we should make a film. Barry taught film at the art school in Sheffield then, and he and his wife were personal friends of mine. We were already aware by then that a 16mm film had a potentially far wider audience because it was more mobile, and although we had a studio discussion after our cable programme we had no way of knowing how many people watched it.

When we said to Barry that we didn't know anything about 16mm film, his reply was, 'Yes, but you know about programme-making. It's the ideas that count. Don't worry about the technology. If you need any support, I'll help you.'

Also he introduced us to Yorkshire Arts Association. Because we had come into film-making, not from arts school but through political involvement, we didn't, at that time, have any knowledge of the arts structures and the arts funding mechanisms. He said, 'Apply to Yorkshire Arts.' So, we applied and that's when Sheffield Film Co-op was born, because we had to fill in an application form and the first question was, 'name of organisation'. At that time the group was the original four, but soon after that we were joined by a film student from the art school, Moya Burns.

MD—In the end wasn't your abortion film made for the British Pregnancy Advisory Service [BPAS]?

JW—Not quite. It was our film, a film we wanted to make and we knew there was a distribution network for us around the country, because we could show it in other women's groups. We applied to Yorkshire Arts and the application apparently provoked great discussion on the panel, with people split between a desire for experimentation in terms of formalism and aesthetics and the argument that this was experimentation in terms of content. What we got from Yorkshire Arts was free film stock. We didn't get a grant. We then applied to BPAS, who gave us £300. After the film was finished they also bought six copies to train their staff. We applied to numerous organisations, like Women in Media, the 300 Group, and we got a personal cheque from Muriel Box [feature director, producer and screen writer in the 50s and 60s. Ed.] for £25.

Christine

MD—And what sort of reaction did you get to the film? Did you manage to get it seen?

CB—We got asked to go to all sorts of community centres and trade union meetings and adult education centres – places where women gathered. In those days, every community centre had a film projector and adult education was a thriving thing in Sheffield. Lots of women went and mostly in Sheffield they were working-class women. It was often their first opportunity to get education since, perhaps, a failed attempt at school. These were brilliant locations in which to get to grips with these issues.

Adult education then was quite informal and there were lots of places setting up women's discussion groups, just for women to come and get talking. (Now, of course, they're trying to phase a lot of it out in the colleges, because they don't see it as economically viable.)

Jenny

JW—The next film was a commission. We were approached by the National Women's Aid Federation.

The film we made after that again was a film that we wanted to make. We would decide what we wanted to do next, then look at the nature of it, and say, 'Who might be interested in funding this?' The next film was about women doing jobs that were previously traditionally done by men. We got money from the Equal Opportunities Commission and completion costs from a branch of Manpower Services.

MD—How did you progress to getting funded on a more regular basis?

JW—It seemed a very long process. By that time, of course, we had become much more integrated into the arts and film network and had got involved in the IFA. The IFA and the growing number of film-makers in the regions made an address to the BFI to, one, spend more money on film production and two, channel more of that money to the Regional Arts Associations for film-makers outside of London.

By the late 70s I was on the Yorkshire Arts Film and Video panel. Jim Pearse became the films officer and we decided on a strategy which was an energetic address to the BFI for more money within the region, a strategy to persuade people not to drift down to London but to stay in the region.

MD—You applied to the BFI Production Board, didn't you, and became entangled in the negotiations about the Workshop Contract. Can you explain what happened?

JW—Out of the IFA, as you know, one of the strategies that was developing was designed to create a film infrastructure in Britain of independent film and video workshops. Now, once film-makers went into the ACTT, the policy became refined, some would say, developed, others would say changed out of all recognition. A dialogue developed between the IFA, ACTT, the cultural funding agencies and the newly established Channel Four, and out of that came the Workshop Declaration.

In the middle of that Sheffield Film Co-op had applied to the Production Board to make *Red Skirts on Clydeside*. There had been an angry exchange at the BFI regional conference the year before about what was perceived as London bias, after which the Production Board had designated some of its monies for regional production and, to cut a long story short, we were awarded development money for that year and production money for the next. After we'd learned that we had been successful, we were told by Peter Sainsbury that we couldn't have the money yet because there'd been a huge overspend on Peter Greenaway's *The Draughtsman's Contract*.

Hard on the heels of that came a dispute between the ACTT and the BFI Production Board, because the BFI appeared to be refusing to sign the Workshop Declaration. The BFI was crucial to the strategy, and so the London film division of ACTT successfully put the union into dispute with the Production Board, which meant that no members of ACTT who had been awarded money were able to take it up. The dispute was resolved. The BFI did sign the Workshop Declaration and that meant, I think, that the following year the board had to give us twice the money that they had initially allocated us before, because they had to give four people ongoing wages for the full year.

MD—When did you start doing work for Channel Four?

JW—In 1984–5, we got money for *Let Our Children Grow Tall*. We weren't working for Channel Four, because that was never supposed to be the relationship. [Under the Workshop Declaration. Ed.] We had a programme of work, some of which Channel Four would hope to pick up and broadcast.

MD—How many were in the group during that period?

JW—I think the largest number of paid members that the Co-op had at any one time was five. At one time the group had become very small. Gill and Barbara had left and when we received the grant to research *Red Skirts on Clydeside* there were effectively only two members, myself and Christine. Gill came back part time in 1984. Chrissy joined about 1983–4. Bernadette Maloney came soon after Chrissy. So, then there were two established members and two new members. It was almost a new group with the same name. Angela Martin was with us for the period of a production. I left at the beginning of 1985. Maya Chowdhry came some years later.

MD—How did the relationships in the group develop? Did you continue to rotate jobs as you had on the very first film?

JW—I wasn't there from 1985 and part of the reason why I left was because I thought that, although the Film Co-op in some respects was fulfilling a very useful function, in other ways it wasn't working well, and certainly for me personally I had felt very frustrated for eighteen months before I left.

MD—Why did you think it wasn't working?

JW—Because people were at different stages of development and if you are working in a collective where everybody has equal rights and things are rotated, that means that in a lot of respects things stand still for a long while.

There was an ongoing underlying tension between rotating everything, sharing everybody's experience, passing on skills and everybody becoming a jack of all trades – this is my perception of it – and another perspective, which probably towards the end I held, that if some people are good at one thing and not good at others, and if we were not to waste public money, it would make more sense to concentrate on what you're good at and have a realistic appraisal, both of our individual skills and of the Co-op, what the Co-op was good at.

When it became clear that there was a chance that we were to go on getting funding, we had a discussion at one point where I said, 'Over the past eight or nine years the Co-op has built up a reputation and a market and an audience for educational films. We're not going be funded for ever and we should use this chance to develop that so that we can continue in the future.' The opposing view was, 'If we're going to be funded to do a programme of work, we want to be free to do a much wider range of things,' and that view held sway. Now I thought that was not only unrealistic but self-indulgent.

MD—Do you think those tensions could have been avoided?

JW—To begin with we were heavily influenced by the politics of the early Women's Movement, based on informal collective working and skill sharing. I think one of the things we learned was the need for proper structures and that included grievance procedures and a definition of the responsibilities of the management committee. I know there were times when we were glad that we had clear procedures. I certainly saw later on when I became an ACTT national organiser that it took some groups time to realise that they had moved into being small businesses. When people said to me, 'Oh, but we're friends and we've worked together for years,' I used to say, 'Never mind, the time to get all these things agreed is when there aren't problems, and then you will be glad, if disputes do arise, particularly if you've got close personal relationships, because you'll be lifted out of personality conflicts.' I think that certainly a problem for the Co-op when I was in it, and a problem for other workshops, was to do with that transition when groups suddenly got large amounts of money and were paying themselves proper wages and were employing freelancers from outside and actually, in spite of all their political beliefs, were employers. It's a bit like Labour councillors coming to terms with the fact that they are employers.

MD—What did you do after leaving the Co-op?

Shooting *Bringing It All Back Home* (Chrissie Stansfield, 1987). The crew, not all members of SFC, are (1. to r.) Christine Bellamy, Lynn Colton, Sue Cane, Nina Kellgren, Hilary Buchanan and Chrissie Stansfield.

JW—I went to work at the ACTT as an organiser. Some of us who at various times left the Film Co-op as employed members stepped back to being members of its management committee. We always had some people on the management committee from outside, like Ros Brunt for example, who was and is a lecturer in media at Sheffield Poly (now Sheffield Hallam University). So, I was a management committee member from 1985. Moya Burns was a management committee member.

Christine

CB—When we got the grant for *Red Skirts on Clydeside* it was the first time we'd had real money. It was like winning the pools. But there was a pressure from that. We thought it's got to be really good.

At the time only myself and Jenny were working on the project, but once the film was launched we had about ten women working with us and we gave several people their first break as a cameraperson, for instance, rather than just an assistant. When the film was in the editing room new people had joined the group and each newcomer had some input.

We had some difficulties, because it was our first long film. We had difficulties deciding what to keep in. Our main concern was that the women came over well and that we showed the political struggle. I think we succeeded in this. The film was used in lots of women's history courses. The Scottish Film Archive bought several copies and distributed it in Scotland. So, it carried on our tradition of using film in education, although possibly it was used more in women's studies than out in the community. It was shown on the *11th Hour,* and after that I think we saw the TV audience as the main audience.

MD–Did the distribution become less important?

CB–We were still sending films out but we were not so involved in that. It was important in raising revenue but not for contact with the audience.

Theory, Practice and the Film Establishment

Jenny

MD–When you started to get involved at a national level with film culture, what were your views on the various arguments taking place around the IFA?

JW–I can only speak personally about this. About the time we finished our abortion film, the London Women's Group had also made an abortion film. Now you must remember that we didn't come from arts backgrounds at all, and we saw it, and halfway through we thought, 'What's happened here? It's gone wrong!' Because the picture disappeared from the screen, there was just black leader and all you heard was voices. And we were sometimes going to places where both abortion films had been seen and quotes 'ordinary women' were saying to us, 'We really liked your film. What was the matter with that other one?'

We discovered after a while that what was raging within the BFI was nothing about women having access to equipment, women being able to make films, but arguments about formalism and structures.

The arguments were couched in such obscure terms that a reasonably intelligent lay person who was outside wouldn't understand a word of it to begin with. I went away and I thought, 'Blow this, I'm not going to be beaten by these buggers. I have got to get to grips with this to be able to get involved in these arguments.' So, I went on a few film courses and I started reading, because I knew that, politically, there was an agenda underneath it all.

MD–And when you did get to grips with it, what did you think?

JW–I still have enormous problems with a lot of the films that were made during that period. They were essays about visual conventions in visual language and some of them worked and some of them didn't.

MD–But against that what did you see yourselves as doing?

JW–What we were doing was political, we had a political agenda.

MD–But surely the argument was that language is political and that because you were interesting your audience in the same way as television does, you weren't really influencing them very much?

JW–But my problem was that they weren't influencing them at all, if nobody can understand them.

I went on a weekend school run by Ben Brewster and we were halfway through watching an experimental film when whoever was projecting it said, 'I'm terribly sorry', very red-faced, and stopped the projector because he had run it end out and nobody knew. And that confirmed at least some of my opinions.

MD—How was this related to the IFA? The IFA membership was very mixed, wasn't it?

JW—To begin with we were very wary about getting involved in the IFA, because we saw the IFA as a group that held meetings at which people read papers in obscure language and banged on about the BFI.

My memory is that we didn't get involved in it until about 1979. But I do remember going to a meeting where Claire Johnston gave a paper, and coming away very angry about it and very angry about the whole movement, and going through the paper – I was an English teacher – writing it out in plain English paragraph by paragraph and finding it meant something quite banal and quite ordinary. And it did seem to me that there were a lot of people trying to build their own academic reputations – or maybe that's unfair – trying to build academic respectability for a whole new area of activity. It was the time that film studies and media studies were struggling to establish themselves as academic subjects.

MD—Did you feel that the theorists lacked experience of the kind of practical work you were doing, showing your films to people who had nothing to do with the media and hadn't necessarily been through higher education?

JW—Yes, I felt they were totally divorced from the real world. But I don't think that is necessarily the case with academics.

MD—But did the ideas affect your work at all?

JW—In my opinion an awareness of all those arguments had a negative effect upon our film-making, and I would say that the early films that Sheffield Film Co-op made were more interesting, when we were unaware of the arguments and they were therefore much more instinctive, our first priority being what do we want to say? How do we say it to people so they understand it and so that it raises questions for debate and argument? People have said to us things like, 'You had house style; there were very distinctive features about your film-making; there was much more humour in your films; the construction was much more imaginative.' *Red Skirts on Clydeside*, to my mind, was an absolute disaster. It was a film made by a committee.

MD—When you say you made them instinctively, you must have been informed by ...

JW—... By popular television, by people like Ken Loach and Tony Garnet. By political theatre, particularly Joan Littlewood's work at the Theatre Royal in Stratford. *Oh What a Lovely War, Sparrows Can't Sing,* and Arnold Wesker's work at the Royal Court.

MD—Another argument in the IFA revolved round the issue of workshops versus individual film-makers. What was your view on that?

JW—The workshops at that time were a minority. But already then the term 'workshop' was beginning to have more than one meaning. Now in Sheffield we were members of Sheffield Film Co-op, which was a film-making collective. We, as individuals, were also members of the other kind of workshop, Sheffield Independent Film, which we had helped found in about 1976–7, and that was an open-access workshop.

MD–How did Sheffield Independent Film work?

JW–Over the years it has fulfilled a very important function in Sheffield, but around that time there were difficulties with how an open-access workshop ran, because if you raised money and bought equipment, that in turn meant lots more people who hadn't necessarily got any money to make a film would want to join. So, you've got all sorts of tensions like: should we just be here to administer equipment? If we have just bought a rather sophisticated camera, do we hire it out to people who join the group just in order to make their first film and might damage it?

You must see this also against the background of the debates about film culture: Colin McArthur's notion of integrated practice meant that every group like Sheffield Independent Film which wanted money from the BFI had to be engaged in exhibition, education and distribution.

MD–But you as a group did take your films out to audiences?

JW–Yes, we did, and this was what we perceived to be the irony of our situation. We were genuinely involved in film production, film distribution and what we saw as education. The problem was how the BFI and some RAAs saw activities like ours was that it wasn't film education; it might be political education; it might be social education; it might be feminist education, but showing films and having a discussion about the film, was not in itself film education.

MD–You felt under pressure to do something else?

JW–It was all trimming here and there according to the needs, the perceived needs, of the funding bodies. That's how we ended up getting funded by the Community Arts Panel for a while instead of the Film Panel of Yorkshire Arts. We said, 'Alright, we're not film-makers, because we're not engaged in formal experimentation. We are working with groups of people in the community.' So all the time during the 70s and early 80s, the question bounced backwards and forwards: is this political activity, is this community activity or is it film-making?

Chronology: Organisation and Funding

Figures on funding were provided by members of the group. Those marked 'approximately' were from memory. Figures from 1985 came from written records.

1972   Sheffield Women's Group makes radio series, *Not Just a Pretty Face*,
            for BBC local radio.

1973   Informal group formed by four women to make programmes for
            Rediffusion local cable television. First programme made and
            transmitted.

1975   Group adopts name of Sheffield Film Co-op.
            First application to Yorkshire Arts for *A Woman Like You*. Receives
                £100 and film stock.
            First project funding: £250 from British Pregnancy Advisory Service.

1976   Complete first film, *A Woman Like You*. Start distribution and
                exhibition around the film.

1977   First commission from the National Women's Aid Federation for
                That's No Lady.

1980   Registered as a workers' co-operative.
            First public revenue funding: Yorkshire Arts Community Arts Panel
                and Sheffield City Council.
            First continuously waged work.
            Members joined ACTT.

1981   Grant from Community Arts Panel: approximately £7,500. Income
                from distribution: approximately £1,000.

1982   Becomes an ACTT-franchised workshop.

1983   Funding from Sheffield City Council: £8,826; £41,916 from BFI as a
                first tranche for *Red Skirts*.
            Income from distribution, speakers' fees, equipment hire, etc.:
                £5,148.

1985   First Channel Four funding. Total grants and fees: £92,653.

1987   Year of maximum funding. Total for year: £161,943.
            BFI   £39,000
            CFour (workshop)   105,000
            CFour (other)   14,020
            Income from distribution etc.   3,923

1989   Last workshop funding. Total for year: £133,901.
            BFI   £39,030
            CFour (workshop)   62,500
            CFour (other)   268
            Income from distribution etc.   32,103

1990   Channel Four commission for *Running Gay*.

1991   Ceased trading.

From 1985 to 1990 total grants and fees: £724,728.

Productions

Descriptions are based on Sheffield Film Co-op (SFC) publicity and on viewing.
Producer and director credits are given only where individuals are named.
VHS Viewing copies of most of the production are held by SFC.

1973   *Women and Children Last* 1 inch Tape. B/W. Approximately 20
              mins., followed by studio discussion.
              For Rediffusion local cable TV. A look at Sheffield city design and
              transport planning from the point of view of mothers with babies
              and young children.
              Location of extract: SFC.

1974   *My Child* 1 inch Tape. B/W. 30 mins.
              Programme for Rediffusion local cable TV on child-minders.

1976   *A Woman Like You* 16mm. Col. 18 mins.
              Dramatised documentary showing the difficulties experienced by a
              married woman with two children trying to get an abortion on the
              NHS.
              Location of archive material: NFA.

1977   *That's No Lady* 16mm. Col. 14 mins.
              Dramatised documentary about violence in the home. Domestic
              scenes illustrate the kinds of experiences and relationships which
              can develop in the life of any woman who gets battered.
              Alternating with these are scenes from a working men's club where
              a comedian is telling jokes about women.
              A commission from the National Women's Aid Federation.
              Location of archive material: NFA.

1979   *Jobs for the Girls* 16mm. Col. 29 mins.
              Drama about a girl who decides to get a job as an apprentice motor
              mechanic. It raises for discussion the pressures acting on girls to
              conform to traditional feminine patterns.
              Funded by the Equal Opportunities Commission, Manpower Services
              and Yorkshire Arts Association.

Location of archive material and viewing print: NFA.

1982   *A Question of Choice* 16mm. Col. 18 mins.
        Documentary made with a group of low-paid women workers who
            work in a school and community centre in Sheffield. The title
            refers to the limited choices available to women who see family
            commitments as their first priority.
        Funded by Yorkshire Arts Association and Sheffield City Council.
        Location of archive material: NFA.

1984   *Red Skirts on Clydeside* 16mm. Col. 40 mins.
        Documentary about the 1915 Glasgow rent strike and the process of
            rediscovering women's history.
        Funded under the Workshop Agreement by the BFI.
        Location of archive material and viewing print: NFA

1984   *Women of Steel* Hi band U Matic. Col. 27 mins.
        Documentary about the part played by women in the Sheffield
            munitions factories during the Second World War.
        Location of archive material: NFA.

1984   *Changing Our Lives – Five Arches Community Centre* Low band
            U Matic. Col. 18 mins.
        Documentary made with a group of women on a Sheffield council
            estate who struggled to open the community centre to serve local
            needs.
        Location of archive material: NFA.

1986   *Let Our Children Grow Tall* 16mm. Film and betacam. Col. 52 mins.
        Research and Co-dir. Gill Booth; Film Lighting and Dir. Christine
            Bellamy.
        Documentary. Women with children living on low wages or benefits
            present their analysis of the impact of the Conservative
            government policies on their living standards.
        Location of archive material and viewing print: NFA.

1986   *For a Living Wage* Low band U Matic. Col. 15 mins.
        Documentary about low pay and how individuals, trade unions and
            government can combat it.
        Funded by Sheffield City Council, London Borough of Greenwich,
            COHSE, T&GWU, GLC, Jobs Year Campaign.
        Location of archive material: NFA.

1987   *Bringing It All Back Home.* 16mm. Col. 48 mins.
        Dir. Chrissie Stansfield; Prod. Gill Booth.
        Using interviews with developers, economists, trade unionists and
            women's representatives, the film compares developments
            attracted to Britain's declining industrial regions with those in
            some industrialising countries of the third world. In both cases
            women are in demand as labour.
        Location of archive material and viewing print: NFA.

1988   *Diamonds in Brown Paper* 16mm. Col. 52 mins.
        Writer/Dir. Gill Booth; Prod. Maya Chowdhry and Bernadette
        Maloney.

Drama documentary about the working lives of 'Buffers' – women
who work polishing cutlery in the 'Sheffield Trade', following a
group of buffers from 1928 to the present day.
Location of archive material and viewing print: NFA.

1990   *Women Can Make It Work* U Matic. 22 mins.
Northern Nottingham's women's training scheme offers over twenty-
three taster courses for crafts such as plumbing, mechanics, driving
heavy goods vehicles, electrical work, electronics, painting and
decorating. A look at five women who had been through the
courses.

1990   *Thankyou, That's All I Knew* Betacam SP. 43 Mins.
Dir. Christine Bellamy.
Inspired by Sheffield's Yemeni Literacy Campaign, which was
launched in 1988 as a partnership between Sheffield City Council's
Education Department and the Yemeni Community Association.
An interesting profile of a significant minority group in a large city.
Location of archive material: NFA.

1991   *Running Gay* Betacam SP. 20 mins.
Dir. Maya Chowdhry; Prod. Chrissie Stansfield.
Item for *Out*, the Channel Four strand of programmes on lesbian and
gay issues.
Location of archive material and viewing print: NFA.

Black Audio Film Collective

The following text is taken from extracts from two interviews: with Lina Gopaul in February 1996 and with John Akomfrah, Eddie George and Avril Johnson in May 1996.

Influences

John Akomfrah, Eddie George and Avril Johnson

MD–Were there key experiences for any of you which pushed you towards politics or films?

AJ–I was interested in politics before I was interested in films and I think the whole film thing for me was an accident. I worked with the BBC for two years before I did my degree, doing the finance and administration for the hair and make-up department. It was just by chance. I had two A levels and could type and was looking for a job.

MD–Did the experience change your perspective?

AJ–Yes, it made me think I never want to do this ever again! Because I come from a background where, when people say something, you believe what they say, you don't look for hidden agendas, and there are lots of hidden agendas in the BBC. I couldn't stand it and it so happened that, at the time, I was also doing another A level – psychology – and I was so gob-smacked that I passed that I applied to do a degree in psychology.

EG–It's difficult to say where you first bucked up on politics or when politics discovered you. For me, it's really boring: we had books in the house and I read them.

MD–So, were your parents political?

EG–No. My mother's husband was a schoolteacher, so he had a shit load of books – Sartre, Fanon, Malcolm X – and I used to hang out in anarcho bookshops and read bits of Marx, not making any particular sense of it – don't get the idea that anything was settling in – and I went to art school. So, I just drew a lot of stuff, read a lot of books.

MD–But it's not every kid who will pick up Marx, whether they understand it or not!

EG–No, I just liked it. And punk was very important. Punk rock made my life, because about 1976–7, when I was a kid, the idea came along that you can just do anything you want, like a flashback of 1968 – that and some of the radical currents found in black music at the time. That's the nexus.

By 1979 I had found out about the French lot – Barthes and Foucault – still not making any particular sense of it but getting into it anyway, still riffing on that sense of openness and making your own connection between things, foregrounded, I suppose, by a kind of post pan-Africanist politics.

MD–Where were you living at the time?

EG–I was in Hackney. That was the other thing, where I come from the idea that you could do things like make films, write books, make records, in 1976 or 1979, no, that was not one of the possibilities that was open to you, especially the class that I come from. My mother came here when she was eighteen. Her grandmother sold cakes in Dominica, which is nowhere central even for the Caribbean. So, going to college, doing a degree, that was something really, really new.

I met Trevor Mathison in 1979 and he said, 'You should come to college with me. There'll be girls, there'll be drugs, it'll be great!' So, I went.

JA–I was always interested in films. When I was fourteen I applied for an apprenticeship scheme at the BBC with a Spanish friend whose father worked there. He got in and I didn't. Then, when I was about nineteen or twenty, I applied to the National Film School, not knowing that you needed particular qualifications, and again they turned me down.

By the time I was twenty-one I had a sense of a world of cinema which I knew very well, because I lived off the Fulham Road, and just round the corner from us was a cinema called the Paris Pullman where I went quite regularly. I remember seeing Bob Rafelson's *The King of Marvin Gardens*, *Five Easy Pieces*, all the early Tarkovsky, Antonioni's *The Red Desert*, Bergman, most of the 60s and 70s art cinema. When I was confident enough I then went down to the Gate Cinema in Notting Hill, and these were very difficult places to go, because I was quite young and most of the films didn't really make much sense ...

MD–Why did you go then?

JA–I was intrigued. Up until I started going to the Paris Pullman I just assumed that there was one particular way of making films, a Hollywood way. (I had seen a few Indian and Chinese films, but I just thought they were perversions of the original, which was Hollywood.) So, going to the Paris Pullman was a discovery of a whole new way of thinking about film.

MD–Do you know why you were drawn to that? Why didn't Hollywood satisfy you?

JA–Now I can tell you why, but then I didn't know. With hindsight I think I was discovering that films were made by people, with particular kinds of viewpoints. I think it was really with *Solaris* and *Pather Panchali*, I suddenly realised that you could have something called an authorial vision.

MD–You hadn't, presumably, heard of 'authorial visions' at that time?

JA–No, but it was partly the way they programmed things: 'Tarkovsky's *Solaris*', or 'a Bob Rafelson double bill', and then the names of the films themselves – very small. So, just the act of going to those cinemas gave you the impression that there were individual film-makers – visionaries – and I bought into that way of looking at cinema. It didn't strike me then that it might be flawed. I just watched.

MD–What kind of background do you come from?

JA–My mother worked at City and East London College. She used to run the canteen there and teach on an HND course. It's an exile family and with exile families there's a certain faded glory ... It's as if somebody's always appealing to something bigger elsewhere that you've missed or you could have had ...

MD–Was it your father or your mother who'd been in politics?

JA–Both of them. My father, who died in 1963, was a member of the Nkrumah government. My parents met here and had gone back to Ghana where I was born, and then my father died and we left Ghana, wandered around for a bit and arrived here in 1965.

MD–So, you'd have been about eight? Do you have much memory of living in Ghana?

JA–I do, actually. Until I was about fifteen or sixteen I lived in this double world, where I compared things that happened here to how they used to happen when I was a child. After a while it didn't seem a very fruitful way of leading your life.

MD–You were wishing you were back in Ghana?

JA–I never did. It wasn't a place I missed until I was much older. In fact, in some ways I was very happy to be out of it, because I preferred the close-knit quality of English life or what appeared then to be a close-knit quality. People always thought of extended families as kids going in all sorts of directions and all these people around, but the flip side of that is that most of the time there is no one that you bonded with, because the grown-ups just carried on with their life. So my childhood in Ghana was really one of being left alone.

MD–Were your parents plugged into English socialism? A lot of English socialists were very interested in Ghana ...

JA–My father joined the Communist Party when he was here, but I think a couple of the younger pan-Africanists put him right when he got to Ghana, because a number of the major pan-Africanists of the time had been members of the Communist Party and had left because they'd followed the machinations of the Communism International and its relationship with the race question. George Padmore, for instance, was in the Comintern in the 20s. He was from Trinidad and went to America and from America to the Soviet Union, but left in the 30s, broke with communism, because he felt that the Communist International just wasn't dealing with the liberation question. So he set up an organisation called the Bureau of African Affairs in London in the 30s, which had quite a lot to do with the Independent Labour Party. He drew people like Stafford Cripps into the bureau and harangued them and leafleted them and pushed them to take a position on anti-colonialism, but also started training young Africans like Kwame Nkrumah, Jomo Kenyatta. He was a very important figure who's been forgotten.

MD–Going back to your own past, you applied for film school, didn't get in and then went to Portsmouth and met the others there?

JA—No. I met three of the original seven at Portsmouth, but I'd met Avril, Lina and Reece before, because we were at the same O level college, in Whitechapel. We'd fallen into this group of black students who were all interested in more or less the same stuff: the American political scene, African liberation theory, Jean-Paul Sartre. (Marxism was a later edition. I think that started to come in in 1978–9, from a mixture of chance encounters with people in the SWP [Socialist Workers' Party], Big Flame and a renegade Trotskyite think-tank called the Intervention Collective.) So, I met four of the group before Portsmouth. We'd got involved in student activism as FE students and then got expelled from Southwark College.

MD—You were expelled for political activity or things that went with it?

JA—For organising too many occupations. I would have expelled us – we were a bloody nuisance!

AJ—I was the one that wasn't part of this. I thought they were all mad. I was a part-time student and they were full time. I was paying for my education at that point, doing an administrative job for the Workers' Education Association. So, I was paying and couldn't understand all this politics, playing at politics. Then later on, as I said, I was working at the BBC.

MD—But you met up again at Portsmouth. Was it a popular college for black students?

AJ—No.

MD—Did you get to know each other quickly because there weren't many black students there?

EG—It wasn't just that it was all black, because I remember getting there and meeting a bunch of people that I just thought were tossers. I wouldn't have gone out with them if they were white, black, green, whatever. A lot of the black students were saying, 'Let's get a black students' society together,' and out of that group you suddenly realise there are people you can talk to and people you didn't have anything in common with other than you were all black.

Lina Gopaul

LG—Where did I get my politics from? A deep sense of injustice from education. A deep sense of racism from things that have happened to me all my life. You can't pinpoint that. Race isn't something that knocked us on the head when we went to college. You've got to put it in the context of race and racism in that time we were growing up. You're talking about the 60s and 70s and a very hostile racial background, a racialised Britain – Enoch Powell.

MD—What was your own family like? Were your parents political?

LG—No. They are both factory workers and they were too busy out there trying to feed us and clothe us and house us. Most working-class black parents were doing that.

None of us in Black Audio, barring John, come from political backgrounds in that way. I think our parents had a great belief in a British system of education and fairness that would be enough to get us through, but what we encountered was not that. I came out of school with a very basic education and I knew why. If you're black and you're growing up in Britain in the 60s your colour could not have escaped you, from the children teasing you and abusing you to the lack of expectation from the teachers. It was Hackney, a very poor area. Racism was rife.

MD–Did that influence what you chose to study?

LG–I wanted to change things. I'll be quite honest. I thought that through studying I would be able to change things.

Prior to university I read everything I could get my hands on to do with race and women, but I knew I needed a way of organising all those thoughts and I felt that going to university was a way of doing that.

MD–What was the most most valuable thing it gave you?

LG–Time and the means of living. And it was a place where you were allowed to study politics. I suppose it's a chance a lot of young working-class kids will never have again, because if I'd had to pay for that I couldn't have done it.

Forming Black Audio

John Akomfrah, Eddie George and Avril Johnson

EG–We didn't start out with the idea that we were going to form a production company and make films. We started out doing installations, performance pieces, sound design. Then I left college with Trevor in 82, and we began the process by trying to find out where we could set up a workshop ...

MD–What was your experience of workshops? Did you know anyone already in one?

JA–No. In 1980–1 Simon Field, who later ran the ICA cinema, used to teach film at Portsmouth, which meant showing films and students who weren't on the course could watch them too. A couple of us saw Berwick Street Collective's *Nightcleaners* and some Cinema Action stuff, so we knew that there were English groups (although I didn't hear of Amber until much later). We'd also seen the SLON stuff from Chris Marker's outfit, and I think we knew more about the Latin American collectives than English ones.

MD–You'd got the picture that what you were going to form was, in some sense, a collective?

EG–No. I got the picture that we were going to set up more a SLON kind of outfit, where different people could work. The collective came about a year or two later.

MD–Why did you change?

JA–Because it felt that having the two was the way forward. I thought, personally, that it was really clear that we were beginning something new that had never taken place, because there had been one or two black film-makers before but none of them worked together, and we looked at the history of how they managed to survive and realised that, on the whole, they tended to get isolated.

So, the desire to set up a collective was definitely part of an attempt to think of where next to take black film-making. We'd also looked at other models of black art coalitions and the more successful ones, the Black Art movement in the States, for instance, tended to be groups, where people came together to formulate manifestos and lay down a certain kind of idea of what they wanted to do.

It also became clear that we were going to do something the independent film movement in this country hadn't managed to do, which was to make race and questions of race a central object or interrogation. That hadn't happened even after 1981, although the most convulsive social event at that time was the riots in the early 80s. Thatcher had just got into power and suddenly questions of national identity were definitely on the cards, and the groups which were interrogating political landscape using the concept of class seemed to be missing something very central that was going on in England at the time.

MD—When you talk about setting up something, what was it exactly?

JA—We drew up a constitution which said we were going to be a collective and everything I said to you just now was in that constitution: a workshop to pursue black film culture, a group where audiovisual research into race would take place and so on. It was very high-falutin, very general, but the idea was definitely to set up a black film workshop with the collective at the centre using the workshop, which we saw in very literal terms as a space with equipment and personnel, a bit like Andy Warhol's factory. It was only much later that we realised a workshop could have all those other connotations.

MD—But this document was only for the group? It didn't have a legal basis?

JA—No, not at all.

MD—But when you did form a legal entity, was it a straightforward company or a co-operative?

JA—It was a co-operative. When we finally set up a company it was with the ICOM rules, the Institute of Common Ownership Movement.

The First Years

Lina Gopaul

LG—In 1982 we were trying to look for a name which would represent all our interests. We spent many discussions and hours discussing the name, and through that you went into endless discussions about what we were going to do.

MD—How did you subsist until Black Audio was viable?

LG—We all had little jobs that we rushed off to get so we could survive. We used those jobs to finance a tape/slide production. We couldn't afford film but we could afford tape/slide. And we were making applications to the GLC and GLAA, the BFI, and none of them were being taken seriously, because we hadn't done anything. At the same time we were trying to get ourselves onto short film courses and trying to get experience by working on productions. We worked on *On Duty*, a film by Julien Henriques and Cassie McFarlane about the closing of a hospital in Kensal Rise.

The GLC was important to us, because there was the ethnic-minorities unit which began to nurture black arts as well as putting money into established black art forms and we were one of the nurturing projects. In 1985 we got a small grant and it enabled us to get premises and set up a very small training course and an exhibition programme. The GLC was putting together the Third Eye Film Festival and we helped with the programme and writing programme notes. We were also working at places like the Rio and Four Corners organising exhibition programmes. We were going to meetings, taking part, trying to put black media issues on the agenda. There were a lot more meetings then. We were making links with the union and the independent film-makers. Sankofa was also there and at that point we started linking with them. We first met Isaac (Julien) at Four Corners in 1983. It was a time when lots of things were bubbling and you felt you could engage in those debates and have some kind of influence.

MD–You were concentrating on the independent film world rather than the mainstream. What drew you in that direction?

LG–A very deliberate choice. We knew we probably could have got into the BBC, but we wanted to work outside the mainstream so we were not constrained by anybody else's views and ideas, especially those notions of objectivity we were constantly being told about. We declared proudly that we wanted to make our own

Handsworth Songs (John Akomfrah, 1986).

subjective account. We wanted to make films that were off the beaten track. We wanted to make 'ourstories'. We wanted to be experimental.

MD—How did you manage to make your first film, *Handsworth Songs*?

LG—That was before we had any workshop funding. We'd completed our tape/slide and we were exhibiting it. We got it into universities and colleges on media courses, and a lot of the money that came from that went into *Handsworth Songs*. We financed it ourselves, except that right at the end we managed to change about £2,500 for research from the GLC into work on the production.

MD—So, did you sell it later to Channel Four?

LG—We had a strategy for *Handsworth Songs*. We pushed it to every festival and we wanted it in the cinema. It was picked up very quickly and at the time Channel Four and the BBC were both chasing it. We wanted to have a relationship with Channel Four under the Workshop Agreement and we used *Handsworth Songs* as part of the deal.

MD—Did your priorities change after that?

LG—After *Handsworth Songs* we found that our exhibition, our training courses, were not giving us what we set out to achieve. It seemed to us that people took more notice of productions than anything else and at that point, because we had the one film, we needed to prioritise the productions so we would not ever be in a position of not having a rostrum of work behind us.

Independent Film Culture, Race, Experimentation

John Akomfrah, Eddie George and Avril Johnson

MD—So after negotiations Channel Four bought *Handsworth Songs* and gave you a workshop contract?

AJ—We always had a relationship with Alan (Fountain), who kept saying he wanted to give us a contract, but we weren't a fully franchised workshop. We became franchised by the end of the making of *Handsworth Songs* and so at that point there was no problem, but he didn't give us a contract until a year later, after the success of *Handsworth Songs*.

JA—It was very clear then that the institutions we went to see – the BFI and GLAA, Channel Four, the Arts Council – had in their mind a time-table by which black film groups should be set up. At the top was Ceddo, because it was made up of people they'd heard of, who had made films that they had seen. Everybody would say they'd deal with us after Ceddo, but suddenly there was another group, Sankofa, who were coming at the thing from a different angle, saying, 'We're going to deal with sexuality and gender.' So we then got moved behind them and we didn't help our case, because we kept insisting on the question of experimentation and form. I remember at the Arts Council being told that you couldn't have a black experimental film group, and I think there was an idea that there was already an established way of making films which black film-makers were simply going to provide new characters for. So, white film-makers made film about, I don't know, avant-garde constructivism and black film groups would make things about carnival – and because we kept in the foreground the question of form and experimentation, I think at times we made people uneasy.

MD–But Sankofa were keen on experimentation too, weren't they?

JA–Yes, except Sankofa seemed to be able to foreground a cultural politics which could be identified. They seemed to be able to say that the forms were to come out of the cultural politics, whereas we always put the question of form first.

MD–Films which have that reflexive quality can be difficult to watch. Did you have discussions about your audience and how viewers would react to this problematising?

JA–One of the things that we were very clear about was that there was no constituency for what we wanted to do. We didn't take for granted the assumption that there was a black audience for a black film. We ourselves having come from very diverse backgrounds knew that there were very different kinds of black people and we wanted to target and create a specific kind of interest group within black circles for a certain kind of film.

MD–Just in black circles?

JA–Initially, yes, that was the thing that interested us most, and so there was a real paradox when white people started liking the film.

MD–But if it got shown widely wasn't it bound to pick up a sizeable white audience?

JA–That didn't worry us. I'm being slightly dishonest by saying we'd only targeted the black audience. At the back of my mind, there was always a sense that we were talking to a national audience, because the issues were of national significance. What sense people made of race seemed to me to be not just of interest to black people. But also, behind all of that, the broader project was definitely to inaugurate black film culture, to bring more young people like us to the gate.

MD–Were you conscious of doing this at a time when film culture generally was in decline?

JA–Yes, I used to refer to us as the bastard children of 1968, to get across the idea that there was this out-of-sync quality to our activities.

MD–But did you think you could inaugurate a black film culture without there being a wider film culture?

EG–No, not necessarily. We were interested in the debates, and within two years of starting to work with film we'd come into contact with most of the people in the larger independent film movement, from Simon (Hartog), to Willemen to Ellis.

JA–By that time we'd already been through the London Film-Makers' Co-op and the two avant-gardes theory . . .

MD–How do you mean, 'through the Co-op?'

JA–Some of our first screenings were at the Co-op and we had friends that were members. We never belonged as a group, but Trevor and I joined as individuals to use the equipment.

MD—Were there other groups who were helpful before you got your own equipment?

JA—Four Corners were very, very useful. Mary Pat Leece was always very keen for Four Corners to be a place where black film-makers felt at home.

Group Dynamics

John Akomfrah, Eddie George and Avril Johnson

MD—After *Handsworth Songs* how did you finance your next films: *Testament*, for instance, and *Twilight City*?

AJ—They were under the Channel Four contract.

MD—Which was the first film that wasn't part of the contract?

AJ—*Seven Songs*. That was a combination, because by then all the other contracts had run out but we still had a year to go and Channel Four couldn't avoid the contract, but they didn't want to work under the Declaration, so it wasn't strictly a workshop film.

MD—And after *Seven Songs*?

AJ—Then it's all straightforward commissions.

MD—So, then you had to do your budgets in the orthodox way, where the rates of pay relate to a hierarchical wage structure?

AJ—But we always did our budgets like that. On the films people were paid according to grade. The difference was that before people were paid outside of the films and then they were paid the same. So, while we were under the Workshop Declaration, say, Lina and John were making *Seven Songs*, they would be paid the same, but if Eddie was the writer he would be paid for the writing. Right from the word go, we had allocated roles in which we wanted to work in the television industry – producer, director, writer, whatever and we would then pay ourselves accordingly. We wouldn't think because we're a collective we've all got to be paid the same.

JA—We had differentials from, I think, after *Testament*.

MD—So, in what sense would you say, your organisation is now any different from an ordinary company owned by a group of film-makers?

JA—What has always distinguished us was that the decision-making on what sorts of films were made and how they were made was always done collectively, and the discussions about the direction the company should take.

MD—On the discussions about films, would you all be involved or do you tend to form smaller groups of, say, producer, director, writer, around particular films?

JA—It was always done in the messy, old-fashioned collective way.

EG—That's pretty much survived and that's probably what's kept us going.

MD—The membership of the group has hardly changed, has it, since you set it up?

JA—There's only one person who's not still in it – Claire – and one who came in later – David.

MD—Are any of you also personal partners to each other?

JA—At college, Lina and I were already going out with each other from 1977.

MD—I'm asking, because quite a lot of workshops begin with at least one couple among the members and sometimes it seems to be a source of strength, but it can also cause tensions.

JA—There were actually three couples in the group, because I was going out with Lina, Avril was going out with Reece ...

EG—... I was going out with Claire.

MD—And was it a problem for the group when Avril and Reece split up?

JA—I think it always is, because you learn to work in a particular way and then you have to adapt. I always think that change is difficult for big organisations, but actually change is probably even more difficult for smaller organisations, where the bonds are much more tangible. But thankfully, we lived through it ...

AJ—In my mind there was never a question of whether or not I would leave the group, so in that sense that wasn't a problem. And although we're close, people are allowed to have their privacy and their space, although that's not always a good thing I might add.

JA—I think that there's a formal recognition that although we all work together that we don't get into each other's lives twenty-four hours of the day, seven days of the week. There's a recognition I think, conscious or unconscious, that people need to develop on their own as well as with the group, and so I think that that has been a strength in lots of ways which has enabled us, I suppose, to weather the storms.

Lina Gopaul

MD—Do you find that you can function as a collective in relation to the outside world?

LG—Whenever you confront the banks etc., there's always a reaction of 'What is this notion of the collective? who's in charge? who's the responsible person?'

MD—How did you deal with that in relation to Channel Four?

LG—The Workshop Declaration covers that.

MD—But now with ordinary commissions, don't they insist on a contract signed by someone in charge? They won't accept collective responsibility will they?

LG—No. So we do put two people up there in that capacity.

MD—How do you organise the technical work on the films? Do you employ people or do you divide it among yourselves.

LG—We did parts of *Handsworth Songs* ourselves.

MD—And subsequently?

LG—We did go down that route, but then people found those weren't the areas they wanted to go into. Trevor is a sound man and does all the music, but he's about the only one. So we're all directors and producers.

MD—So you have to employ other people now? Do you regret that at all?

LG—No. It has been part of our expanding strategy, rather than tying everybody up in one production. That has always been important.

John Akomfrah, Eddie George and Avril Johnson

MD–How do you share administrative work in the group?

AJ–We have a flexible approach to it depending on what the individual's doing, but largely I'd say me and Lina and David do the administration.

MD–Has it ever been an issue? It does sound like there's a rather conventional gender division between being creative and providing back-up?

AJ–It's a criticism that we've had for years and that's because people think that all the creativity would come from the director, but right from the word go we have our input in terms of what films we want made. We argue about how a film should be made and when we go into the cutting room we argue about the cuts.

MD–So, in a sense an outsider like me probably doesn't realise how much of you and Lina are in some of the films that get written up in the papers as being primarily, say, John's?

EG–But that's because you've got all these different structures to interlock really well: you've got this hierarchical production company structure; you've got the classical SLON-style floating collective structure; you've got informal links, partnership links, cross-currents of shared interests; and when it comes to getting a project from the paper to the can it works, but there's not a critical language for making sense of that.

MD–How far do you think that is to do with being a black group and how far is it to do with individual factors and having evolved patterns of work that function well for you all personally?

EG–For me the real trick is to find another way of talking, because it's not just the blackness and it's not just the group, it's the way one thing turns on the other.

JA–My sense is that like all organisations that work people find what their strengths are and play to them. I think all of us are aware that we have limitations and things that we're not very good at, and what I like about it is that people seem to want to help each other, to compensate for each other. It's a method of working where you're endlessly looking out for each other and you know that no one's ever going to let you drop into something, you're never going to be in a place where you're out of your depths. It's a mutual-aid approach.

Chronology: organisation
Figures for funding are not included, at the group's request.

1982   Informal group formed.

1983   Black Audio Film Collective established as a co-operative under
            ICOM rules.
            First applications for grant funding – unsuccessful. First screenings.

1984   Made tape/slides programmes.

1985   First grant from the GLC Ethnic Arts Committee.
            Set up premises in Hackney. Start first film, *Handsworth Songs*.

1986   Complete *Handsworth Songs*.
            Become a franchised workshop.

1987   Obtain a Channel Four contract under the Workshop Declaration.

1992   Channel Four workshop contract runs out.
            Move to premises in Camden.

Productions

The list does not include productions produced or directed by members of Black
Audio as individuals working for other companies. John Akomfrah has directed
several programmes for other companies since 1994. Where descriptions are taken
verbatim from Black Audio publicity they are marked [BAFC].

1983–4   *Signs of Empire* Tape/Slide. 30 mins.

            Images of Nationality Tape/Slide. 30 mins.

1986   *Handsworth Songs* 16mm. Col. 58 mins.
            Dir. John Akomfrah; Prod. Lina Gopaul.
            A documentary on the contours of 'race' and 'civil disorder' in 80s
                Britain. Set in Birmingham and London, *Handsworth Songs*
                presents a diversity of responses to the 'riots' of autumn 1985.
                From an Asian councillor's loss for words to a funeral procession
                commemorating the tragedy of lost loved ones, it contextualises
                the events of that Autumn in an 'alternative frame' to that of a
                current affairs documentary ... The 'Songs' of the title are the
                lamentations from the dramas of industrial decline; the elegies of
                an increasingly dissatisfied 'surplus' class; the falling debris of
                shattered hopes and broken dreams. ... In the twilight of old and
                new technologies, the film develops through a key phrase: 'There
                are no stories in the riots, only the ghosts of other stories.' [BAFC]
            Seven awards including Grand Prize Kaleidoscope, International
                Immigrant Film Festival, Stockholm, 1986; Paul Robeson Prize for
                Cinema, FESPACO Film Festival, Burkino Faso, 1987; British Film
                Institute Grierson Award, London, 1987.
1988   *Testament* 16mm. Col. 80 mins.
            Dir. John Akomfrah; Prod. Lina Gopaul and Avril Johnson.
            A film about exile and dispossession. Filmed on location in Ghana.

Five awards including Grand Prize Riminicinema International Film
    Festival, 1988.

1989   *Twilight City* 16mm. Col. 52 mins.
            Dir. Reece Auguiste; Prod. Avril Johnson.
            Documentary. After thirty-five years of living in London, Olivia's
                mother returns to Dominica vowing never to return. They parted
                after a long and tortured silence. Ten years later a letter breaks the
                silence. Eugenia wants to come 'home' and she wants to be invited.
                Olivia is a journalist researching 'The New London and the
                Creation of Wealth'. Watching the London of her childhood sink
                in the shadows of redevelopment, she is not sure what answer to
                give her mother. [BAFC]

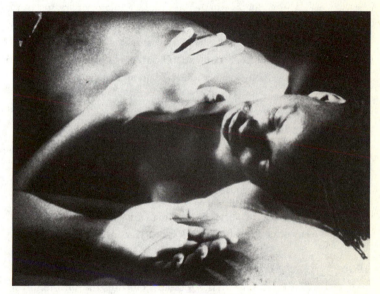

Seven awards including Grand Prize, Melbourne International Film
    Festival; Gold Hugo for Documentary, Chicago International Film
    Festival, 1989.

1991   *Mysteries of July* 16mm. Col. 52 mins.
            Dir. Reece Auguiste; Prod. Avril Johnson.
            Documentary for *Critical Eye* about deaths in British police custody.

            A Touch of the Tar Brush Betacam SP. 40 mins.
            Dir. John Akomfrah; Prod. Lina Gopaul.
            BBC documentary. A personal portrait of mixed race life in
                Liverpool.

Who Needs a Heart? 16mm. Col. 80 mins.
Dir. John Akomfrah; Prod. Lina Gopaul.
Channel Four and ZDF. Investigates the life and times of Michael X –
urban bandit, mystic, British Black Power leader – by looking at the
lives of a group of friends who are acolytes of Michael's.

1993   *Seven Songs for Malcolm X* 16mm. Col. 58 mins.
Dir. John Akomfrah; Prod. Lina Gopaul.
Documentary examining the biography, the myth and the political
   background using interviews with friends and family and
   reconstructions of incidents in Malcolm's life. The Channel Four
   showing was timed to coincide with the London opening of Spike
   Lee's *Malcolm X*, and scenes of Lee promoting the film in the
   United States situate the simple, adulatory narrative as part of the
   context. *Seven Songs*, by contrast, uncovers the less well-known
   parts of the story, from aspects of Malcolm's background to details
   of the political context and differences between the civil rights
   movement, the Nation of Islam and Malcolm X.

1994   *Dark Side of Black* 16mm. 45 mins.
Dir. Isaac Julien; Prod. Lina Gopaul.
For BBC2 *Arena*. Documentary about the social and political
   influence of Rap and Ragga music.

1994   *Black Cabs* 16mm. Col. 28 mins.
Dir. Rupert Gabriel; Prod. Lina Gopaul.
Documentary about black cab drivers in London.

1995   *Mothership Connection* 16mm. Col. 25.5 mins.
Dir. John Akomfrah; Prod. Lina Gopaul and Avril Johnson.
George Clinton's music is a starting point for an exploration of links
   between slavery and science fiction.

1995   *Three Songs on Pain, Time and Light* Betacam SP. 22 mins.
Dir. Eddie George; Prod. David Lawson.
Programme about an artist who has sickle-cell anaemia.

1995   *Last Angel of History* 16mm. Col. 45 mins.
Dir. John Akomfrah; Prod. Lina Gopaul and Avril Johnson.

1995   *Martin Luther King. Last Days of Hope* Digibeta. 57 mins.
Dir. John Akomfrah; Prod. Lina Gopaul.

Select Bibliography

Aaronovitch, Sam, *The Road from Thatcherism* (London: Lawrence and Wishart, 1981).

Abbott, Frank, 'The IFA: Film Club or Trade Association?', *New Cinema Workshop Bulletin* issue 7, May 1982.

Abbott, Frank, 'On the Air', *Screen* vol. 24 no. 1, January/February 1983.

Afterimage 'English Independent Cinema', no. 6, Summer 1976.

Akomfrah, John, 'Sneaking Ghosts through the Back Door', *Black Film Bulletin* vol. 1 no. 1, Spring 1993.

Akomfrah, John, 'Wishful Filming', *Black Film Bulletin* vol. 1 no. 2, Summer 1993.

Aldgate, Anthony and Richards, Jeffrey, *Britain Can Take It: The British Cinema in the Second World War* (Edinburgh: Edinburgh University Press, 1986) revised 1994.

Anderson, Lindsay, 'A Possible Solution', *Sequence* no. 5, Autumn 1948.

Anderson, Lindsay, 'Only Connect: Some Aspects of the Work of Humphrey Jennings', *Sight and Sound* vol. 23 no. 4, April/June 1954.

Anderson, Lindsay, 'Stand Up! Stand Up!', *Sight and Sound* vol. 26 no. 2, Autumn 1956.

Anderson, Perry, 'Origins of the Present Crisis', *New Left Review* no. 23, January/February 1964.

Artrage nos. 3/4, Summer 1983.

Aspinall, Sue, 'This Sadder Recognition', *Screen* vol. 23 nos. 3/4, September/October 1982.

Aspinall, Sue, 'The Space for Innovation and Experiment', *Screen* vol. 25 no. 6, November/December 1984.

Association of Cinematograph and Allied Technicians, *Film Business Is Big Business* (London: ACT, 1939).

Association of Cinematograph and Allied Technicians, 'A State Film Industry?', *The Cine Technician*, May/June 1941.

Association of Cinematograph and Allied Technicians, *The Film Crisis* (London: ACT, 1949).

Association of Cinematograph and Allied Technicians, *Films: Trade Union Policy* (London: ACT, 1956).

Association of Cinematograph and Television Technicians, *Survival or Extinction: A Policy for British Films* (London: ACTT, 1964).

Association of Cinematograph and Television Technicians, *48 Times the Usual Junk: The ACTT Committee Report on Cable TV* (London: ACTT, 1973).

Association of Cinematograph and Television Technicians, *Nationalising the Film Industry: Report of the Nationalisation Forum* (London: ACTT, August 1973).

Association of Cinematograph and Television Technicians, *Patterns of Discrimination against Women in the Film and Television Industries* (London: ACTT, 1975).

Association of Cinematograph and Television Technicians, *Action. 50 Years in the Life of a Union* (London: ACTT, 1983).

Association of Independent Producers, *Recommendations to the Government following the Prime Minister's Working Party Report on the Future of the British Film Industry and the Interim Action Committee's Report on the Setting up of the British Film Authority* (London: AIP, 1978).

Attile, Martina, 'Black Women and Representation', *Undercut* nos. 14/15, Summer 1985.

Attile, Martina, 'The Passion of Remembrance: Background', *Framework* nos. 32/33, 1986.

Auguiste, Reece, '*Handsworth Songs*: Some Background Notes', *Framework* no. 35, 1988.

Baehr, Helen and Spindler Brown, Angela, 'Firing a Broadside: A Feminist Intervention into Mainstream TV', in Helen Baehr and Gillian Dyer (eds), *Boxed in: Women and Television* (London: Pandora, 1987).

Berry, David, *Wales and Cinema. The First Hundred Years* (Cardiff: University of Wales Press, 1994).

Black Film Bulletin 'Home from Home', vol. 1 nos. 3/4, Autumn/Winter 1993/4.

Blackburn, Alexander and Cockburn, Robin (eds), *Student Power – Problems, Diagnosis, Action* (Harmondsworth: Penguin, 1969).

Blanchard, Simon, *The Distribution and Exhibition of Film and Video in London. A Report to the GLC* (London: GLC, 1983).

Blanchard, Simon and Harvey, Sylvia, 'The Post-War Independent Cinema – Structures and Organisation', in James Curran and Vincent Porter (eds), *British Cinema History* (London: Weidenfeld and Nicolson, 1983).

Blanchard, Simon and Morley, David (eds), *What's This Channel Fo/ur?* (London: Comedia, 1982).

Board of Trade, *Tendencies to Monopoly in the Cinematograph Film Industry*, report of a committee appointed by the Cinematograph Films Council (London: HMSO, 1944).

Bond, Ralph, *Monopoly: The Future of British Films* (London: ACT, 1946).

Boyden Southwood and Comedia for GLAA, *Developing the Independent Film and Video Sector* (London: GLAA, 1988).

Burton, Alan, *The People's Cinema: Film and the Co-operative Movement* (London: National Film Theatre, 1994).

Caughie, John, '*Because I Am King* and Independent Cinema', *Screen* vol. 21 no. 4, 1980/1.

Caute, David, *Fanon* (London: Fontana, 1970).

Chanan, Michael, *Labour Power in the British Film Industry* (London: BFI Publishing, 1976).

Channel Four and Media, *Audiovisual in the Regions* (Newcastle: Amberside, 1988).

Chittock, John, 'Turning on the TV Tap', *Sight and Sound* vol. 54 no. 1, Winter 1984/5.

Clarke, Jane, for the IFA London Region, letter in *Screen* vol. 18 no. 1, Spring 1977.

Cleave, Alan, 'Middleman with a Mission', *Moviemaker* vol. 1 no. 7, September 1967.

Cook, Chris and Sked, Alan, *Post-War Britain* (Harmondsworth: Penguin, 1979).

Cottringer, Anne, Dickinson, Margaret and Petley, Julian, '*Dream On* and *Hush-a-bye Baby*, a Dossier', *Vertigo* vol. 1 no. 1, Spring 1993.

Curling, Jonathan and McLean, Fran, 'The Independent Film-Makers' Association – Annual General Meeting and Conference', *Screen* vol. 18 no. 1, Spring 1977.

Curling, Jonathan and Oppe, Fizze, 'A Declaration of Independence', *Screen* vol. 24 no. 1, January/February 1983.

Curtis, David (ed.), *The Directory of British Film and Video Artists* (Luton: John Libbey Media, 1996).

Curtis, David and Dusinberre, Deke (eds), *A Perspective on English Avant-Garde Film*
(London: Arts Council of Great Britain, 1978).

Dickinson, Margaret and Street, Sarah, *Cinema and State* (London: BFI Publishing, 1985).

Dovy, Jon, 'Old Dogs and New Tricks', in Tony Dowmunt (ed.) *Channels of Resistance*
(London: BFI in association with Channel Four, 1993).

Doyen, Marion, paper for the BFI Regional Conference Cultural Industries panel,
(London: BFI, 1988).

Dwoskin, Steve, *Film Is* (London: Peter Owen, 1975).

Ellis, John, 'The Future of the British Film Industry' in 'Film Culture', *Screen* vol. 17 no. 1,
Spring 1976.

Ellis, John (ed.), *British Film Institute Productions; a Catalogue of Films Made Under the
Auspices of the Experimental Film Fund 1951–66 and the Production Board 1966–76*
(London: BFI, 1977).

Ellis, John, 'Art, Culture and Quality: Terms for a Cinema in the Forties and Seventies',
Screen vol. 19 no. 3, Autumn 1978.

Ellis, John, 'Channel 4: Working Notes', *Screen* vol. 25 no. 2, March/April 1984.

Ellis, John, *Visible Fictions* (London: Routledge Kegan Paul, 1982) revised edition 1992.

Ellis, John, Flynn, Barry, Gardner, Carl, Merck, Mandy, Sheppard, Julie, Stoneman, Rod
and Wyver, John, 'Channel 4 – One Year On', *Screen* vol. 25 no. 2, March/April 1984.

Elstein, David, 'Political Movies', *Film and Television Technician* vol. 36 no. 297, February
1976.

Elvin, George, 'Advances in Twenty-One Years', *The Cine Technician* May 1954.

Farrell, Graeme, 'Which Avant-Garde?', *Afterimage* no. 2, Autumn 1971.

Field, Simon, 'Editorial 1', *Afterimage* no. 2, Autumn 1971.

Film and Television Technician 'The Strike, the March and the Movies', vol. 36 no. 307,
December 1970.

Film and Video Extra 'The Last Nine Years of Video UK', interviews with John Hopkins,
Steve Herman and Chris Evans in no. 9, Spring 1978.

Fitzgerald, Kitty, 'Diary of Distribution', *Vertigo* vol. 1 no. 1, Spring 1993.

Fountain, Alan, 'Questions of Democracy and Control in Film Culture', in *The New Social
Function of Cinema* (London: BFI, 1981).

Fountain, Alan, Spry, Caroline and Stoneman, Rod, *The Work of Channel 4's Independent
Film and Video Department* (London: Channel Four, 1986).

Framework no. 19, 1982, for series of articles on *So That You Can Live*.

Freidman, Lester (ed.), *British Cinema and Thatcherism* (London: UCL Press, 1993).

Future of the British Film Industry report of the Prime Minister's Working Party, January
1976, Cmnd 6372.

Garnham, Nicholas, 'TV Documentary and Ideology', *Screen* vol. 13. no. 2, Summer 1972.

Garnham, Nicholas, *Capitalism and Communication: Global Culture and the Economics of
Information* (London: Sage, 1990).

Gidal, Peter, 'The Anti-Narrative', *Screen* vol. 20 no. 2, Summer 1979.

Giddens, Anthony, *Beyond Left and Right* (Cambridge: Polity Press, 1994).

Gillet, John, 'Happening Here', *Sight and Sound* vol. 34 no. 3, Summer 1965.

Gilroy, Paul, 'Bridgehead or Bantustan', *Screen* vol. 24 nos. 4/5, July/October 1983.

Gilroy, Paul, 'Black and White', *Vertigo* issue 2, Summer/Autumn 1993.

Glaessner, Vera, 'Community Film: Who Cares', *Time Out*, October 12–18, 1973.

Glasgow University Media Group, *War and Peace News* (Milton Keynes: Open University Press, 1985).

Greater London Enterprise Board, *Altered Images* (London: GLEB, 1986).

Gutch, Robin, 'Whose Telly Anyway?', *Screen* vol. 25 nos. 4/5, July/October 1984.

Harris, Robert, *Gotcha! The Media, the Government and the Falklands Crisis* (London: Faber, 1983).

Hartog, Simon, 'The États Généraux du Cinéma', *Cinema Rising* no. 2, May 1972.

Hartog, Simon, 'The Estates General of the French Cinema', *Screen* vol. 13 no. 4, Spring 1972/3.

Hartzell, James, Morris, Robert and Sibley, Peter, 'Video Power', *Vertigo* issue 4, Winter 1994/5, p. 12.

Harvey, Sylvia, *May '68 and Film Culture* (London: BFI Publishing, 1978).

Harvey, Sylvia, *Independent Cinema?* (Stafford: West Midlands Arts, 1978).

Harvey, Sylvia, 'Whose Brecht?', *Screen* vol. 23 no. 1, May/June 1982.

Harvey, Sylvia, 'Interview with Platform Films', *Screen* vol. 25 no. 6, November/December 1984.

Harvey, Sylvia, 'The Other Cinema – A History: Part I 1970–1977', *Screen* vol. 26 no. 6, November/December 1985 and 'Part II', *Screen* vol. 27 no. 2, March/April 1986.

Harvey, Sylvia, 'Channel 4 Television from Annan to Grade', in Stuart Hood (ed.) *Behind the Screens: The Structure of British Television in the Nineties* (London: Lawrence and Wishart, 1994).

Hill, John, *Sex, Class and Realism: British Cinema 1956–1963* (London: BFI Publishing, 1986), reprinted 1995.

Hillier, Jim and Lovell, Alan, *Studies in Documentary* (London: Secker and Warburg in association with the BFI, 1972).

Hogenkamp, Bert, *Deadly Parallels* (London: Lawrence and Wishart, 1986).

Hood, Stuart, *On Television* (London: Pluto Press, 1980).

Houston, Penelope, '*March to Aldermaston*', *Sight and Sound* vol. 28 no. 2, Spring 1959.

Hoyland, Wisty and Nicholls, Jill, 'One Two Three', *Spare Rib* no. 39, September 1975.

Hutton, Will, *The State We're in* (London: Jonathan Cape, 1995).

IFA TV 4 Group, *Channel 4 and Independence* (London: IFA, 1979), reprinted in *Framework* no. 11, Autumn 1979.

Independent Cinema West, *Festival Programme of the First Festival of British Independent Cinema* (Bristol, 1975).

Independent Film, Video and Photography Association, *Strangling the Cities* (London: IFVPA, 1984).

Independent Film, Video and Photography Association, North of Ireland, 'Report on the Funding of Grant-Aided Film and Video in Northern Ireland', in *Fast Forward*, 1988.

Independent Film-Makers' Association, *Independent Film-Making in the '70s* (London: IFA, May 1976).

Independent Film-Makers' Association, *Submission to the Parliamentary Under Secretary for State on 'The Future of the British Film Industry'* (London: IFA, July 1978).

Independent Film-Makers' Association, *Channel 4 and Innovation. The Foundation* (London: IFA, February 1980).

Isaacs, Jeremy, *Storm Over 4* (London: Weidenfeld and Nicolson, 1989).

Jenkins, Tricia, *British Film Production: the Independent Sector: An Introductory Guide* (London: BFI South Bank Education, 1996).

Johnston, Claire, 'Film Journals in Britain and France', *Screen* vol. 12 no. 1, Spring 1971.

Johnston, Claire, 'The Subject of Feminist Film Theory/Practice', *Screen* vol. 21 no. 2, Summer 1980.

Johnston, Claire, 'Towards a Feminist Film Practice', *Edinburgh Film Festival Magazine* 1, 1976, reprinted in Bill Nichols (ed.), *Movies and Methods* vol. II (Berkeley and London: University of California Press, 1985).

Johnston, Claire and Willemen, Paul, 'Penthesilea, Queen of the Amazons: Interview with Laura Mulvey and Peter Wollen', *Screen* vol. 15 no. 3, Autumn 1974.

Johnston, Claire and Willemen, Paul, 'Brecht in Britain – The Independent Political Film', *Screen* vol. 16 no. 4, Winter 1975/6.

Johnston, Claire, Karlin, Marc, Nash, Mark and Willemen, Paul, 'Problems of Independent Cinema', *Screen* vol. 21 no. 4, 1980/1.

King, Noel, 'How Welsh Are My Eyes?: *So That You Can Live* Textual Analysis and Political Cinema', *Undercut* nos. 10/11, Winter 1983.

Knight, Julia (ed.), *Diverse Practices: A Critical Reader on British Video Art* (Luton: Arts Council/John Libbey Media, 1996).

Knight, Julia, 'In Search of an Identity: Distribution, Exhibition and the "Process" of Video Art', in *Diverse Practices: A Crititical Reader on British Video Art* (Luton: Arts Council/John Libby Media, 1996).

Lippard, Chris (ed.), *By Angels Driven: The Films of Derek Jarman* (Trowbridge, Wilts: Flicks Books, 1996).

Loisos, Peter, *Innovation in Ethnographic Film* (Manchester: Manchester University Press, 1993).

Lovell, Alan, 'The BFI and Film Education', *Screen* vol. 12 no. 3, Autumn 1971.

Lovell, Alan (ed.), *The British Film Institute Production Board* (London: BFI, 1976).

Lovell, Alan, 'That Was the Workshop That Was', *Screen* vol. 31 no. 1, Spring 1990.

MacCabe, Colin, '*Days of Hope*', *Screen* vol. 17 no 1, Spring 1976.

MacCabe, Colin, 'Memory, Phantasy, Identity: *Days of Hope* and the Politics of the Past', *Edinburgh '77 Magazine* no. 2, 1977.

Macpherson, Don (ed.), *Traditions of Independence* (London, BFI Publishing, 1980).

MacPherson, Rob, *Independent Film and Television in Scotland: A Case of Dependent Cultural Reproduction*, University of Sterling unpublished thesis for M. Litt., 1991.

Marcuse, Herbert, *One Dimensional Man* (London: Sphere Books, 1968).

Marshall, Stuart, 'Video Technology and Practice', *Screen* vol. 20 no. 1, Spring 1979.

Martin, Murray, *Toward a Policy on Workshops*, NOW papers, n.d., probably 1981/2.

Marx, Karl, 'Critique of the Gotha Programme', in *Karl Marx and Frederich Engels Selected Works Volume II* (Moscow: Foreign Languages Publishing House, 1962).

Maziere, Michael, 'Towards a Specific Practice', *Undercut* no. 12, Summer 1984.

McArthur, Colin, '*Days of Hope*', *Screen* vol. 16 no. 4, Winter 1975/6.

McCarthy, Matt, 'Free Cinema – In Chains', *Films and Filming* vol. 5 no. 5, February 1959.

McCarthy, Sarah, 'Independent Film Workshops – A Perspective from Swingbridge Video', *Co-operative History Workshop Conference Report*, 1994.

McIntyre, Steve, 'Art and Industry: Regional Film and Video Policy in the UK', in Albert Moran (ed.), *Film Policy* (London: Routledge, 1996).

McLeod, Lewis and Russell, Elisabeth, 'The End of Free Cinema', *Film and Television Technician* vol. 25 no. 172, April 1959.

McQuail, Denis and Siune, Karen, *New Media Politics: Comparative Perspectives in Western Europe* (London: Sage, 1986).

Mercer, Kobena (ed.), *Black Film British Cinema* ICA Documents 7, 1988.

Merz, Caroline and Parmar, Pratibha, 'Distribution Matters: Circles', *Screen* vol. 28 no. 4, July/October 1987.

Milner, Peter, 'The London Film-Makers' Co-op: The Politics of Licence?', *Undercut* nos. 10/11, Winter 1983.

Mulgan, Geoff and Worpole, Ken, *Saturday Night and Sunday Morning* (London: Comedia, 1986).

Mullally, Frederick, *Films: An Alternative to Rank* (London: Socialist Book Centre, 1946).

Mulvey, Laura, 'Visual Pleasure and Narrative Cinema', *Screen* vol. 16 no. 3, Autumn 1975, reprinted in *Visual and Other Pleasures* (Bloomington: Indiana University Press, 1989).

Mulvey, Laura and Wollen, Peter, 'A Written Discussion', *Afterimage* no. 6, Autumn 1976.

Mulvey, Laura and Wollen, Peter, 'Riddles of the Avant-Garde', *Framework* no. 9, Winter 1978/9.

Nash, Mark and Neale, Steve, 'Film History Production/Memory', in 'Reports from the Edinburgh Festival', *Screen* vol. 18 no. 4, Winter 1977.

Neale, Steve, 'Art Cinema as Institution', *Screen* vol. 22 no. 1, Winter 1981.

Nicolson, Annabel, 'The London Film-Makers' Co-operative', *Framework* no. 9, Winter 1978/9.

Nigg, Heinz and Wade, Graham, 'Liberation Films', in *Community Media: Community Communication in the UK – Video, Local TV, Film and Photography; a Documentary Report on Six Groups* (Zurich: Regenbogen-Verlag, 1980).

O'Pray, Michael, *Derek Jarman, Dream of England* (London: BFI Publishing, 1996).

O'Pray, Michael, 'The British Avant-Garde and Art Cinema from the 1970s to the 1990s', in Andrew Higson (ed.), *Dissolving Views: Key Issues in British Cinema* (London: Cassell, 1996).

O'Pray, Michael, *The British Avant-Garde Film* (Luton: John Libbey Media, 1996).

Orbanz, Eva, *Journey to a Legend and Back: The British Realistic Film* (Berlin: Edition Volker Spiess, 1977).

Owoo, Nii Kwate, 'You Hide Me', *Vertigo* issue 2, Summer/Autumn 1993.

Perry, George, *The Great British Picture Show* (London: Hart-Davis, MacGibbon Ltd, 1974).

Petit, Chris, 'Whither the Avant-Garde ... the ICA Biennial', *Vertigo* issue 5, Autumn/Winter 1995.

Petley, Julian, *Landmarks: Independent Film and Video from the British Workshop Movement* (London: British Council, 1989).

Petley, Julian, 'Crisis in the Northeast', *Vertigo* issue 5, Autumn/Winter 1995.

Pines, Jim, 'Left Film Distributors', *Screen* vol. 13 no. 4, Winter 1972/3.

Pines, Jim, 'Territories Interview with Isaac Julien', *Framework* nos. 26/7, 19, 1985.

Pines, Jim, 'The Passion of Remembrance. Interview', *Framework* nos. 32/3, 1986.

Power, Nigel, *Twenty Years On* (London: IFVPA, 1987).

Raban, William, 'William Raban Talks to Michael Maziere', *Vertigo* issue 6, Autumn 1996.

Root, Jane, 'Distributing a *Question of Silence*', *Screen* vol. 26 no. 6, November/December 1985.

Rose, Gillian, 'The Cultural Politics of Place: Local Representation and Oppositonal Discourse in Two Films', *Transactions of the Institute of British Geographers* 19, 1994.

Rotha, Paul, 'The Government and the Film Industry', in *Rotha on the Film* (London: Faber and Faber, 1958).

Rowe, Marsha, 'The Art of Women's Liberation Propaganda', *Spare Rib* no. 38, August 1975.

Sainsbury, Peter, 'Editorial 2', *Afterimage* no. 2, Autumn 1970.

Sainsbury, Peter, 'The Financial Base of Independent Film Production in the UK', *Screen* vol. 22 no. 1, 1981.

Screen vol. 12 no. 3, 1971, 'An Open Letter to the Staff of the BFI' and 'A New Screenplay for the BFI'.

Stamp, Andy and Stone, Georgia, 'Reasons to Be Cheerful. Part 2 Working in Libraries', *Independent Media* no. 73, January 1988.

Stoneman, Rod (ed.), *Independent Film Workshops in Britain* (Torquay, Devon: Grael Communications, 1979).

Stoneman, Rod, 'Film Related Practice and the Avant-Garde', *Screen* vol. 20 nos. 3/4, Winter 1979/80.

Stoneman, Rod and Thompson, Hilary (eds), *The New Social Function of Cinema: Catalogue of British Film Institute Productions 1979–1980* (London: BFI, 1981).

Taylor, Richard, 'Opportunities Knocked? Regional Broadcasters and Grant-Aided Film Production', *Vertigo* issue 5, Autumn/Winter 1995.

Turner, Sarah, 'Pandemonium', *Vertigo* issue 6, Autumn 1996.

Turner, Sarah, 'The Lux Centre: Eastward Ho!', *Vertigo* issue 7, Autumn 1997.

Undercut, Special Issue: 'Cultural Identities', no. 17, Spring 1988.

Undercut, 'A Decade of British Experimental Film and Video Art', no. 19, Autumn 1990.

Wade, Graham, *Street Video – An Account of 5 Video Groups* (Leicester: Blackthorn Press, 1980).

Walton, Paul and Winston, Brian, 'Virtually Free', *Vertigo* issue 6, Autumn 1996.

Willemen, Paul, 'Notes on *Rocinante*', *Framework* nos. 32/3, 1986.

Willemen, Paul, 'The Loss of Visions: An Interview', *Framework* nos. 32/3, 1986.

Willemen, Paul, *Looks and Frictions* (London: BFI Publishing, 1994).

Williams, Granville, 'Media Meltdown', *Vertigo* issue 6, Autumn 1996.

Williams, Raymond (ed.), *The May Day Manifesto 1968* (Harmondsworth: Penguin, 1968).

Williams, Raymond, *Technology and Cultural Form* (London: Fontana, 1974).

Winston, Brian, *Claiming the Real* (London: BFI Publishing, 1995).

Wollen, Peter, *Signs and Meaning in the Cinema* (London: Secker and Warburg, 1969).

Wollen, Peter, 'The Two Avant-Gardes', *Studio International* November/December 1975.

Wollen, Roger (ed.), *Derek Jarman, a Portrait* (London: Thames and Hudson, 1996).

Wood, Jane, *Gala Day and the Challenge* (BA humanities thesis, Ealing College of Higher Education, 1982).

Wyver, John, 'Gardening the Net', *Vertigo* issue 6, Autumn 1996.

Index